Soldiering On in a Dying War

Soldiering On in a Dying War

The True Story of the Firebase Pace Incidents and the Vietnam Drawdown

WILLIAM J. SHKURTI

UNIVERSITY PRESS OF KANSAS

Library of Congress Cataloging-in-Publication Data

Shkurti, William J.

Soldiering on in a dying war : the true story of the Firebase Pace
incidents and the Vietnam drawdown /William J. Shkurti.

p.   cm. — (Modern war studies)

Includes bibliographical references and index.

ISBN 978-0-7006-1781-4 (cloth : acid-free paper)

ISBN 978-0-7006-3403-3 (pbk. : acid-free paper)

1. Vietna   War, 1961–1975—United States. 2. Disengagement
(Military science)—Social aspects—Vietnam—History—20th
century. 3. Soldiers—United States—History—20th century.
4. Military bases, American—Vietnam—History—20th century.
5. United States. Army—History—Vietnam War, 1961–1975.
6. Insubordination—United tates—History—20th century.
7. Insubordination—Vietnam—History—20th century.
8. Sociology, Military—United States— History—20th century.
9. Vietnam War, 1961–1975—Press coverage. 10. Vietnam War,
1961–1975—Social aspects. I. Title.

DS558.2.S55 2011

959.704′342—dc22

2011002773

British Library Cataloguing-in-Publication Data is available.

Printed in the United States of America

10 9 8 7 6 5 4 3 2 1

The paper used in this publication is acid free and meets the
minimum requirements of the American National Standard for
Permanence of Paper for Printed Library Materials Z39.48–1992.

Dedication

This book is dedicated to the memory of those soldiers who gave their lives to protect their comrades at Fire Support Bases Pace and Lanyard:

Specialist Four Chris Behm

Warrant Officer Fred Hebert

First Lieutenant Gary Lynn Pace

Specialist Four Ron Ricks

Warrant Officer Tom Stansbury

Contents

(A photo gallery follows page 148)

List of Figures and Tables   ix

Preface   xi

List of Abbreviations   xiv

PART ONE: THE SIEGE

    1. Winding Down   3

    2. Proud Americans   10

    3. Sappers in the Wire   20

    4. Bad Omen   25

    5. Sky Troopers   33

    6. ARVNs, BUFFS, and Other Friends   38

    7. Incoming   43

    8. Confusion on the Ground   52

    9. Welcome to Prime Time   58

    10. Under New Management   63

    11. Leave No One Behind   70

    12. Whiskey and Kool-Aid   77

PART TWO: THE SOLDIERS

    13. The Grunts   85

    14. Artillery and Other Combat Support Troops   98

    15. Beyond Pace   108

    16. Soldiering On in MR I   114

    17. REMFs, Fraggers, Dopers, Slackers, and Other Losers   123

    18. Follow Me   130

    19. A Thousand Calleys?   140

PART THREE: THE PRESS

    20. Richard Boyle vs. the Powers That Be   167

    21. The Press and the White House   173

    22. The Press and the M-Word   184

PART FOUR: THE BIGGER PICTURE

    23. South Vietnamese Allies   197

    24. North Vietnamese Enemies   209

    25. Vietnamese Verdun   218

    26. Pace as History   228

    27. Lessons Learned?   236

    28. Conclusions: A Difficult End to a Long War   246

Epilogue   249

Appendix A: Order of Battle MR III—U.S. Forces, Fall 1971   255

Appendix B: Order of Battle MR III—North and South Vietnamese Forces   256

Appendix C: Inspector General's Report, October 11, 1971   257

Appendix D: Fact Sheet, Fire Support Base Pace Incident, October 22, 1971   263

Appendix E: Letter from Senator Kennedy to SP4 Al Grana, October 18, 1971   267

Appendix F: Letter from MG Donnelly Bolton to SP4 John P. White   268

Appendix G: Valorous Unit Award for Extraordinary Heroism to the 2/32d Field Artillery and Attached Units, July 3, 1972   270

Notes   273

Bibliography   313

Index   323

Figures and Tables

FIGURES

2.1. Area Northwest of Saigon   13
2.2. Fire Support Fans at the Cambodian Border, July 1970   16
4.1. Military Regions, 1971   26
4.2. Fire Support Base Pace   28
5.1. Area Northwest of Tay Ninh   37
6.1. Krek–War Zone C Battle, September 26–October 22, 1971   39
7.1. Activities around Fire Support Base Pace, September–October 1971   45
22.1. Combat Incidents, 1969–1971   185
23.1. Cambodian Border Region, 1971   200
25.1. The Easter Offensive in Military Region III, April 1972   219

TABLES

4.1. Redeployment of Major U.S. Ground Combat Units, Military Region III, 1969–1972   30
4.2. Redeployment of Medium and Heavy Artillery Battalions, Military Region III, 1969–1972   31
14.1. Court-Martial Statistics for 2/32d Field Artillery Battalion   99
14.2. Article 15 Punishments for 2/32d Field Artillery Battalion   101
23.1. U.S. and South Vietnamese Casualties, Tay Ninh Border Area, September 26–October 13, 1971   205

Preface

This book is about the soldiers who served in the last ground combat units in Vietnam. It begins with one of the most controversial incidents of the war. On the evening of October 9, 1971, a group of six First Air Cavalry Division GIs at a position surrounded by enemy troops balked at conducting a night ambush. The next day, sixty-six of their comrades, including thirteen noncommissioned officers, signed a petition supporting their actions. Even though this incident occurred at an isolated firebase, word spread quickly. Within twenty-four hours, the story of Firebase Pace appeared on all three TV networks and in the pages of most major newspapers. It prompted an immediate call from Congress for an investigation. Four days later, a second group of twenty soldiers from a different unit, but at the same firebase, refused an order to conduct a daylight patrol. This incident also found its way into the national news and prompted an inquiry from a worried White House.

On October 22, the twenty-seven-day siege of Fire Support Base Pace came to an end. The remaining American troops were hurriedly evacuated by helicopter, leaving their heavy guns and most of their vehicles behind. To many, these incidents served as yet additional evidence of the collapse of discipline and morale of the remaining American ground troops in the long pullout from Vietnam. Even though almost forty years have passed since these events took place, many of the key facts remain missing or in dispute. At least seven different versions exist in print or on various Web sites. Each one reflects a differing point of view, but no one has yet taken a comprehensive look at these events from beginning to end.

Originally incorrectly reported as a mutiny, the actions of these soldiers still raise a number of questions. Who were these men and how far were they willing to go in defying their commanders? What role did South Vietnamese allies play, if any? Did the press just report accurately what happened, or did it play a role in provoking or sensationalizing the story? And, what about the soldiers' commanders—did they exert any leadership, or were they victims of something they couldn't control? While this story stands on its own, it also serves as an entry point to better understanding the unique set of challenges facing soldiers on the ground conducting a strategic withdrawal in the face of a determined enemy. In that sense it tells us a lot about larger questions, such as why soldiers fight (or don't), what the press regards as newsworthy (or not), and how commanders cope (or don't).

This book is divided into four parts. Part 1 tells the story of the 1971 siege of Fire Support Base Pace in chronological sequence. Part 2 looks more specifically at the performance and motivation of U.S. ground troops in this period, not only at Pace but also elsewhere in Vietnam. In part 3, the role of the press is examined both in relationship to the events at Pace and in the broader context. In part 4, broader issues are examined using the siege of Firebase Pace as a starting point. This includes the performance of South and North Vietnamese soldiers at Pace and elsewhere, how historians viewed these events, and an examination of lessons that may be learned from this difficult period in American military experience.

In the fall of 1971 I was stationed at Fort Meade, Maryland, with Howitzer Battery, 1st Squadron, 6th Armored Cavalry Regiment. I had been back from Vietnam for about seven months and looked forward to completing my enlistment. In just seven weeks I would become a civilian again. I picked up the *Washington Post* on October 23 and saw a photograph from Vietnam that looked eerily familiar. The caption identified it as a night shot from Fire Support Base Pace on the Cambodian border. The shot was identical to one I had taken from the watchtower at Firebase Lanyard nine months earlier. I later learned that Lanyard had been renamed Pace after a Lieutenant Pace who had been killed there. As I read the accompanying story by *Washington Post* Saigon Bureau Chief Peter Jay, something he wrote would stay with me: "The troubles at Pace had come to symbolize, in a small way, the unpleasant dilemma confronting those few American officers and men still on the ground in a combat role in Vietnam."

Seven weeks later I mustered out of the Army and moved on with my life, but I struggled to find some meaning in the sacrifices of all the soldiers who fought and died in those last stages of America's withdrawal from Vietnam. For nearly forty years I collected bits and pieces of information off and on, but it didn't come together in any way until I read a copy of the 2/32d Field Artillery daily logs obtained from the National Archives. The 2/32d was the parent unit of the artillery battery at Pace. These documents gave me a framework to fit the seemingly disparate pieces together and helped me realize there was a much more significant story here that needed to be told. This book is a product of that effort.

There are a number of people I would like to individually thank for their help in preparing this book. First is my typist, Patty Egger, who soldiered on through multiple drafts, bad handwriting, and a barrage of military acronyms and Vietnamese place names. My thanks to Ohio State University graduate students Rob and Megan Clemm, who prepared the maps; to my son, Tom Shkurti, and to Kathleen Murphy, who helped digitize the photographs. Thanks also to two of my OSU colleagues who made unique contributions to this work, Professor Joe Guilmartin, whose invitation to speak to his classes on the Vietnam War helped crystallize a lot of the ideas reflected in this book, and Sharon West, associate professor of journalism, who provided important insights on the practice of that craft.

Martin Gedra and Rich Boylan at the National Archives were extremely helpful in identifying key documents, as was Greg Cummings at the Richard Nixon Presidential Library. Dale Andrade at the Center for Military History provided both useful information and sound advice. A special thanks to my editors at the University Press of Kansas, Michael Briggs, Jennifer Dropkin, and their colleagues, who helped transform this manuscript into a book. Thanks to John Prados and Jim Willbanks—two exceptional historians in their own right—for their valuable counsel regarding this work. I want to express my appreciation to the veterans of Lanyard and Pace who gave generously of their time to be interviewed for this project. Any errors of omission or commission are mine and mine alone.

To my wife, Renee, whose love and support contributed mightily to my ability to complete this project, a heartfelt thanks. And, finally, I want acknowledge Keith William Nolan. Although not a veteran himself, Mr. Nolan demonstrated a keen understanding of what it was like to be in the shoes of the soldiers on the ground in this difficult time. His three volumes on the later stages of the Vietnam War (*Ripcord*, *Into Laos*, and *Sappers in the Wire*) did so much to tell the story of these soldiers when other historians were not interested. Unfortunately, Keith William Nolan passed away in 2009 at the age of forty-five.

Abbreviations

AFVN	Armed Forces Radio and Television Networks
AO	area of operation
AP	Associated Press
APC	armored personnel carrier
ARVN	Army of the Republic of Vietnam (South Vietnam)
CMH	Center for Military History, United States Army
COSVN	Central Office for South Vietnam
LZ	landing zone
MACV	Military Assistance Command, Vietnam
NARA	National Archives and Records Administration
NCO	noncommissioned officer
NLF	National Liberation Front
NVA	North Vietnamese Army
OCMH	Office of Chief of Military History
ORLL	*Operational Report / Lessons Learned*
ROTC	Reserve Officers' Training Corp
RPG	rocket-propelled grenade
S&S	Stars and Stripes Vietnam Bureau
TOT	time on target
TRAC	Third Regional Assistance Command
TTVVA	Texas Tech University Virtual Vietnam Archive
UPI	United Press International
VC	Vietcong
VTNA	Vanderbilt University Television News Archive

Soldiering On in
a Dying War

PART ONE

The Siege

Chapter One

Winding Down
January–September 1971

By the fall of 1971 most Americans had had enough of Vietnam and were ready to move on. For the administration of President Richard M. Nixon, this meant an opportunity to open a new relationship with the People's Republic of China after more than twenty years of hostility. For the Army's leadership, it meant looking forward to an all-volunteer force rebuilt free of the difficulties in Vietnam. And, for Americans of military age, declining draft calls meant they could get on with their lives without the nagging uncertainties of involuntary military service. But, for the dwindling number of American soldiers on the ground in Vietnam, getting on with their lives and other thoughts of home would have to wait. Some would never come home again. Two hundred thirteen American soldiers would lose their lives that September of 1971—more than any month prior to February 1966, when the American buildup was well under way.[1]

Although the loss of these 213 lives was regrettable, it was still substantially less than the peak of 540 a month in late spring of 1969. Since President Nixon initiated phased troop withdrawals in July of that year, the number of U.S. troops in Vietnam declined steadily at the rate of 10,000–14,000 a month. By September 1971 only a little over 200,000 remained—more than 300,000 fewer Americans than were there twenty-seven months earlier.[2] The level of combat for U.S. troops also declined as the South Vietnamese army grew in size and strength and the North Vietnamese and Vietcong shied away from major confrontations with U.S. ground forces. But the decline in the intensity of U.S. military operations and escalating tensions at home created a whole new set of challenges.

The Army in Vietnam now found itself combating soaring drug abuse and racial friction among its soldiers. The reported incidences of disobedience and physical violence against officers and noncommissioned officers increased dramatically. Scandals that reflected poorly on the Army's leadership dominated the news headlines. Just when they were needed the most, the Army started losing experienced NCOs and junior officers in droves. Soured by increasingly reluctant draftees and a perceived lack of support from above, career soldiers chose not to reenlist and found other ways to avoid service in Vietnam. Those who did stay were often assigned roles as advisers in a crash program to build up the combat proficiency of the South Vietnamese. As a result, most of the dirty and dangerous jobs in U.S. ground-combat units—riflemen, machine gunners, artillery crews, tank and personnel-carrier drivers—were left in the hands of young and increasingly reluctant draftees who had no interest in military careers. In many cases the inexperienced sergeants and lieutenants who commanded them shared their lack of enthusiasm.[3]

Late in 1970 *Newsweek* sent a small army of reporters out to the field to talk with and observe these soldiers where they lived and worked. They presented their conclusion in a January 11, 1971, lead story titled "The Troubled Army in Vietnam." The issue featured the photograph of a smiling GI on the cover with two bandoliers of M60 machine-gun rounds draped over his shoulders and a peace medallion hanging from his neck. After reeling off the usual litany of problems—drug abuse, racial tension, the cultural gap between regular GIs and lifers, and general disillusionment—*Newsweek* observed,

> Worst of all, American troops have never before experienced the pervasive bitterness, regret and frustration that stems from a final national retreat. As one top ranking American officer in Saigon puts it, "Vietnam has become a poison in the veins of the US Army." . . . For the US Army in Vietnam is being asked to do something that no citizen army is equipped to do: Conduct a prolonged strategic retreat from a war the nation now detests. So far, the degree of demoralization in Vietnam is not immediately dangerous. When they have to, U.S. troops fight—and fight well. . . . The central question, however, is whether an army that has begun to wilt can manage to wilt just a little.[4]

During the remainder of 1971 the U.S. Army in Vietnam would wilt a lot. The year began on an optimistic note, but even that would create a controversy of its own. Talking with reporters from all four TV networks (ABC, CBS, NBC, and PBS) in a wide-ranging interview on January 4, 1971, President Nixon noted that the number of American GIs killed in Vietnam during the past year (1970) was down a third from what it was two years earlier in 1968. "We now can see the end of the American combat role in Vietnam. We can see that coming."[5]

Defense Secretary Melvin Laird elaborated on that point two days later at a Paris news conference while in route to a tour of Southeast Asia. He predicted the United States would end its "combat responsibility in Vietnam by mid summer." In response to a reporter's question about whether this meant all American ground troops might be pulled out of Vietnam by the end of 1971, Laird responded: "the American combat responsibility will be removed as far as South Vietnam is concerned." He went on to say, "We are approaching that position on our May 1 troop ceiling deadline. The position of American forces in South Vietnam after the midsummer period of 1971 will be such that we will have a logistic role, we will have an air support role, and the combat forces which will be assigned to the logistic, support and artillery roles, will not be a combat mission, but will be a security mission. They will be there to protect and to secure the forces that are assigned these roles."[6]

Sensing his January 6 remarks may be misinterpreted, the secretary issued a further clarification at a January 11 press conference in Saigon. He said he didn't envision a security mission, "where you stand around a fence 24 hours a day." The remaining troops would be "on the alert, but careful at the same time, and ready to pursue and seek out the enemy when the time comes. I don't want to give anyone the impression here that the security forces which are stationed with American logistics, artillery and air units will not be used to protect the lives of Americans stationed here," he concluded.[7]

The subtleties of "defensive" patrols around artillery bases versus "offensive" patrols would prove to be a bone of contention between the country's political leaders and the troops on the ground later that year, but during the second week of January the news from the field seemed to support the administration's upbeat assessment. On January 9 the U.S. Command in Vietnam failed to issue a morning press release for the first time in more than three years. "There just wasn't anything to report," a spokesman said. "Normally we report B-52 strikes in Vietnam. There were no B-52 strikes. Normally we report indirect fire attacks against U.S. personnel. There were no indirect fire attacks. Normally we report ground actions involving U.S. troops. There were no ground actions."[8] Later that same day, the New York Times quoted "reliable reports" that the United States would pull out 20,000 more combat troops from the area surrounding Saigon over the next four months. This would leave one brigade, or about 5,000 soldiers, with the task of providing security for all U.S. bases and installations in the area.[9]

While the defense secretary was still in Saigon, reports surfaced of two ugly incidents of U.S. soldiers turning on each other. The first occurred at the 5th Mechanized Division base camp at Quang Tri. Two Army officers, both majors, were shot following an argument with four enlisted men over a loud phonograph. One died, the other was wounded. Both officers were white; the four enlisted men were black.[10] The next night, January 11, military police had to be called in to break up a riot involving U.S. soldiers at the base camp at Tuy Hoa that included one American soldier tossing a live hand grenade into a group of fellow soldiers at an enlisted man's club. Twenty-seven soldiers were injured.[11] When asked about the morale of American troops, Secretary Laird put the best face on that he could by saying the current morale problems "are good problems for our commanders to have"—because they are indicators of a reduced level of combat. But he added he would still not be satisfied "until those casualties get down to zero."[12]

February brought a respite from stories about fighting among American troops as most reports focused on the South Vietnamese incursion into Laos in Operation Lam Son 719. The effort was aimed at disrupting the enemy logistics network along the Ho Chi Minh Trail, but South Vietnamese units ran into unexpectedly strong resistance and soon found themselves being pursued back across their own border by the North Vietnamese. TV reports featured images of retreating South Vietnamese soldiers desperately clinging to helicopter skids while trying to escape. A Harris Poll the second week of March showed a majority of Americans thought the Vietnam War was "morally wrong," and a similar majority thought the president was not telling them the truth about the war. Their evaluation of President Nixon's handling of the war dropped to its lowest level since he took office.[13]

By the end of March, fighting, or lack of fighting, by U.S. troops crept back into the headlines. Five miles west of the Laotian border, a *Time Magazine* reporter came across an armored column stopped on Route 9. He asked what was going on. It turned out they had been ordered to move down the road to secure a downed helicopter and other equipment to keep it from falling into enemy hands. The GIs from the Americal Division's 1/1 Armored Calvary refused, saying it was too dangerous. In all, fifty-six men were involved.[14] The unit had to be pulled out and replaced with a different unit that finished the job.

Two weeks later, the Army revealed that a team of North Vietnamese commandos operating under the cover of darkness snuck into an Americal Division forward base named Mary Ann fifty miles south of Danang. Before they were finished they had killed thirty-three GIs and wounded seventy-six more, many while they slept. The enemy lost less than ten of their own before slipping out into the darkness.[15] The debacle at Fire Support Base Mary Ann would be one of the Army's most embarrassing defeats of the war. Accusations and speculation swirled about possible drug use and carelessness of the soldiers involved. An infuriated General Creighton Abrams initiated an investigation that resulted in disciplinary action against several officers in the unit who he held responsible.[16]

That same day, the Army announced the conviction of First Lieutenant William Calley for his role in the massacre of 500 unarmed civilians in the village of My Lai three years before. Although the My Lai massacre was old news by this point, the continuing drumbeat of ugly revelations about the actions of American soldiers and the resultant cover-ups further eroded faith in the Army and its leadership. A month later Colonel Oren K. Henderson, the highest ranking officer charged in the cover-up of the killings by troops under his command, defended himself by telling reporters, "Every unit of brigade size has its My Lai hidden some place."[17]

April brought more disturbing news about violence directed against GIs by other GIs. The Pentagon released figures about the dramatic rise in fragging incidents—the use of fragmentation grenades, usually by lower ranking enlisted men, against senior officers or noncommissioned officers. The Pentagon reported the number of fraggings in Vietnam had more than doubled from 96 in 1969 to 209 in 1970, even though the number of troops stationed in Vietnam had declined. Senate Majority Leader Mike Mansfield, who had asked the Pentagon for the numbers after one of his constituents lost their son in such an incident, said the fraggings were "just another outgrowth of this mistaken, this tragic conflict."[18]

The month ended with a massive antiwar rally in Washington, D.C., that featured a group of Vietnam veterans throwing their decorations over a White House fence to protest continuation of the war. The week's events included the televised testimony of decorated Vietnam veteran John Kerry, who implored the Senate Foreign Relations Committee: "How do you ask a man to be the last man to die for a mistake?"[19]

One enemy rocket produced a tragic outcome that made headlines in May. It slammed into a small sixteen-by-thirty-two-foot bunker at an American base called Charlie 2 just south of the demilitarized zone. The rocket, armed with a time delay fuse, penetrated six feet of protective earth and planking before exploding. Thirty GIs were killed and nearly an equal number were wounded. When asked why they had violated the preferred practice of dispersing when being shelled, one of the few remaining survivors explained they were all eating dinner and ran to the nearest bunker when the attack started.[20] Days later, enemy commandos snuck into the supposedly well-defended base camp at Cam Ranh Bay and blew up one and a half million gallons of aviation fuel. They escaped undetected. The base at Cam Ranh Bay had once been considered the safest place in Vietnam—so safe President Johnson was able to visit U.S. troops there four years earlier.[21]

May ended with renewed emphasis on the growing drug problem in Vietnam. The Pentagon disclosed that an estimated 30,000 drug addicts were serving in Vietnam, or about one soldier out of every eight. Those figures applied only to soldiers addicted to opiates or cocaine. It did not include soldiers addicted to amphetamines, barbiturates, LSD, or other drugs. Nor did it include regular or occasional marijuana users. In which case, the percentage was reported to exceed 50 percent.[22]

The most scathing attack on the performance of the U.S. Army in Vietnam to date came that June. It came not from antiwar critics in the press or in Congress, but in the usually circumspect *Armed Forces Journal*—a publication whose core audience consisted of career military people and military contractors. Writing in the June 7 issue, Robert Heinl offered this assessment, "By every conceivable indicator our army that now remains in Vietnam is in a state approaching collapse, with individual units avoiding or having refused combat, murdering their officers and non-commissioned officers, drug-ridden, and dispirited where not near mutinous."[23]

What gave Heinl's assessment added resonance was not only its publication in a respected pro-military publication but also his own background. He was no young antiwar reporter, but a retired marine colonel. He went on to issue a particularly ominous warning, "All the foregoing facts—and mean more dire indicators of the worst kind of military trouble—point to widespread conditions among American forces in Vietnam that only have been exceeded in this century by the French Army's Nivelle mutinies of 1917 and the collapse of the Tsarist Armies of 1916 and 1917."[24]

At first Heinl's salvo laid there—similar to a secret someone had dropped at a family dinner table. No one was sure what else to say. No one wanted to touch it. Everyone hoped someone would change the subject. That would happen on June 13 in the form of an even more startling revelation. The *New York Times* published the first in a series of leaked secret reports, known as the "Pentagon Papers."[25] These documents were originally compiled by the Johnson administration to trace the history of U.S. involvement in Vietnam from 1954 to 1968. First released by the *New York Times*, then other newspapers, the Pentagon Papers would dominate the news over the summer of 1971. Although the once top-secret subject matter dealt with events that preceded the Nixon administration's Vietnam policy, the succession of revelations about deliberate government lying and obfuscation further eroded public trust in the military and civilian leadership.

As summer faded into fall and the Pentagon Papers ran their course, other media outlets picked up on the themes outlined in Heinl's June indictment. "The bitter Vietnam experience has left the United States Army with a crisis in morale and discipline as serious as any of its oldest and toughest soldiers can remember," B. Drummond Ayres wrote in a front-page story for the September 5, 1971, edition of the *New York Times*.[26]

Conservative columnists Rowland Evans and Robert Novak chimed in with a September 17 piece titled "Last GI's in Bitter Mood." The combination of the gradual nature of Vietnamization and declining war support at home "has led to American forces so dispirited that, in the view of many officers, they constitute nothing less than a national disgrace."[27]

In mid September, the *Washington Post* ran a weeklong series titled "Army in Anguish." A team of the *Post*'s top reporters spent three months visiting U.S. troops at home and abroad, laying out the Army's wrenching difficulties with discipline and morale, crime and drug abuse, racial tension and leadership. The final story of the series on page 1 of the September 20 edition included this observation from Alfred B. Pitt, the Pentagon's former manpower chief: "I think Vietnam's been an unmitigated disaster for the country, for the armed forces and for the Army. I've often pondered since I've left the Pentagon how we managed to make a mess of things. . . . I wish I could find some consolation, some suggestion that all those people have died in a cause that was worth it, but I don't find such consolation."[28]

By now the GIs developed their own name for their efforts in Vietnam—the Four U's:

We are the
Unwilling, led by the
Unqualified, to do the
Unnecessary, for the
Ungrateful.[29]

For those who thought the Four U's were too subtle, the GIs had an expression for that too: "Fuck it; it don't mean nothin'."[30]

Thus, as the fall campaign season in Vietnam loomed, senior U.S. civilian and military leaders had to wonder: what if North Vietnamese forces made a move against American troops, or if American troops were just in the way? Would such a dispirited group of soldiers even be able to defend themselves?

CHAPTER TWO

Proud Americans
November 1965–February 1971

The "Proud Americans" of 2/32 Field Artillery were one of the first Army ground units to arrive in Vietnam. They would be one of the last to leave. In between, they fired more than 500,000 rounds in support of U.S. and Vietnamese troops. Thirty-seven artillerymen from 2/32 would give their lives.[1]

The 2/32 Field Artillery was organized in August 1918. Activated too late for World War I, it disbanded four months later. The unit was reconstituted in 1929 and saw service in World War II in support of the Army's 1st Infantry Division in North Africa, Italy, France, and Germany. It was demobilized again after World War II and did not participate in the Korean War. However, it was reactivated in January 1963, just in time to serve in Vietnam. The battalion arrived in Saigon on November 4, 1965. Two months later, the 2/32 moved its base camp to Cu Chi, northwest of Saigon, where it supported elements of the 1st and 25th Infantry Divisions.[2]

If the infantry was the queen of battle, the field artillery saw itself as the king. The helicopter gunships and the jet fighter bombers might get all the glory, but when the chips were down, it was the artillery that would put steel on the target. The gunships were powerful, but they carried limited payloads, were vulnerable to ground fire, and couldn't operate in bad weather. The fighter-bombers were flashy and carried bigger payloads, but they were not always precise (especially in bad weather) and could take a long time to arrive from distant airfields. The field artillery on the other hand could respond quickly (usually in a minute or less), accurately (in some cases as close as fifty yards), and, most important in Vietnam, in any kind of weather, night or day.[3]

The guns of the 2/32 epitomized the saying "bringing in the heavy artillery." Its eight-inch howitzers and 175mm guns were the biggest in the Army's inventory. Each of its three firing batteries consisted of two of these powerful howitzers and two long-range guns. The M110 Eight Inch howitzer, known to the troops as the "Short Stubby," fired the heaviest round in the Army's Vietnam arsenal. It could fire an eight-inch diameter, 200-pound projectile 16,800 meters, or ten miles. The burst covered an area more than half the size of a football field (30 x 80 meters) and spit off deadly shrapnel up to 500 meters away.[4] It was also the most accurate piece in the Army's arsenal, which made it ideal for bunker and tunnel busting.

The M107, 175mm "Long Skinny" was the longest range artillery piece the

Army had. It could fire a 150-pound projectile 32,700 meters, or almost twenty miles, out of its thirty-five-foot long barrel.[5] The muzzle velocity from the long tube was so great that in early versions it would wear out after only 400 rounds and would need to be replaced.[6] It was not the most accurate weapon in the arsenal, but its long range made it extremely valuable in the drawdown period of the war, as fewer and fewer American troops were left to cover a wider and wider area. From a single firing position, one Long Skinny could cover nearly 1,400 square miles.

Both the M107 and M110 were mounted on self-propelled tractor chassis, so they were, in a sense, mobile. But their size and weight (about thirty tons each) restricted movement pretty much to roads and level ground. Each gun or howitzer required a crew of ten to keep it firing. The sustained rate of fire was one round every two minutes, although they could fire at twice that speed for short periods of time. Because of their size and range, these weapons seldom fired at targets the crew could see. Instead, sighting depended on map locations called in by ground observers, air observers, and other intelligence sources such as radar, sensors, and infrared intelligence. They were usually grouped into four gun batteries to achieve concentrated fire power.[7]

In addition to four ten-man gun crews, a firing battery required about forty to fifty men in direct support. This included a fire control section, battery headquarters, communications, maintenance and supply personnel, and the battery medic. The battery required about thirty vehicles to provide support and supplies, mostly light and medium trucks. Battalion provided additional fire support, communications, maintenance, and supply personnel.[8] As powerful as these big guns were, they were also vulnerable. Not only were they big targets, but the gun platforms were too big to be protected by an armored enclosure the way other self-propelled guns were. Crews were exposed and in the open when firing. This would prove to be a difficult challenge when nearby enemy troops could sneak to within mortar and small arms range.

Consequently, Army doctrine called for co-locating the Long Skinnies and Short Stubbies with medium or light artillery wherever possible. The 155mm howitzers of the medium artillery could hurl a ninety-five-pound high explosive projectile about ten miles.[9] The ubiquitous 105mm howitzer represented the light artillery. It could fire a thirty-three-pound round up to six miles.[10] Although they lacked the range and punch of the heavy artillery, the 155mm and 105mm howitzers were much more effective at close-in defense because of their lower profile (less of a target) and more rapid rate of fire.

In April 1967 the 2/32d battalion headquarters moved to Tay Ninh City, which at that time was the logistics hub for all U.S. forces operating in Tay Ninh Province.[11] It would remain there for the next four and a half years. Tay Ninh City lay fifty miles northwest of Saigon, astride one of the historical invasion routes to the populous heart of Vietnam. Tay Ninh Province jutted into neighboring Cambodia, which surrounded it on three sides. The border between the two countries squiggled back and forth, producing distinct outlines on military maps with names that would become familiar to American GIs, such as the Parrot's Beak, Angel's Wing, Dog's Head, and Fish Hook.

Dense, tropical forest covered the area. Fanning out to the north, northeast, and northwest from Tay Ninh, it covered 1,500 square miles of sparsely inhabited terrain. This proved to be ideal concealment for enemy forces and had remained a Communist stronghold since the days of the Viet Minh's war with the French beginning in the late 1940s. The French had divided the region around Saigon into four zones: A, B, C, and D. The area northwest of Saigon became War Zone C. Heavily wooded and sparsely populated, War Zone C (and War Zone D next to it) became favorite base areas for Vietcong and North Vietnamese troops operating between Saigon and the Cambodian border (see fig. 2.1).[12]

By late 1966 U.S. forces were strong enough to begin forays into the edges of War Zone C. In February 1967 they struck at the heart of this enemy base area. Under the code name "Junction City," over 50,000 soldiers, including those from the 2/32d, charged into this area in a combined land and air assault in what would be the largest U.S.–South Vietnamese operation of the war to date. The stated goal was to "destroy COSVN [the Communist headquarters for all of Vietnam] and VC/NVA forces and installations."[13]

By the time the operation concluded in May, the U.S. Command would claim a significant victory, saying enemy forces had been "trounced," leaving behind a confirmed body count of 2,728 enemy dead. In fact, only one of the three stated objectives had been achieved. Allied forces did report destroying 5,000 enemy bunkers and other military structures and capturing hundreds of tons of weapons and supplies.[14] But, the vast majority of enemy soldiers escaped across the Cambodian border, along with COSVN, to return at a time and place of their own choosing. That time and place would be the 1968 Tet Offensive less than a year later. The offensive, which featured attacks on cities and towns throughout Vietnam (including Tay Ninh City), failed to achieve its objective of a public uprising and was eventually repulsed by U.S. and South Vietnamese troops. However, the strength of the offensive demonstrated that the war was far from over and raised serious questions about the ultimate U.S. strategy.[15]

The last half of 1968 and the first half of 1969 brought major changes in the way the war would be conducted, both in War Zone C and across Vietnam. These changes helped shape the battle for Fire Support Base Pace three years later. In November 1968 the American voters elected Richard M. Nixon president. He promised to bring an honorable end to the Vietnam War. In June 1969 he and South Vietnamese President Thieu jointly announced how they proposed to do this. While still attempting to negotiate with the enemy, the United States would

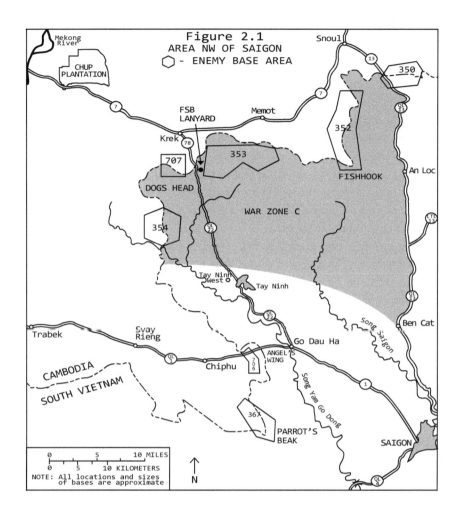

Figure 2.1
AREA NW OF SAIGON
◯ - ENEMY BASE AREA

Mekong River
CHUP PLANTATION
Snoul
350
FSB LANYARD
Memot
352
Krek
707
353
DOGS HEAD
FISHHOOK
An Loc
WAR ZONE C
354
Tay Ninh West
Tay Ninh
Trabek
Svay Rieng
Go Dau Ha
Ben Cat
Song Saigon
CAMBODIA
SOUTH VIETNAM
Chiphu
ANGEL'S WING
Song Vam Co Dong
361
PARROT'S BEAK
SAIGON

0   5   10 MILES
0   5   10 KILOMETERS
NOTE: All locations and sizes
of bases are approximate
N

gradually withdraw its ground forces, their place to be taken by upgraded South Vietnamese troops.[16]

General William Westmoreland, senior U.S. commander in Vietnam since 1964, rotated back to the United States in August 1968. He was replaced by his deputy, Creighton W. Abrams. By mid-1969 Abrams had redirected U.S. ground troops away from large multi-division sweeps with high body counts to focus on smaller, more mobile battalion and company level strike forces aimed at the enemy's logistical support structure.[17] One of Abrams's first actions was to transfer the powerful 1st Cavalry Division from Quang Tri Province, just south of the Demilitarized Zone, south to the Cambodian border area north and northwest of Saigon. Highly mobile, with four times more helicopters than the typical U.S.

infantry division, the 1st Cav, supported by other units, including the 2/32d Field Artillery, began to methodically push Vietcong and North Vietnamese units away from Saigon and Tay Ninh and other population centers.[18]

By Spring 1970, after more than a year of sustained effort, the North Vietnamese in War Zone C had been pushed out of Vietnam almost entirely.[19] The North Vietnamese that remained struck back with a series of mass assaults against remote 1st Cavalry firebases near the Cambodian border. The enemy counterattacks reached a climax on April 1, 1970, when units of the NVA 9th Division—the same unit the U.S. had "trounced" three years earlier in Junction City—attacked Fire Support Base Illingsworth.[20] Illingsworth was situated in the Dog's Head part of Tay Ninh Province, only about ten kilometers (six miles) from where FSB Pace would be constructed a year later.

The attack by an estimated 600 NVA regulars began under cover of darkness at 0218 hours with a 300-round mortar-and-rocket barrage against Illingsworth. It ended two hours later with the enemy in retreat after a combination of tactical air strikes, helicopter gunships, artillery barrages from nearby firebases, direct fire from artillery at Illingsworth, small arms, and even hand-to-hand combat on the perimeter. The failed assault cost the Communists sixty-five dead soldiers left behind, but it cost the United States twenty-four killed and fifty-four wounded.[21] U.S. casualties included three soldiers killed and twelve wounded from A Battery 2/32 Field Artillery, which had two eight-inch howitzers deployed at Illingsworth. It would be the 2/32d's third largest one-day loss in the war.[22]

The fighting on the Vietnamese side of the Cambodian border sputtered out quickly after Illingsworth. But the overthrow of the neutralist Sihounok government in Cambodia by the pro-U.S. General Lon Nol in April gave the United States an opening to do what many military planners had wanted to do for years—go after the Communist sanctuaries across the border. Advocates for such a move found a strong supporter in President Nixon. The immediate military objectives were similar to the operations at Junction City three years earlier: destroy enemy forces and base camps and hopefully find and destroy COSVN, which was now believed to be in the jungle near the Cambodian town of Memot.[23]

But the 1970 Cambodian operation was much broader in scope than Junction City geographically. Instead of just focusing on the northern part of Tay Ninh Province, Operation Toan Thang (Total Victory), as it was known, covered the Cambodian border area all the way from the Mekong Delta to the Central Highlands in the north. Two batteries of the 2/32d (Charlie and Bravo) followed U.S. troops into Cambodia and set up firebases there. When U.S. and South Vietnamese troops crossed into Cambodia near the Dog's Head and Fish Hook in early May, the 2/32 provided fire support to the tune of 18,000 rounds over a two-month period.[24]

In a little over sixty days of operations, Allied forces claimed a resounding success. This included more than 8,000 NVA killed or captured in Military Region III alone (compared to 2,300 in Junction City), 1,800 crew served weapons captured or destroyed (compared to 100 in Junction City), and 6,500 tons of rice captured (compared to 810 tons in Junction City).[25] But, in the end, Toan Thang produced an outcome frustratingly similar. Enemy infrastructure had been destroyed, but the bulk of the enemy forces escaped deeper into Cambodia to fight another day and, with them, the perpetually elusive COSVN.[26]

That left MACV with a difficult dilemma. If Communist forces were allowed to reoccupy their Cambodian border sanctuaries, much of the success in destroying their physical infrastructure would be lost. But President Nixon had already promised all U.S. forces would leave Cambodian soil by June 30. Many of those units would have to leave Vietnam entirely over the next six to twelve months to meet the president's phased withdrawal timetable. This included two-thirds of the 1st Cavalry Division.[27]

The South Vietnamese Army, on the other hand, operated under no such constraints and could stay in Cambodia as long as needed. The problem was that they lacked the ability to provide sophisticated fire support, particularly both fixed and rotary wing aircraft and medium and heavy artillery.[28] The aircraft could be based in Vietnam and still fly into Cambodia. The artillery could stay in Vietnam and fire into Cambodia. Consequently, the U.S. Command decided to position medium and heavy artillery in an interlocking chain of firebases along the entire length of the Vietnamese-Cambodian border. In this way they could provide support to the South Vietnamese units ten to twenty miles deep into Cambodia, while those units formed a screen to keep the North Vietnamese out (see fig. 2.2).[29]

Fire Support Base Lanyard was one of those bases. Built to accommodate a battery of four heavy guns and a battery of six medium guns, it could provide around-the-clock, all-weather fire support to the South Vietnamese forces, then miles away, trying to keep the North Vietnamese out of the Chup Rubber Plantation.[30] Lanyard was positioned at the neck of the area known as the Dog's Head just 300 yards from the Cambodian border. It was less than one-quarter mile from the abandoned border village of Xa Mat. Although not known to Allied Intelligence at the time, Xa Mat had been the reported location of COSVN, the Central Headquarters for all Communist forces in South Vietnam. It relocated to Cambodia when U.S. forces flooded the area in the first half of 1970.[31]

Vietnam-era firebases were muscular descendents of the cavalry forts of the American West a hundred years earlier. These isolated outposts, deep in hostile territory, were designed to be able to defend themselves against all comers. They served as a secure base of operations for mobile forces that scoured the countryside for hostiles and protected key transportation lines. While there were many similarities, there were differences as well. Unlike a hundred years ago, when hostile Indians would very rarely attack the fort itself, the North Vietnamese

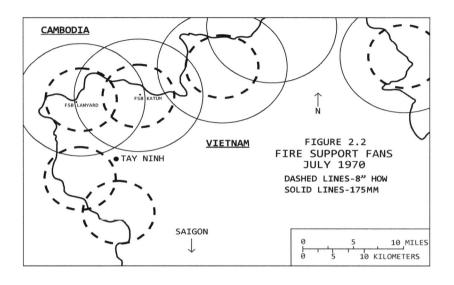

CAMBODIA

FSB LANYARD

FSB KATUM

VIETNAM

● TAY NINH

↑
N

FIGURE 2.2
FIRE SUPPORT FANS
JULY 1970
DASHED LINES-8" HOW
SOLID LINES-175MM

SAIGON
↓

| 0 | | 5 | | 10 MILES |
| 0 | | 5 | | 10 KILOMETERS |

and their Vietcong allies were not nearly so reticent. They had a variety of deadly weapons at their disposal. They could choose a standoff attack, bombarding the position with rockets and mortars. They could mount a direct frontal assault with massed infantry (usually under the cover of darkness). Or, they could attempt a sneak attack using a small group of highly trained commandos (or sappers) to sneak through the perimeter defenses and destroy key installations and equipment with explosives and small arms, again under the cover of darkness.[32]

Over the course of the war, U.S. forces developed a series of countermeasures to protect remote firebases, including passive measures such as barbed wire and Claymore mines, as well as organic weapons such as machine guns and rifles in the hands of the base occupants. American artillery units that occupied these bases were almost always paired with American infantry units that would provide additional protection for the firebase against direct enemy attacks. A firebase the size of Lanyard would expect to have at least a company of 100 or so infantry assigned to protect the artillery. Often, firebases would also have a battery of four Dusters (twin 40mm cannon mounted on a tank chassis) and/or Quad Fifties (fifty caliber machine guns mounted on a truck chassis) for close-in defense. Originally designed for anti-aircraft defense in World War II, these weapons were also extremely effective against mass ground assaults. In addition, firebases were placed close enough together to mutually support each other with artillery fire in case of attack.[33]

This system worked reasonably well but began to show strain as U.S. ground troops, particularly infantry, began to be redeployed in mid-1969. The gap was supposed to be filled by South Vietnamese units, but the remaining U.S. ground troops were skeptical as to whether these soldiers could really be trusted when the chips were down.[34] However, additional artillery could help. A medium artillery battery of six howitzers provided two major advantages when it came to protecting the base. First, it meant eighty more sets of eyes and ears to perform guard duty and provide perimeter defense. Equally important, the 155mm self-propelled howitzers were much better suited to close-in defense. They lacked the impact of the 2/32d's heavy guns but could fire a much wider array of ammunition much more quickly. Their crew compartments were protected with armor plate, which meant they could fire back while being fired upon.

Charlie Battery 2/32d Field Artillery pulled into newly constructed Firebase Lanyard from Cambodia on June 28, 1970.[35] They were joined by a second battery of six 155mm self-propelled howitzers from Bravo Battery of the 1/27th Field Artillery.[36] Even though their sanctuaries in Cambodia had been destroyed and their soldiers chased into the hinterlands, the enemy was still able to make its presence felt. On June 27 they ambushed the 1/27th Field Artillery's convoy on its way to Lanyard just a half mile northwest of that base. They scored a hit on the lead jeep with a rocket-propelled grenade, wounding the battery commander's driver.[37] Additional protection for the heavy and medium artillery at Lanyard was provided by a platoon of infantry from the U.S. 25th Infantry Division, a company of South Vietnamese soldiers, and a mixed battery of two 40mm Dusters and two Quad Fifty machine guns.[38]

Defensive countermeasures notwithstanding, the North Vietnamese welcomed their new neighbors with a series of mortar barrages every day for a week. Fortunately, these were hit-and-run attacks and did not do much damage.[39] But these attacks would begin anew with much greater intensity fifteen months later.

In mid-August the North Vietnamese returned, ambushing a U.S. Artillery convoy on Highway 22 just south of Lanyard. Tanks from the U.S. 25th Infantry Division were called in to assist South Vietnamese forces securing the road. In what was characterized as a "massive reconnaissance in force," ARVN infantry and American tankers unearthed four huge bunker complexes, one of which was seventy yards long. The positions were subsequently described as "heavily fortified and seemingly withstood air strikes, heavy artillery and tank fire." The structures were destroyed, eleven NVA killed and two more captured, with the loss of two ARVN soldiers killed and no U.S. casualties. The operation was declared a success, but it was clear the North Vietnamese were not going to leave this area without a fight.[40]

The units protecting Lanyard had to be reshuffled as troop withdrawals from Vietnam accelerated in the second half of 1970. The platoon of U.S. infantry defending Lanyard left when its parent unit, the 25th Infantry Division, pulled out as part of Increment V of MACV's withdrawal plan.[41] The six 155mm howitzers of B/2/27th were next, leaving in November 1970. They were replaced, at least temporarily, by B/2/35th Field Artillery and a 155mm self-propelled howitzer battery.[42]

The men of B/2/35 took great pride in their skill in all aspects of field artillery gunnery, but particularly their prowess in close-in defense. This self-assurance stemmed from the successful defense of Fire Support Base Rising Sun in Bin Tuy Province on May 29, 1970. A large enemy force attacked Sun shortly after midnight with mortars, machine guns, and small arms. B Battery responded by lowering the barrels of its six 155mm howitzers and firing away at point-blank range, breaking the back of the massed ground assault. The enemy withdrew, leaving behind forty-one dead. B Battery didn't lose a man.[43] B Battery soldiers earned four Silver Stars for heroism that night.[44] Their battalion commander was so appreciative of their efforts, he asked the battery commander to draw up a list of training points he could share with the other batteries.[45]

After arriving at Lanyard six months later, in November 1970, the artillerymen of B/2/35th decided the South Vietnamese Ranger Company assigned to Lanyard was too inert to provide sufficient security. Consequently, by using volunteers from their own ranks, they began running reconnaissance patrols to the tree line around the base's perimeter to make sure any enemy activity did not go undetected.[46]

The North Vietnamese were still able to make their presence felt. In the first part of January they mortared Lanyard twice for the first time in several months. No U.S. troops were hurt, but several South Vietnamese in the compound across the road were wounded.[47] A couple of days later, the NVA ambushed a South Vietnamese convoy south of Lanyard, causing heavy losses.[48]

On February 5, 1971, the six howitzers of B/2/35 departed Lanyard as part of Increment VI of MACV's withdrawal plan.[49] As B/2/35's convoy disappeared in the dust of Highway 22, the eighty men of Charlie Battery 2/32d remained alone with no U.S. infantry and no medium artillery for the first time since the base opened.

The MACV did not want to abandon Lanyard and its other firebases on the border because South Vietnamese forces fighting North Vietnamese regulars in Cambodia north of Lanyard still needed the support of Charlie Battery's long-range guns. Rumors persist among some officers and enlisted men stationed at Lanyard at the time that the base had to be moved because it was really located in Cambodia—which was prohibited.[50] However, there is no credible evidence to support this.[51] What is clear is that Lanyard had been constructed for two artillery batteries, not one. In addition, living conditions at Lanyard were not good. It occupied a small clearing of low-lying ground that flooded into a muddy morass whenever it rained—and it rained a lot. In fact, a detachment of engineers was assigned to pump water out of Lanyard almost constantly between November 1970 and February 1971.[52] The ultimate solution was to build a new "model" firebase for one battery of heavy artillery a little farther away from the border on higher ground. It would be called Lanyard II.[53]

CHAPTER THREE

Sappers in the Wire
March 1971–August 1971

Gary Lynn Pace loved to build things. After he graduated from high school he attended Clemson University to learn civil engineering. Clemson at that time (1965) required all male students to take two years of ROTC. He decided to stay with Army ROTC for all four years. An active athlete, he played basketball in high school, but a friend convinced him to try soccer even though he'd never played it before. Gary Pace ended up being All Atlantic Coast Conference second team goalie.[1]

When Gary Pace graduated from Clemson in 1969, he was awarded a commission as a second lieutenant in the U.S. Army Reserve and headed off for additional training at Fort Jackson and Fort Belvoir. He was surprised to learn he was being assigned to Vietnam, but felt a strong sense of duty to serve his country in whatever capacity he was asked. He later told friends that even though his wife, Pat, whom he met and married while he was at Clemson, opposed the war in Vietnam, she also strongly supported him and his decision to serve in uniform.[2] Lieutenant Pace arrived in Vietnam in December of 1970. He joined the 31st Combat Engineers at the big U.S. base at Bien Hoa, where he spent an uneventful first three months in the country. But in mid-March he found himself in Tay Ninh and then Fire Support Base Lanyard on the Cambodian border. The 31st Engineers were building a new firebase to be called Lanyard II. Lieutenant Pace took the place of another officer there who had left on R&R.[3]

After a relatively quiet month between mid-February and mid-March, activity increased. A Special Forces officer dropped by Lanyard to warn the troops against going outside the perimeter without armed escort because of an increased enemy presence.[4] On the evening of March 22, Lanyard reported four rounds of incoming from an unknown source. One detonated near U.S. hooches without causing any casualties or damage. A second round detonated in the ARVN compound killing one soldier and wounding another. Two others landed inside the base but failed to explode. An explosive demolition team flew in the next morning to inspect and disarm the two unexploded devices. Officially they were deemed to be "bomb like devices 8–10 inches in diameter."[5] Unofficially, they appeared to be packages of C-4 explosives seated in a bell-shaped device by the VC or NVA, no one was sure which. They were apparently launched at Lanyard from the tree line using a wooden plank as a catapult-like device.[6]

Meanwhile, the construction of Lanyard II continued. Various work details, including Gary Pace and the other engineers, would leave Lanyard I in the morning and make the 1.2 kilometer trek (or about three-quarters of a mile) to the construction site, then return back to Lanyard I every evening for hot meals and a place to sleep. Lieutenant Pace struck up a friendship with the artillerymen there, and every evening after supper he went to the Charlie Battery Fire Direction Center to join the artillerymen in their nightly pinochle game.

At about 2200 hours on the evening of March 29, something detonated a trip flare in the tree line about 300 meters east of Lanyard, interrupting the card game. Not sure if it was enemy approaching the base, an animal of some sort, or just a random event, the base commander ordered the Dusters and Quads to hose down the area.[7]

After that things quieted down. Not knowing what set off the trip flare, the garrison returned to its usual routines. Except for those on guard duty or manning the Fire Direction Center, people gradually turned in. What they didn't know was the trip flare had been set off by a squad of NVA sappers—soldiers specially trained to penetrate the perimeter of allied firebases and similar installations.[8] In fact, it had been sappers who had destroyed Fire Support Base Mary Ann in the northern part of Vietnam just the day before. Later a POW revealed that Dusters and Quads at Lanyard wounded three sappers that night, one of whom was probably killed. Those that remained regrouped to plan a second attack.[9]

At 0430 bright flashes and the crash of explosions rocked the firebase. Under the cover of a barrage of mortars and rocket propelled grenades (RPGs), a team of enemy sappers quickly breached the perimeter wire on the east side of Fire Support Base Lanyard. However, before they could move in for the kill they needed to breach one additional barrier, a line of cyclone fencing originally constructed to protect Lanyard's 155mm howitzers from RPGs.

The delay gave the embattled engineers and artillerymen just enough time to scramble out of their sleeping quarters into defensive positions. Lieutenant Pace led a group of his 31st Engineers toward the direction of the attack. A ferocious firefight ensued in the Motor Pool as both attackers and defenders sought protection around and under the parked vehicles. Red and green tracer rounds streaked through the darkness. Before long, three wounded engineers lay in the open among the burning trucks. Fearing his men would be killed if not moved to safety, Lieutenant Pace ran out to pull Specialist Five Kenneth E. Williams out of harm's way. Standing six foot three, Pace presented a big target to the intruders. They gunned him down, killing him instantly. But by firing at Lieutenant Pace the enemy revealed their position and were in turn fired on by the remaining engineers in his platoon.[10] Two enemy sappers died a fiery death when the fuel truck they were hiding under exploded. Another was crushed by the differential when the tires supporting the water truck he was under collapsed in a hail of bullets.[11]

By the time the firing ceased, five North Vietnamese sappers lay dead. A sixth was wounded and taken prisoner. One South Vietnamese soldier was killed and five wounded. Six trucks were destroyed or badly damaged. Eight Americans were reported wounded. Only one American, Lieutenant Gary Pace, was killed.[12] He was to be the first and only American soldier killed at Lanyard. A group of his comrades carried his body out on a stretcher to the helipad at the main gate and waited with him until it was safe for the helicopter to land to pick him up.[13]

It took a week to ten days for Lieutenant Pace's body to make it back to his hometown of Greenville, South Carolina. His family was stunned when they heard Gary had been killed. Since he was in the engineers, they didn't think he would see hostile action. The family was so upset they had to ask an uncle to go to the funeral home to identify the body. His brother, Steve Pace, later described the visitation and funeral as "the saddest occasion I have ever experienced."[14] In recognition of his heroism and sacrifice, the Army awarded Lieutenant Pace the Silver Star, the Army's third highest award for valor. For Gary's wife, it had to be a particularly difficult time. She had lost the man she loved to a war she had so strongly opposed.

After the March 29 sapper attack was repulsed, enemy activity declined except for the mining of Route 22. Lanyard received a warning a second sapper attack might happen on May 4, but nothing materialized.[15] Meanwhile, preparations for moving to Lanyard II stepped up, including visits from assorted VIPs. Major General Wagstaff, commanding general of all of Military Region III, stopped by on May 14 and told his troops he was "pleased."[16] Army officials also decided to rename Lanyard II in Lieutenant Pace's honor. Lanyard II officially became Fire Support Base Pace when Charlie Battery 2/32d occupied it on May 23.[17] By 1235 hours on May 23, all four of Charlie Battery's guns had been moved to Pace and emplaced.[18] Five days later, the enemy ambushed a resupply convoy 2 kilometers south of Pace on Route 22. One GI was slightly wounded.[19]

As the summer monsoon season dragged on, enemy activity died down significantly. Without that to worry about, if someone still had to be in Vietnam, somewhere like Firebase Pace was not a bad place to be. Remote and isolated, it was a safe distance from the top brass and all the hassles in the rear areas. But because it was a fixed position, soldiers there had it much better than those in the bush. Everyone had a cot to sleep on and a roof over his head. Cooks prepared three meals a day. It was still Army food, but it wasn't out of a cold can, and everyone could eat as much as they wanted. The resupply choppers would also bring mail and news from home every day. Postage was free, and GIs could mail order stereo equipment at rock-bottom prices from the Pacific Exchange catalog and have it shipped home.

Hot and cold running water was not part of the accommodations, but an enterprising trooper could enjoy a warm shower by filling an empty powder canister with water and letting it sit out on the roof of the bunker all day until the water got warm. Then he could fill a canvas bucket hung from a wooden frame called an "Australian shower," turn on the showerlike nozzle, and pretend it was just like home.

Electronic devices were plentiful, including the latest innovation, portable cassette player/recorders. GIs could exchange music and messages with loved ones by mailing cassette tapes back and forth. But the entertainment mainstay for homesick GIs was the perpetually upbeat voice of Armed Forces Radio. Its powerful signal from the transmitter in Saigon came in loud and clear even in the border area. With a small transistor radio, soldiers could enjoy the same music their civilian counterparts heard on Top 40 radio back home, or what the troops called "back in The World." Of course, they had to endure the Army's antidrug commercials, but they could also listen to singer/songwriter Carol King lament "It's too late, baby," from her best-selling *Tapestry* album, or to the Undisputed Truth warn that "smiling faces tell lies (and I've got proof) sometimes." All these electronic devices took batteries, and that could be a problem at remote firebases. Enterprising soldiers could get friends to buy them at the PX when they went to the rear, have family and friends ship them in care packages from the States, barter with their better-supplied South Vietnamese allies, or "liberate" them from the Army's user-unfriendly supply system.

For those seeking more adventure, the running war with the rats was always looking for new recruits. Vietnamese firebase rats were known for their cunning and durability. Seemingly impervious to conventional rat traps and poisons, they were everywhere. "Tons of rats" is how one GI described them. Another GI at Pace complained rats would drop from the sandbag ceiling of his hooch whenever the big guns fired directly overhead. For those soldiers willing to take on the enemy, elaborate countermeasures were available. A favorite was to bait a trap with C-ration peanut butter, then blow the rat away with a chunk of C-4 explosive when it took the bait. A more proactive approach was to go out hunting at night on a rat search-and-destroy operation. Removing the slug from an M16 and replacing it with waded paper or candle wax produced a projectile that was fatal to rats but presumably not dangerous to humans. However, effectiveness of this method required quick reflexes and excellent night vision. A less sophisticated approach called for burning out their nests with unused powder.[20]

In mid-July, a CBS news team visited newly named Fire Support Base Pace on the Cambodian border. Correspondent Ed Rabel, accompanied by a sound and film crew, came to Pace for part of a CBS series on what it called the "special problems" for U.S. GIs as the Vietnam War wound down.[21] Rabel began his report by pointing out that Pace was one of about fifty outposts where U.S. troops were still in a combat role. In addition to footage of Pace's big guns firing into Cambodia, Rabel's report showed some of the diversions that made life a little more tolerable for the troops—mail call, hot meals, cold beer for sale, and friendly volleyball games to pass the time. Still, it was far from home, where most of the GIs wanted to be.

There were other concerns as well. Second Lieutenant Wayne Alberg of Long Beach, California, complained about all the high-ranking visitors who kept dropping in to see this "model" firebase. Second Lieutenant Jim Dupree of Tucson, Arizona, told Rabel his cannoneers were frustrated because they didn't know if they were hitting anything. Their targets were ten or fifteen miles away in Cambodia and often came from classified intelligence sources such as ground sensors and infrared sensors.[22] Rabel also reported that the men feared a nighttime sapper attack similar to the one that killed Lieutenant Pace a little over three months earlier. "The men at Pace believe the Army is getting ready to turn over the firebase to the South Vietnamese who have already taken over most of the combat in Vietnam," Rabel concluded, "and for these men the consensus is, the soonest that can take place is not soon enough."[23]

On August 4, 9,000 miles away in Washington, D.C., President Nixon held his first press conference since June. Major topics included the famine in East Pakistan, the president's upcoming trip to the People's Republic of China, and inflation. But the last question dealt with casualties in Vietnam—did the President think the recent decline to twelve servicemen killed per week was an aberration or would they continue to decline?

"No, they are not an aberration," Nixon explained. "They are the result, frankly, of, first, an American withdrawal. American forces in Vietnam today, as you can tell from reading the reports, are in defensive positions. We are frankly just defending the area in which we have responsibility and there are less of them."

He went on to explain that casualties were also down because "the enemy doesn't have the punch it had. . . . What has happened is that the two operations, Cambodia and Laos, so very severely disrupted the enemy's ability to wage offensive actions that for both Americans and South Vietnamese the level of fighting is down."

"There again will be aberrations up and down, I would assume. Nobody can predict that. But the war is being wound down and, as far as Americans are concerned, we trust it will continue to go down," the president concluded.[24]

CHAPTER FOUR

Bad Omen
September 22, 1971

Veteran soldiers believe that if several layers of command above you take a sudden interest in your defensive preparations, it's not a good sign. Fire Support Base Pace always had a lot of visitors, but beginning the third week in September they took a sudden interest in Pace's defenses. Among them was Major General Jack J. Wagstaff, the senior commander for all U.S. forces in Military Region III, who came out to personally inspect the base on September 22.[1]

General Wagstaff commanded the entire area surrounding Saigon. It stretched from the southern border of the central highlands in the north to the northern border of the Mekong Delta in the south, and from the South China Sea in the west to the Cambodian border in the east (see fig. 4.1). He reported directly to General Creighton Abrams, commander of all U.S. forces in South Vietnam. Wagstaff, sixty-three, had served as an infantry officer in World War II after receiving an ROTC commission from the University of Oregon. He completed a law degree after the end of the war and then went on to serve as chief of staff for the U.S. troops in postwar Berlin. He also commanded troops in Europe and Korea. Wagstaff assumed command of Third Military Assistance Command in May 1971.[2] Now he wanted to personally inspect Pace's defenses and then Katum's before making a decision: pull out or stand and fight.[3]

Approaching Pace from the vantage point of his command helicopter, Wagstaff could see the problem confronting him and his troops: a blue-green sea of treetops stretched all the way to the horizon in all four directions. After years of war, these forests had been bombed, shelled, strafed, burned, and sprayed with defoliants. Yet enough of them still remained to provide cover for the Vietcong and North Vietnamese base camps. A concentrated effort by U.S. and South Vietnamese troops in the spring of 1970 cleared out the North Vietnamese. The enemy fled into Eastern Cambodia, their supplies confiscated, fortifications burned and bulldozed. But everyone knew at the time that they would be back—maybe twelve months, maybe eighteen, but they would be back. Now, fifteen months later, General Wagstaff's intelligence operation told him the North Vietnamese were on the move in alarming numbers. One regiment of North Vietnamese regulars had already moved into the woods near Firebase Pace, with indications of two additional divisions possibly joining them. A third division was moving on Katum. Additional unidentified forces were also believed to be concentrating in

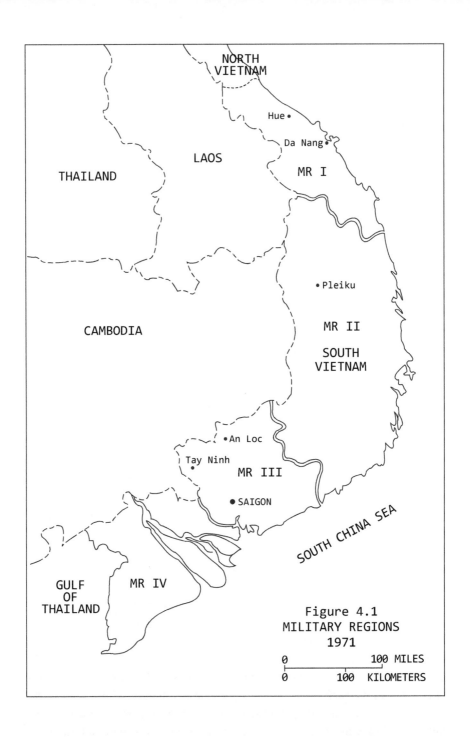

NORTH
VIETNAM

Hue •

Da Nang •

LAOS

THAILAND

MR I

• Pleiku

CAMBODIA

MR II

SOUTH
VIETNAM

• An Loc

Tay Ninh
•

MR III

• SAIGON

SOUTH CHINA SEA

GULF
OF
THAILAND

MR IV

Figure 4.1
MILITARY REGIONS
1971

0   100 MILES
0   100   KILOMETERS

the south between the border and Tay Ninh. In all, there were possibly 20,000–25,000 enemy soldiers in the border area.[4]

The helicopter banked and began its descent toward Pace, an ugly little brown scar sitting like an island amid this sea of forest. Immediately to the right of Pace was a straight, narrow brown line cut through the trees, a two-lane dirt road running north and south, optimistically labeled National Highway 22—Pace's only land route for supplies from Tay Ninh and Saigon. Looking out over the trees, Wagstaff could see how truly isolated Pace was. A mere 300 yards from the Cambodian border, the nearest friendly forces were a company of South Vietnamese soldiers next to Pace and a small South Vietnamese garrison at the former Special Forces camp at Thien Ngon, three and a half miles to the south. The nearest major forces were the South Vietnamese near Krek in Cambodia, more than ten miles away, and they had their hands full. The nearest Americans were fourteen miles away as the crow flies—Charlie's sister battery at Firebase Katum, also on the Cambodian border.[5]

As he walked the base, it was clear to General Wagstaff that the engineers had done a thorough job. The base itself was a square, about 100 meters by 100 meters, circled by an access road and surrounded by an earthen parapet and barbed wire. Charlie Battery's nerve center, the Fire Direction Center, stood in the center of the base, protected by three layers of sandbags in a sturdy bunker. Charlie Battery's four big guns surrounded it, each one dug into circular position protected by an earthen wall four feet high. Ammunition was protected in sandbag-covered dugouts nearby, as were sleeping quarters for the crews. Spread out between there and the perimeter was a mess hall and maintenance and storage facilities. Fuel was stored separately in a protected area (see fig. 4.2). All the phone lines were buried to provide additional protection. Kleg lights were embedded into the perimeter to provide illumination at night. It also included new secret ground surveillance radar that could detect enemy movement in the woods around Pace. And, most important, from the GI's point of view, Pace was built up to remain dry most of the time, as compared to Lanyard, which was under water most of the time.[6]

A four-foot-high earthen parapet ringed the entire perimeter, complete with protected firing positions for rifles and machine guns. But the real firepower would come from the four Quad Fifty machine guns strategically placed at each of the four corners so they could interlock fire. Known officially as .50 cal MG M55, the four 50-caliber machine guns sat on the back of a five-ton flat bed truck. Each gun could put out as many as 1,800–2,000 rounds a minute. Four could put out 7,200–8,000 rounds per minute, shredding everything in their path.[7] Out beyond the perimeter the engineers had cleared twenty-six acres of jungle to provide a 360-degree killing zone around the entire base.[8]

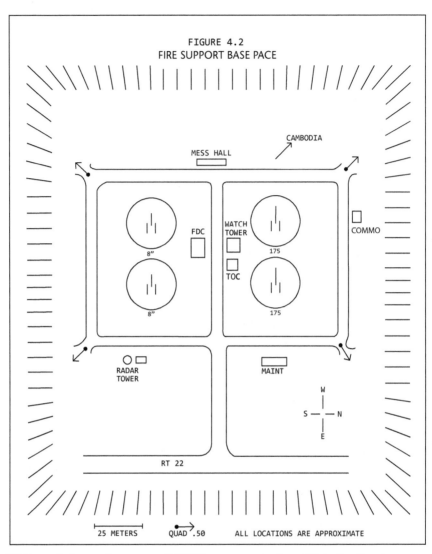

FIGURE 4.2
FIRE SUPPORT BASE PACE

TOC = tactical operations center; COMMO = communications; FDC = fire direction center; MAINT = maintenance.

The Quad Fifties were fearsome but also extremely vulnerable. They sat on high, bulky gun mounts presenting a tempting target for RPGs, mortars, and other close-in weapons used by Communist troops. Army doctrine called for protecting these valuable weapons from close-in attack by direct fire from supporting artillery, machine guns, and riflemen. But Pace had no organic infantry and no supporting fires. There was a company of South Vietnamese infantry encamped nearby, but no one knew if they could be depended on. It didn't take a lot of imagination to see what would happen. Working at night or in bad weather, the North Vietnamese would collect in the surrounding woods. They would sneak up under darkness and a mortar barrage and try to knock out the Quad Fifties and machine gun positions with RPGs and satchel charges. Then, either with commandos or a full-blown ground assault, they would try to storm the place.

The North Vietnamese clearly had the capability to hit hard at a time and place of their own choosing. Just two days earlier, an enemy force estimated at 600 attacked the South Vietnamese Trang Lon base camp near Tay Ninh, twenty miles to the south of Pace. They killed twenty and wounded sixty-three.[9] Since the casualties were all South Vietnamese, it didn't get much attention back in the States, but if these had been American GIs killed and wounded, it would make the uproar over the debacle at Firebase Mary Ann look calm by comparison.

Wagstaff stayed at Pace for about fifty minutes before heading off to Katum. Before he left, he told the soldiers there he was impressed with what he had seen regarding Charlie Battery's defensive preparations.[10] No one could know for sure what the North Vietnamese were up to, or when or where they would strike. His intelligence people speculated they would do something to create a destabilizing embarrassment of the Allies prior to the South Vietnamese presidential elections scheduled for October 3—but exactly what, when, and how was anyone's guess.

To make matters worse, after two years of troop withdrawals, Wagstaff was left with only five maneuver battalions of U.S. combat troops.[11] This translated to about 5,000 GIs to cover an area of 150,000 square miles of military region—only one soldier for every thirty square miles. Of course, he could move one of those battalions or parts of them to protect Pace and Katum, but to do so would show a lack of confidence in the South Vietnamese.[12] And, if he did, that would leave some other area unprotected. Wagstaff had to be aware of the second guessing of General Westmoreland's decision to reinforce the embattled outpost at Khe Sanh in 1968. Critics claimed North Vietnamese General Giap had outsmarted Westmoreland by focusing his attention on Khe Sanh while the real action was aimed at the populated areas targeted as part of the Tet Offensive.

But even if he moved more U.S. troops in to protect Pace and the other border firebases, would it be enough? By now the impact of President Nixon's commitment to withdraw U.S. troops was clearly felt on the ground. Troop withdrawals began in August 1969 at the rate of 10,000 per month, while 524,000 U.S. troops were still in the country. By mid-1971 the withdrawal rate had increased to 14,300 a month, with a goal of having U.S. troop strength at no more than 184,000 by December 1, 1971.[13] The results had dramatically changed the nature of the war in Military Region III. Between April 1970 and April 1971, the U.S. ground combat forces operating in the area had dropped from 3 2/3 divisions with thirty-two maneuver battalions to just 1/3 division with five battalions (see table 4.1). A similar

Table 4.1. Redeployment of Major U.S. Ground Combat Units, Military Region III, 1969–1972

Unit	No. of Maneuver Battalions	Arrived	Departed
Redeployed prior to April 1970:			
3d Brigade 82d Airborne Div	3	September 1969	December 1969
Redeployed April 1970–April 1971:			
1st Infantry Division	9	October 1965	April 1970
199th Light Infantry Brigade	4	December 1965	October 1970
11th Armored Cavalry Regiment (-)	2*	September 1966	March 1971
25th Infantry Division	11	March 1966	April 1971
1st Air Cavalry Division (-)	6	November 1968†	April 1971
Total, April 1970–April 1971	32		
Redeployed after April 1971:			
3d Brigade 1st Air Cavalry	5*	April 1971	June 1972

Source: Shelby Stanton, *Vietnam Order of Battle* (Washington, DC: U.S. News Books, 1981), 71–85, 375–380.
* 2d Squadron, 11th Armored Cavalry, assigned to 3d Brigade, 1st Air Cavalry, April 1971.
†Date arrived in III Corps; arrived in Vietnam September 1965.

drawdown affected the availability of medium/heavy artillery, where the number of battalions had dropped from 10 in April 1970, to only 2 1/3 in September 1971 (see table 4.2).

This meant Wagstaff had to engage in an entirely different way compared to his predecessors. Before he assumed command, his position carried the title of commanding general, Second Field Force Vietnam, the equivalent of an Army Corps. Now his title was commander of the Third Regional Assistance Command (TRAC), where his role was to represent MACV (the U.S. Military Assistance Command for all of Vietnam) and act as the senior adviser to the South Vietnamese Commander of III Corps, who was supposed to be running the show now.[14]

That would be Lieutenant General Nguyen Minh, commander of all the South Vietnamese troops in III Corps. On paper they were a formidable force. Minh could claim a quarter of a million soldiers under his command, including sixty-three maneuver battalions.[15] Since early 1969 the U.S. Command had been engaged in a crash program of Vietnamization to improve the capability of South Vietnamese Armed Forces as U.S. forces withdrew. The South Vietnamese received large infusions of more up-to-date equipment, including the same M16 rifles used by American GIs, as well as armored vehicles and light artillery.

Table 4.2. Redeployment of Medium and Heavy Artillery Battalions, Military Region III, 1969–1972

Battalion	Weapon(s)	No. of Tubes	Arrived	Departed
Redeployed April 1970– September 1971:				
8/6 FA*	155 T/8"	22	October 1965	April 1970
3/13 FA*	155 T/8"	22	April 1966	December 1970
1/27 FA	155 SP	18	April 1967	December 1970
2/35 FA	155 SP	18	June 1966	March 1971
11 ACR (-)†	155 SP	12	September 1966	March 1971
7/8 FA	8"/175	12	June 1967	July 1971
2/12 FA‡	155 T	18	September 1969	August 1971
6/27 FA	8"/175	12	November 1965	September 1971
Total		134		
Redeployed after September 1971:				
2/32 FA	8"/175	12	November 1965	January 1972
5/42 FA	155 T	18	April 1965	April 1972
How/2/11 ACR†	155 SP	6	September 1965	April 1972
Total		36		

*Mixed 155 T/8" battalion includes eighteen 155mm howitzers and four 8-inch howitzers.
†One squadron and a supporting artillery battery reassigned to 3d Brigade, 1st Cavalry Division in March 1971.
‡Activated using assets of 3/197th Artillery of New Hampshire National Guard, which arrived in Vietnam in September 1968.

Manpower was increased and training was substantially upgraded from privates to general officers.[16] But, could they fight?

U.S. observers felt the ARVN performed well alongside U.S. troops in the Cambodian operation of May and June 1970, but subsequent operations had not gone well.[17] Lieutenant General Do Cao Tri, the aggressive commander of South Vietnamese forces in Military Region III, died in a February 1970 helicopter crash just after his troops launched an offensive against Communist base areas in Cambodia. General Minh succeeded him, and things took a turn for the worse. Minh, who was much more cautious than Tri, decided to halt the offensive and pull his troops back to the border. The North Vietnamese ambushed them repeatedly as they tried to withdraw. The retreat turned into a rout.[18]

Five months later, Minh would finally try to take the offensive, this time to relieve an embattled ARVN position near Snoul across the border in Cambodia. Wagstaff had been in command for only a month at that point. What he witnessed concerned him. Once again, Minh tried to rescue a beleaguered garrison. Once again the North Vietnamese sprung deadly ambushes. Once again the South Vietnamese were overmatched and retreated across the border in a costly and humiliating retreat.[19]

Now the Communists were on the move in the northwest corner of Military Region III. Would they make Pace or one of the other firebases in the border area a target to bait a trap for the ARVN? Would Minh buckle again and this time draw American troops into the cauldron? If that wasn't bad enough, two weeks earlier defense of the area around Pace had been assigned to the 25th ARVN Division.[20] The 25th had long had a reputation as one of the worst units in the South Vietnamese Army. One U.S. adviser reportedly described them as "the worst division in any army anywhere."[21] A change in commanders in 1969 improved the unit's performance some, but according to the U.S. Army's own official history, it was still rated "mediocre, even by South Vietnamese standards."[22]

One option would be to pull out entirely and declare victory. A problem with that was it could also be interpreted as a lack of confidence in the South Vietnamese Army to protect the remaining American troops, which in turn would undercut the goal of strengthening their self confidence. A more immediate problem was rounding up enough lift capacity to evacuate both Pace and Katum by road or by air. That would take time, and Wagstaff wasn't sure he could pull it off with the North Vietnamese so close already. One thing was for certain—nothing would be worse militarily than to be attacked while an evacuation was in progress.

They could decide to make a stand and fight, but that had its own set of risks. To have a legitimate chance of survival, these bases would have to be reinforced with ground troops—but from where? As he headed off for Katum, Wagstaff knew his options were limited. His resources were few. His intelligence was fragmentary. His margin for error was nonexistent. Time was running out. Someone had to make a decision and that someone was him.

CHAPTER FIVE

Sky Troopers
September 23–28

They were called grunts, ground pounders, crunchies, boonie rats, or eleven bingos. Like any unit that spent most of their time in the field, they did not look parade ground fresh. Their uniforms were well worn. Their hair, sideburns, and mustaches pushed the edge of Army regulations. Some even wore colored beads or peace medallions on their necks. But to the defenders at Pace, all that mattered was that they would have additional protection. The newcomers brought with them M16 rifles, M79 grenade launchers, M60 machine guns, Claymore antipersonnel mines, and fragmentation grenades. The artillerymen at Pace already had these same weapons and were supposed to be able to use them to defend themselves, but there was a big difference between having someone dedicated to the task of close-in defense and trying to do it yourself while simultaneously working the big guns. Even better, these grunts brought with them two 4.2-inch M30 mortars, also known as "Four Deuces."[1] The Four Deuces lacked the accuracy, range, and punch of field artillery but more than made up for it in flexibility and rapid rate of fire. Unlike the Short Stubbies and Long Skinnies, the Four Deuces were perfect for close-in defense.

Officially, the fifty soldiers disembarking from helicopters the afternoon of September 23 were the Sky Troopers from Charlie and Echo Companies, 1st Battalion, 12th Cavalry Regiment, 3d Brigade (Separate), 1st Cavalry Division (Airmobile).[2] Their arrival meant the U.S. Command had decided to stay and fight and that Firebase Pace now had the close-in infantry support to protect the Quad Fifties that protected the base.

The 12th Cavalry Regiment traced its origins back to 1901 when its members chased Mexican bandits on the Texas border and guerrillas in the Philippines. In 1933 they became part of the newly organized 1st Cavalry Division. They fought the Japanese in New Guinea and the Philippines in World War II.[3] The 12th Cavalry was deactivated after World War II but reactivated as part of the new 1st Air Cavalry Division before it shipped out to Vietnam in September 1965. In the ensuing six years, the 1/12th fought the Vietcong guerrillas and the North Vietnamese regulars all over Vietnam. At first they fought in the Central Highlands, including the Ia Drang Campaign in 1965 and the legendary defense of LZ Bird in 1966. In 1968 they participated in the relief of the besieged garrison at Khe Sanh.[4]

Later that year, the 1st Air Cavalry Division moved south to lead the effort to push Communist forces out of their historic base areas northwest of Saigon. Within eighteen months, they had succeeded admirably, chasing North Vietnamese and Vietcong all the way back to the Cambodian border. Then they led the assault into Cambodia in May 1970, kicking the North Vietnamese even further back into the hinterlands. The Nixon administration declared the Cambodian operation a success. It turned over defense of the approaches to Saigon to the South Vietnamese and continued bringing U.S. combat troops home.

By fall 1971 only one brigade of the 1st Cavalry remained (the 3rd Brigade), including the 1/12th Cavalry, three other cavalry battalions, and an armored cavalry squadron from the 11th Cavalry Regiment.[5] Their role was to serve as the reserve, or "Fire Brigade," for all of Military Region III surrounding Saigon. For most of September, the 1/12th Cavalry operated out of Fire Support Base Timbuktu in Long Khanh Province about 100 miles northeast of Saigon, aggressively patrolling for Communist bases and supply caches.[6]

On the morning of September 23rd, 2d Platoon of Charlie Company and a mortar platoon from Echo Company were hastily airlifted to Fire Support Base Pace while the rest of Charlie Company was shipped to Katum.[7] The next day, the U.S. Command shifted units around to add two platoons from Alpha Company and one platoon from Delta Company to Pace and moved Charlie Company to Katum. That left Pace with seventy infantrymen and eleven mortar personnel. Pace's new defenders spent the next day strengthening its fighting positions and living quarters with the help of the combat engineers stationed there.[8]

Captain Jack Adams commanded Alpha Company. He had spent a previous tour in Vietnam as an aerial observer. He immediately took a helicopter on an aerial reconnaissance of the area surrounding Pace. He found no evidence of enemy activity, but he knew from two previous tours in Vietnam that that didn't mean they weren't out there.[9]

On the early morning of September 26, the North Vietnamese struck. They lit up the northwest corner of Tay Ninh Province and the area between the Vietnamese border and the Cambodian town of Krek. Eight South Vietnamese positions were hit with rocket and mortar attacks and two others with ground assaults.[10] One American position was hit as well—Fire Support Base Pace. Between 0800 and 1830, Pace took twenty-four incoming mortar rounds. Most of them landed outside the perimeter, but one barrage of half a dozen rounds hit on or near the berm about 1000. Three GIs were wounded seriously enough to require medical attention back at the 24th Evacuation Hospital near Saigon.[11] More than 100 rounds of incoming fell on or near Pace over the next two days. The casualty total rose to twenty-one GIs over three days, almost all from shrapnel. Fortunately, no American soldiers were killed, but ten required medical evacuation.[12] At the rate of seven wounded a day, the entire garrison stood a 100 percent chance of being wounded within a month. In addition, one Kit Carson scout assigned to Alpha Company (former North Vietnamese or VC soldiers who rallied to the South Vietnamese and were employed as scouts) was killed by incoming and three others were wounded.[13]

The drumbeat of intelligence reports warning of enemy activity was even more troubling. On the afternoon of the twenty-sixth, 23d Artillery Group received a report that 400 North Vietnamese soldiers were massed in the woods south to southwest of Pace, with the goal of establishing roadblocks and springing ambushes along Route 22, Pace's only land link to the rear.[14] Then came a report that elements of three North Vietnamese Infantry Divisions—the 5th, 7th, and the 9th—were believed to be in the area with up to 25,000 men.[15] An American liaison officer reported that a Cambodian soldier told Vietnamese intelligence he had spotted eight to thirteen enemy tanks hidden in the Chup Rubber Plantation just north of Pace.[16]

The threat of tanks was so alarming because the defenders at Pace weren't trained or equipped to stop them. The North Vietnamese weren't even supposed to have tanks this far south. Pace's big artillery pieces were too slow and too exposed to be effective against tanks. The Quad Fifties could shred the light aluminum skin of aircraft, but their slugs would bounce off tank armor. Pace's defenders had access to LAWS (Light Antitank Weapons Systems), a single-shot, disposable 66mm rocket patterned after World War II bazookas, but these worked only at close range and required a defender with nerves of steel to expose himself to enemy fire to use it. Helicopters and fighter bombers could be helpful, but the North Vietnamese were presumably smart enough to attack at night or in bad weather when aircraft would be grounded or ineffective because of limited visibility.

Perhaps this explains the instruction Charlie Battery received from higher headquarters that same day. They were told to develop a "contingency plan" for destruction of their guns to prevent their capture by enemy forces.[17] Disabling the heavy artillery was neither time consuming or complicated. A thermite grenade inserted into the open breech (rear end) of the barrel, followed by slamming shut the breech block, fused the moving parts together, rendering the cannon useless forever. What this contingency did not address was what would happen to the now gunless artillerymen and the infantrymen defending them. That's where the nearby firebase at Thien Ngon came in. About four miles south of Pace, it was the closest friendly position. If worse came to worse and they couldn't be evacuated by air, either a relief could be mounted from Thien Ngon, or the defenders of Pace could go there if they had to escape over land.

Thien Ngon opened as a Special Forces Camp in December 1967. It served as a base of operations for reconnaissance and interdiction by small teams of Special Forces assisted by Vietnamese and Cambodian irregulars (mercenaries) against the elaborate enemy logistics system in northwest Tay Ninh Province. Designed to hold a small force bordering enemy territory, it boasted stout construction and clear fields of fire. The base withstood numerous mortar attacks in its history, as well as a direct ground assault.[18]

In September 1970 it was turned over to the South Vietnamese Army and became the northernmost base in a series of small bases protecting the critical supply line along Route 22 from Tay Ninh across the Cambodian border to Krek (see fig. 5.1). The South Vietnamese base at Thien Ngon was the only base close enough to actively protect Pace. The mix of South Vietnamese 105mm light howitzers and 155mm medium howitzers emplaced there provided close-in protective fire for Pace called in via radio. Of equal importance was Thien Ngon's counter mortar radar, which proved extremely effective in locating enemy firing positions.

Now the North Vietnamese seemed to be taking an even bigger interest in Thien Ngon than Pace. On the twenty-seventh, North Vietnamese gunners lobbed 150 rounds at Thien Ngon and followed up with two separate ground attacks, which fortunately were repulsed.[19] On the twenty-ninth, they attacked again and were repulsed again.[20] What American commanders didn't know was if the attacks on Thien Ngon were just a random event or part of a larger strategy to knock out Thien Ngon as a prelude to an all-out assault on Pace. As the sun set on September 28, what the people defending Firebase Pace had to worry about was a disturbing trend line: increasingly ominous intelligence from the field about enemy capability, with increasingly threatening enemy activity close by. If in fact their principal objective was to embarrass the U.S.–South Vietnamese war effort prior to the October 3 presidential election, the time was fast approaching to make a move—and there Pace sat, either in the way or as the target.

Captain Tom Timmons, twenty-six, of Melvin, Iowa, had assumed command of Charlie Battery 2/32 Field Artillery on September 7. When he first arrived at Pace he was struck by how clean it looked. His biggest problem seemed to be how to keep it that way for the endless parade of VIPs visiting his model firebase. Now, two weeks later he found himself at the epicenter of what was shaping up to be a big showdown with the suddenly resurgent North Vietnamese. If anyone should have been happy to see the Sky Troopers from the 1/12th, it was him. But he was beginning to have doubts. As the noose around Pace tightened, Timmons began to wonder if they weren't just sitting ducks. He'd suggested to the infantry commander that they conduct reconnaissance patrols outside the perimeter to find the NVA and keep them off balance. The grunts did not seem so inclined.[21]

Timmons called all his section chiefs together for a special conference. He told them Pace was surrounded by enemy troops, with up to 25,000 North Vietnamese regulars in the area. This meant Pace was cut off from resupply by land and would have to be resupplied by air. No one knew yet what the North

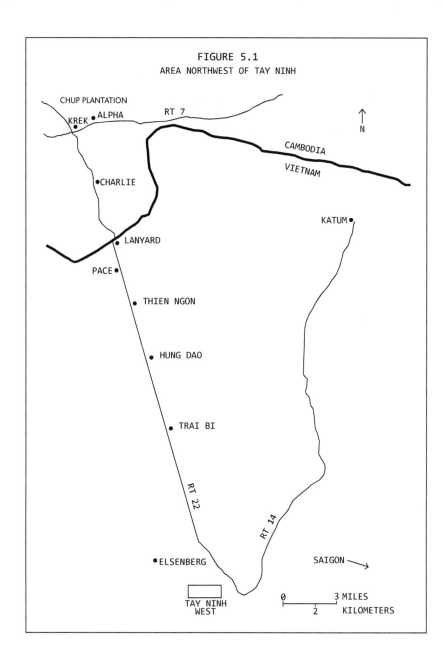

FIGURE 5.1
AREA NORTHWEST OF TAY NINH

CHUP PLANTATION
KREK • ALPHA   RT 7
N

CAMBODIA
VIETNAM

• CHARLIE

KATUM •

• LANYARD

PACE •

• THIEN NGON

• HUNG DAO

• TRAI BI

RT 22

RT 14

• ELSENBERG

SAIGON →

TAY NINH WEST

0   3 MILES
         2   KILOMETERS

Vietnamese's ultimate objective was, but this much was clear: this was serious business. There would be no U.S. reinforcements beyond the soldiers already committed. They would all have to pull together and stay together if they hoped to make it through.[22]

CHAPTER SIX

ARVNs, BUFFs, and Other Friends
September 29–October 3

Sometimes help can come from the most unexpected places. On September 29 Lieutenant General Nguyen Van Minh, General Wagstaff's Vietnamese counterpart, announced a major counteroffensive in northwestern Tay Ninh Province and the Cambodian border regions. Two brigades of the elite South Vietnamese Airborne Division were released from the Strategic Reserve in Saigon to lead the assault. A column of 1,500 men struck northward from Tay Ninh up Route 22. A second column was airlifted to Krek and headed south down Highway 22. The goal was to clear the vital supply line (see fig. 6.1).[1]

Concurrently, the U.S. Command announced moving approximately 1,500 of its own troops into Tay Ninh West, including the 1/12th Air Cavalry and the 2d Squadron of the 11th Armored Cavalry, to secure base camps and supply lines. These efforts came out of a daylong meeting involving top U.S. and South Vietnamese Army and Air Force commanders. Also coming out of that meeting was a decision to play the allies' ultimate trump card—unleashing the B-52s. This would mark the first time in almost a year that B-52s would work over this area.[2] Nicknamed BUFFs (Big Ugly Fat Fellows), the eight-engine jet bombers were designed in the early 1950s to be able to carry nuclear bombs to targets deep within the Soviet Union and safely return. But in the Vietnam War they were used as a way of delivering heavy doses of high explosives to suspected enemy concentrations and base camps on both sides of the Vietnam border.

Flying out of airfields in Thailand and Guam, a flight of three B-52s could carry a load of high explosives sufficient to decimate an area 3 kilometers deep and 1 kilometer wide, or the equivalent of thirty football fields. As the number of American soldiers in Vietnam started to decline after mid-1969, the use of B-52s to fill in the gaps on the ground increased. But, like many powerful weapons, the B-52's destructive power was also its greatest liability. This was before widespread use of so-called smart bombs, so fear of friendly casualties meant that B-52 strikes had to be kept at least one and a half kilometers, or 1,500 yards, away from the nearest friendly troops.[3] Soon the North Vietnamese figured this out, so if B-52s were believed to be in the area, the North Vietnamese would move as close as they could to allied troops—what they called "belt buckle to belt buckle." At Pace, where dense tree cover started 300 yards from the camp perimeter, there were still plenty of places to hide.

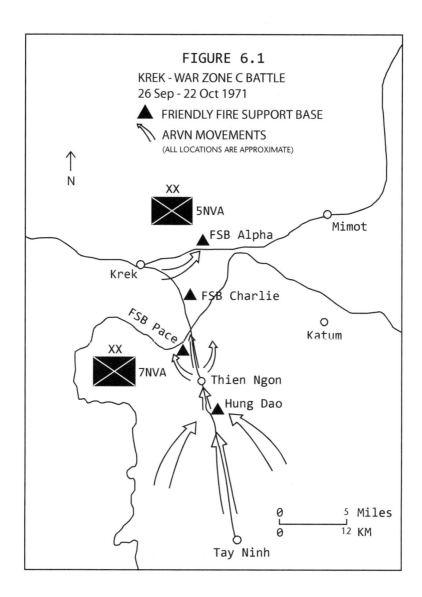

FIGURE 6.1

KREK - WAR ZONE C BATTLE
26 Sep - 22 Oct 1971

▲ FRIENDLY FIRE SUPPORT BASE

↖ ARVN MOVEMENTS

(ALL LOCATIONS ARE APPROXIMATE)

N

XX
5NVA

▲ FSB Alpha

Mimot

Krek

▲ FSB Charlie

FSB Pace

Katum

XX
7NVA

Thien Ngon

▲ Hung Dao

0   5 Miles

0   12 KM

Tay Ninh

This knowledge prompted the 7th Air Force to deploy a new procedure to better protect Pace and other installations. By using a combination of radar and high-powered beacons, they could bring strikes safely to within 1,000 yards. The bombing started just a little after midnight on the twenty-ninth and continued round the clock for the next twenty-one days.[4] Because of the dense terrain and enemy control of the area, it was difficult to precisely assess the damage. But the power was unmistakable. Strong shockwaves could be seen and felt as they cut through the humid air. The ground shook and huge geysers of smoke and dust spit high into the sky.[5] Surely no living things could endure such a pounding and survive. In fact, the U.S. Command reported on October 1 that one B-52 strike had "wiped out" a North Vietnamese supply point near the Cambodian border three and a half miles east of Pace. B-52 and tactical air strikes had inflicted "heavy ammunition and material losses" on the enemy.[6]

On September 29 an officer showed up at Pace from General Wagstaff's headquarters. He brought with him an olive drab box about the size of a present-day computer printer. He instructed the GIs at Pace to place it near the center of the base, report the distance from the berm, then turn it on whenever calling for air support. The troops quickly labeled the instrument the "black box."[7] By using the radio signals from the black box as a homing device, allied aircraft could bring in fire much closer than before. Among them were the AC-130 Spectre gunships. Originally designed as cargo carriers, these aircraft were reconfigured with elaborate detection devices, including radar, infrared, television, searchlight, and laser capability. The aircraft carried lethal weapons, including two 7.62mm Vulcan miniguns, two 40mm Vulcan Cannon, one 40mm Bofors automatic gun and, in some cases, an airborne 105mm cannon.[8] A test run in the early morning of September 30 produced a secondary explosion in the woods around Pace, indicating they hit something. A similar test at FSB Katum produced six secondary explosions.[9] The first time Spectre gunships fired into the woods surrounding Pace after the test run, the rounds were so close that frightened South Vietnamese and American soldiers on the perimeter complained to their superiors to call them off. They were not called off, but Pace suffered no casualties from friendly aircraft in this period.[10]

By the third day of the counteroffensive (October 1), the South Vietnamese command announced that its Tay Ninh based column had busted through to the embattled South Vietnamese firebase at Tran Hung Dao, just six miles south of Thien Ngon and ten miles south of Pace. A second column, moving south from Krek, reported killing thirty-three North Vietnamese while moving to relieve the siege of Fire Support Base Alpha, three miles away.[11] A third column spearheaded by the 11th Armored Cavalry met no resistance as it cleared the road from Tay Ninh all the way to Katum.[12]

If the North Vietnamese were intimidated by all this, they weren't letting on. Instead, they seemed to be focusing on the helicopters supporting Pace. With Highway 22 still blocked, all of Pace's supplies, including food, water, ammunition, and spare parts, had to be delivered by helicopter. The base could probably survive a few days with reserves on hand of food and water, but ammunition and spare parts were another matter, especially for the artillery and the Quad Fifties.

Air resupply for Pace required at least half a dozen flights per day.[13] The ammunition had to be brought in by helicopters, such as the CH-47 Chinook and CH-54 Flying Crane. These big, slow cargo aircraft became favorite targets of the

North Vietnamese anti-aircraft gunners hidden in the woods east of Pace. In the first few days of the siege, a couple of helicopters had been hit. One CH-54 had been chased away by enemy fire, but no aircraft were shot down and no crewmen were killed or injured.[14]

This all changed on the afternoon of September 30. At about 1500 hours, two UHIC Huey gunships from the 117th Assault Helicopter Squadron were traveling parallel to Route 22 providing protection for resupply helicopters. Although the resupply ships flew as high as 5,000 feet, they still received ground fire from the woods east of Pace. Chief Warrant Officer Tom Stansbury commanded the trailing gunship, which operated under the call sign *Sidewinder Four*. Stansbury, who was the unit's scheduling officer, volunteered for the flight, replacing a less experienced pilot because he knew it would be a dangerous mission.[15]

About one and a half miles south of Pace, *Sidewinder Four* began taking ground fire from North Vietnamese .51 caliber machine guns. Stansbury and pilot Warrant Officer Fred Hebert kept the helicopter between the enemy machine guns and the more vulnerable supply ships, even though it began taking hits. Slugs from the .51 caliber machine guns slammed into the ship's engine, starting a fire. Stansbury and Hebert tried to stabilize the aircraft while the crew tried to put out the fire. At between 300 and 500 feet, the tail boom failed, and the helicopter flipped over and crashed. The four crewmen aboard were killed: Fred Hebert of Richmond, Virginia, age twenty; Tom Stansbury of Houston, Texas, age twenty-four; Specialist Four Chris Behm of Pensacola, Florida, age nineteen; and Specialist Four Ron Ricks of Dallas, Texas, age twenty-five. All four men were posthumously awarded Distinguished Flying Crosses.[16] The ship had crashed just south of Pace. GIs at Pace made an effort to recover the bodies but were driven off by heavy enemy fire.[17]

The following day, half a dozen helicopters reported hits from ground fire, wounding three pilots or crew members. Fortunately, none were shot down.[18] Meanwhile, South Vietnamese Airborne slowly worked their way up Route 22. Allied air and artillery continued to pound the surrounding forests, but North Vietnamese gunners to the west of Pace continued to lob 81mm mortar rounds at the base. They missed more often than not but still put enough rounds on target to wound additional GIs. On October 1, two GIs had to be evacuated for medical treatment, one with shrapnel wounds in both feet and another with a wound to the head. Their medical evacuation helicopter took fire as well. A rocket propelled grenade fired from the tree line passed through the base but fortunately didn't hit anyone.[19] Two days later, enemy mortars hit the POL dump, starting a fire.[20]

The South Vietnamese presidential elections went ahead as scheduled on October 3, despite the highest number of enemy mortar and rocket attacks across Vietnam in one and a half years. Pace took twenty-one rounds of incoming that day, but the massive attack everyone feared failed to materialize. President Thieu received 90 percent of the vote amid widespread charges of voter fraud and intimidation.[21]

Concurrently, both of Charlie Battery's sister batteries evacuated their border firebases. Bravo Battery moved overland from Katum on the twenty-ninth, escorted by most of the 2d Squadron of the 11th Armored Cavalry, as well as supporting artillery and gunships. The evacuation of Katum was successful in that it was accomplished without the loss of life. However, it consumed an enormous amount of resources, including the better part of two battalions of air cavalry and armored cavalry, two field artillery batteries, nearly 800 hours of helicopter time, plus additional fixed wing, engineer, medical, and communications support. Even with this support, assorted communications and logistical problems delayed the evacuation. Three vehicles were disabled by mines and six GIs were wounded, three of them seriously.[22] On October 2, Alpha Battery was extracted from Fire Support Base Elsenberg without incident.[23]

Charlie Battery and its supporting infantry and Quad Fifties now stood alone as the only Americans on the Vietnam-Cambodian border in all of Tay Ninh Province. The guns at Pace were still needed to protect South Vietnamese forces still fighting near Krek in Cambodia. In addition, the road extraction from Katum and Elsenberg was possible because the enemy was not active, whereas Route 22 from Pace was still blocked.[24] In any event, the evacuation of Katum must have impressed upon the Third Regional Assistance Command the difficulties of a withdrawal while enemy forces are still active and probably influenced the outcome of the decision to evacuate Pace later in October.

With the South Vietnamese presidential elections now over and the enemy unable to deliver an October surprise, the defenders at Pace should have been at least able to look forward to a more manageable state of equilibrium. After all, the grunts were now dug in to provide closed-in protection. The black box–guided AC-130s constantly raked the North Vietnamese positions in the surrounding woods. Elite South Vietnamese airborne units chased the enemy through the surrounding jungle, and BUFFs plastered enemy base areas and supply lines for miles in all directions. Surely the embattled garrison could assume they had put the worst behind them. In fact, the most difficult days still lay ahead.

CHAPTER SEVEN

Incoming
October 4–8

Command responsibility for the guns and their crews at Pace rested with forty-two-year-old Lieutenant Colonel Robert McCaffree of Seattle, Washington. McCaffree first entered the Army in 1946 as a seventeen-year-old enlisted man. After discharge, he used the GI bill to go to college. He reenlisted in 1950, graduated from the Field Artillery Officer Candidate School at Fort Sill, Oklahoma, and received a commission as a second lieutenant. He served as an artillery forward observer in the last days of the Korean War, where he was decorated for bravery for evacuating a wounded soldier.[1]

Over the next eighteen years McCaffree held a number of command and staff positions but had not served in Vietnam. He volunteered for duty there in 1971. He assumed command of the Proud Americans of the 2/32d Field Artillery on August 20.[2] Charlie Battery at Pace reported to him, as did the battalion's two other firing batteries and various support units. McCaffree in turn reported to Colonel Richard Hoffman, commanding officer of the 23d Artillery Group. Hoffman reported to General Wagstaff's headquarters in Saigon.

Colonel McCaffree operated primarily out of the 2/32d forward headquarters at Tay Ninh West, where he could easily maintain radio contact with Charlie Battery twenty miles away at Pace. He had access to his own command helicopter (an OH-58 Kiowa) and used it to visit Pace as needed. His forward headquarters at Tay Ninh gave him radio, teletype, and direct phone line communication with the battalion base camp at Phu Loi and his superiors at Long Binh near Saigon.[3]

With both Alpha and Bravo Batteries of the 2/32d pulled out of their border firebases at the end of September, McCaffree was free to concentrate on the operations of Charlie Battery at Pace. The language of official documents, such as daily operating logs, is usually bland, but it's easy to see the increased frustration seeping through during the first nine days of October. For example, the entry in the 2/32d battalion log for October 3 at 0910 hours reads: "Pace reports when men man guns they take incoming without failure."[4]

It's not hard to imagine why this was a problem. Loading and firing an 8-inch howitzer or 175mm gun was a labor-intensive process that hadn't changed much since breech-loading cannons were adopted in World War I. Two men would have to manhandle a 150–200 pound projectile out of its bunker, screw off the nose cap, screw on and set a fuse, and then carry it to the automatic loader-rammer to be pushed into the open breech. If the automatic loader-rammer wasn't working properly (which was often the case), then the heavy projectile would have to be hand loaded into the breech. Another team would need to load the powder charge and ram it in after the projectile. Then, a primer had to be inserted and the lanyard hooked up.

Concurrently, the gunner would need to set the deflection (direction) through a telescopic sight, and the assistant gunner would set the elevation (barrel angle) using a device similar to a carpenter's leveler. The command would then need to be read back for accuracy, the air checked to make sure no friendly aircraft were in the way, the fire command given, the lanyard pulled, and the breech reopened and swabbed to remove any sparks.[5]

The whole time this was taking place, the crew was out in the open, exposed to flying shrapnel from enemy mortars and rockets. Shrapnel consisted of jagged, white-hot pieces of metal sprayed in random directions every time a mortar or rocket exploded. The artillery crews were supposed to wear steel helmets and nylon flak jackets for protection. The steel helmets protected the top of the head pretty well, and the flak jackets protected the torso, but this still left the face and neck, as well as arms and legs subject to painful and potentially deadly shrapnel wounds. The artillerymen at Pace knew this, and before long their commanders began worrying about slow response times because the crews were increasingly reluctant to leave their bunkers and expose themselves to hostile fire.

The North Vietnamese weapon of choice in these cases was usually a Korean War vintage Chinese or Russian made 82mm mortar. Deceptively simple—a four-foot tube attached to a base plate and bipod with a crude arming device. Weighing only 123 pounds, it could quickly be assembled or dismantled by a three-man crew. It could hurl a six-pound projectile up to 3,000 yards.[6] Although its explosive charge was puny compared to a 200-pound 8-inch howitzer round, for example, the shell fragments were deadly to personnel in the open.

Because the mortar fired a high arc, an even minimally competent crew could drop two or three rounds into the tube in quick succession, then scramble back into a protected bunker before impact fifteen seconds later. Covered with layers of dirt and logs, these prepared positions could survive just about anything except a direct hit from a B-52. And, by placing their bunkers in the woods, less than 1,000 yards from Pace, the enemy could steer clear of B-52 strikes.

Most rounds fired this way missed the target completely. But just enough landed inside the berm to create a nagging problem. The Americans and South Vietnamese threw everything they had at the North Vietnamese gunners: tactical air strikes; helicopter gunships; heavy, medium, and light artillery; Four Deuces; Quad Fifties; and M79s. Using the Q4 countermortar radar from Thien Ngon, they could even plot firing points with precision (see fig. 7.1) but still could not stop the bombardment.

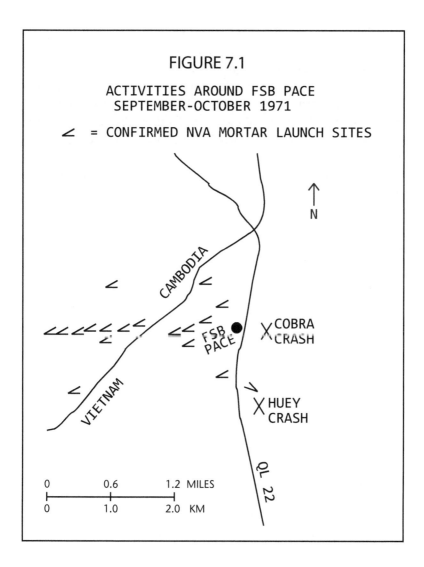

FIGURE 7.1

**ACTIVITIES AROUND FSB PACE
SEPTEMBER-OCTOBER 1971**

∠ = CONFIRMED NVA MORTAR LAUNCH SITES

Fortunately, the mortar's long flight time usually gave the intended targets an opportunity to take cover. The defenders at Pace kept the Quad Fifty closest to the tree line manned twenty-four hours a day as an early warning post. As soon as the sentry heard the telltale hollow metal clunk from the tree line, he could alert the rest of the base. Exposed personnel would then have ten to fifteen seconds to seek cover.[7] But even that wasn't foolproof. Operating the hydraulics on the big guns required the engine to be running. When the engine was running, it was difficult to hear anything over the noise.[8]

The North Vietnamese also added a few twists of their own. For example, whenever someone would go out in the open area of the base to lay the guns (an artillery term for realigning the sights so the guns fired accurately), that individual would immediately draw fire.[9] Relaying the guns was important because the recoil from the blast associated with hurling a 150–200 pound projectile ten to twenty miles could actually lift the front of a thirty-ton gun carriage several inches off the ground. The carriage would settle back in, but a difference of even less than an inch in the alignment of the sights or the gun barrel could cause a firing error of disastrous consequences down range. Consequently, the guns at Pace had to be relayed at least daily.[10] The North Vietnamese knew this and seized on the opportunity to fire on exposed personnel. Rumors persisted among the troops that the enemy either had a forward observer hidden somewhere near the perimeter or a spy among the ARVNs.[11]

The shelling of Pace was not as intense as experienced elsewhere. For example, Fire Support Base Illingsworth endured a barrage of over 300 rounds in just a few minutes when it was attacked in April 1970.[12] Pace, by comparison, was taking 20–30 rounds a day, and no U.S. soldiers had been killed by incoming in the two weeks since the enemy offensive began. But neither the artillery or infantry personnel at Pace had come under enemy mortar fire before to this degree, and a number of gruesome injuries due to flying shrapnel put people on edge. One soldier reportedly lost his leg. A second lost his foot. A third lost his eyesight because of metal fragments in his eyes. A fourth had a jagged piece of shrapnel penetrate his wrist and come out the other side.[13] Meanwhile, every time enemy rounds were in the air, the alert would sound and everyone on the base would have to stop what they were doing and either seek cover or continue to risk death or injury to keep the base and its four guns operating.

In addition to mortars, the North Vietnamese surrounding Pace were close enough to bombard the base with RPGs and recoiless rifles. Originally designed as a weapon to protect infantry against armor, the RPG operated similar to a World War II bazooka. It could be fired from the shoulder by one man and hurled a fist-sized charge up to 500 yards. Not only could it penetrate steel, it could also be deadly against sandbags and bunkers.[14]

Unlike mortars, whose payload is fired in a high arc, RPGs had a flat trajectory and arrived quickly with little warning. The best defense against them consisted of cyclone fencing (known as an RPG screen) set off two to three feet in front of a bunker or doorway, which would cause the charge to explode prematurely before it could do any damage. But the RPG screens could interfere with return fire, and taking them down left the gun crews and their guns vulnerable to RPGs. In fact, McCaffree got into an argument with his executive officer at Pace because the latter refused to take down an RPG screen in order to allow one of his 8-inch howitzers a clear shot at a suspected enemy mortar position.[15]

Colonel McCaffree's first communication to higher headquarters about security at Pace came at 0105 hours on October 1. In a confidential message to 23d Artillery Group he pointed out that the insertion of a South Vietnamese Airborne Brigade near Trai Bi (south of Pace) allowed the ARVN 25th Division to shift more of its forces north to the area around Pace, but that Pace "has not yet felt the benefit of this more concentrated power." He went on to complain that the two U.S. platoons from Alpha Company 1/12 Cavalry were insufficient to adequately defend the firebase. "If the Vietnamese forces cannot reduce the threat at Pace by 3 Oct 1971 to a point where it can be adequately resupplied and its equipment maintained," he warned, "I will recommend a U.S. Infantry Battalion be given the mission of defending the base primarily by maneuver within the current TAOR (Tactical Area of Responsibility)."[16]

There is no record of a response from 23d Group. Later that day, two GIs had to be evacuated with shrapnel wounds, including one with a wound to his head.[17] The following day (October 2), Pace reported incoming at 0955, 1025, 1205, 1255, and 1310, but no casualties or damage. On October 3 they reported incoming "all day." That afternoon, enemy mortars hit the POL (fuel) supply, starting a fire.[18]

McCaffree did not follow up his threat to request a battalion sweep by October 3. Instead, on October 4 he helicoptered out to visit the besieged firebase for three hours. After being briefed on the continuing interruptions caused by incoming mortars, he pulled aside Captain Jack Adams, commanding officer of Alpha Company 1/12th Cavalry. He told Adams that since enemy mortars were too close and too well dug in to be effectively engaged by artillery, Adams should send his men out into the tree line west of Pace under the cover of darkness, but guided by the ground radar at Pace. Then, at first light, they could sweep the area, pitching grenades into the enemy spider holes as they moved along.[19]

The ground radar McCaffree referred to was the Army's most advanced—a highly sophisticated ground surveillance system also known as Camp Sentinel Radar, or CSR III. Sending out electronic impulses from a hundred-foot antenna, it could "see" through foliage and detect movement by an individual soldier for 360 degrees around Pace's perimeter. Originally designed by MIT's Lincoln Laboratory, five units were sent to Vietnam.[20] One ended up at Pace after the March 29 sapper attack.[21] It effectively placed an electronic fence around the firebase; whenever something moved it was immediately engaged by the Quad Fifties or other organic weapons at Pace. ARVN patrols sent out the next day would report blood trails, but no weapons or bodies were ever found.[22] The technology was so sensitive that U.S. soldiers at Pace were told they were not to let the trained crew fall into enemy hands under any circumstances.[23]

The wonders of CSR III notwithstanding, Captain Adams was less than enthused. According to McCaffree, Adams claimed he had a "foxhole strength" of only fifty-five (excluding headquarters personnel) and therefore did not have enough men to successfully conduct such a maneuver. According to McCaffree's account, Adams also said he'd been ordered to stay inside the firebase.[24] By whom, McCaffree didn't say, but in a later message he told 23d Group he thought it was Lieutenant Colonel Stan Tyson, commanding officer of the 1/12th.[25]

Both Tyson and Adams dispute this. Tyson says he never gave such an order.[26] Adams does not recall receiving such an order.[27] What Adams does recall is that Tyson told him to expect to be outranked when he arrived at Firebase Pace on September 24. He was. Major Larry McCullum of the 2/32d Field Artillery greeted him when he arrived and told him that Colonel McCaffree had charged him (McCullum) with the responsibility to oversee all operations at the base. According to Adams, he and McCullum agreed to concentrate on improving the base's defenses, including repositioning the two 8-inch howitzers so they could protect the base with direct fire in all four directions.[28] Two days later, on the twenty-sixth, the North Vietnamese emerged from their hiding places and launched attacks throughout the area, including mortar attacks on Pace.

The available documentary evidence, including the daily journals for the 1/12th Cavalry, supports Tyson and Adams on this point. They show Adams did send out a daylight patrol on the afternoon of September 29, but they turned back after receiving small arms fire about 700 meters out.[29] Two more daylight patrols went out on October 5 and 6.[30]

On the other hand, the daily journals show that Alpha at Pace was severely under strength, as McCaffree claimed in his message. On September 25, one day before the enemy offensive began, all of Alpha Company's three platoons were at Pace, along with the Company Headquarters. On the twenty-sixth, one platoon was pulled out and sent to Firebase Nui Chau Chan 100 miles to the east, but it was replaced with a platoon from Delta Company. The next day, September 27, a second platoon was pulled out of Pace to go to Nui Chau Chan but was not replaced. This left Captain Adams with only two platoons instead of the usual three, and one of them belonged to a different company. It stayed this way for the remainder of Alpha's stay at Pace.[31]

It is important to remember that Adams was no rookie. The son of a career Air Force serviceman, Adams spent three years on active duty as an Army enlisted man and another five years in the Ohio National Guard before earning a commission as an artillery second lieutenant. Adams spent two tours in Vietnam. His first tour in 1966–1967 he spent as an aerial observer with the 25th Infantry Division. In his second tour he served as senior district adviser in Hau Ngia Province just south of Tay Ninh before being wounded and evacuated back to the United States. After being discharged from the hospital, he completed his college degree and also decided to request a branch transfer to the infantry, to "be closer to the action." He was sent back to Vietnam for a third tour and assumed command of

Alpha Company 1/12th Cavalry in August 1971 at age thirty-five. Colonel Tyson jokingly told him he had to be "the oldest captain in the Vietnam."[32]

In all likelihood, what happened is that Colonel Tyson gave Captain Adams, whose judgment he trusted, quite a bit of leeway but told him not to take any unnecessary chances. Adams saw a night operation of the kind McCaffree envisioned to be unnecessarily risky and elected to do daytime patrols instead. Adams did send out a daylight patrol on October 5. They reported finding a two-and-a-half-ton truck painted yellow hidden in the bushes at the side of the road. It apparently had been used to haul dirt by persons unknown. They went back out the next day and blew it up. But the issue of more aggressive action remained unresolved when Alpha rotated out two days later to be replaced by Bravo Company.[33]

On October 5 Pace took six rounds of incoming around 1200 hours that wounded three ARVNs and left one GI with severe shrapnel wounds in both legs.[34] McCaffree decided he'd had enough. Thirty minutes later, McCaffree formally sent a request to 23d Group asking for an infantry battalion to sweep the area around Pace.[35]

If this had been 1967 or 1968, the U.S. Command would have jumped at the opportunity to force the VC or NVA to stand and fight. But running up big body counts, as such an operation would have provoked, was no longer a part of U.S. strategy. There weren't enough American troops to conduct an operation of this size anyway. The South Vietnamese had the ground troops, at least in theory, but they already had their hands full. So McCaffree's superiors in Saigon told him they would do a B-52 strike instead.[36]

October 6 began like the day before and the day before that. Five rounds of incoming at 1102. Four mortar rounds and one rocket at 1200, wounding four ARVNs. Two more mortar attacks between 1340 and 1410. U.S. and South Vietnamese artillery responded with at least ten rounds of fire for every mortar round fired against them, but to no apparent affect.[37] In addition, the enemy now appeared to be using RPGs and recoilless rifles to arc rounds over the protective screens on the west and south sides of the perimeter into the positions on the east side of the perimeter.[38]

That morning McCaffree received some additional bad news. He found out he would have to replace Captain Timmons, Charlie Battery's commanding officer, because Timmons had broken his arm and dislocated his shoulder in a fall from a noncombat-related accident.[39] But McCaffree was still able to report that morale was high among the artillerymen at Pace, even though twelve men from Charlie Battery had suffered shrapnel wounds, three of them serious. "Some 'short-timers' are a bit shaky," he reported to 23d Group, "but general tenor is strength and confidence."[40]

That confidence would be tested at 1530 hours, when Pace received a disturbing message from Third Regional Assistance Command in Saigon. They reported three different intelligence sources had predicted a North Vietnamese ground attack against Pace that night. McCaffree and his staff, along with staff from 23d Group and TRAC, scrambled to provide additional protection for the isolated garrison. A B-52 strike was lined up for that night to plaster a box one kilometer wide and two kilometers deep just 600 meters west of Pace. Napalm strikes were scheduled along the tree line to the west. Additional air strikes and flare ships were laid on for that evening. Two AC-130 Spectre gunships were earmarked to come on station beginning at 2000 hours.[41]

Then half an hour after the first message, TRAC sent out a revised message. The threat of an "imminent" attack that night was changed to a "possible attack," at some undefined point in the future.[42] The wary garrison spent a nervous but uneventful night.

Meanwhile, the South Vietnamese command continued to report progress in clearing Route 22. On October 6 General Minh announced the North Vietnamese had withdrawn from the area after suffering heavy losses from ground and air attacks. The relief column moving north from Tay Ninh had reestablished security on Route 22 in the twenty-mile stretch from Tay Ninyh to Thien Ngon, he explained, but the road was still largely impassable due to structural damage to the roadway. He acknowledged that enemy forces were still operating between Thien Ngon and Krek, but pressure in that area (including Pace) had decreased.[43]

Minh also claimed he surprised the Communists with the speed by which he redeployed his troops. He explained that the Communists thought his forces were so preoccupied with the October 3 presidential election that they "thought we didn't dare move from Saigon and other places in the military region." He said the North Vietnamese were planning to ambush the ARVNs as they moved up Highway 22 and then attack Tay Ninh itself. "But the VC were wrong because we shifted quickly," Minh explained. "It surprised them. It disrupted their plan. We turned it back to them." He added that even though these units were pulling back, fresh units could replace them and continue the offensive.[44]

The next day (October 8) the Saigon Command announced new fighting just south of Pace. The enemy unit involved was identified as the 209th Regiment of the NVA Seventh Division. It was believed to be about 1,500 strong. U.S. and South Vietnamese officers said they believed the 209th was a rear guard covering the withdrawal of the main force back into Cambodia.[45]

If the 209th was just a rear guard, they were doing a superb job of harassing Pace. The number of rounds fired at the base increased every day between October 5 and October 8: October 5, fifteen rounds; October 6, twenty rounds; October 7, thirty rounds; and October 8, thirty-one rounds. Only one U.S. soldier was wounded, but in this period thirteen South Vietnamese soldiers were wounded seriously enough to require dust-off in four separate attacks.[46] Medical evacuation helicopters and gunships continued to take fire as well. Both the 2/32d and

23d Group daily logs recorded that General Wagstaff, when he was briefed during a visit to a forward headquarters at Tay Ninh West on October 8, expressed surprise that Pace had taken so many casualties.[47]

By the evening of October 8, a frustrated Colonel McCaffree knew he couldn't just pick up and leave. He knew he wouldn't get reinforced, but he felt his men shouldn't have to just sit there and take it. Something had to give.

CHAPTER EIGHT

Confusion on the Ground
October 7–9

Even though it would mean a roof over his head and other amenities, Specialist Four Al Grana was not looking forward to Firebase Pace. Along with the rest of his company, Grana had spent most of his tour in the bush chasing after VC and NVA. The twenty-four-year-old Los Angeles native was older than most of his fellow soldiers. He was just a few courses short of a degree in business and economics at California State University, Los Angeles, when he decided to enlist. He wanted to believe what his recruiter had told him, that he'd have a better chance of getting a good assignment than he would by waiting to be drafted. So Grana signed up for a two-year hitch but found himself as an infantryman in Vietnam anyway, with Bravo Company 1/12th Cavalry. Being one of the smallest men in the company earned him the nickname "Big Al," but it didn't save him from drawing an assignment of carrying heavy belts of 7.62mm machine gun ammo as an assistant machine gunner.[1]

Although it wasn't what he'd initially wanted, Grana got used to being out in the field. It was always dirty and sometimes dangerous, but he valued the sense of camaraderie with his fellow soldiers and the freedom from the hassles in the rear. He and the rest of his company had seen some action, mainly brief firefights with groups of two or three enemy soldiers who would fire off a few shots then flee. He had stayed free of wounds and trouble for ten months and looked forward to getting out of the Army when his tour was up in December.

What he didn't like was what he'd been hearing about Bravo Company's impending assignment to Firebase Pace. The rumor mill had been churning for a week and nothing he'd heard was encouraging. Pace was surrounded. Troops there had taken 30 percent casualties. The bodies of dead NVA hung menacingly in the perimeter wire. But, like it or not, Specialist Grana and the rest of Bravo Company were headed for Pace on the morning of October 7. They were to take Alpha Company's place when Alpha rotated out after a two-week stay.[2]

Grana's helicopter flew low and fast to avoid the anti-aircraft fire surrounding Pace. He was relieved not to hear anything shooting at him until after he'd jumped off the helicopter. As he landed he fell over from the weight of ammunition he carried with him. A tall older man grabbed him by the arm to help him up. He noticed the black oak leaf cluster of a lieutenant colonel on the man's uniform. Lieutenant Colonel Robert McCaffree told Grana he needed to get moving and get under cover.

As Grana headed for the nearest bunker he noticed a couple of things at Pace he'd never seen before, despite nearly ten months in the field. The first was a line of circling helicopter gunships blasting away at the tree line below with rockets and miniguns. Then there were the four big guns, 8-inch howitzer and 175mm cannon barrels, pointed toward the horizon in the direction of Cambodia. Suddenly a Quad Fifty opened up on something, filling the air with noise, smoke, and sheets of flame. Seeing all this fire power told him that he and Bravo Company had stepped into something bigger than they had ever seen before.[3]

Grana and his section finally settled into Bunker 6 on the west side of the base facing the Cambodian border. It didn't take long for the Welcome Wagon to arrive. Every time someone moved outside the bunker it seemed to provoke an enemy response followed by a shout of "Incoming!" Grana was convinced the North Vietnamese in the tree line had zeroed in on Bunker 6. Each time they took incoming, someone from Grana's squad popped out of the bunker long enough to fire a LAWS at the suspected location in the tree line. It would grow quiet for a while, only to repeat the cycle a few minutes or a few hours later. Over the next two days, the members of Bravo Company settled into the routine of garrison duty at Pace, which meant helmets and flak jackets when outside the safety of their bunkers, C rations only, and no showers, because hot food and showers invited enemy fire.[4]

Bravo Company's third day at Firebase Pace (October 9) began with a burst of AK-47 fire from the North Vietnamese, who had dug into the tree line east of the base. Pace responded with one of its Quad Fifties, and the firing ceased.[5] Fifty minutes later, the AK-47 fire started again. The Quad Fifties responded again. The firing stopped again.[6] At 1010, three mortar rounds landed just outside the perimeter. There were no casualties, but one field range and two field burning units were damaged.[7]

Shortly before 1100 hours, Colonel McCaffree got an important message from 23d Group. Major General Wagstaff had talked with Brigadier General Jonathan R. Burton, commanding officer of the 1st Cavalry Division's 3d Brigade, the 1/12th's parent unit. Wagstaff told Burton the rifle company assigned to Pace was under the operational control of the local artillery commander (McCaffree) and was "to respond to his orders." More specifically, operations could be conducted outside the perimeter as long as "a certain amount of caution was used."[8] In McCaffree's view, this order resolved a two-week-long aggravation. According to Army protocol, the senior officer on site was always supposed to be in charge, but his infantry colleagues seemed to see things differently. Now Wagstaff had intervened and backed him up. That meant it was time for the infantry to get out there and protect Pace the way it should be protected.[9]

McCaffree had already flown out to Pace that morning. He now sought out Captain Robert Cronin, commanding officer of Bravo Company, 1/12th Cavalry. The twenty-five-year-old native of Somerville, Massachusetts, was easy to identify because of his distinctive Boston accent, ever-present cigars, and the short-barreled M-16 Rifle he carried with him. An ROTC Distinguished Military Graduate, Cronin had been in command of Bravo Company for only a month but carried a lot of Vietnam experience. He'd been in country since October 1970 and had already extended his tour. He had volunteered for Vietnam and strongly believed in what his country was trying to accomplish there.[10]

Cronin and McCaffree quickly agreed that Bravo Company would send out a reinforced squad (about fifteen men) on an ambush that evening. They would slip out of the perimeter under the cover of darkness and set up in the woods about 500 yards east of Pace. Using Claymore mines and their own rifles and machine guns, they would ambush North Vietnamese soldiers moving from the Cambodian border to resupply or reinforce the enemy units still active around the base.[11]

First Lieutenant Richard Coreno of Atlanta, Georgia, commanded 2d Platoon. Coreno recalls Captain Cronin first offering the mission to his platoon.[12] Coreno and Cronin did not get along well to begin with. Coreno and some of the other members of his platoon felt Cronin disliked them and singled them out for undesirable assignments.[13] SP4 Grana remembers Cronin referring to 2d Platoon as the "Mod Squad" because of their longish hair and telling them they were hypocrites because they wore peace symbols on their uniforms.[14]

Coreno told Cronin he didn't think the night ambush was a good idea. Coreno argued that because his platoon manned the west side of the perimeter (nearest the Cambodian border), his men had been under fire constantly since they'd arrived. Five men had already been wounded, and the rest of the men were tired and jumpy due to lack of sleep. Coreno maintains Cronin called him a "pussy" and threatened to send the patrol out with just the platoon sergeant, leaving Coreno behind. Coreno returned to his bunker, not sure of what would happen next.[15]

Captain Cronin does not recall any such conversation with Lieutenant Coreno and maintains he would not have used the terminology Coreno attributed to him. Cronin does remember assigning the mission to First Lieutenant Ron Shuler's 3d Platoon because he felt Shuler was his strongest platoon leader.[16] Meanwhile, the North Vietnamese in the woods west of Pace continued to go about their business. Between 1200 and 1925 hours, they mortared or rocketed Pace seven more times:

- 1240—A rocket blew up outside the perimeter with no casualties. But two minutes later, two 82mm mortar rounds exploded inside the perimeter, causing no casualties but damaging twenty-five bundles of clothes.

- 1350—Pace took three more rounds, one of which destroyed 2,000 feet of electrical cable stored on the berm.
- 1445—Four more rounds landed, causing no casualties but damaging six berm lights and eight footlockers.
- 1535—Pace took seven rounds of 82mm mortar and two rockets. These wounded ten ARVN soldiers who required medical evacuation.
- 1725—Two rounds of 82mm mortar were fired at Pace. One exploded inside the compound and wounded one GI with head and back injuries. Pace called for a dust-off but was told that the weather was too bad and that the wounded soldier would have to wait until first light the next day.
- 1820—Another rocket landed outside the perimeter. No casualties.
- 1925—A mortar round landed near one of the generators.

In total, Pace took more than thirty rounds of incoming that day.[17]

To add insult to injury, McCaffree's superiors at 23d Artillery Group, seventy miles away and safely inside the sprawling U.S. base at Long Binh, got on him over late reports. After McCaffree returned to Tay Ninh West that afternoon, Captain J. F. Ryan, the 23d Group's assistant S-3, telephoned and told him his units "were submitting insufficient spot reports. Personnel were not knowledgeable concerning number of rds or incoming, caliber of weapons, surveillance, direction of attack or action taken by the unit."[18] Military protocol provides that captains are not supposed to chew out lieutenant colonels, but Captain Ryan's message was clear. Higher headquarters was not satisfied. "LTC McCaffree sends a daily update but rarely in time to meet our requirements," Captain Ryan noted in the 23d Group's daily log for October 9.[19]

But as the afternoon faded into evening, the phone call from Captain Ryan was the least of Pace's problems. Lieutenant Shuler picked his men and told them to get their gear together to be ready to move out after dark.

It was Specialist Four Ernest French's turn to take point. The twenty-four-year-old had worked at an arsenal near his hometown of Maltoon, Illinois, where he had a draft deferment. He left that job, got drafted, and found himself with the 1/12th Cavalry in January 1971. French recalled being at the end of the column during his first firefight. He was scared to death because he could hear shooting in front of him but couldn't see what was going on. He decided he'd be better off up front and volunteered for point duty.

Because of the stress involved with the position, each squad had a lead point and a backup. The backup would relieve the point whenever he got tired. French ended up being paired with Sergeant Nick Demas, a twenty-one-year-old draftee from Elkhart, Indiana. They quickly became close friends. Demas credits French with saving his life and the lives of other members of his squad during a fight in

May when he disarmed an enemy Claymore pointed directly at them. French was awarded a Bronze Star for valor for his actions that day. By the time they arrived at Pace, they'd worked together for nine months.[20]

Now, as word circulated around the base about that night's mission, French, Demas, and the other members of the patrol didn't like what they were hearing. The GIs from Charlie Battery told them the engineers had set booby traps (including Claymore mines) out in that area when they were working on building Pace six months earlier. "I wouldn't go there if I were you," one of the artillerymen reportedly advised.[21] Standard Operating Procedure in the 1st Cavalry Division called for mapping all booby traps and automatic ambushes to protect friendly troops. French asked for a map of the Claymores east of the base but was told by his superiors there was no map because there were no Claymores out there. French, Demas, and the others talked amongst themselves in what was later described as a two-hour gripe session. Finally, French and five other men told Lieutenant Shuler they would not go without the maps.[22]

Word eventually got back to McCaffree, who by now was at Tay Ninh West. He decided this was serious enough to report up the chain of command. At 1931 hours he sent the 23d Artillery Group a message that six of fifteen men refused to go out on the mission, and that he was considering continuing the ambush but with substitute personnel.[23] Then twenty minutes later the ground radar detected seventeen to twenty-four enemy personnel moving in on Pace from the Cambodian border area to the west.[24] Was this just a probe or a precursor to some sort of ground assault? Rumors circulated among the base's defenders that the enemy may be tunneling toward Pace, but no one knew for sure.[25] What they did know was that the berm lights were not working and the flare ships they called for earlier in the day had to be canceled because of bad weather.[26] Twenty-seven minutes later, at 2007 hours, Thien Ngon reported taking small arms and automatic weapons fire from the south. Thirty minutes after that, they received a barrage of thirty mixed mortar and rockets over thirty minutes.[27] Would Pace be next?

Meanwhile, Captain Cronin learned from a liaison officer assigned to the South Vietnamese that two companies of South Vietnamese soldiers were also out in night defensive positions in the same area. Cronin then decided to cancel the patrol altogether for fear of running into friendly units in the dark, and McCaffree agreed.[28] At 2325 hours McCaffree notified 23d Group with a message reaffirming the six men had not refused a direct order since the patrol had been canceled. The commanding officer of the Cav "will handle it as an internal matter," he concluded.[29]

That matter out of the way, McCaffree fired back an answer to 23d Group about the slow response time. He blamed it partially on "too much confusion" in the Fire Direction Center at Pace.[30] He explained that the Fire Direction Center's mini computer had been down since the third week in September, meaning all calculations had to be made and checked by hand, that incoming had naturally slowed down response times. He also pointed out that the slow response time from the gun crews reflected their knowledge that these were noncontact fire missions, and the crews had to contend with incoming at the same time.[31] There is no record of the 23d Group's immediate response, but it is doubtful they found this explanation fully satisfactory.

Back in "The World," October 9 marked the opening of the 1971 World Series in Baltimore. Oriole pitcher Dave McNally bested Pittsburgh's Doc Ellis by a score of 5–3 on a game carried live by Armed Forces Radio. But at Pace the inhabitants settled in for an uneasy night serenaded by the thump, thump of B-52 strikes in the surrounding woods as word of the 3d Platoon's refusal spread to other platoons.

In Bunker 6, Al Grana and other members of 2d Platoon talked among themselves about what to do. They all agreed the night ambush was a bad idea. They also worried that if the higher ups resurrected the idea of a night ambush again the next day and the 3d Platoon refused to go, they could be ordered to go. They wanted to show support for 3d Platoon's refusal. What they hadn't decided was how.[32]

The location of the South Vietnamese to the east of Pace provided a face-saving solution for everyone involved—for now. But six men had still refused an order for a time. Would failure to punish them lead to even more defiance? Even at this stage of the war, a military unit depended on some sort of discipline to survive. The enemy was stirring. Air support was grounded because of bad weather. The troops were increasingly anxious. The last thing Pace needed right now was some reporter poking around asking questions.

CHAPTER NINE

Welcome to Prime Time
October 9–13

A sometimes freelance journalist, sometimes freelance photographer, sometimes author and committed antiwar activist, Richard Boyle hardly fit the description of a typical reporter for a typical mainstream news organization. In fact, he had no press credentials at all. Born and raised in San Francisco, Boyle had always wanted to be a reporter or, even better, a war correspondent.[1] He lied about his age to enlist in the California National Guard, where he served in the Air Defense Artillery.[2] In 1965 he went to Vietnam at the age of twenty-one to fulfill his ambition. He stayed in Vietnam for awhile, then traveled for awhile, only to return in 1969 as a freelance photographer. He covered the siege of Ben Het and then took a job with *Overseas Weekly* in Saigon to pay his bills.[3] Boyle's stay in Vietnam was cut short when in 1970 he was kicked out by the South Vietnamese government for participating in an antiwar demonstration.[4]

Now, in October of 1971, he was back, having slipped across the Cambodian border. A colleague told him there was a lot of activity at Firebase Pace, so Boyle thought that would be a good place to get additional material for a book he was doing on dissent in the military.[5] It took him three tries. He finally got there sometime on the afternoon of October 9 by hitching a ride from Tay Ninh on a Vietnamese army helicopter. Boyle was twenty-eight at the time, so he didn't look much older than the typical GI. He wore a set of camouflage striped Army fatigues with no insignia and a haircut and mustache that blended in with the troops. Even at that, the other GIs were somewhat distrustful of this stranger, suspecting he was some sort of Army spy or undercover agent.[6]

According to Boyle, he introduced himself to Captain Cronin and Lieutenant Colonel McCaffree and then went over to the enlisted men of Bravo Company to talk with them. There he learned about the night ambush planned for later that night and sympathetically listened to the men complain about it.[7]

One of the soldiers Boyle got to know was Specialist Four Grana. According to Boyle, they both shared an interest in politics. Grana told Boyle that the enlisted men were fearful that the six who refused to go out on patrol the night before would be court-martialed. They wondered if a show of solidarity would help. Grana said men in all three platoons had talked about sending a letter to Senator Edward Kennedy of Massachusetts—one of the war's severest critics in the U.S. Senate. Grana claimed more than half the company was willing to sign. It's not clear whose idea the letter was originally. According to Grana, one of the GIs who had been an English major in college had agreed to draft it but wasn't getting anywhere. Grana finally volunteered to finish it. He'd been stewing about the night ambush since he'd heard about it the day before. The words came out quickly after that. They agreed Boyle would take the letter with him when he left.[8]

The letter read as follows:

> We the undersigned of Bravo Company, First Battalion, Twelfth Cav, First Cav Division, feel compelled to write you because of your influence on public opinion and on decisions made in the Senate.
>
> We're in the peculiar position of being the last remaining ground troops that the U.S. has in a combat role and we suffer from problems that are peculiar only to us. We are ground troops who are supposedly in a defensive role (according to the Nixon administration) but who constantly find ourselves faced with the same combat role we were in ten months ago. At this writing we are under siege on Firebase Pace near the city of Tay Ninh. We are surrounded on three sides by Cambodia and on all sides by NVA. We are faced daily with the decision of whether to take a court-martial or participate in an offensive role. We have already had six persons refuse to go on a night ambush (which is suicidal as well as offensive), and may be court-martialed. With morale as low as it is there probably will be more before this siege of Pace is over.
>
> Our concern in writing you is not only to bring your full weight of influence in the Senate, but also to enlighten public opinion on the fact that we ground troops still exist. In the event of mass prosecution of our unit, our only hope would be public opinion and your voice.[9]

While the letter worked its way from bunker to bunker for signatures, one of the other members of Grana's platoon, Specialist Four Mike McNamara of Chicago, Illinois, scrounged up a portable cassette recorder. Boyle agreed to take the recorded statements of Bravo Company personnel as evidence too.[10] The following comments are typical:

> "We're not supposed to be fighting this war anyway. We're supposed to be turning it over to them [the South Vietnamese]."
>
> "Do any of the people back in the world know that [Defense Secretary] Melvin Laird said something to the effect that our combat role has ended?"
>
> "It's always the higher highers, and they don't have to go out there. They just send us out there. They get to sit back here and talk."
>
> "You know, there's a thing about giving an order, and there's a thing about using your head, too. It's really like everybody's insane. It's a suicide mission. You're just not using your head when you order fifteen men to go out there

when they know goddamn well there's mortar tubes out there and there's probably around five or six hundred dinks and they tell fifteen men to go out there. That ain't using your head."

"Back in basic training they said all you can use in Vietnam is common sense."

"If you go out there at night, say you take thirty or forty men, they'll never find you no more. That'll be the last they see of you, once you walk off this firebase. 'Cause if they can't go out there to get those dudes out of that chopper that crashed about four days ago, they ain't going to go out there looking for you in the jungle, man."

"Who's going to go out there and get us?"

The letter came back with sixty-six signatures, or about two-thirds of Bravo Company. The signatures were mostly those of privates first class and specialist fours, but also included twelve of Bravo Company's sergeants.[11]

Carrying the letter and the tapes, Boyle decided it was time to get out of there and file his story. He was convinced he was being stalked by an undercover operative posing as an *LA Times* photographer.[12] He hitched a ride on an American helicopter that afternoon back to Tay Ninh. From there, he caught a bus to Saigon.

Boyle later wrote he was worried that if he gave his account to the wrong news outlet (like a wire service), they would first call the U.S. Command for verification. MACV would deny it, and his story would be killed. Since he was back in Vietnam without credentials, he was also worried about what could happen to him—including being jailed by the South Vietnamese government. Consequently, he gave the story to Roland Paringaux of Agence France-Presse. Boyle had known Paringaux from covering the war in Cambodia. He next worked to get himself out of Vietnam before all hell broke loose. Claiming he'd been hit by shrapnel at Pace and near exhaustion from his ordeal, Boyle persuaded the Vietnam Press Office to grant him a special exit visa on humanitarian grounds. A few hours later he was on a Pan Am 747 headed for San Francisco.[13]

The French daily newspaper *LeMonde* printed Boyle's characterization the next day, describing the refusal as a "mutiny."[14] It was then picked up by both the Associated Press and United Press International, who did their own follow-up. ABC and CBS News reported on the AP version of the Pace story the evening of October 11. It was the lead on ABC and the second item on CBS.[15] The following day the events at Pace appeared in daily newspapers across the country, including the *New York Times, Washington Post, Chicago Tribune,* and the Pacific edition of *Stars and Stripes.*[16] These reports quoted Army officials, not Boyle, in describing the incident. For example, the Associated Press featured Lieutenant Colonel McCaffree saying the men had not actually refused an order because the patrol was canceled and the unit went out the next day.

The following day (October 12), AP carried a follow-up piece saying the Third Regional Assistance Command announced that Bravo Company, the unit involved in the incident, had been pulled out of Pace by helicopter and replaced with another unit. The article quoted General Jack Wagstaff saying Bravo Company was moved out "because of all this goddam flak, the possible harm it could do to company morale and in line with normal rotation policy." Wagstaff continued, "There was never any confrontation, never any refusal. There was never an opportunity. The only refusal, if you want to call it that, is that they told a newsman they weren't going to go." Wagstaff concluded by saying there would be no disciplinary action because "nothing was violated."[17] Both CBS and ABC briefly mentioned the AP account that evening.[18] The *Washington Post* ran it on page A17 on October 13.[19]

On October 12 Bravo Company was reassigned to Fire Support Base Timbuktu about ninety miles to the east of Pace and much quieter. There the Army allowed inquisitive reporters to talk to the enlisted men while, at least according to *Newsweek*'s Nicholas Proffitt, Captain Cronin "hovered" nearby.[20] Cronin's presence didn't seem to inhibit the troops from expressing themselves. "The patrol was suicide, senseless suicide," Proffitt quoted one squad leader. "I had six men who had never been in combat before. We were supposed to go out in the dark and we didn't know the area. You get shot up, and the guys go wild simply because they don't know what's going on."[21]

ABC sent reporter Ron Miller to Timbuktu and ran a nearly three-minute segment on the ABC Evening News October 13. Miller interviewed Specialist Al Grana, as well as Specialist Four Joe Reiger of Edwardsville, Illinois, and Sergeant Walter Wernli of Three Rivers, Texas. Grana reiterated his point about defensive versus offensive operations. Wernli, a squad leader, defended his men. "They're not even cowards. I've been with these guys four months now. On September 1 and September 3 we were in contact and there wasn't a man out there that wouldn't have risked his life if someone else was in trouble out there." Specialist Reiger explained it this way, "We would like the people back in the world to know things haven't changed for the guys still over here. We're still doing the same thing that I've been doing for the last 13 months and things haven't changed one bit. We just want people to know that."[22]

Meanwhile, Boyle, after a short press conference in San Francisco, headed to Washington to deliver the letter and tapes to Senator Edward Kennedy. He was told Kennedy was out of town, so he met with two aides. They promised to arrange a meeting. Boyle did finally get to meet with Kennedy long enough to deliver the letter, and Kennedy did call for a Pentagon investigation but went no further.[23] In his book, Boyle quoted Ed Martin, Kennedy's top aide, as explaining Kennedy had been "clobbered" for criticizing the assault on Hamburger Hill two years earlier and didn't want to appear to be using the GIs for political purposes.[24]

Boyle blamed "divisiveness within the veterans' anti war groups." He singled out one of Kennedy's constituents active in the antiwar movement for Kennedy's reluctance. He claimed John Kerry had flown to Washington to advise Kennedy's staff to "stay away" from the Pace affair.[25]

CHAPTER TEN

Under New Management
October 10–11

October 10 began with what now had become routine for the garrison at Pace: AK-47 fire from the south at 0540 hours. The early morning AK-47 fire was by now so familiar that Pace's defenders nicknamed the suspected perpetrator(s) "Ricky Recoilless." Every morning he'd fire off a few AK-47 rounds timed to disrupt breakfast preparations. Every morning Pace would respond by hosing the area down with Quad Fifties and small arms fire. Ricky Recoilless would presumably disappear into a well-camouflaged bunker or spider hole, only to return the next morning.[1]

At about 1300 hours North Vietnamese gunners in the tree line shot up a Cobra gunship, which then had to make an emergency landing at Pace. Bravo Company quickly sent out a squad to provide a protective perimeter for the downed helicopter. One of the pilots was wounded so badly he had to be medevaced back to the hospital at Long Binh.[2] At 1355 hours Pace reported five mortar rounds impacting inside the perimeter and two rockets outside, but no casualties or damage.[3]

Meanwhile, Captain Cronin decided he needed to get his men "back to doing what they needed to do" and put the drama of the night before behind them. They would conduct a recon patrol into the tree line to the east, the same area that sparked the refusal the night before—except this time it would be in daylight and Cronin would accompany them himself.[4]

From this point, recollections of the participants differ. Sergeant Demas remembers Cronin lining up the 3d Platoon and asking each man if he knew that he could be court-martialed if he didn't join the patrol. Cronin maintains that he did not threaten to court-martial anyone, but that he would have if he thought it was necessary. Sergeant Tex Wernli remembers a platoon meeting where Cronin asked for volunteers and gave 3d Platoon a brief period of time to think over what they wanted to do. Wernli, Demas, and French all remember the response as being less than enthusiastic. In addition to the unmarked Claymores, they worried about being cut down by machine guns in the tree line as they crossed an open field in broad daylight.[5]

Finally, the platoon leader, First Lieutenant Ron Shuler, a 1969 graduate of the University of Pittsburgh, volunteered to take point. Tex Wernli, a squad leader in Shuler's platoon, admired Shuler but thought he was too inexperienced to take point on such a dangerous mission. Just eight hours short of a degree in chemistry, the twenty-four-year-old Wernli got drafted when he dropped out of school to pay for the birth of his first daughter. Even though he now had a wife and a two-year-old daughter back home in Texas, he felt his experience as a hunter raised on a farm in rattlesnake country gave him an edge in detecting mines and booby traps. He volunteered to take point.[6]

As the small group consisting of Wernli, Shuler, Cronin, and a radioman headed toward the main gate, French and Demas reluctantly decided to join them rather than let them hang out there by themselves. A few others joined as well, so that about a dozen men moved out together.[7]

Once they crossed Highway 22 they traversed an open field with grass a foot high. About seventy-five meters out, Sergeant Wernli spotted a trip wire off to the right. Lieutenant Shuler spotted one to the left. At the same time, someone shouted from further back in the formation. "There was a lot of yelling going on," Wernli recalled later, "as you can imagine, and fear was rampant."[8]

Sergeant Demas was the first man to yell out. He'd felt a wire brush against his trouser leg. Being an experienced point man he knew what it meant. He yelled "Automatic!" and froze in place. The wire was attached to Claymore mines in what was known as a daisy chain. Claymores were American-made antipersonnel mines about the size of a paperback book. They could be detonated by command or by a trip wire. Each would spray 700 steel pellets in a fan-shaped pattern 50–100 yards, shredding unprotected personnel.[9]

Demas and his colleagues knew they couldn't just cut the wire, because the mines were emplaced with a triggering device that would set off the charge. They also knew Demas could not step backward or forward, because jostling the trip wire would also set off the charge. They all agreed to send the rest of the patrol back so that they would not be endangered if the mines went off. Then French, assisted by Lieutenant Shuler, carefully followed the wires, being sure not to set off anything. Each Claymore had to be found, felt underneath for booby traps, and then disarmed by removing the blasting caps. It took several agonizing minutes while Sergeant Demas stood there, knowing he was twenty-eight days short of going home, and knowing that if he moved, what was left of him would be going home in a body bag.[10]

When French and Shuler completed their work, they gathered up the Claymores and headed back toward the relative safety of the base. Just as they approached the front gate, enemy mortars opened up on the other side of the perimeter. Shuler, French, and Demas hit the ground and waited until the firing let up; then, as French recalls, they "ran like hell" back to the base.[11] French and Demas remember carrying the two armloads of Claymores back to the base and dumping them in front of one of the senior artillery officers (most likely Major McCullom), telling him, "Here are the Claymores you said didn't exist."[12]

Sergeant Wernli remembers a heated conversation between Captain Cronin and one of these same officers, but Cronin recalls he and McCaffree jointly agreed to call off the patrol.[13]

Afterward, Cronin sat down at his desk and composed a three- to four-page after-action assessment addressed to his battalion commander, Lieutenant Colonel Al Tyson, and sent it to the rear via courier. Battalion sent it on to Brigadier General Burton at brigade, who sent it on to General Abrams's headquarters.[14]

While Captain Cronin's report was working its way from Pace back through the 1/12th Cavalry's chain of command, the 2/32d chain of command was being totally revamped. The newcomers included First Lieutenant Mark Diggs, twenty-four, of Jonesboro, Arkansas. Diggs began his Vietnam tour as a forward observer assigned to the 1st Brigade, 5th Mechanized Division, near the DMZ and Laotian border. There he experienced quite a bit of combat while supporting the ARVN incursion into Laos, where he was wounded and awarded a Purple Heart.[15]

When his unit redeployed to the States, Diggs was reassigned to the 23d Artillery Group and eventually found himself with B 2/32d Artillery at Katum. There he served first as a fire direction officer, then executive officer, or second in command. When he learned Katum was evacuated at the end of September, he entertained thoughts of passing the remainder of his time in Vietnam quietly until it came time to redeploy back to the States. But this was not to be.

A couple of days after the Katum pullout was completed, Lieutenant Colonel McCaffree showed up at Bravo Battery's camp at Tay Ninh West asking to speak to Lieutenant Diggs and his chief of firing battery, Sergeant First Class Masters. McCaffree told them the situation at Pace was very tense and he needed his strongest and most experienced team out there to address what he felt was a breakdown in leadership.[16] Diggs was no stranger to the situation at Pace. Two weeks earlier he'd been a passenger on the helicopter flying participants back to Pace and then Katum after the Commanders Call in Tay Ninh on September 26. Diggs suspected something was wrong as he watched the traffic on Highway 22 below them—there was none, even though the road was always busy.

When their helicopter approached Pace he understood why. They began taking ground fire and executing evasive action. As passengers, Diggs and the others were not connected to the helicopter's communication system, but they could tell the landing would not be a walk in the park. The GIs at Pace rushed to move one of the 8-inch howitzers off its pad so the helicopter could land inside instead of outside the perimeter.[17] As it landed, Diggs could see incoming exploding around the base and GIs in helmets and flak jackets running back and forth. Someone started throwing wounded onto Diggs's helicopter until someone else spotted a medevac helicopter approaching, so the wounded were offloaded, and the pilots lifted Diggs's helicopter out of Pace as quickly as possible. Before heading on to

Katum, the helicopter had to refuel. The pilots remembered a refueling facility was available at the Thien Ngon airstrip. Flying fast and low along Route 22 to conserve fuel, they noticed a large group of Vietnamese moving along the road. They waved. The Vietnamese waved back. Then they landed at the refueling point at Thien Ngon, at the end of a grassy runway. None of the South Vietnamese who usually worked the pumps were anywhere to be found, so they fueled up the helicopter on their own and proceeded on to Katum.[18]

They learned later Thien Ngon was about to come under attack. The Vietnamese near the road were the NVA/VC attacking force, who probably waved back at the low-flying helicopter because they were as surprised as the occupants overhead.[19] The helicopter dropped off Lieutenant Diggs and his battery commander at Katum without further incident. For the next week, while Diggs's battery at Katum prepared for evacuation, he heard the radio traffic from Pace over the command net.

When Diggs's battalion commander asked him to volunteer for this mission, he feared it would be a mini Dien Bien Phu. Diggs asked McCaffree, whom he respected, if this was a suicide mission. McCaffree didn't answer directly. Diggs felt he and Masters had no choice but to "volunteer" or be sent anyway, so he volunteered, with a request that he and Sergeant Masters be transferred back to B Battery once his work at Pace was complete. McCaffree agreed.[20]

Lieutenant Diggs, Sergeant Masters, and the rest of the new command team arrived at Pace via helicopter at approximately 1510 hours on October 10. Accompanying Diggs and Masters were Captain Richard Ashley, a West Point graduate from Quincy, Florida, who would be the new battery commander for Charlie Battery, and Major Russell Davis, who up to that point had served as 2/32d's executive officer. The mission of the new leadership team was described as follows in the 23d Artillery Group's daily staff journal: "(c) Fm CO, 2–32: MAJ Davis, CPT Ashely, LT Diggs, SFC Masters have gone to replace other personnel at Pace. Slow response to fire missions caused by reluctance of men to man the guns and get out of their bunkers. This problem may be overcome with the new leadership."[21]

Diggs recalls that as the helicopter landed, Pace was under fire from mortars or recoilless rifles. He headed for the nearest 8-inch howitzer to begin directing counter battery fire, except no one was to be found. He spotted a lone GI in a nearby bunker and asked, "Where the hell is the gun crew?" The GI pointed to another bunker nearby. Diggs ran into the bunker and found them inside. After he confirmed they were the crew, he instructed them to follow him.[22]

"Where are you going?" they replied.

"To the gun to fire back at those assholes." They still didn't seem inclined to move. "Look," Diggs said, "I don't like sticking my ass out there any more than you do. But it is the only way you are going to get them to stop shelling us. You can either sit in your hooch scared and hunkered down, or you can get pissed and start giving back some of what they've been dishing out." He then asked for two of them "with enough balls to help me man the gun and the rest of them could be chickenshits if they wanted to."[23]

The entire crew came out, although reluctantly, and fired several rounds of what artillerymen called "Killer Senior." The technique was pioneered by the 25th Infantry Division Artillery to protect firebases at close range. By setting the time fuse on a projectile at a predetermined setting, it could be made to explode about thirty feet off the ground at ranges between 200 and 1,000 meters, spraying everything below with deadly shrapnel.[24] Diggs's makeshift crew fired several rounds, and the enemy shelling eventually stopped. No one was wounded in the exchange, and Diggs felt that set the tone from then on for a more aggressive response.[25] Now every time Pace came under fire, both 8-inch howitzers would reply.

Responsibility for managing this new team fell to nineteen-year Army veteran Major Russell Davis. The thirty-seven-year-old major started his career in 1952 as a private. He went on to earn a commission from Field Artillery Officer Candidate School at Fort Sill in 1959. He did his first Vietnam tour in 1966 as an adviser in Can Tho Province in Military Region IV. Davis began his second tour in Admiral McCain's headquarters, the theater command that oversaw all U.S. activities in Southeast Asia, but asked Admiral McCain to get him a slot with a line unit.[26]

Davis knew he had work to do at Pace. He remembers Charlie Battery's response time at Pace as "slow or nonexistent." While still 2/32d executive officer, he initiated a time-on-target (TOT) exercise to confirm his concerns about the performance of his units at the battery level. TOT described the technique of massed fire from guns at multiple locations on one point at one time in order to maximize shock and effect. The technique was first developed at Fort Sill during World War II and was used on the Germans and Japanese with devastating impact. In order for it to work, each participating battery had to separately compute its firing data to take into account distance from the target and time of flight with a high degree of accuracy. It was a complex procedure, but one every artilleryman was expected to master. Davis ordered all three of the firing batteries of the 2/32d to participate in a TOT exercise under his supervision. Alpha and Bravo batteries executed the mission flawlessly. Charlie Battery did not. In fact, they never got around to firing the mission at all.[27]

While Lieutenant Diggs worked to get the gun crews out of their bunkers and back to their guns, Major Davis worked on other measures to improve overall discipline and morale. He inspected all the battery's bunkers. He found the living quarters in particular to be dirty and uncared for, even by field standards. In one section he found one side of the bunker filled with trash, including C-ration boxes, empty cans, and even human waste. He arranged to get a five-ton truck to do trash pickup around the base. They filled the truck five times. He also found multiple bags of unused powder, which was supposed to be burned daily to prevent fire hazards. He collected it and had it burned off. With Lieutenant Diggs's help, he began drilling the gun crews to make sure they could reposition their guns to fire in a 360-degree environment.[28]

The 1/12th chain of command did some shuffling on October 10 as well. A different helicopter unloaded Major Joseph D. Dye, thirty-four years old, from Portland, Oregon. Dye was sent by General Burton, commander of the 3rd Brigade, 1st Air Cavalry Division, 1/12th's parent unit. His mission: get in there and fix whatever was wrong. Dye brought with him a wealth of experience. In ten years in the Army he was already on his third tour of duty in Vietnam. In 1964–1965 he served in the 5th Special Forces Group as a detachment commander in the Mekong Delta. In this second tour (1967–1968) he served as a training adviser, again in the IV Corps (Mekong Delta Area) and also worked with the Revolutionary Development cadre. When he returned the third time in 1971, he worked as executive officer for the 1/7th Cav (one of the 1/12th's sister units) until they departed in May. Now he'd taken over as S-3 (operations officer) of the 1/12th.[29]

He recalled the place being "a mess . . . morale was low, positions needed rebuilding, etc." He also found relations between himself and the artillery command, particularly Colonel McCaffree, to be "frosty." Dye felt McCaffree interpreted his presence as a lack of confidence in his ability to defend his firebase.[30] According to Dye, he and McCaffree had already clashed before. When the ARVN Airborne first arrived in early October, Dye wanted to move a battery of their 105mm howitzers onto the base for added protection.[31] The big advantage the ARVN 105's possessed was the ability to fire the XM546 beehive round, which McCaffree's big guns were not capable of firing. The XM546 was a direct descendent of the canister and grapeshot rounds of the Civil War era. When fired, they let loose 8,000 1 1/4 inch steel fleshettes that would shred everything in a path 50 yards wide and 150 yards deep.[32] Named "beehive" because of the frightening buzz they made, they were a perfect weapon for defense against mass enemy troops. In fact, skillful use of beehive was credited with helping the 1/12th Cavalry save Fire Support Base Bird in 1966.[33] Why McCaffree resisted Dye's suggestion is not clear. Perhaps he had safety concerns. Perhaps he didn't like the way Dye approached him.[34] But, four of the ARVN 105's were moved to Pace on October 2.[35]

On October 11 MACV announced three B-52 strikes against bunkers and antiaircraft positions near Firebase Pace.[36] That and Lieutenant Diggs's killer senior rounds notwithstanding, the enemy bombardment continued. The morning of October 11 began with an RPG round whooshing across the compound and out the other side at 0710 hours. Two hours later, three 82mm mortar rounds landed at or near the base. They damaged four mermite cans, two immersion heaters, three garbage cans, two 2 1/2 ton truck tires, and two generators. Fortunately there were no casualties.[37]

At 0700 hours that day, the Battalion Headquarters of the 2/32d Artillery logged a message from General Burton of the 3d Brigade, 1st Cavalry Division, that read as follows: "CG of 1st CAV relates that officer of infantry is under operational control of arty CO. Infantry may be used for limited operations outside the berm. May be used in woodlines where C/2/32 has been taking incoming."[38]

Before the day ended, Fire Support Base Pace got two additional visitors. The inspector general of 3d Brigade, 1st Air Cavalry Division, Major William S. Tozer, accompanied by Deputy Brigade Commander Colonel Spence, flew in with an escort of two Cobra gunships. They had been sent there by Brigade headquarters to determine if, in fact, there was a combat refusal on the part of Bravo Company on October 9 and 10 and to assess the state of morale and welfare of the men.[39]

Tozer and Spence first talked with Captain Cronin and Lieutenant Shuler, and then with a group of approximately fifteen enlisted men. After completing these discussions, the two men boarded their helicopter to go back to Bien Hoa and file their report.[40] Tozer remembers being surprised they were not fired on when they arrived, given everything they had heard about the intensity of enemy anti-aircraft fire around Pace. They were not so lucky going out. Green tracers streaked by as their helicopter corkscrewed out of the hostile airspace over Pace.[41]

At 1830 hours, North Vietnamese gunners finally hit the jackpot. Five to seven rounds landed on or near the guns. Five men were wounded, although none seriously enough to be evacuated. But two of Pace's four guns suffered direct hits and became inoperable. One of the 8-inch howitzers lost its sights, and one of the 175mm guns lost its loader rammer.[42]

Just before 2200 hours, Headquarters 1/12th Cavalry reported receiving two messages from higher headquarters. The first said that the next day Bravo Company would be pulled out and replaced with another company. The second said Major Dye would now be in charge of the base defense.[43]

CHAPTER ELEVEN

Leave No One Behind
October 12–21

The Sky Troopers of Delta Company, 1/12th Cavalry arrived at Firebase Pace at about 1300 hours in the afternoon of October 12.[1] For Specialist Four Paul Marling it would be an arrival he would never forget. Standard operating procedure called for one of the company's medics to ride on the first helicopter landing in a potentially hot LZ. Marling drew the assignment of accompanying the first chopper in, along with three other GIs. Marling, a nineteen-year-old draftee from Wassaic, New York, had been in Vietnam just over a month.[2]

As the four Hueys and accompanying Cobra gunships approached Pace from about 2,000 feet, Specialist Marling could see the green tracer rounds from North Vietnamese gunners rise toward them from the woods below. The door gunners in the Hueys hammered back with their machine guns. Marling's helicopter suddenly dropped to treetop level for its approach. Now he could see the flashes of North Vietnamese mortars and machine guns in the tree line surrounding the base. The Quad Fifties and other weapons responded in kind. Bright red tracer rounds flashed toward the tree line. The door gunner tapped him on the shoulder—his signal to jump. He landed on his feet and ran for the front gate as fast as he could. As he had been briefed the night before, he turned left and jumped into the first bunker. The smell of cordite filled the air.

Suddenly, a lieutenant appeared. He was the same one who had briefed them the day before at the Tay Ninh airstrip. He reminded Marling of a young Kirk Douglas. "Boys, a Cobra just crashed into the tree line. He was protecting us; now it's our turn to protect him. Are you with me?"[3] All sixteen men from Delta Company's first wave dropped their rucksacks, grabbed their weapons, and followed First Lieutenant Richard Lee out the front gate they had just sprinted past. They ran across the road to the wood line east of the base road and worked their way southeast about one and a half kilometers.[4]

The downed Cobra belonged to F Battery, 79th Artillery, located at Tay Ninh West. Its mission that day was to escort a UH-1 Huey supply ship and provide suppressive fire. Just south of Pace three North Vietnamese anti-aircraft machine guns opened up on them from the trees below. Slugs riddled the fuselage. The engine stopped immediately. The hydraulics also failed. One of the pilots, Warrant Officer Eddie Rickenbacker Jr., spotted a clearing ahead and tried to guide the falling four-ton helicopter to it. It crashed into the trees just short of the clearing.

The downed Cobra started to burn, and Rickenbacker heard an explosion from the rear. He got out as quickly as he could while shouting for his copilot, Captain James McLaughlin, to get out as well.

"I can't. I can't get out!" McLaughlin yelled back.[5] His leg had been fractured at the thigh. Rickenbacker helped pull him out of the cockpit as the flames reached higher. They were able to take cover behind a large ant hill as the rockets and machine gun ammunition aboard the Cobra began to cook off. They counted at least nine separate explosions before the burning ship quieted down. Rickenbacker decided they shouldn't just sit there and wait. They weren't very far from the base, but McLaughlin was in no condition to move. "Do you have your weapon?" Rickenbacker asked.

"No. I left it in the snake [Cobra]."

"Here, take mine. I'm going to try to make it to Pace." Rickenbacker handed him the pearl-handled pistol and headed off. That's where McLaughlin was when Lieutenant Lee's patrol found them minutes later.[6]

Specialist Marling examined McLaughlin, who was still conscious, and determined he had a compound fracture of his left leg and burns on his face, hands, and legs. The fifteen remaining GIs from Delta Company established a protective perimeter around the two men while Marling gave the injured pilot a shot of morphine to ease his pain and tried to stabilize his fracture. He quickly realized McLaughlin was in no condition to be moved back to the firebase, so he gave him a second shot of morphine while Lieutenant Lee called for a medevac.

With other helicopters providing suppressive fire, a medical evacuation ship arrived and dropped a jungle pulley into the small clearing. Marling and others strapped McLaughlin into a stretcher, and the helicopter crew pulled him up. They headed back to the hospital, where he fully recovered. Marling remembered McLaughlin later asking him if he had seen any NVA in the wood line. Marling answered no, but he did hear voices. McLaughlin then told him he could see movement over Marling's shoulder. With the aid of the CSRJII radar, other members of the platoon were able to find Rickenbacker who returned to his unit and was back flying again two days later. Only later did they learn Rickenbacker was the grandson of World War I flying ace Eddie Rickenbacker.[7]

Marling and the other members of the patrol returned to the relative security of the firebase. The rest of Delta Company had arrived without any further incident, and things began to settle down for the evening. While Marling was seated outside their bunker, Lieutenant Lee walked by. "Doc, you did a good job out there," he told Marling.

"Piece of cake, L.T., piece of cake," replied Marling. As Lee walked off, Marling decided he needed a cigarette. He was shaking so much he couldn't get the lighter and the cigarette steady enough to light. He finally prevailed only by bracing both elbows against his knees.[8]

Sergeant Michael Stevens also landed with Delta Company that day. The native of Newton, Pennsylvania, remembered that while his unit was waiting at Tay Ninh West to be shuttled into Pace, they were told to get some chow. The cooks asked them where they were going, and when they found out it was Pace, they came back with steaks from the officer's mess. One of the cooks also handed one of Sergeant Stevens's colleagues a bag of marijuana. "Take this. You're going to need it," he said.[9]

As they descended into Pace, they were told they had to unload and reload the helicopter within five seconds in order to minimize exposure to enemy ground fire. Then, just before they landed, the crew chief yelled that one of the Cobra gunships escorting them had been shot down. Stevens recalls the face of the man seated next to him who'd just arrived in the country. It was "white as a ghost."

Stevens and the others jumped off their helicopters and headed for the nearest bunkers. He noticed the bunkers were all wrapped in cyclone fencing to protect against rocket-propelled grenades. Stevens remembered it was the first time he'd seen anything like that. He also noticed the .50 caliber machine guns bristling from the bunkers, and the Quad Fifties on the perimeter, and he realized they had just descended into "deep shit."[10]

While North Vietnamese anti-aircraft gunners knocked down a Cobra gunship, North Vietnamese mortars continued to bombard Pace. On October 12 Pace took twenty-six rounds of incoming in ten separate attacks, beginning at 0100 hours and ending at 2245 hours. Pace lost two fire extinguishers. Six GIs were wounded, but none seriously enough to require evacuation.[11] By working all night, gun crews were able to repair the 8-inch howitzer that had been knocked out of action the day before. Fortunately, it was up and operational when the South Vietnamese garrison at Thien Ngon reported a battalion-size ground attack at 1700 hours. Aided by helicopter gunships and both 8-inch howitzers from Pace, the defenders were able to fight off the attack. The 175mm Long Skinny knocked out on the eleventh could not be repaired and remained out of action for the next ten days.[12]

That same day (October 12) the inspector general released his report to Brigadier General Burton, commanding officer of 3d Brigade. Major Tozer concluded there was no combat refusal on October 9 or 10, that the welfare of the company was good, "considering their location," and the morale of the men in the company was "fair." He recommended no further action and that the case be closed.[13] Later that same day a verbal message was passed on to Captain Cronin from General Abrams, who had read his report. "Tell the young Captain he did good," Abrams reportedly said.[14]

Delta's second day at Pace (October 13) began with incoming at 0120, 0145, 0215, 0255, and 0540 hours. Pace responded with its organic mortars. There were no casualties or known damage.[15] At 0930 word came down to Delta Company to load up for a patrol to the wood line east of Pace, the same area Bravo Company had been assigned four days earlier. When the lieutenant in charge of 3d Platoon went to his second squad, they told him they wouldn't go.[16] The GIs in Delta Company had heard about Bravo Company's refusal over the Armed Forces radio while they were out in the field. They agreed among themselves that if they replaced Bravo Company, they wouldn't go out on that patrol, either.[17] Two of the GIs who refused said they had participated in the rescue of the two downed Cobra pilots (McLaughlin and Rickenbacker) the day before.[18] "Before we came here we were told we were not going out on any offensive patrols," Special Four Dennis VanOder explained later. "We are here for the defense of the artillery," agreed Private First Class David Scott.[19]

The frustrated platoon leader called in Delta's commanding officer, Captain Kenneth Smith of Nebraska City. Smith reportedly told the soldiers they could be court-martialed for refusing an order. When he didn't get any response, he instructed the entire platoon to step to the other side of the bunker if they refused to go. Twenty of the twenty-six men did so. Major Dye was called in. He explained to the men their mission would be to screen the tree line where the Cobra was shot down the day before in order to provide security for incoming aircraft resupplying the base. He offered to lead the patrol personally, if that's what it took for them to go out. Within thirty minutes they had their gear on (including all the men who had refused earlier) and headed out with their platoon leader.[20]

The patrol searched the tree line and returned to Pace without incident. But the North Vietnamese gunners west of Pace continued to lob 82mm mortar rounds at the base. At 1415 hours, a round seriously injured two soldiers, one with wounds to the head, shoulders, and back, and the other with a concussion. They were both medevaced to Saigon.[21]

Meanwhile, the units at Pace received a confusing set of orders from headquarters regarding preparations to withdraw from Pace. On October 12, Lieutenant Colonel McCaffree requested fourteen complete wheels (tire, wheel, tube, and air) for five-ton trucks, as well as batteries and sling equipment, obviously in preparation for an evacuation over land.[22] At 0150 hours on October 13, McCaffree received a call from General Wagstaff himself telling him the move from Pace had been postponed until further notice.[23] On October 15, at 1240 hours, McCaffree was told by 23d Group they would decide if Charlie Battery would be replaced by another battery from the 2/32d. They weren't.[24]

At 1300 hours on October 13, 1/12th Cavalry reported receiving an order that all U.S. personnel would be evacuated from Pace by air, but all heavy equipment would be put in "Admin Storage" because of a lack of air assets.[25] At 1010 hours the next day, they were told all activity was on hold for twenty-four hours. On October 15 they were told D Company would stay at Pace at least until October 21.[26]

At 2315 hours on October 17, 23d Group notified Colonel McCaffree they wanted a report on the overall morale of his troops at Pace and a list of any measures to improve the situation, as well as numbers of rounds fired and casualties and vehicle status, and they wanted it by 0400 hours that morning.[27] McCaffree reported back at 2300 hours on October 18 that after some ups and downs, current morale was "uniformly high," and no additional measures were required.[28]

Over the next week, life at Pace settled into a familiar but uneasy routine. Sergeant Stevens and the others adapted as best they could to the ever present threat of incoming. They found the camp's latrine was on the north end of the base, which required them to cross over open ground every time they needed to heed nature's call. So they built their own makeshift outhouse out of ammo boxes close by, "in the interest of personal safety," as Stevens described it.[29]

Under Major Dye's watchful eye, Delta Company continued to send out regular daylight reconnaissance patrols: sometimes northeast, sometimes east, sometimes southeast, but reported no contact.[30] Under the watchful eye of Major Davis and his team, the gunners in Charlie Battery continued to work the remaining three guns in service, firing into Cambodia. They reported to 23d Group they had destroyed seventy-three bunkers and three hooches over the last eight days. Damage assessments reported blood trails but no enemy bodies.[31] Meanwhile, the rumbling of B-52s filled the air and shook the ground, delivering what were described as some of the heaviest strikes of the entire war.[32] And three, four, or five times a day, the North Vietnamese lobbed one, two, three, or half a dozen mortar rounds at Pace. Sometimes they hit something; sometimes they didn't. The defenders at Pace could trace the location of the enemy firing point with great precision on their countermortar radars. They fired twenty or thirty rounds back for every round fired at them, but with no apparent effect. Casualties mounted, especially among the South Vietnamese, and everyone waited to see if the Americans at Pace would be pulled out.

Occasionally the monotony was broken by something unusual. On October 18 ARVN paratroopers clashed with elements of the 209th NVA Regiment in a firefight between Pace and Thien Ngon. The South Vietnamese army reported twenty-eight enemy killed and a loss of seven of their own.[33] But minutes later friendly aircraft mistook the South Vietnamese for enemy soldiers. Eighteen more South Vietnamese soldiers lost their lives when U.S. aircraft mistakenly dropped two 500-pound bombs directly on them.[34]

The next day, NBC sent a camera and sound crew out with correspondent Arthur Lord to report from the embattled firebase. Lord began with an aerial view of the base from a helicopter, explaining that Pace was home to about 200 American soldiers, including an artillery unit and an infantry company. Then, with visuals of an 8-inch howitzer firing, he described the mission of the big guns was to support the South Vietnamese forces nearby in Cambodia. The next shot was of infantrymen heading out on a daylight patrol. Lord reported that the purpose of the patrols was to keep the thousands of enemy troops in the area away from small-arms range of the base. No mention was made of the earlier refusals.[35]

Lord explained that the single road to Pace had been cut off. Showing two Chinook helicopters carrying a heavy load under a sling, he said aircraft delivered vital food, mail, and ammunition to Pace. He concluded the ninety-second segment standing in front of one of the Short Stubbies preparing to fire: "There aren't many Americans engaged in an active combat role in Vietnam anymore. But here, enemy mortar rounds hit the base every night, and there are thousands of North Vietnamese troops in the area. To the men stationed here, at least, the war that is winding down still seems very real. Arthur Lord, NBC News, at Firebase Pace near the Cambodian border."[36]

By the beginning of the third week in October it became increasingly clear that Fire Support Base Pace's days as the last U.S. outpost on the Cambodian border were coming to an end. The artillery had begun sending nonessential equipment back to the rear on a regular basis.[37] Rumors of an impending pullout grew in frequency.

For the grunts of Delta Company it meant completing two last dangerous but necessary tasks. On October 17 a Delta Company patrol headed into the tree line east of the base and recovered the black box and other sensitive equipment from the Cobra shot down on October 13, the day Delta arrived.[38] On October 21, Delta mounted a patrol south of Pace to recover the remains of the four helicopter crewmen killed when the Huey gunship crashed on September 29. A captain from their parent unit (117th Assault Helicopter Company), a tracker dog, and his handler accompanied them.[39] Delta Company Medic Paul Marling was told to join the patrol as well, although nobody told him exactly why. "Just make sure you have some Compazine," his squad leader warned. Compazine was treatment for a queasy stomach.[40]

They found the downed helicopter about a mile south of Pace near the bend in the road. As the only medic along, Specialist Marling inherited the unpleasant task of collecting the remains. The stench of death hung in the humid air. The bodies had badly decomposed after three weeks in the sun. Marling didn't have any rubber gloves with him, so he tried to pick up the shards of bone and decomposing tissue with sterile battle dressings. It didn't work, so he resorted to scooping up the remains with his bare hands.

After the patrol had returned to the relative safety of the firebase, an officer asked Marling how many bodies he'd recovered. He told the officer, "Two, perhaps three." Knowing the remains of one or two soldiers had been left behind would haunt Marling for at least a decade after he returned from Vietnam. He finally found some measure of relief when he visited the Vietnam Veterans Memorial in Washington, D.C., years later. All four names were up there and the code indicated all four had been recovered. "I have always said that was the most difficult task I did while in Vietnam," Marling said later, "but also the one I am most proud of."[41]

CHAPTER TWELVE

Whiskey and Kool-Aid
October 21–22

Every evening Sergeant Michael Donze walked around his 8-inch howitzer, "Cool Hand Luke," to make sure everything was in working order before darkness set in. He knew Charlie Battery would be pulled the next day, so this would be his last night at Pace.[1] What he didn't know was that he would soon become the last American soldier to be seriously wounded there.

Donze came from the small town of Ste. Genevieve, Missouri, that believed in honoring its active duty servicemen; every month Donze was the only GI at Pace to receive a care package from his entire hometown. Even though Donze was drafted, he believed in what his country was trying to do in Vietnam, so he agreed to attend the NCO academy at Fort Sill.[2] There the Army took selected enlisted men who seemed to have leadership potential and gave them additional training and a sergeant's rank to fill much-needed noncommissioned officer slots in Vietnam and elsewhere, particularly in the combat arms.[3]

After graduation from the NCO academy, Donze was sent to Vietnam, where he ended up as a section chief with Charlie Battery. As Donze walked around his howitzer that night, he heard the familiar shout of "Incoming!" He looked to the west side of the base, where the enemy seemed to be walking a string of 82mm mortar rounds straight for him. He threw himself under the chassis of the thirty-ton steel beast for cover.[4]

A round exploded with a bright flash and loud clang just in front of him. He thought at first the worst he would get out of this was a mild concussion, but then he felt a stinging in his chest and legs. Something warm ran across his skin—his own blood. He cried out for a medic. Because he was under one of the howitzers and it was getting dark, it took some time for his men to find him. When they did, they immediately called for an emergency evacuation for what were described as "serious wounds" around his chest and legs.[5]

Donze passed out but remembers waking up to the sight of tracers following his helicopter as it lifted off. They stopped off at Tay Ninh so a doctor could join them and keep him alive for the remainder of the trip to the 93d Evacuation Hospital at Long Binh. Sergeant Donze eventually recovered, but only after numerous operations and nine months in and out of various hospitals.[6]

Charlie Battery spent the remainder of the night firing off all their ammo. The next morning (October 22) an armada of armed helicopters from F Battery, 79th

Aerial Rocket Artillery, filled the air over Fire Support Base Pace. It included at one time or another ten Cobra gunships, a smoke ship, and rocket-firing ships.[7] Their job: suppress enemy anti-aircraft to allow the evacuation of Fire Support Base Pace by air. The 2/32d had been backhauling equipment for three days. Over that period of time a steady stream of heavy equipment had been removed via eighteen Chinook sorties.[8] Now it was time to finish the job.

The first person to be evacuated was First Lieutenant Diggs. He'd been wounded in the hand by shrapnel two days earlier, and his superiors feared it would become infected if not treated soon. He left via OH-58 Ranger. The helicopter twisted and turned so much doing evasive maneuvers that Diggs thought for sure they'd crash before any infection could get him.[9]

The first CH-47 Chinook arrived at 1130 hours. A CH-54 Flying Crane joined the exercise shortly thereafter. The last elements of the artillery battery and supporting personnel (five officers and fifty-six enlisted men) landed at Tay Ninh West at 1310 hours.[10] They celebrated with whiskey and Kool-Aid.[11] D Company, 1/12th Cavalry began its evacuation at 1320 hours. Six officers and 102 men departed in ten UH1 Hueys. Evacuation was completed at 1358 hours. At 1444 hours on October 22, General Wagstaff sent a message to General Abrams indicating the evacuation went according to plan and was completed without incident or enemy interference.[12]

While the soldiers at Pace were all relieved to finally be leaving, it left a bad taste for the artillery officers and noncommissioned officers. The Air Cavalry moved around a lot anyway, so leaving Pace was no big deal. For the artillery, it was a big deal.[13] They had been taught from the first day they arrived at Fort Sill to abide by one simple concept: an artilleryman never abandons his guns. They had all heard the story of Lieutenant Alanzo Cushing, Battery A, 4th U.S. Artillery, at Gettysburg. Although mortally wounded, Cushing stood by his guns at Bloody Angle on Cemetery Ridge long enough to fire one last round of canister, helping to break the back of Pickett's charge and save the day for the Union army. Now it was time to board the helicopters and leave the guns behind. Sure, it was logical and much safer to evacuate by air. Taking the breech blocks meant the enemy could never use the guns, and later the guns would be recovered. But it still didn't seem quite right. In its own way, it reflected the unsatisfying end to the war itself three and a half years later.

Left behind, in addition to the South Vietnamese soldiers, was the equipment deemed too heavy to lift out by air—two M107 guns (minus breech blocks), two M110 self-propelled howitzers (also minus breech blocks), four Quad Fifty machine guns on five-ton trucks, two bulldozers, two five-ton trucks, one bucket loader, and one M557 armored personnel carrier.[14] Two enlisted men, Specialist Four William C. Comer of Somerville, Georgia, from Charlie Battery 2/32d Field

Artillery, and Sergeant Steven W. Belt of Waxahachie, Texas, from D Battery 71st Artillery (Quad Fifties), volunteered to stay behind as custodians.[15]

Belt and Comer told the Associated Press that they felt very safe at Pace because the South Vietnamese paratroops defending the base "are really squared away. If anyone can protect us, they can." Both men were approaching the end of their tours in Vietnam. Sergeant Belt, a career soldier, had two months left. Specialist Comer, a draftee, had three months left, after which he planned to "get out and stay out." Both had a wife and child back in the States. When asked what their wives would think of their decision to stay behind, Belt replied, "Tell them not to worry; we're doing just fine."[16]

Sergeant Belt said later he thought he was volunteering to lead a breakout, which had been rumored for some time, so he stepped forward. When he realized he had instead volunteered to stay with the equipment being left behind, his first thought was, "Oh shit!" His next thought was to gather up whatever he could use. He and Specialist Comer, the other "volunteer," spent the next couple of hours going through the abandoned hooches gathering up food and anything else they could use. For several days Pace had been on short rations of food (one C ration per man per day) and water, so "we felt like kings in heaven with what we found," Belt said later.[17]

Also staying behind at Pace were four American advisers assigned to the 6th ARVN Airborne Battalion. Captain Ray Rhodes, senior adviser to the ARVN 6th Airborne, was the ranking officer left in charge. Rhodes had taken over from Major Mike Anderson, who had been wounded by incoming at Pace and had to be evacuated.[18] When asked by a UPI reporter if he was confident his troops could hold Pace against any enemy attack, Rhodes replied, "I'm not worried. These airborne troops are good. They can take anything."[19]

While the evacuation occurred without incident, the controversy associated with Fire Support Base Pace continued to swirl. On October 18 Senator Kennedy replied to the October 10 letter sent by Specialist Four Al Grana and his colleagues. He thanked them for their courage and bravery under fire and let them know he had forwarded the letter to the secretary of defense and requested his comments on recent events at Pace.[20]

On October 21 the White House asked the Pentagon to find out what was going on. The next day, a "Fact Sheet on Fire Support Base Pace Incidents" was forwarded to the White House over the signature of Lieutenant General Walter T. Kerwin Jr., deputy chief of staff for personnel.

"Recent allegations by news media concerning soldiers refusing to accompany their unit on patrols on two separate instances in the vicinity of Fire Support Base Pace, Republic of South Vietnam, have been investigated," began the report. After summarizing both the Bravo Company refusal on October 9th and the Delta

Company refusal on October 13th, the two-page report concluded: "There were no combat refusals. Consequently, there are no grounds for disciplinary action. . . . The underlying cause of the incidents was the fact that the men had talked themselves into a negative frame of mind. Once the soldiers understood their mission, no further incidents arose."[21]

On October 22 UPI put out the story on Delta Company's temporary refusal a week earlier. The story ran in the Washington Post and the Pacific edition of Stars and Stripes.[22] The evacuation itself was dutifully reported on all three network news programs the evening of October 21 and in major newspapers on October 23.[23]

Richard Boyle continued to lobby Congress. After a tepid response from Senator Kennedy, he visited Representative Ron Dellums (D-CA), whom he described as "sympathetic"; Senator Fred Harris (D-OK), who asked for a congressional inquiry; Senator Mike Gravel (D-Alaska), who "expressed interest" in his information; and even Senator Barry Goldwater (R-AZ), who Boyle said told him there had been revolts at other times in American history, even the Revolutionary War.[24]

He finally got a response more to his liking from Representative Pete McCloskey. The California Republican was an ex-Marine and outspoken opponent of the war. He'd already announced he would run against President Nixon in the New Hampshire primary. Boyle described McCloskey as "visibly moved." The congressman invited Boyle to dinner at his home, and they decided to hold a joint press conference. McCloskey invited Senator Kennedy to the press conference, but Kennedy declined to appear.[25] McCloskey and Boyle went ahead with a press conference in the Capitol hearing room. Then, on October 28, McCloskey entered the petition from Bravo Company into the Congressional Record.[26]

Back in Vietnam, the South Vietnamese moved quickly to claim victory. In an October 23rd interview with the Associated Press, Lieutenant General Minh declared a major setback for Hanoi, claiming the North Vietnamese 7th Division, which included the 209th Regiment, had been forced to retreat after suffering 2,200 killed out of an estimated strength of 4,000 to 5,000 committed to the battle. This included "confirmed kills" of 1,100 by body count on the ground and another 1,100 from air strikes reported by aerial observers. This compared to a loss of 187 killed and 800 wounded among the 25,000 South Vietnamese troops committed to the battle. Minh also said 2,000 troops from the North Vietnamese 5th Division, who were involved in the fighting around Krek, had also retreated deeper into Cambodia.[27]

As a result, Route 22 had been secured along its entire length, although it would take about a week to repair the road surface so that convoys could travel the last five miles from Thien Ngon to the border. "In the last 24 hours there have been no mortars or rockets on Route 22," Minh concluded, adding that the enemy had been hurt so badly, "I don't believe they'll come back. If they want to do something, it will take them six more months."[28]

By November 2, Highway 22 was in good enough shape for the guns and other equipment from Charlie Battery to be evacuated by road from Pace.[29] Sergeant Steve Belt accompanied the convoy that evacuated the remaining vehicles out of Pace. He remembers being struck by the sight of dead vegetation and torn-up ground south of the firebase from all the bombing and shelling. "There appeared to be craters everywhere," he recalled.[30]

The rest of the evacuation by road proceeded successfully, but not without one last tense moment. One of the tractor trailers carrying an 8-inch howitzer went off the road between Tay Ninh and Phu Loi. It was too late in the day to call for a wrecker, so Lieutenant Colonel McCaffree made the decision to let the rest of the convoy move on while leaving someone behind to guard the disabled vehicle. Major Jack Garner, carrying only a pistol, got that assignment, along with a very nervous-looking platoon of ARVN. The night passed slowly but without incident, and the remaining howitzer made it to Phu Loi the next day.[31]

The last member of the 2/32d Field Artillery to be killed by hostile fire in Vietnam would not come from Firebase Pace or from Charlie Battery. Instead, the misfortune would fall to Specialist Four David L. Hamm, twenty-one, of Kingsport, Tennessee. He was killed when a 122mm rocket landed near him at Tay Ninh West on October 3.[32] Ironically, David and the other members of Bravo Battery had been evacuated from the exposed position at Katum to the relative safety of the Tay Ninh base camp just a few days earlier.[33]

If Specialist Hamm's concern was that he would be forgotten, he needn't have worried. The memorial to him on the Vietnam Veteran's Memorial Web site includes remembrances from both his friends back home and his comrades in arms. This January 6, 2002, message from Jessee Edwards is typical:

My Best Friend
I will always, remember as kids, David coming down to play. He had, a
speech impediment and would ask, if he could have some speakettea, to eat.
I would, make him say it over and again and we would laugh. I remember, all
the good times, we had as kids. While, I went to the funeral, I could not see
them lay him down and now, when I visit the grave I have problems, going
near the site. David was, a true friend and he will, never be forgotten by all,
who knew him. When together, we often mention him and think, about his
family. I miss you, big guy. Jessee[34]

In late November the South Vietnamese announced a new drive into the Chup Rubber Plantation—5,000 troops in the lead and another 10,000 to back them up.[35] On December 14 they captured the rubber plantation town of Chup.[36] On

December 30 they declared the operation a success and redeployed the ARVN Airborne to the central highlands.[37] Before he left Pace with the Airborne, Captain Rhodes removed the plaque commemorating Lieutenant Gary Pace and sent it back to Army officials in the States for safekeeping.[38]

On January 22, 1972, the Proud Americans of 2/32d Field Artillery officially left Vietnam to return to the States as part of Increment X of MACV's withdrawal plan.[39] The Sky Troopers of the 1/12th remained with most of the 3d Brigade through June 1972.[40] The North Vietnamese had no intention of withdrawing for any length of time, General Minh's declaration of victory notwithstanding. We now know the North Vietnamese command decided in December 1971 to go for broke with a major dry season offensive in 1972.[41]

PART TWO

The Soldiers

CHAPTER THIRTEEN

The Grunts

In the 1970 movie *Kelly's Heroes*, Donald Sutherland plays a lethargic, unkempt GI named Oddball, somewhere in France in 1944. When asked by another GI, played by Telly Savalas, why he and his tank had avoided combat for four months while his comrades fought their way from the Normandy beachhead, Oddball smirks, "We see our mission as essentially defensive in nature . . . we are holding ourselves in reserve in case the Krauts mount a counteroffensive which threatens Paris . . . or maybe even New York."[1] It is often said that movies say more about the time they were made than anything else. Add a reefer and a peace medallion and Oddball would have easily fit the image many Americans had of the 1970–1971 American GI in Vietnam—dirty, undisciplined, hippiefied, and combat averse.

This kind of soldier (or nonsoldier) is what Robert Heinl wrote about when he described "an Army in a state approaching collapse" in his June 1971 *Armed Forces Journal* article. "By every conceivable indicator, our Army that now remains in Vietnam is in a state approaching collapse, with individual units avoiding or having refused combat, murdering their officers and non-commissioned officers, drug-ridden, and dispirited where not near mutinous," Heinl charged.[2] This point of view was shared by some still on active duty in the Army. For example, Brigadier General Theodore Mataxis, who had led troops both in Vietnam and Korea, declared, "It's been the opposite of Korea. There we went in with a bad army and came out with a good one. In Vietnam we went in with a good Army and came out with a bad one."[3]

As combat draws to a close, soldiers turn skittish about risking their lives in what appears to be a foregone conclusion. This was true in Vietnam, but not only in Vietnam. Sometimes even the best units are affected. One such case occurred in February 1945 about ninety days before the end of the war in Europe. In the book *Band of Brothers*, Stephen Ambrose chronicles the story of Easy Company, 506th Parachute Regiment, 101st Airborne Division, one of the best and most highly decorated group of soldiers in World War II. But, when ordered to run a risky night reconnaissance patrol across the Moder River near Haguenau, a patrol the Company Commander considered suicidal, they elected to fake the patrol (what would be later called "ghosting" in Vietnam). Afterward some of the men got drunk and got into a fight.[4] No reporters were around, so the excellent reputation of the unit remained intact.

The lingering stalemate in Korea seven years later provides an even better example. Peace talks dragged on for two years before an armistice was signed, a process that cynical GIs dubbed "die for a tie." Even the Army's official history of the conflict acknowledged the problem: "With rotation as the carrot dangling before his eyes, the individual soldier's main concern was to stay alive until his year of combat service expired. Neither officers nor enlisted men were particularly interested in taking undue chances under these conditions and an air of caution arose. As the reluctance to jeopardize lives grew, the effort to substitute firepower for manpower increased."[5]

But Heinl and other critics claimed the problem was worse in Vietnam, "by several orders of magnitude," as Heinl put it.[6] Not everyone agreed. An unnamed Army officer interviewed by *Washington Post* reporter Peter Jay in the aftermath of the refusals at Firebase Pace explained it this way: "Obviously, no one wants to be the last man killed here," he said. "No one wants to take risks in a cause the country's given up on. Of course there are incidents. But the jobs are still being done."[7]

Job still being done or Army on the verge of collapse? Which of these two alternate realities better describes what was happening on the ground at Firebase Pace in September and October 1971? And what does it tell us about the state of the ground forces in Vietnam at the time, and about why soldiers fight or don't? Author Myra MacPherson attempted to address those questions more than a decade later in her 1984 book, *Long Time Passing: Vietnam and the Haunted Generation.* After referring to Firebase Pace as an "insurrection," she laid out the following statistics in support of her description of a military in "disarray." She argued that a 1971 random group of Army soldiers would produce:

Seven acts of desertion
Seventeen AWOL incidents
Twenty frequent marijuana smokers
Ten regular narcotics users
Two discipline charges
Eighteen lesser punishments
Twelve complaints to Congressmen[8]

MacPherson cites as her source David Cortright's 1975 book, *Soldiers in Revolt: GI Resistance during the Vietnam War.* Cortright draws his information from a series of congressional hearings, much from Pentagon testimony, and uses it to conclude that as many as one-fourth of all enlisted men "engaged in some form of rebellion against military authority. . . . No armed force can function properly when faced with such internal disruption and resistance."[9] While the presentation of information in this way might be an eye-catching way of making a point, it can also be extremely misleading. What Cortright makes clear, but MacPherson does not, is that these figures are Armywide averages. They include not only GIs serving in Vietnam but also soldiers in Europe and the United States. This includes trainees who are likely to have higher incidences of AWOL and discipline failure, for example.

What averages of this nature also do is mask important differences between units or groups of units. Combat in Vietnam was often on the small unit (company or platoon) level, where unit leadership and the unique circumstances of that time and place were much more meaningful than Armywide averages. For example, the ORLL for the 23d Artillery Group for the period ending October 31, 1971, lists 37 men wounded between April and October, or an annualized loss of about 1.5 per 100. So, an average 23d Group Artillery Battery would face one or two soldiers wounded a year due to enemy action in this period. What these averages don't show is that 30 of these 37 losses occurred in Charlie Battery 2/32d over twenty-seven days in September and October at Firebase Pace, or an annualized rate 270 times higher, at 406 per 100.[10]

The incidence of desertions is another good example of how the story told by a group of statistics varies depending on how those statistics are presented. Deserting one's comrades is a serious offense and a legitimate indicator of morale. An August 11, 1971, report in the *Washington Post* revealed that the Army's worldwide desertion rate for the first ten months of fiscal year 1971 was approaching the World War II peak of 63 per 1,000, reached in 1944. However, it also showed that desertions among soldiers serving in Vietnam *had fallen* every year since 1967 and were down to 4.0 per 1,000 by fiscal year 1970, the last year for which figures were available.[11]

The profile of units still in harm's way in Vietnam presents a very different picture from MacPherson's or Cortright's Armywide averages, in part because they were more experienced soldiers, and in part because they faced a tangible enemy. Frontline soldiers in Vietnam had a powerful incentive to stay focused on the job at hand and be protective of each other, regardless of the political context. The Army did not publish statistics for the 1/12th Cavalry for 1971, but it did collect some statistics for the 3d Brigade (Separate) of the 1st Air Cavalry Division, 1/12th parent unit.[12] The figures for April 30, 1971, to October 31, 1971, which include the time Pace was under attack, show the following instances of bad behavior, normalized at an annual incidence per 100 (about the size of an infantry company or the garrison at Pace):

Crimes of Violence (murder, rape, assault, robbery) 0
Property Crimes (burglary, larceny, theft) 8
Drug Convictions 6
AWOL 3

These figures are based on arrests by the provost marshal's office, so there may be some underreporting, especially regarding drug use. On the other hand, they represent figures for the entire brigade, which includes rear echelon support units, where crime and drug use tended to be higher than in units out in the field at places like Fire Support Base Pace. They also do not distinguish between one offense by one person and multiple offenses by one person, so they may overstate the degree of bad behavior of individuals in units actually engaged with the enemy. Although the definitions in this report are different than those used in Cortright's book, the differences, where they are comparable, are stark. For example, Cortright identifies an AWOL rate of 17 per 100, while 3d Brigade 1st Cavalry division had only 3. The incidence of violent crimes is so small it rounds out to 0 per 100.

This evidence strongly suggests that the grunts at Pace, and in the rest of the 3d Brigade, were not at war with themselves anywhere near the degree Heinl, MacPherson, and Cortright suggest, at least in terms of criminal behavior. But, looked at in isolation, these figures do not tell us what these soldiers were doing (or not doing) in terms of accomplishing their mission of protecting American units and installations while the withdrawal continued.

The first place to look for this information are the records the Army itself kept on the activities of the infantry units assigned to protect Fire Support Base Pace. Those documents have since been declassified and provide almost a day-by-day, hour-by-hour record of what went on. It is important to recognize that even though these are official reports, they are not necessarily 100 percent accurate or complete. They were compiled in the heat of the moment, for the most part, based on what the person(s) preparing the report understood to be the case. So, wherever possible, key events have been verified not only through unit records but other sources as well, including eye-witness accounts from people in the position to see and understand what was happening. Much of the story aligns, but in some cases it does not.

The infantry's mission in protecting Pace can best be described as follows:

- Defending the perimeter in the event of a ground attack. Fortunately, this never occured, so it is not known how they would have responded.
- Defending the base with indirect fire from the company's mortars. A two-mortar section from E Company stayed at Pace for the entire period, firing both high explosive and illuminating rounds as needed. The two-man crews working the 4.2-inch mortars at Pace operated in an open pit with no overhead cover, thus exposing themselves to enemy incoming fire, much like the artillery crews.[13] Private 1st Class Steve Lonchase, who spent time at Pace as a mortar crewman, recalls firing at least ten to twenty rounds a day of counter mortar and illumination.[14] This part of the mission was clearly fulfilled.

- Conducting reconnaissance patrols outside the perimeter wire in order to detect possible enemy movement and enemy intentions. These important patrols allowed the garrison to prepare for whatever came their way. They also caused the most controversy.

All four line companies of the 1/12th Cavalry spent time at Fire Support Base Pace over a twenty-nine-day period from September 24 to October 22, 1971. Charlie Company arrived first but spent only one day at Pace before being shuttled off to FSB Katum.[15] The other three companies spent significant time at Pace and left behind a verifiable record of what they did or did not do.

Alpha Company defended Pace for fourteen days, from September 24 through October 7, when some of the most intense enemy activity took place. As described previously, Alpha ran at least three patrols outside the perimeter wire over this period.[16] Differences between Alpha Company's leadership and the artillery commanders at Pace surfaced over the frequency and aggressiveness of these patrols, but at least some patrols were conducted. There were no refusals, and at least eight members of the company suffered wounds from shrapnel during their stay at Pace.[17]

Alpha rotated out on October 7 to be replaced by Bravo Company. Two days later, on October 9, six members of Bravo Company refused to go out on a night ambush. Aggressive reconnaissance is a standard expectation of defenders of any fixed position like a firebase. It keeps potential attackers off guard and provides defenders advance warning of possible enemy activity.[18] The members of Bravo Company did not object to reconnaissance for defensive purposes, but to this particular mission, which they saw as needlessly risky. In fact, General Wagstaff, talking later about the incident, seemed somewhat sympathetic. Speaking with a reporter two days after Pace was evacuated, he said: "They were trained in air mobile tactics in which when a unit gets in trouble there are always reinforcements available. Their reinforcements at Pace were the Vietnamese, who fought damn well there. But it took them some time to get used to operating away from their own battalions."[19]

In addition, the bad weather conditions that night made it chancy, at best, to count on helicopters for fire support, delivery of supplies, or medical evacuation.[20] More important, the men had legitimate concerns about the wisdom of the mission. The 1/12th was a veteran unit that instinctively knew what made sense and what didn't. Going out at night in small numbers over unfamiliar terrain littered with unmarked booby traps and without adequate support was unusually risky.

Three of the individuals directly involved in the temporary refusal on October 9—Sergeant Demas, Sergeant Wernli, and Specialist Four French—were veteran soldiers with good records. They all raised the issue of the unmarked Claymores as a major concern.[21] Their fears turned out to be well founded. Staff Sergeant Cibolski, who was an experienced veteran soldier, confirmed their existence prior to the patrol being sent out. Cibolski's warning turned out to be justified when the patrol came across a string of Claymores the next day.[22] Captain Cronin realized this and wisely canceled the mission. Fortunately, no one was hurt, but the concerns raised prior to the mission came from veteran soldiers wary of unnecessary risks, not mutineers interested in shirking their duty.

What Bravo Company did before and after its appearance at Pace is informative as well. Presumably, if this were a collection of slackers and malcontents, some signs would have surfaced before the refusal. Even more likely, once these soldiers had crossed the line, disobeyed an order and not been punished, the shirkers should have the upper hand and more refusals would follow. In fact, the record indicates the opposite. From May through September 1971, Bravo Company was out in the field regularly, along with the other line companies of 1/12th Cavalry. They operated from seven major firebases and a host of minibases in Long Khanh Province and uncovered twenty tons of flour in a four-day period. In the first week of September, Bravo Company clashed with enemy soldiers on three occasions, with five members of the company wounded by enemy fire.[23]

Another perspective on the status of the grunts at Pace comes from the October 12 report from Major Tozer, inspector general of the 1st Cavalry Division's 3d Brigade. After visiting Pace on October 11, and talking with the soldiers involved, Major Tozer concluded there was no combat refusal on October 9 or 10.[24]

Tozer went on to make some other helpful observations. He noted that the soldiers involved were "intelligent, concerned and willing to discuss the matter openly," which is not the mark of a gang of conspirators or heavy drug users.[25] Also, because of poor weather on October 9, a soldier lightly wounded with a head injury was not medevaced until the next day, which some of the troops misinterpreted as a lack of support.[26]

The men were not of one mind as to how far they would have gone had they received a direct order to go. Some clearly would have gone; some were more reluctant.[27] This observation is consistent with the recollection of First Lieutenant Richard Coreno, the leader of 2d Platoon, whose members initiated the letter to Senator Kennedy. Coreno, who disagreed with Captain Cronin on the merits of this particular mission, felt some of the discussion among the enlisted men was "just talk."[28] Griping is a longtime soldier prerogative, especially among the infantry. According to Tozer, "When I talked with them collectively, they were considerably more defiant than when I had private conversations with them."[29]

Finally, Tozer pointed out that approximately eighty-five of the GIs in Bravo Company were scheduled to rotate back to the States in sixty days or less.[30] If one-year tours were distributed evenly during the year, a company-sized unit would expect only fifteen to twenty men to be short sixty days or less. Although Major

Tozer didn't say it in so many words, short-timers fever had to be at play here. Soldiers who have endured a lot and have the end of their peril in sight are much less likely to take risks. In fact, the members of Bravo Company described themselves as "very close," particularly the members of 2d Platoon.[31] "We were angry, more nervous and more cynical because we'd been in Vietnam so long," Specialist Four Grana recalled later.[32]

After leaving Pace on October 12, Bravo Company was back out in the field on a night ambush north of Xuan Loc.[33] There were no reports of combat refusals or other disciplinary issues. It is probably more than coincidence that although both Bravo and Delta Companies ran patrols in their thirteen days at Pace, no effort was made to resurrect a night ambush, which implies that their commanders recognized this was not a good idea in the first place.

Then there is the issue of the letter/petition to Senator Kennedy. An open letter to an elected official from a line combat unit questioning strategy is very unusual, even in the contentious political environment of the Vietnam War. Sixty-six members of Bravo Company signed the letter, including many of the company's junior NCOs. Tozer mentioned the latter in his report, but he didn't say much more about it.

First of all, the letter is authentic. Although a printed version appears in Boyle's book, *Flower of the Dragon*, copies of the original document in Al Grana's handwriting were made. The GIs listed as signatories are on Bravo Company's roster, and a spot-check of individuals who signed confirmed that they did sign the document. In the years since, no one has come forward to challenge the authenticity of the letter in any way.

The reference to "defensive role" in the letter was not a creation of the petition's authors. At least some of the troops were aware of the public relations offensive President Richard Nixon and Secretary Melvin Laird began in January 1971 about how America's combat role would be ending by May 1. "I don't want to mislead anyone," Secretary Laird said in a January press conference in Bangkok. "There will still be United States combat forces there (in South Vietnam) but *their assignment will not be a combat responsibility as such* (emphasis added). It will be primarily a security responsibility."[34] It came up again in August, just two months before events at Pace reached a boiling point. On August 6, the Pacific Edition of *Stars and Stripes* carried an Associated Press story about Defense Secretary Laird's address to delegates of the American Legion Girl's Nation. Laird was elaborating on President Nixon's statement the day before, when the president told a Washington press conference that U.S. troops "are frankly just defending areas which we occupy."[35]

"Phase I of the Vietnamization program has been virtually completed with the President's announcement that US ground forces had moved into defensive positions," Laird explained; however, this did not mean an end to all "combat activity," the Associated Press report noted. It quoted Laird as saying, "It should be clear to all there will be action by American military units, to protect remaining American bases and support units." Everything Secretary Laird said was factually correct in this case, but the headline in the Army's quasi-official newspaper summarized it this way: "GI Combat Role in Vietnam Nearly Ended—Laird."[36] This creative word parsing had to raise the level of cynicism among those soldiers, including the ones at Pace, who were still being shot at on a daily basis when their combat role was supposed to be nearly ended.

The letter to Senator Kennedy initiated with Specialist Grana and members of 2d Platoon, but the refusal itself began with Specialist French and members of the 3d Platoon. Although members of 3d Platoon did sign the letter, these men maintain they did not object to going out on patrol per se but to the specifics of this patrol, particularly the unmarked Claymores. Their platoon leader seemed to agree. "There's no doubt in my mind that if an order came down they would have gone," Lieutenant Shuler later told *Stars and Stripes*.[37] The fact that men from 3d Platoon, including French, Demas, and Wernli, did go out on patrol the next day (although reluctantly) also supports Shuler's interpretation. Members of 2d Platoon were more outspoken about the mission in general. Members of 2d Platoon did not volunteer to go out on patrol the next day, and some maintain they were unwilling to go under any circumstances, but they did participate in future missions.[38]

Does this mean Richard Boyle just reported on what was happening or did he turn this into something bigger than it was? Boyle's opposition to the Vietnam War was no secret. Boyle's offer to take this information out and share it with Agence France-Presse helped bring this issue into the national headlines.[39] However, it is clear that while Boyle may have embellished this story, he didn't single-handedly make it up. The frustrations were brewing and most likely would have boiled over whether he was there or not. What he did influence was how initial press reports came out.

It is also important to note that concerns over a disconnect between what administration officials were describing to the people back home and what the GIs saw happening to them and to their comrades did not limit itself to Bravo Company. Specialist Four Paul White, a draftee and a May 1970 graduate of the University of North Carolina at Greensboro joined Delta Company, 1/12th Cavalry in May 1971. He was steadily given more responsibility and became the battalion's chief radio telephone operator by the time he arrived at Pace along with Delta Company in October. White was so incensed by Secretary Laird's September 3 statements regarding the diminished combat role of U.S. ground troops that he wrote the secretary a personal letter. He did receive a reply from Major General Donnelly P. Bolton, director of operations."[40] However, he did not find the letter persuasive. "It was really disgusting to me," he wrote his parents on September 25.[41]

General Bolton's reply was not a form letter, and it did correctly emphasize that the overall level of combat activity had declined for U.S. troops. Bolton also acknowledged that the statement that Americans have relinquished all combat roles to the South Vietnamese was incorrect. That statement came from the United Press International wire copy and was not a direct quote from Secretary Laird.[42] Nevertheless, the Nixon administration, including Secretary Laird, continuously downplayed the degree to which U.S. ground troops were at risk for domestic political reasons, and that is what justifiably rankled Specialist White and the other GIs who still regularly found themselves under enemy fire.

On October 31, 1971, the *Chicago Tribune*, a newspaper that editorially supported the Nixon administration and its conduct of the war, ran a story about reporter Donald Kirk's visit to McGuire Air Force Base in New Jersey. Kirk's assignment was to talk to returning Vietnam veterans to gauge their views on the war they had just left.[43] Kirk interviewed a recently returned veteran identified as twenty-year-old Specialist Four James Wilson, of Pittsburgh, Pennsylvania. Wilson served with the 11th Armored Cavalry Regiment and was part of the unit that protected Bravo Battery 2/32d's evacuation from FSB Katum in late September. "It was senseless," Wilson said in describing his view of what was going on in Vietnam. When asked what he thought about the two combat refusals at Pace, he replied, "I'm with them."[44]

Even though the actions of Bravo Company generated support from other GIs at Pace and elsewhere, not everyone in Bravo Company, or in any of the other units, were all of one mind regarding the wisdom of the war, or the strategy to fight it. With the American public split over conduct of the Vietnam War, it should not be surprising that its soldiers possessed differing views as well. But one thing soldiers in Vietnam and civilians at home shared in common, whether they supported the war or not, was a belief that the country's politicians and senior leaders had mismanaged the war. Those who supported the war were angry at their leaders for fighting a war without doing what they needed to do to win. Those who opposed the war blamed their leaders for pursuing a war they knew they couldn't win.[45]

Thus, while some GIs supported Bravo Company's actions for varying reasons, others did not. For example, First Lieutenant Wayne Alberg of Charlie Battery 2/32d Artillery, an assistant executive officer at Pace, was reassigned to 1/7th Cavalry as a forward observer after the 2/32d stood down. What he found was that some of his colleagues in the 1/7th thought their colleagues in Bravo 1/12th had embarrassed the whole 1st Cavalry Division by making headlines over their refusal.[46] CBS reporter John Laurence found the same negative reaction from other units after he broke the story of a temporary refusal by Charlie Company 2/7th Cavalry in April 1970.[47]

Looking back on these events now, Specialist Grana wonders if their letter escalated what would have been a family disagreement into more than it needed to be. "We were willing to take on Cronin, but not the whole Army," he recalls. "Without the letter, it could have been resolved."[48] Having said that, Grana and his enlisted colleagues from Bravo Company who signed the letter still feel as strongly now as they did then that, for a variety of reasons, the night ambush was a bad idea.[49]

Delta Company, the unit flown in to replace Bravo Company on October 12, soon found itself part of a similar controversy. Delta had been out in the field regularly since June. Just two days earlier they had uncovered 3,000 pounds of flour stored near FSB Round Rock in Binh Duong Province.[50] Delta participated in a temporary combat refusal of its own on October 13 after rescuing the two helicopter pilots the day before. This time it involved a daylight mission to secure a tree line just east of the base so that resupply helicopters could take off and land safely—a much more straightforward defensive mission than a night ambush. The soldiers involved acknowledged that they had heard about Bravo's refusal four days earlier.[51]

At this point, the situation at Pace came closest to unraveling into a contagion of rebellion. If Delta refused to follow orders, it left their commanders with a series of unpleasant choices—court-martial the men and/or replace them with yet another unit and run the risk of a spreading insurrection, all under the glare of national publicity. Finally, Major Dye was called in. He talked with the men, explained why the mission was necessary for the defense of Pace, and offered to lead the patrol himself. After about an hour of deliberations the men agreed to proceed under the leadership of their platoon leader. The patrol returned safely, and for the next ten days Delta remained at Pace running reconnaissance patrols necessary for base defense on nearly a daily basis with no further incidents.[52] This included two dangerous missions—one to recover equipment from the downed Cobra, the other to recover bodies from the downed Huey.[53] Two days after Pace was evacuated, Delta went back to Fire Support Base Round Rock and was back out in the field on patrol looking for enemy supply caches.[54]

Charlie Company, the remaining line company of 1/12th, only spent one day at Pace (September 23) before being air lifted to Firebase Katum, where it provided security for Bravo Battery 2/32 until the base was evacuated three days later. Like the other companies of 1/12th, Charlie Company was a veteran unit that conducted itself well without incident before and after the refusals at Pace. A week after Pace was evacuated, Charlie Company was back out in the field when it detonated two booby traps, killing one man and wounding five.[55]

Looking over 1/12th Cavalry's entire record for the second half of 1971, it clearly does not resemble an Army on the brink of collapse or rebellion. Nor is it an Army willing to blindly follow orders. So what is it? Perhaps the best explanation came from veteran CBS correspondent John Laurence, who spent time in the field with another 1st Calvary unit, Charlie Company 2/7th, eighteen months earlier in the spring of 1970.

Laurence and his camera and sound crew went out with Charlie Company on a patrol near the Cambodian border not far from where Pace would be built twelve months later. He filmed a combat refusal by veteran GIs to walk down a road they thought was too dangerous. He later commented on what he saw in his award-winning documentary, "The World of Charlie Company." He focused on the difference in attitude among the line infantry—the grunts—between his first tour in 1966–1967 and those he saw in the spring of 1970:

> A certain sense of independence, a reluctance to behave according to the military's insistence on obedience, like pawns or puppets. Sometimes there was open rebelliousness. The grunts were determined to survive. Since they were forced to endure the most extreme physical hardships, they insisted on having something to say about the making of decisions that determined whether they might live or die. It happened among other units in Charlie Company.[56]

And eighteen months later it happened in Bravo and Delta Companies 1/12th. This pattern of behavior showed itself pretty clearly when the GIs of Bravo Company objected to the night ambush on October 9. It surfaced again on October 13 when Delta Company temporarily refused to conduct a daylight patrol.

But to stop there and view these soldiers as a bunch of dissidents would be totally unfair. After all, the same soldiers who initially refused on the thirteenth rushed out into an enemy-infested area on the twelfth to rescue two Cobra pilots without a moment's hesitation.[57] These same soldiers did later agree to go out on the daylight patrol after their meeting with Major Dye. And, in the following days they again ventured into enemy controlled areas to recover equipment from the downed Cobra, as well the remains of the crew from the downed Huey. Bravo Company did the same thing, protecting the downed Cobra that crash landed near the main gate on October 9.

"These men are not cowards," insisted B Company squad leader Tex Wernli in a subsequent ABC interview.[58] Their commanders supported this position. Bravo Company's commanding officer, Captain Cronin, who probably went through more grief than anyone for Bravo's refusal on October 9, described the two individuals who sparked the refusal and the letter to Senator Kennedy, Specialist Four Ernest French and Specialist Four Al Grana, as good soldiers who had not gotten involved in any trouble before or after the incident.[59] Lieutenant Colonel Stan Tyson, 1/12th's commanding officer during this period, described how fistfights broke out among some of his soldiers over who would be able to participate in

Operation Thundering Hooves after Pace was evacuated because there wasn't enough lift capability to take everyone who wanted to go.[60]

What could explain such apparently contradictory behavior? How do soldiers decide what's worth fighting for and what isn't? Military historians have been struggling to answer such questions for centuries. What seems to best explain it is that the willingness to take risks in battle has little to do with country or cause, with president or king. What holds units together under the stress of combat or impending combat is the willingness to fight for each other.[61] In closing out his account of E Company 506th Regiment, 101st Airborne Division, Stephen Ambrose put it this way: "They thought the Army was boring, unfeeling, and chicken, and hated it. They found combat to be ugliness, destruction, and death, and hated it. Anything was better than the blood and carnage, the grime and filth, the impossible demands made on the body—anything, that is, except letting down their buddies."[62] The various infantry companies of the 1/12th Cavalry at Pace did not face the same degree of intense combat as the veterans of Normandy and Bastogne. But in the end, the similarities of their experience in Vietnam were stronger than the differences. And when those similarities were clear, they rose to the occasion.

The same outlook carries over to the current combat in Iraq and Afghanistan. Sergeant Zack Bazzi, who served with the New Hampshire National Guard in Iraq, put it this way: "Some love our president; some don't. And some of the guys just don't give a damn about politics. . . . Soldiers on the ground have no politics. When you're out there in the field, you're not doing it for a political cause or for a flag. You're doing it for your buddies, left and right. That's how it's always been, and that's how it should be."[63]

Were the actions of the infantry units assigned to Firebase Pace further evidence of an Army in collapse or an Army that could still get the job done? The preponderance of evidence lines up on the side of getting the job done. Yes, there were signs of rebelliousness and resistance that would have been unthinkable in 1965. But this was no longer 1965, when almost everyone inside the Army and out seemed united behind a common purpose and eventual expectation of victory. Six years of stalemate in Tay Ninh Province and elsewhere had taken its toll.

Consequently, a review of the available evidence supports the following:

1. The standard statistics used to illustrate the collapse of discipline and morale among U.S. forces in 1971 are not relevant in this case. They fail to take into account the unique circumstances at the small unit level and the overwhelming focus on survival for those units facing hostile forces.
2. The combat refusals at Pace were temporary and not part of a pattern of poor discipline or mutinous behavior. In fact, the pattern of behavior exhibited by these soldiers was just the opposite.

3. The temporary refusals on October 9 and 13 at Pace reflected an understandable reaction on the part of veteran soldiers who had legitimate concerns. Once these were addressed, the units involved returned to their normal duty.

Although the infantry at Pace may have generated headlines back home, their role was to protect the artillery, who in turn supported the ARVNs fighting ten miles away in Cambodia. Thus, any judgment on how well the soldiers at Pace performed their duty needs to be informed by how well the artillery was able to accomplish its mission.

CHAPTER FOURTEEN

Artillery and Other Combat Support Troops

The Sky Troopers from 1/12th accounted for about half the U.S. troops at Pace. The other half included about sixty artillerymen from Charlie Battery 2/32d; about twenty men from D Battery, 71st Artillery, who formed the crews of the Quad Fifties; and a sprinkling of other combat support troops. The Army did not report separate crime statistics for the 2/32d Artillery Battalion; however, II Field Force (parent unit of 23d Artillery Group) did report certain categories of offenses for the quarter ending April 30, 1971. It showed the annualized incidence of assault at less than 1 per 100 and larceny at slightly more than 1 per 100. Drug offenses were slightly higher at 3 per 100; hardly a crime wave.[1]

The 2/32d Artillery did track courts-martial consistently from mid-1966 through the time Pace was evacuated in October 1971. Some of these reports have gotten lost over the years, but most are still on file with the National Archives. While these documents reflect the experiences of just one battalion among many, they do provide insight into life on the ground for one of the few units to participate in the ground war from start to finish. They show that the rate of courts-martial varied quite a bit, and establishing a clear trend is elusive. While it is true the two six-month reporting periods ending in April and October 1971 did reflect the highest back-to-back incidence of courts-martial for a twelve-month period, the single highest incidence occurred in January 1969, more than two years earlier. The third highest incidence occurred in April 1967 (see table 14.1).

The reports by the 2/32d did not break these court-martial numbers out by nature of the charges, but the 23d Artillery Group did for the six months ending October 31, 1971. That comparison showed drug-related charges accounted for nearly half of all courts-martial.[2] This strongly suggests that a pattern of drug abuse and behavior related to it was the number one discipline and morale problem facing units in this period.

Concerns about drug use by American GIs in Vietnam first surfaced late in 1967.[3] At first the U.S. Command downplayed the issue, but by 1971 the U.S. Command acknowledged it had a problem. According to one historian, by the later stages of the war "many commanders in Vietnam had begun to view drug abuse as a more formidable enemy than the North Vietnamese or the Vietcong."[4] The Army's own surveys estimated that 45 percent of GIs used drugs of some sort.[5] Anecdotal evidence indicates the presence of some drugs, including marijuana and heroin, at Lanyard and Pace, but not as much as in the rear areas.[6] Official reports confirm this.

Table 14.1. Court-Martial Statistics for 2/32d Field Artillery Battalion

Six Months Ending:	Number	Annualized Rate per 100
July 31, 1966	3	1
April 30, 1967	16	6
July 31, 1968	6	2
January 31, 1969	19	7
July 31, 1969	9	3
January 31, 1970	10	4
July 31, 1970	2	1
April 30, 1971	14	5
October 31, 1971	17	6

Source: Headquarters 2/32d Field Artillery, ORLL, NARA.
Note: Includes general, special, and summary courts-martial. The six-month period ending April 30, 1967, includes the three months ending April 30, 1967, and the three months ending October 31, 1966, because the report for the three months ending January 1, 1967, is missing from the files of the National Archives.

"Drug abuse continues to be a problem within this battalion," Lieutenant Colonel M. R. Whitaker, commanding officer, 2/32d Field Artillery, wrote in his ORLL for the quarter ending April 30, 1971. "There appeared to be an increase in availability and use of hard drugs (Heroin) during the reporting period."[7] He went on to point out that twenty-eight battalion GIs, or 6 percent of the battalion's strength, had participated in the MACV's Drug Amnesty Program over the previous three months. Twenty-seven of them were admitted heroin addicts.[8]

Lieutenant Colonel McCaffree made the same observation in his report six months later. "Drug abuse continues to be a problem within the battalion," he concluded. He went on to point out there had not been a significant increase in hard drugs, but twenty-nine soldiers had stepped forward for the drug amnesty program over the last six months.[9]

The 23d Artillery Group, 2/32d's parent unit, identified a similar problem. They found in one artillery battalion (not the 2/32d) that "dangerous drugs are available and are in common use among the troops." They went on to find "frequent use of marijuana, with between 10% and 30% of the troops in every battery of a least one battalion using marijuana on a more or less regular basis."[10] These numbers are consistent with other studies at the time.

Faced with such widespread drug use, it's a wonder these units were able to function at all. One explanation is that in combat units in proximity to the enemy, the troops policed themselves, if for no other reason than self-protection. Someone who might light up a joint while off duty at a relatively secure base camp near Saigon would not be so inclined to do so while on guard duty in proximity to the enemy at a firebase like Pace. And, if they did develop a reputation as a heavy user, they would be likely to be sent to the rear. Investigators for the Senate

Subcommittee on Alcoholism and Narcotics told the committee members the same thing. In April 1971, after a visit to U.S. bases all over the world, including Vietnam, they concluded, "While we were made aware of rare, isolated instances where marijuana had been used in combat situations in Vietnam, we saw no evidence that any mission or operation has been jeopardized by drug abuse."[11]

The 2/32d ORLL reached the same conclusion: "While this battalion can and does accomplish its mission, drug abuse has caused degradation in mission accomplishment; however this degradation can't be qualified."[12] The readiness of the artillerymen and combat engineers at Lanyard and Pace got its sternest test in the early morning hours of March 30, 1971, when at 0400 hours a group of sappers attacked Fire Support Base Lanyard, which was at that time occupied by Charlie Battery 2/32d Field Artillery and a platoon of combat engineers. The heroism of First Lieutenant Gary Pace is recounted in chapter 3, but Lieutenant Pace did not operate alone. Once that attack started, cannoneers and engineers had to leave the safety of their living quarters and engage the enemy at close range. They kept at it until the attacking force was wiped out.[13] Had a significant portion of the GIs at Lanyard that night been strung out on drugs or otherwise unable to defend themselves, the results could have been much different.

The 2/32d ORLL also provide information on lesser levels of disciplinary actions. These are called Article 15 or nonjudicial punishments. Usually administered at the company level, they can cover a variety of infractions. They are intended to give company commanders a great deal of discretion on less serious offenses, such as not wearing a proper uniform or returning late from leave. Punishment is usually limited to fines or a reduction in rank.[14] These are presumably what Myra MacPherson was referring to when she said a company-sized unit could expect nineteen such offenses.[15]

Once again, these numbers show a high incidence of disciplinary actions in 1971. In this case, the rate of 42 Article 15s per 100 soldiers between October 31, 1970, and April 30, 1971, is the highest for any of the nine reporting periods. However, the overall picture is less consistent. The six-month reporting periods immediately before October 1970 and after April 1971 show a much lower incidence of Article 15s (19 per 100), while the next highest incidence rate is found in the periods ending June 1970 and July 1966, respectively (see table 14.2).[16]

Armywide trends for both courts-martial and Article 15s are addressed in chapter 17, but the figures for the 2/32d demonstrate the difficulty in making sweeping generalizations. While it is clear this artillery battalion struggled with increased drug abuse and other disciplinary issues during the drawdown period, it is also clear it was not overwhelmed by them.

When it comes to evaluating the combat effectiveness of artillery units, the Army's record-keeping system does provide some additional insight. Artillery pieces, especially big ones, are dangerous to be around. They involve a volatile

Table 14.2. Article 15 Punishments for 2/32d Field Artillery Battalion

Six Months Ending:	Number	Annualized Rate per 100
July 31, 1966	82	30
April 30, 1967	71	26
July 31, 1968	49	17
January 31, 1969	77	27
July 31, 1969	37	13
January 31, 1970	87	31
July 31, 1970	54	19
April 30, 1971	117	41
October 31, 1971	53	19

Source: Headquarters 2/32d Field Artillery, ORLL, NARA.
Note: The six-month period ending April 30, 1967, includes the three months ending April 30, 1967, and the three months ending October 31, 1966, because the report for the three months ending January 1, 1967, is missing from the files of the National Archives.

mix of flammable propellant, high explosive projectiles, moving heavy machinery, and hydraulic and fuel lines in a confined space. Danger zones exist both in front of and behind the guns when they fire. Consequently, the Army puts a great deal of effort into training crews in appropriate safety procedures for maintaining and firing the guns, both for the safety of the crews, who are at risk if the piece malfunctions, and of friendly troops, who are at risk if artillery rounds land where they are not supposed to, or so-called friendly fire incidents.[17] Therefore, if crews on the guns or in the fire direction center are fogged out by drugs or alcohol, or are otherwise incapable of performing their jobs, firing accidents can occur. An investigation normally ensues shortly thereafter, even in a combat zone. In fact, a 1976 book about the investigation of such an incident in Vietnam reached the national best-seller list.[18]

In addition, the constant firing of "Killer Senior" at Pace (an eight-inch projectile designed to explode just above ground at short range) meant everyone in and around the guns had to be constantly alert. When the round exploded, it would often send the heavy steel base plate hurling back toward the howitzer that fired it. The outcome could be deadly to anyone too careless to keep their head down.[19]

Army records show that in September and October 1971, Charlie Battery 2/32d fired 2,102 rounds of 8-inch howitzer ammunition and 1,238 175mm rounds from Fire Support Base Pace.[20] If drug abuse among the crews directing fire or working the guns was at all prevalent, there would have been plenty of opportunities for it to have shown up in either accidents on the guns or friendly fire incidents when the rounds landed. Instead, Army records show a flawless safety record with no incidents of either kind, despite nearly continuous firing for twenty-seven straight days. This information was confirmed by first-person accounts from officers on the scene. In the words of one officer, "Those kids [the gun crews] busted their ass."[21]

Nearly all of the officers and enlisted men interviewed for this book acknowledged drug abuse problems in the U.S. forces in 1971. But they also pointed out a strong sense of peer pressure and self-policing at forward bases like Pace, where survival meant less tolerance for behavior that threatened the safety of the group. And, those individuals who were incapable of performing were sent back to the rear.[22]

While Charlie Battery gun crews demonstrated a good record for safety and accuracy in this period, it is clear higher headquarters was concerned about incomplete reporting and slow response times.[23] It is not clear, however, how much of this was a problem on the guns or in the fire direction center, or both. The officers and men most familiar with the guns speak highly of the commitment of the gun crews.[24] Colonel McCaffree's October 9 message to Colonel Hoffman listed a number of possible explanations.[25] This was also the period of uncertainty between Captain Timmons's departure and Captain Ashley's arrival, so that may have played a role.[26] In any event, the messages back and forth about slow response times and reporting disappeared after the new leadership team arrived on October 10.

As pointed out previously, the enemy shelling at Pace was not intense by Vietnam War standards. By comparison, the Marines at Khe Sanh endured an average of 100 rounds of incoming a day for seventy-seven days in early 1968. On some days the number of incoming rounds reached 1,000. Pace took 20–40 rounds a day for twenty-seven days. But the Marines at Khe Sanh were dug in over an area of two square miles. The GIs at Pace were crammed into a perimeter a little over 100 meters square. The Marines at Khe Sanh believed they were fighting one of the decisive battles of the war. The GIs at Pace knew the war was supposed to be coming to an end. Even at that, the enemy bombardment still took a toll psychologically on the battle-hardened Marines at Khe Sanh. "The shelling slowly wore them down," wrote historian Robert Pisor. "It wasn't the weight or accuracy, but the persistence of enemy shelling that slowly eroded the Marine's cocky readiness for battle."[27] So, if steady shelling could wear down battle-hardened marines at Khe Sanh, it could also wear down the relatively inexperienced GIs at Pace. That doesn't mean either group were bad soldiers.

On October 18 Colonel McCaffree sent a confidential message to 23d Group regarding morale at Pace. It provides an excellent summary of the emotional roller coaster the troops had to deal with during this operation.[28] McCaffree reported that morale seemed to improve when the infantry first arrived but then dipped when Katum was evacuated and Pace was not. Morale went back up after the Vietnamese presidential elections on October 3, only to plummet when the shelling intensified after that.

It dropped further when Specialist Four Brooks was hit the next day by a 75mm recoilless rifle while presumably protected in his bunker. The blast stripped the flesh from one leg and badly injured the other, which he eventually lost. On October 6 Colonel McCaffree flew out to Pace and met with each section in Charlie Battery. He offered to replace any individual who wanted to leave. His men told him they were doing a job no other unit could do as well, and they would leave together or not at all.[29] Morale went back up with the arrival of a new leadership team on October 10 and the announcement of plans to evacuate the base. McCaffree reported that the impact on morale of the refusal by the infantry on October 9 was unknown, but the media attention afterward actually had a positive effect. Then, on October 16 morale plummeted again when it was announced that the move was off. However, according to McCaffree, a personal visit from Colonel Hoffman, commanding officer of the 23d Artillery Group, to let the troops know they would be extracted shortly had a positive effect. McCaffree concluded that morale was currently good and no additional action was required.[30]

The issue of drug abuse in the 1/12th Cavalry did not surface in the 3d Brigade ORLL reports of the six months ending October 31. This may reflect a reluctance to admit a problem, or it could mean that drugs were less of an issue because the soldiers were in the bush so much that they didn't have an opportunity to use. However, drug use was far from unknown in the 1/12th. For the most part, they were used in the rear during stand down, but there were scattered instances of drug use in the field. In most of those cases, heavy users were sent to the rear just as they were in other units.[31]

Fragging, the deliberate murder or intimidation of officers or noncommissioned officers via live hand grenades, was also widely believed to be occurring in epidemic proportions in 1971 and usually involved drugs. One of the most notorious cases occurred in the 1st Cavalry at the Bien Hoa base camp in March 1971. An officer was killed and the perpetrator was never found.[32] The 23d Group reported an unsuccessful attempt to frag a sergeant in 5/42 Artillery on September 25.[33] Official records and interviews with both enlisted men and officers confirm no incidents of violence or threats of violence among the troops at Pace during this period.

In 1948 President Harry Truman officially desegregated the Armed Forces, but old habits die hard. Tensions over racial discrimination intensified as the Vietnam War dragged on, especially after the assassination of Dr. Martin Luther King in 1968.[34] Private First Class Levell Hinton of Detroit, Michigan, remembers being told by other black GIs that his training as a field artillery fire direction specialist didn't matter; he would be assigned a menial job just because he was an African

American. Hinton was pleasantly surprised when he was slotted in a position he was trained for at the Fire Direction Center at Firebase Pace.[35] He and many of the other GIs at Pace—both white and black—felt the situation there muted racial conflicts because of the need for everyone to look out for one another. But, similarly, once back to the relative safety of the rear, both races tended to self-segregate and racial conflict increased.[36]

This analysis would not be complete without addressing the other combat and combat-support troops at Pace, which included the crews from D Battery, 71st Artillery, who manned the Quad Fifty machine guns at Pace. Working the Quad Fifties also required exposure to enemy fire. Over the twenty-seven-day siege of Pace, seven members of D Battery were injured by flying shrapnel, with a casualty rate of close to 25 percent.[37] The other two wounded soldiers at Pace came from other support troops. There was no evidence of combat refusal or discipline issues with any of these units. In fact, the section chief of the Quad Fifties praised his troops for constantly exposing themselves to enemy fire in order to return fire when needed.[38]

Three other groups of soldiers were on the ground at Pace and actively participated in its defense. One was Chief Warrant Officer Bunyan Wicker and a crew of four enlisted men who operated the CSR III ground surveillance radar that played such an important role in protecting Pace's perimeter from intruders. Although these soldiers operated out of a heavily protected bunker and were not exposed to enemy fire, they were a high value target to the North Vietnamese and very much at risk if captured or threatened with capture.[39]

Two technicians from the 19th Maintenance Company, 185th Maintenance Battalion, 29th General Support Group also stayed at Pace for an extended period to keep the Short Stubbies and Long Skinnies serviced.[40] Unlike their counterparts at Bien Hoa or Phu Loi, Specialist Fours Wade Heckman and David DeLeon were out in the field sharing the same dangers as the gun crews at Pace.

The most dangerous job at Pace, if fatalities are considered, was not artillery crewman or foot soldier, but helicopter pilot or crew member. Supply and medical evacuation helicopters had to take off and land while under fire from North Vietnamese anti-aircraft guns in the woods east of Pace. Helicopter gunships circled nearby to provide protection. Four crewmen lost their lives when Chief Warrant Officer Stansbury's Huey was shot down on October 29. Two more pilots had their gunships shot down but survived. At least one other Cobra pilot was severely wounded. The GIs at Pace understood those pilots risked their lives for them, which is why they didn't hesitate to mount a rescue mission when the situation called for it.

Most of the heavy lifting in terms of tangling with the North Vietnamese around Pace was done by the ARVN Airborne. Headquarters for the 6th Airborne Battalion moved into Pace in early October supported by a team of six American officers and senior NCOs.[41] Not only did they share the dangers of incoming at Pace, they spent time in the bush with the South Vietnamese troops exposed to enemy fire. In fact, the senior adviser, Major Mike Anderson, was wounded there and had to be evacuated. When the other Americans left Pace on October 22, most of them stayed behind.

The experiences at Pace and Lanyard also reveal some of the issues involved in waging war with soldiers from different countries and cultures. Although Richard Boyle embellished some of what he saw at Pace, he wasn't far off the mark in his observation that some of the barbed wire was placed there to keep South Vietnamese soldiers out. U.S. GIs, who were much better paid, worried about loss of watches, cameras, tape recorders, and other valuables due to theft.[42]

U.S. commanders in this period struggled to make sure their own troops treated their South Vietnamese counterparts respectfully. For example, in January 1971 the headquarters of the 2/35 Artillery Battalion felt it necessary to issue an edict to subordinate units banning the use of the term "Little People" from the battalion radio network to describe their South Vietnamese allies.[43] In October, senior commanders at 2/32d Artillery had to instruct the crew of one of the 8-inch howitzers to repaint the nickname on the barrel of their piece from "Cool Hand Gook" to "Cool Hand Luke," as the ARVN Airborne Battalion Headquarters moved into the base.[44]

Not all the encounters were negative, however. Captain Rhodes recalls inviting the GIs at Pace to visit the French-trained South Vietnamese battalion surgeon for the ARVN Airborne unit there, since many of them were not permitted to leave the base to receive treatment for minor ailments. At first, the men expressed a reluctance to let themselves be examined by a Vietnamese doctor, but after the first few souls emerged as satisfied patients, the number of GIs visiting the dispensary grew rapidly. [45]

In many ways, the two competing versions of the combat performance of U.S. troops at Pace is representative of the larger debate over the performance of the entire Army in Vietnam in this period. Retired Army Lieutenant General Phillip B. Davidson took on this issue in his 1988 book, *Vietnam at War: The History 1946–1975*. Davidson was MACV's senior intelligence officer for two years in the late 1960s. He referred to a July 19, 1971, message Lieutenant General William J. McCaffrey (Abrams's deputy and no relation to Colonel Robert McCaffree) sent to his subordinate commanders. General McCaffrey acknowledged that since 1969 "discipline in the command has eroded to a serious but not critical degree."[46] Davidson concluded, "It is easy to exaggerate this collapse of morale and discipline in Vietnam. The truth probably lay somewhere between McCaffrey's judgment of 'serious but not critical' and Heinl's 'approaching collapse.'"[47]

This glass half empty, glass half full line of argument continues to this day. In his 2009 book, *Vietnam: The History of an Unwinnable War, 1945–1975*, John Prados recounts the outcome of a discussion at the Vietnam Center at Texas Tech University that included almost two dozen men who had commanded battalions in Vietnam during the 1970–1971 period. In a show of hands, about half agreed their units were "fully able," the other half "less than capable," with all kinds of variation in between. Prados continues to pose the question to people who commanded a battalion in Vietnam—about forty in all—and he finds they still divide "roughly evenly."[48]

Where the two battalion commanders with units at Pace come out on this issue is reflective of the lack of anything close to a simple answer on anything to do with the performance of U.S. troops in Vietnam. Both men agreed to be interviewed for this book. Lieutenant Colonel Stan Tyson clearly came down on the side of rating his unit, the 1/12th Cavalry, as fully capable.[49] However, some of his artillery colleagues at Pace might dispute this because of differing expectations regarding the aggressiveness of patrolling. For example, in his ORLL for the period including operations at Pace, Colonel McCaffree wrote the following: "Individual thoughts on FSB defense jeopardized the mission of the base. . . . At one FSB infantrymen had been brought to the fire base to help defend it, but the mission was jeopardized after it was discovered that many of the individual soldiers had developed their own ideas of how the base should be properly defended."[50]

Colonel McCaffree was equally hesitant to rate his own troops as fully capable. To him, fully capable for an artillery unit meant the ability to "move, shoot and communicate." McCaffree expressed a particular concern about the poor condition of the vehicles at Pace.[51] Many of them were no longer operable because repeated shelling had shredded tires and punctured radiators. But was this the fault of his troops, who were under attack and unable to move for three weeks? McCaffree acknowledged he was proud of his men for accomplishing their mission, which is how he seemingly felt at the time.[52] On October 17, 1971, he issued a personal commendation to the soldiers at Pace. "For the actions at Pace," he wrote, "every man has earned the admiration of his comrades in arms. For this action, I am pleased to command with pride the gallant men of Pace."[53]

As for the Army itself, it seemed more than satisfied with the performance of the soldiers at Pace. On July 3, 1972, the U.S. Army in Vietnam issued General Order No. 1484, the Valorous Unit Award for Extraordinary Heroism. Described as the unit equivalent of the Silver Star, it was awarded to the members of the 2d Battalion, 32d Field Artillery, and assigned and attached units, including all four line companies of the 1/12th Cavalry for what was described as "extraordinary heroism and devotion to duty . . . in keeping with the highest traditions of military service and reflect great credit upon themselves, their units, and the United States Army."[54] This level of recognition was awarded sparingly. The 2/32d Field Artillery received two such awards in the five years served in Vietnam; the 1/12th Cavalry, three in seven years.[55]

After examining official records and the accounts of both officers and enlisted men who were there, a clear pattern emerges, and it is not the pattern of a mob on the edge of collapse or of fermenting rebellion. Instead, it is one of very ordinary citizen soldiers coping with extraordinary challenges. Despite the gun shyness that afflicts every army near the end of the war, despite the confusion furthered by the public statements of highest civilian officials, despite the erosion of trust in established authority, despite a growing problem associated with drug abuse in the ranks, and despite differences in approaches between the senior leadership in the infantry chain of command and the artillery chain of command, these soldiers, and the soldiers who supported them, did what they needed to do.

The artillerymen, albeit reluctantly, braved enemy fire to keep their guns firing. And the infantry, for their part, protected the pilots that were shot down, protected Pace with their mortars, and, albeit reluctantly, left the relative safety of their bunkers to patrol the base as well. The helicopter pilots and the fixed wing pilots dodged enemy fire regularly to protect Pace, resupply it, and evacuate its wounded. They all stood toe to toe against a skillful and determined foe, and long after their country had turned away they soldiered on.

Perhaps the most telling indicator of morale during this entire period was Colonel McCaffree's observation that the interviews with correspondents and photographers after the October 9 refusal "probably had a good effect."[56] What that seems to say, more than anything else, is that these men felt they were being good soldiers. All they wanted in return from their countrymen back in The World was a little recognition that what they were doing mattered in some way to someone. Unfortunately, that recognition would be a long time in coming.

Chapter Fifteen

Beyond Pace

The defense of Firebase Pace involved, at one time or another, one U.S. artillery battery, four infantry companies, and a handful of other U.S. support troops over a little less than a month. As informative as Pace may be symbolically, it leaves open the question of what other U.S. ground troops were doing all over Vietnam in the twenty-two months between the end of the Cambodian operation in June 1970 and the start of the North Vietnamese Easter Offensive in April 1972.

In Military Region III surrounding Saigon, the battle for Firebase Pace stands out clearly as the most significant action in that period. However, that does not mean U.S. troops not involved with defending Firebase Pace were idle or out of harm's way. After the Cambodian operation ended, the entire 25th Infantry Division, two-thirds of the 1st Cavalry Division, and two-thirds of the 11th Armored Cavalry Regiment packed up and headed home, along with a proportionate share of artillery and other combat support troops. While these soldiers concentrated on the activities necessary to ship out, including inventorying equipment and closing down installations, different elements continued to conduct reconnaissance patrols and other activities necessary to maintain security. Both the 2d Brigade of the 25th Infantry Division and the 1/5th Cavalry Battalion of the 1st Cavalry Division have been recognized by historians for continuing to soldier on right up to their departure date.[1]

By April 1971 the five battalions (5,000 men) of the 3d Brigade (Separate) of the 1st Cavalry Division remained as the only U.S. ground maneuver element left in Military Region III.[2] Since 1971 has been identified by a number of historians as the period when discipline and morale began to deteriorate rapidly, the experiences of these five battalions of the 3d Brigade during this time is a good place to start an assessment of the U.S. Army in Vietnam outside of Pace.[3]

According to the 3d Brigade's ORLL for May 1, 1971, to October 31, 1971, the 3,500 square mile AO was the largest ever assigned to an American brigade-sized unit during the entire Vietnam War.[4] The 3d Brigade's mission was an aggressive one, not only because of the size of its AO, but also in light of the administration's claim that U.S. offensive ground operations would cease by mid 1971. Specifically, the 3d Brigade was tasked with the following:

1. Destroy enemy forces in the AO with priority to the 33rd NVA Regiment.
2. Attack the enemy command and control system with priority to MR7.

3. Neutralize the enemy logistical system.

4. Support the Vietnamese government's 1971 Community Defense and Local Development efforts with emphasis on Bin Tuy and Long Khanh provinces.

5. Be prepared to execute assigned contingency plans.[5]

The brigade vigorously pursued these goals but met with only mixed success. It wasn't for lack of trying, but it was clear that except in rare instances (Pace being one), the enemy was hiding and not looking for confrontations with U.S. troops. Capitalizing on the mobility provided by the 1st Cavalry's helicopters, 3d Brigade maneuver elements actively sought out enemy supply points and base camps in company and platoon size units. Overall, 3d Brigade maneuver units reported opening forty-two firebases in this period, or one almost every four days. Constituent units reported 370 enemy soldiers killed and five tons of rice captured, while losing 30 of their own killed due to hostile action and 247 wounded.[6]

By comparison, during the three months preceding the Cambodian operation (February–April 1970), the entire 1st Cavalry Division reported opening or closing eighty firebases, or about one a day, but with three times as many soldiers. They reported killing 3,047 enemy soldiers and capturing 262 tons of rice while losing 172 killed and 1,250 wounded due to hostile action.[7] So, while it is clear the intensity of combat declined significantly after Cambodia, the troops were not idle and did continue to make contact with the enemy.

There were no publicly reported cases of combat refusals in the 1st Cavalry in this period, other than the two temporary refusals at Pace. According to historian Shelby Stanton, who is generally very critical of the Army's overall performance in this period, the 1st Air Cavalry "continued to function brilliantly as it headed for standown."[8] In fact, the Sky Troopers of the 1st Air Cavalry would continue to pursue the enemy after pulling out of Pace. Unit leaders coped with drugs and motivational issues in different ways. For example, in the 1/5th Cavalry in early 1971, one company commander explained he tried to isolate "all the slugs I had and put them together in one platoon. I kept them away from the rest of the men. I said if you guys want to smoke dope and get yourselves killed and the system won't help me, then just go off by yourselves and do it."[9]

In the January 24, 1972, edition of *Time* magazine, correspondent Rudolph Rauch reported on his experience in the bush with an unnamed unit of the 3d Brigade. They were operating east of Saigon in search of the 33d NVA Regiment.[10] Rauch described how they spent twelve-hour days hacking through the jungle in heavy packs, stopping ten minutes once an hour to rest, then digging in for the night. They did this for ten to fifteen days at a stretch, followed by a three-day "rest" at a remote firebase with no hot water and minimal facilities; then they would go out for another ten to fifteen days. Every forty-five days troops would earn a much-prized weekend by the sea at the in-country resort at Vung Tau. There they could relax before going out for another forty-five days. In order to stay mobile, they had no barracks, no dress uniforms (they were in storage), and no personal possessions while in the field, except for letters from home.[11] This level of activity was typical of the remaining 1st Cavalry maneuver battalions during this period.

Their work was not only dirty, boring, lonely, and tedious, but also dangerous. Rauch reported the brigade lost two killed and thirty-four wounded in January due to hostile actions from an enemy that had supposedly been chased into Cambodia. News reports revealed a litany of frustrating losses in early 1972:

> January 3—North Vietnamese forces ambushed a twenty-four-man U.S. patrol forty miles northeast of Saigon. One American was killed and four wounded. Three medical evacuation helicopters marked with red crosses were shot down while trying to evacuate the wounded.[12]
> January 8—Eighteen Americans were wounded when enemy mortar rounds landed at dinner hour at an 11th Cavalry Regiment firebase twenty miles northeast of Saigon.[13]
> January 10—One American soldier was killed and two others wounded when their patrol was ambushed twenty-four miles northeast of Saigon.[14]
> January 29—Ten Americans were wounded, a resupply helicopter shot up, and an armored personnel carrier damaged by a mine in a series of incidents near Xuan Loc, forty miles east of Saigon.[15]

Through it all, the grunts sucked it up and soldiered on. "My mother can't believe I'm in danger," Sergeant Henry Campbell told Rauch with a wry smile. "She says the President says it's all defensive now, so how could it be dangerous."[16]

New York Times reporter Gloria Emerson spoke with Sky Troopers in the field and offered her assessment in the January 22, 1972, *New York Times*. After talking to soldiers of A Company 2/8th Cavalry near Firebase Melanie, seventeen miles east of Bien Hoa, she wrote, "These men are not complainers or whiners. Their officers say they are good soldiers." She described them as more suspicious and confused than in revolt. "Why don't people back home know what we're doing?" one soldier complained. Another told her he wished the people back home did not think "we are all in the rear standing guard duty or lying around on beaches."[17]

This effort would continue through the first half of 1972. The Colors of the 3d Brigade, 1st Cavalry Division (Separate) finally departed Vietnam on June 26, 1972, to rejoin the rest of the 1st Cavalry Division at Fort Hood, Texas. The 1/12th Cavalry left with them.[18] The last Sky Trooper killed in action was Sergeant Mark F. Biagini of Charlie Company. He was reported killed by hostile ground fire on June 13, 1972, after being in the country less than a month. A native of Guam, he was the seventy-first soldier from that territory to give up his life in Vietnam. He left behind a four-month-old daughter.[19]

The 1st Cavalry Division operated exclusively in Military Region III, but MACV had divided South Vietnam into four military regions. Military Region III encompassed the area around Saigon from the South China Sea to the Cambodian border. Military Region IV included all the area south of MR III, including the Mekong Delta. The central highland areas north of MR III constituted Military Region II. The area north of MR II all the way to the borders of Laos and North Vietnam, including the so-called demilitarized zone, made up Military Region I. Vietnamization affected each of these regions differently (see fig. 4.1).

U.S. ground troops were pulled out of MR IV in 1969 with the withdrawal of the U.S. 9th Division, so it was the first to be Vietnamized. Military Region III was mostly Vietnamized during 1970, as previously described. After the U.S. 4th Division left Vietnam in December 1970, the 173d Airborne Brigade at Bong Son was the only major U.S. ground unit in Military Region II, until it departed in August 1971.[20]

Much like the 3d Brigade of the 1st Cavalry Division, the 173d Airborne Brigade stayed in the bush hunting down the enemy until just before its withdrawal date. The brigade's ORLL for November 1, 1970, to April 30, 1971, described this transition as some of the brigade's "most challenging moments" of its six-year stay in Vietnam, because it had to conduct a variety of ambitious operations in far-flung locations.[21]

The brigade's commander, Brigadier General Jack MacFarlane, explained their mission to a *New York Times* reporter as follows: "We're still actively looking for the enemy. We spend 95 per cent of our time looking for the enemy, and 5 percent zapping him."[22] MacFarlane's troops conducted six separate combat operations in this period in Bin Dinh, Pleiku, and Phu Bon provinces in conjunction with the ARVN 22d Division. They reported killing 281 enemy soldiers while suffering 42 killed and 239 wounded among their own ranks.[23]

Military Region I was the closest to North Vietnam and included the most rugged terrain and most entrenched NVA and Vietcong base areas in all of South Vietnam. Consequently, it would be the last place to be totally Vietnamized, and it was the site of most of the heavy action involving U.S. ground troops between June 1970 and April 1972.

In June 1970, MR I remained the home of the entire 101st Airborne Division, 23d (American) Division, 1st Brigade of the 5th Mechanized Division, 3d Marine Amphibious Force, plus artillery and other support troops. However, the Marines, who had started pulling out in 1969, would all be gone after the departure of the 1st Marine Regiment in May 1971. Both the 101st Airborne (ten maneuver battalions) and American Division (twelve battalions) stayed through all of 1971, and the 1st Brigade, 5th Mechanized Division (five battalions) stayed through the end of August 1971. While the Cambodian operation set back the enemy in MR III, the North Vietnamese remained active in MR I from the middle of 1970 to the middle of 1971.[24]

On June 10, 1970, an estimated seventy sappers attacked Fire Support Base Tomahawk in Thua Thien Province. The base was defended by D Company 2/327th Infantry of the 101st Airborne Division. In an attempt to achieve surprise, the attack did not begin with a mortar barrage; instead, the enemy tried to cut through the wire at night. A platoon sergeant walking the perimeter spotted a sapper in the wire and killed him. The sound of gunfire alerted the other defenders, who quickly swung into action. After an intense thirty-five-minute firefight, the enemy withdrew without penetrating the base, leaving twenty-eight dead behind. Only one American was killed.[25] Contrary to the image of complacent, poorly prepared troops, D Company was on alert. The company commander insisted that at least one officer or NCO walk the perimeter at night to check on the guards. The company had also rehearsed its defense drills several times.[26]

The enemy's next target would be Fire Support Base Ripcord, defended by elements of the 1/506th Infantry Battalion of the 101st Airborne Division. Located thirty-eight kilometers due west of Hue near the north end of the A Shau Valley, Ripcord served as a staging area for disrupting the logistics network of the North Vietnamese that operated on the Vietnam/Laotian border. Ripcord had originally been built by the 1st Cavalry Division in 1968. It was closed down and then reopened in April 1970 as part of Operation Chicago Peak.[27]

From July 1 to July 23, 1970, Ripcord was subjected to heavy enemy mortar, artillery, and anti-aircraft fire. On July 18 enemy gunners shot down a CH-47 resupply ship unloading ammunition. The helicopter crashed into an artillery battery at the base, setting off a horrifying series of explosions that destroyed all six guns.[28] Since Ripcord was at a remote location and most of the press corps was still covering the Cambodian incursion, Ripcord got very little attention in the press. But as casualties mounted, the U.S. Command worried about another public relations disaster similar to the 1969 fight for Ap Bia Mountain (Hamburger Hill) that set off a major controversy adversely affecting morale throughout Vietnam. So the division commander decided to pull out both the infantry and artillery by air on July 23 under intense enemy fire. The official U.S. toll was placed at 61 killed in action and 400 wounded in action, compared to 70 killed in action and 302 wounded in action at Hamburger Hill fourteen months earlier.[29]

By all accounts, the infantry, artillery, and aircrews at Ripcord fought bravely and well. There were no reports of combat refusals or of a price on some officers' heads, as there were at Hamburger Hill. Officers later told author Keith William Nolan that some of the enlisted men felt they weren't adequately supported by the higher ups during the battle and threatened to not return to the field for the next operation. But, after the shock of the battle dissipated, the 101st Airborne continued to soldier on.[30]

As 1970 came to a close, MACV, under prodding from the White House, decided to strike hard at the North Vietnamese logistic network one last time in order for Vietnamization to have a chance to succeed. As a result, the first four months of 1971 involved the U.S. ground troops in Military Region I in some of the most intense fighting of the war.

CHAPTER SIXTEEN

Soldiering On in MR I

In the predawn darkness of January 30, 1971, a single bulldozer, headlights blazing, crawled along the treacherous dirt road known as Route 9 toward the abandoned U.S. base at Khe Sanh. An armored task force of the 1st Brigade, 5th Mechanized Division followed closely behind, the spearhead of Operation Dewey Canyon II. Their mission: open Route 9 from FSB Vandegrift to the Laotian border. Nine thousand U.S. troops were committed to what would be the largest U.S. ground operation since the Cambodian incursion nine months earlier.[1]

Behind them a column of about 25,000 elite South Vietnamese troops prepared to advance into Laos, sever the Ho Chi Minh Trail, and destroy the enemy's logistical network. What the 1970 Cambodian operation had done for Military Region III, the Allied Command hoped Dewey Canyon II and Lam Son 719 would do for Military Region I. But conditions going into Laos in the spring of 1971 were very different from those going into Cambodia in the spring of 1970. The Cambodian border region, for the most part, was flat and open. The Laotian border was mountainous and much more conducive to the defense. In addition, it was a lot closer to North Vietnam, which made it much easier for the enemy to resupply and reinforce.[2]

In addition, U.S. forces would have to operate under much tighter geographic constraints. Congress, surprised by President Nixon's foray into Cambodia, was determined to limit his ability to expand the war. Months earlier the Senate had passed legislation restricting use of U.S. ground forces in Cambodia (the Cooper-Church Amendment), but the legislation narrowly failed in the House. In January 1971, the Nixon administration reluctantly agreed to language that prohibited U.S. ground forces (including advisers) in Cambodia or Laos in order to get congressional support for additional financial assistance to the Cambodian government. The compromise did allow use of U.S. airpower in both Cambodia and Laos, and artillery support, as long as the guns and aircraft were based on the Vietnamese side of the border.[3]

South Vietnamese troops fought well at first, but instead of fleeing, as they did in Cambodia, the North Vietnamese decided to stand and fight. Reinforcements poured in, along with artillery and other sophisticated weapons.[4] Forced to operate across the border where their American advisers were not allowed to accompany them, the South Vietnamese had difficulty coordinating with American air support and with each other. Soon they were in danger of being overwhelmed.

Some ARVN units continued to fight well. Others panicked. President Thieu decided not to reinforce at a critical point. By March the remaining South Vietnamese forces in Laos tried to conduct an orderly withdrawal. The North Vietnamese pursued vigorously, turning the withdrawal into an embarrassing retreat.[5] The image of desperate South Vietnamese soldiers clinging to U.S. evacuation helicopters filled TV screens across the United States, adding to the sense of failure.

The U.S. ground troops remaining on the South Vietnamese side of the border would now be called upon to play an unexpected, yet critical, role in this operation. They would have to defend their forward bases against increasing North Vietnamese pressure so the South Vietnamese withdrawing from Laos would have somewhere to withdraw to. They would have to keep Route 9 open on the Vietnamese side of the border so that they could continue to receive critical supplies. And, finally, they would have to extricate themselves from the border firebases once the South Vietnamese had returned. All of this had to be done in extremely difficult terrain while the enemy closed in with growing numbers. It is not an exaggeration to describe these soldiers of the withdrawal Army as facing some of the most difficult fighting of the Vietnam War.

Keeping Highway 9 open would be the primary responsibility of the 1/1st Cavalry, also known as the "First Regiment of Dragoons." Equipped with Sheridan tanks and armored personnel carriers, 1/1st belonged to the American Division but had been assigned to the 1st Brigade of the 5th Mechanized Division for this operation. This was no small task. No more than a narrow dirt road at this point, Route 9 wound through the wooded foothills of northwest Vietnam. Vehicles traveling the road were subject to ambush from many points along the route, thus earning the road the well-deserved nickname of "Ambush Alley."[6]

Although having a reputation among the troops in Vietnam for being a little "flakey," 1/1st had performed well so far.[7] On the morning of March 20, B Troop of 1/1st advanced down Route 9 toward the border to rescue long-range reconnaissance patrol teams. Inserted the day before to keep Route 9 open, they were now pinned down. Then the rescue column itself was ambushed. One GI was killed, five wounded, and two vehicles damaged. Troop commander Captain Carlos A. Poveda pulled his troops back and called in air strikes, then charged forward again. Another trooper was killed in a hail of AK-47 and RPG fire. Poveda pulled back again, called in air and artillery again, and then charged down the road a third time, only to be repulsed again, except this time Poveda's APC hit a mine, disabling it. He and his crew were left behind as the troop retreated back up the road.[8]

After realizing what they had done, Bravo Troop sent two vehicles back down Route 9 to rescue Poveda and his crew. North Vietnamese soldiers surged forward in broad daylight, "like they owned the place," as one historian put it. Bravo Troop rescued Poveda then pulled into a rough circle to defend itself. An enemy

RPG exploded into a track commander's head, spraying the driver below with blood and bits of flesh. The driver went into shock. Realizing their position was untenable, Bravo Troop retreated west back up the road about a mile, then halted in a situation described as "pandemonium" as the casualties were lifted from the vehicles for treatment.[9]

At this point a radio message came in from Lieutenant Colonel Gene L. Breeding, the squadron commander. Breeding wanted Bravo Troop to head back to the ambush site to retrieve sensitive communications equipment from Captain Poveda's disabled APC and a downed helicopter nearby. Poveda's men refused to move, arguing the equipment wasn't worth the risk. Shortly thereafter, Colonel Breeding and his sergeant major arrived by helicopter. Breeding repeated his order to move out. "You must be out of your fucking mind!," one soldier yelled out. Breeding had the sergeant major line the men up and take down the names of those unwilling to go. Two men agreed to go, fifty-three others said no.[10]

By now Brigadier General John D. Hill, the brigade commander, was on the radio wanting to know what was going on. Clearly unhappy with Captain Poveda's response, Hill relieved him of command on the spot. A second unit, 1/77th Armor, was called up to take Bravo troop's place. A *Time* magazine reporter witnessed the incident and reported it back to his office. It made the AP wire the next day.[11]

Unlike 1/1st Cavalry, which had only light reconnaissance vehicles, 1/77th had M48 medium tanks. Lieutenant Colonel Richard M. Meyer commanded the 1/77th Armor. Meyer's orders were to break through the ambush, recover the equipment, and then drive west on Route 9 to Lang Vei and rescue two batteries of U.S. heavy artillery stranded there. Meyer put on a CVC helmet and jumped into the lead tank. As the head of the column passed Bravo Troop 1/1st, many of the Bravo Troop GIs were out of uniform, and half a dozen yelled obscenities and made obscene gestures at the passing column.[12]

Meyer's tanks ran the gauntlet of RPGs, machine guns, and mortar fire for the four miles between Lang Vei and the stranded artillery. They responded with canister rounds from their own tanks' main guns and machine gun fire into the elephant grass on both sides of the road. The column finally roared into the isolated firebase at Lao Bao. Meyer popped out of his hatch to the curious stares of a group of dirt-covered cannoneers who had gathered around his vehicle. One of them confided later that they were concerned when they first heard the tank engines approaching. They feared Soviet-built tanks were about to overrun them. "Are you boys ready to get out of here?" Meyer shouted. "Hell yes, let's go!," the soldiers responded.[13]

The exhausted artillerymen had been on the Laotian border for nearly six weeks at this point, under almost constant enemy attack. They were more than ready to go. Two heavy artillery battalions of 8-inch howitzers and 175mm guns, of the 2/94th and 8/4th field artillery battalions of the 108th Artillery Group, had been set up near Lao Bao since February 9.[14] Lao Bao was about four miles west (closer to the border) than the former Special Forces camp at Lang Vei. By placing these heavy guns so close to the border, MACV hoped to maximize the degree of fire support they could provide South Vietnamese forces moving toward the Ho Chi Minh Trail as Route 9 wound through Laos.

But being so close to the border also made the guns and their crews prime targets for North Vietnamese forces in the area. After all, it was a former Special Forces camp because it was overrun in 1968. The 2/94th reported taking 100–200 rounds of incoming a day while at Lao Bao, including mortars similar to those fired at Pace, as well as 122mm artillery fired at them from across the border in Laos.[15] Now, with the South Vietnamese pulling back through Route 9 across the border, these firebases were in danger of being overrun by surging North Vietnamese. It was Colonel Meyer's job to escort them out.

After rounding infantry in the areas as well, Meyer lined up his makeshift column and headed back through Ambush Alley. North Vietnamese immediately opened up on the column with everything they had. GIs could see NVA in green pith helmets firing at them from the brush on both sides of the road. The column fired back with 90mm cannon, twin 40mm dusters, and machine guns. The column charged forward, passing corpses and burned-out vehicles along the route. They managed to make it back to the relative safety of Lang Vei just before dark.[16]

On March 22, Meyer sent a second convoy, this time including two M88 tank retrievers, to recover the vehicles left behind two days before. They dodged bomb craters, wrecked vehicles, and enemy fire; blew up the remaining ammunition; and towed back a disabled 175mm gun. Another, careened on its side down a steep slope, had to be left behind. The next day (March 23), yet a third convoy ran the gauntlet again to recover a disabled eight-inch self-propelled howitzer.[17] That night, a large team of enemy sappers attempted to overrun the base camp at Khe Sanh. They were repulsed at the cost of three GIs killed and fourteen wounded. Fourteen dead NVA were found, along with numerous blood trails leading into the brush.[18]

Lam Son 719 officially came to an end on April 6, 1971. Whether or not the operation was a "success" generated a lot of debate at the time, and it continues to this day. North Vietnamese suffered heavy casualties and were not able to mount an offensive in the remainder of 1971. However, South Vietnamese forces were not able to cut the Ho Chi Minh Trail as planned and withdrew under pressure. The North Vietnamese recovered quickly and mounted a major offensive a year later.[19]

What is less subject to dispute is the performance of the American troops involved. The skill and heroism of U.S. helicopter pilots in supporting the South

Vietnamese was widely acknowledged at the time. The role of American ground forces was not. The March 20 refusal by Bravo Troop 1/1st on Route 9 was cited at the time and subsequently used as additional evidence of the erosion of morale and combat efficiency among U.S. ground troops in 1971.[20]

But the breakdown of B Troop 1/1st turned out to be the exception rather than the rule. Both the 2/94th and the 8/4th Field Artillery provided timely and accurate long-range fire support to beleaguered South Vietnamese forces in Laos while under constant enemy fire themselves. Colonel Meyer's 1/77th Armor Battalion helped keep Route 9 open despite growing enemy pressure to close it. They ran the gauntlet of Ambush Alley multiple times to rescue men and equipment. They were ably assisted by the Dusters of the 1/44th Air Defense Artillery, who ran the road with them, providing valuable protective fire. The 45th Engineer Group opened up Route 9 in the first place and helped keep it open. Infantry, cavalry, and other support troops from the 1st Brigade, 5th Mechanized Division, 101st Airborne Division, and Americal Division all contributed.

Even Bravo Troop 1/1st Cavalry, which suffered a breakdown of sorts on March 20, had performed well up until then. It turned out to be the only reported combat refusal in this period where another unit had to be brought in to finish the job. But Bravo's refusal came after days of heavy fighting, including three attempts that day to bust through a roadblock with lightly armored reconnaissance vehicles.

With all the documented prevalence of drug abuse and other dysfunctional behavior by U.S. troops in 1971, how could combat performance not be affected? How could some of these units even function? The answer, in large part, comes from Keith William Nolan's 1986 account of the war, *Into Laos*. Using a combination of official reports and extensive interviews, Nolan was able to produce a comprehensive evaluation of this operation that had not been done, either at the time or in the fifteen years that followed.

For example, Nolan interviewed Private First Class James Kenny, a radio operator with C Battery 2/94th Artillery. C/2/94th was a mixed 8-inch howitzer/175mm cannon battery much like C/2/32d. Kenny joined the battery in January 1971 in the sprawling Da Nang base camp. He was appalled at the racial divisions, drug use, and prostitution that he witnessed. Half the battery used marijuana, but what really scared him were the half dozen or so heroin addicts he thought were paranoid enough to kill anyone they suspected would turn them in. A month later, when 2/94 marched into harm's way at the Laotian border, Kenny couldn't believe what he saw next. "The drug use dropped dramatically, and the artillerymen tucked away their differences to work as an effective team."[21]

Nolan reported similar differences between the front lines and the rear in the 101st Airborne Division. Specialist Four Michael E. Daugherty described the difference between the front and the rear as "a shock."[22] Private First Class Michael DeAngelis, an assistant machine gunner with Bravo Company, 1/61st Infantry, 1st Brigade, 5th Mechanized Division told Nolan, "One USO show in the EM Club turned into a race riot among the 1/61 REMFS." According to Nolan,

> DeAngelis was convinced that if the hatreds had been allowed to boil long enough in the rear, some of the grunts would have killed each other . . . but all of the troubles ended the moment they drove past the Quang Tri wire. The common denominator, he surmised, was hating Charlie and taking care of each other. Even the most militant of blacks packed away their prejudices, took some solace in falling into tight-lipped silence around the whites, and soldiered with the best of them. There were no drugs in the field. One of the company potheads was on DeAngelis's track. His nickname was 'Pockets' because he kept everything he owned in them, and he was an original Haight-Ashbury hippie who'd been caught up in the draft. He hated the war, but in the bush, he was a man you could count on.[23]

The challenge of rising to the occasion even affected support troops. Specialist Four John J. Carney, battalion mail clerk for the 39th Transportation Battalion in Da Nang, told Nolan he was "amazed at the transformation among the GIs" when the order came down to mount up and leave Da Nang. "Short-timers, guys who didn't care, dudes whose major concern previously had been to have enough dope to pass the time, all seemed suddenly motivated."[24]

This does not mean these soldiers always faithfully obeyed orders. For example, when it came time to evacuate the border firebases at Lao Bao, the soldiers of Alpha Battery, 2/94th Artillery watched as Bravo Battery was nearly destroyed by enemy artillery fire when they lined up in a regular formation as their battalion commander had ordered. When it came time for Alpha Battery to evacuate, they ignored the order and headed down Route 9 in ones and twos. Once they were out of harm's way, they formed into one column to finish their charge down Ambush Alley. As a result, Alpha Battery had only a fraction of the vehicle losses that Bravo suffered.[25]

Overall, official casualties for U.S. troops in this campaign totaled 215 killed, 38 missing, and 1,100 wounded,[26] including about 100 helicopter pilots and crews on both sides of the border. By comparison, U.S. losses during the 1968 siege of Khe Sanh, which is often viewed as the climax of the ground war in I Corps, were reported to be 205 killed and 852 wounded.[27]

But the GIs who participated in Dewey Canyon II and Lam Son 719 would never receive the recognition from contemporaries or historians to the degree the Marines did at Khe Sanh. Part of it might have been because Lam Son 719 was a South Vietnamese operation; part of it may have been war weariness after three more years of fighting. But part of it may have been the distraction of yet another high-profile example of the disintegration of fighting capability of U.S. soldiers in Vietnam—the defeat at Fire Support Base Mary Ann.

While Dewey Canyon II and Lam Son 719 were still winding down, North Vietnamese sappers successfully attacked Fire Support Base Mary Ann in what would be regarded as another classic example of the failings of the withdrawal Army. On the night of March 29–30, a team of fifty to sixty NVA commandos snuck into the isolated firebase 80 km south of Da Nang. For half an hour they tossed grenades and satchel charges into bunkers, including the base's tactical operations center. They killed thirty GIs and wounded eighty-two more, or about half the entire garrison. They also destroyed numerous bunkers, two artillery pieces, and other equipment before escaping into the night and losing no more than twelve of their own number. The loss turned out to be the largest in a single action in almost two years and one of the Army's most humiliating defeats of the Vietnam War.[28] Immediately, rumors surfaced of heavy drug use at the base and laxness on the part of the defenders. The parent unit, the Americal Division, began an investigation.[29]

Investigators found a number of shortcomings in defensive preparations. Even though one-third of the unit was supposedly on guard, no one saw or heard the intruders. Guards were not posted at key points, nor were they checked periodically by officers or NCOs as required. Reconnaissance outside the perimeter was not conducted on a regular basis. Fields of fire were not marked, and explosives were not properly placed around the perimeter.[30]

General Abrams then ordered a higher level investigation. The final report issued in July by Colonel Robert N. Cook, inspector general of MACV, was even more critical, finding fault up and down the entire Americal Division chain of command, including the division commander, Major General James C. Baldwin. "Consideration should be given to the fact that this incident could very well have happened to other units of the 23rd Infantry (Americal) Division or to combat units in Vietnam today. . . . Nevertheless, it must be recognized that if this type of situation is allowed to prevail, we can expect that in the months to come, there may occur an even greater disaster," the report concluded.[31] In the end, thirteen officers faced corrective action of some sort, from removal from military service to written reprimands—more than were disciplined for the murder of 500 civilians at My Lai, and the subsequent cover-up, three years earlier.[32]

But how typical was lack of alertness? In the two weeks before and after the attack on Mary Ann, enemy sappers attacked three other remote firebases under similar circumstances. On the night of March 18, an enemy sapper team moved against Charlie Battery 2/94, still left at the semi-abandoned firebase at Lao Bao. They were engaged by alert sentries. In the morning, a dozen enemy bodies were found.[33] Four days later, enemy sappers tried to attack the Allied base camp at Khe

Sanh. At 0315 on March 22, perimeter guards spotted them and started shooting. By the time the shooting stopped, three GIs were dead and fourteen wounded, but fourteen NVA bodies were counted with numerous blood trails. The attack had been repulsed.[34] A week later, far away from the action near the Laotian border, a team of enemy sappers tried to overrun Fire Support Base Lanyard. As described earlier, Lieutenant Gary Pace and the artillerymen and engineers with him stopped that attack.[35] So, in three cases out of four, over a two-week period in March 1971, U.S. forces were alert and did stop enemy attacks. Consequently, Colonel Cook's conclusion that this catastrophe could have happened anywhere is not supported by the pattern of actions on the ground. But what about the unit tasked with defending Mary Ann? What kind of record did it have? What kind of leadership did it have?

Keith William Nolan took a detailed look at the 1/46th Infantry in *Sappers in the Wire*. Nolan found many of the problems plaguing the withdrawal Army to be present, including use of drugs in rear base camps and at least two temporary refusals. He also found "the Professionals," as the 1/46th called themselves, to be a good unit and its battalion commander to be a good leader.[36] In the months prior to the attack on Mary Ann, the battalion had chased the enemy across the AO taking prisoners, destroying supplies, and taking a toll on NVA regulars and VC guerillas in the area. "We gave them no rest," one officer told Nolan, "and bit by bit we drove them into the ground."[37]

Clearly the 1/46th let down its guard on the night of March 29–30. Mary Ann had been in a quiet area and was due to be abandoned soon.[38] Immediately, that raised the specter of sentries zoned out on drugs. *Newsweek*'s Nicholas Proffitt took that issue head on when he interviewed survivors in base camp. He witnessed two GIs telling a TV crew about rampant drug use at the base. He got their names and checked against the unit's roster. He concluded it was unlikely either man was even there. He did find one soldier who was. "I ain't saying there's no pot up there," the soldier told Proffitt, "but if we catch anybody doping up heavily, we get him quick." Proffitt concluded that the battalion and its leaders were clearly responsible for a lack of alertness, but not widespread drug use.[39]

The GIs in Military Region I soldiered on for another sixteen months after Mary Ann and Lam Son 719 as troop withdrawals gained momentum. The 1st Brigade of the 5th Mechanized Division was the first to leave, withdrawing by the end of August 1971.[40] The 101st Airborne was next to redeploy, but not until after completing Operation Jefferson Glen in Thua Thien Province. Jefferson Glen was billed as the last major U.S. ground offensive of the war. The operation, which lasted from September 1970 to October 1971, claimed 2,356 enemy killed. U.S. losses were reported at 292 killed in action and 1,299 wounded in action over that period.[41] The 101st Airborne started redeployment in December as part of Increment X. By March 1972 they were gone entirely.

The 23d (Americal) Division was the last U.S. major ground unit to leave. Its maneuver elements were kept in the field as long as possible. While the intensity of combat dropped significantly after Lam Son 719, Americal Division soldiers still found themselves in harm's way. Between July 1, 1971, and October 15, the Americal Division lost 39 of its soldiers killed due to enemy action and another 447 wounded. Enemy losses were claimed at 736 killed.[42] Americal losses came in groups of five or ten in random skirmishes with small enemy units, almost on a weekly basis. The toll for the month of August 1971 is indicative:

August 1—Three soldiers were killed and eight wounded in an ambush of an Americal Division patrol in the hills south of Da Nang.[43]

August 6—Five Americal GIs were killed and two wounded when their APC struck a mine twenty-six miles south of Da Nang.[44]

August 27—Five soldiers were killed and seven wounded in a nighttime attack on an Americal Division position sixteen miles southwest of Da Nang.[45]

This last attack came a day after MACV announced that the previous week's death toll of ten Americans killed in Vietnam was the lowest in six years, when six servicemen were reported killed in August 1965.[46]

Americal Division units began redeployment to the United States in November 1971, but the 196th Light Infantry Brigade did not redeploy until Increment XII in June 1972. The 196th Brigade's 3/21st Infantry was the Army's last ground combat unit to leave.[47] On August 5, 1972, Delta Company, 3/21st Infantry conducted the last patrol by U.S. ground forces in Vietnam. Their mission was to sweep the area eight miles to the west of the Da Nang airfield and base camp looking for enemy troops, particularly rocket launch sites. Ironically, this was the same mission given to the U.S. Marines, who were first on the ground seven years earlier. The next day, two Delta Company GIs were wounded by enemy mines, giving them the dubious distinction of the last ground troop casualties in Vietnam. Two days later they returned to base camp. On August 23 the "Gimlets" of the 21st Infantry were officially deactivated, thus signaling the official end of participation in the war by U.S. ground units.[48]

CHAPTER SEVENTEEN

REMFs, Fraggers, Dopers, Slackers, and Other Losers

The soldiers at Mary Ann, Pace, and other firebases represented the ground troops still in the field in 1971 and therefore the closest to being in harm's way. So, for them, the close proximity of the enemy had an energizing effect that spurred them, for the most part, to stay focused, leave drugs and alcohol alone, put racial divisions aside, and work together for their own safety. But these soldiers (infantry, armor, artillery and combat engineers in forward positions) accounted for only a small portion of U.S. soldiers in Vietnam—probably no more than 20–25 percent.[1]

For the other GIs, most of whom stayed in the large, generally more secure base camps like Bien Hoa or Da Nang, the lack of an immediate threat, idleness, and other factors created a fertile ground for drug abuse, fraggings, and racial tension. Whatever these problems were, they were made worse by the propensity of frontline units to send troublemakers to the rear, simply exacerbating whatever difficulties were already there.

Even at that, the Army's own statistics showed that if measured by the traditional indicators of morale and discipline, U.S. forces in Vietnam in 1970–1971 performed better than U.S. counterparts in Korea or World War II at the later stages of those conflicts, even when both frontline and rear echelon personnel are included. For example, the incidence of general courts-martial (the most serious level of offense) reached 1.4 per 1,000 among Army personnel stationed in Vietnam in 1971.[2] But this rate was lower than the Armywide rate of 2.1 per 1,000 that year and significantly less than the rate of 7 general courts-martial per 1,000 Armywide at the end of the Korean War in 1953.[3] The incidence of all courts-martial (general, special, and summary) was also lower in Vietnam than for the Army as a whole, and less for the Army as a whole in 1971 than it had been in 1953.[4]

Some of these differences may reflect wider use of less severe punishments (such as Article 15s), which were not available to unit commanders until 1964. But even these differences do not support a dramatic breakdown of discipline among troops in Vietnam. The 1971 rate of 162 nonjudicial punishments (Article 15s) per 1,000 in Vietnam was less than the Armywide rate of 212 per 1,000 that year, and less than the Armywide rate of 187 per 1,000 in 1965, before the Vietnam buildup was fully under way.[5] As previously examined, the incidence of desertions in the Army in Vietnam was significantly lower than in U.S. forces during World War II and Korea.[6] What was different about Vietnam was the emergence of problems not seen in large numbers in Korea or World War II—fraggings, drug abuse, and racial tensions.

As part of the Army's official history of the Vietnam War, William M. Hammond was commissioned to write *Public Affairs: The Military and the Media, 1968–1973*, published in 1995. Entire chapters are devoted to race and drugs, discipline and dissent, My Lai and other atrocities, and morale and the unique challenges of 1971. In describing the issues involving support troops, Hammond clearly errs on the side of understatement when he concludes that "the problems the military faced in the rear, especially race relations, assaults against officers and drug abuse thus became a staple for them (reporters) and a continuing source of trouble for public affairs officers."[7]

"Fragging" is the term used to describe the crime of attempting to kill or injure an officer or noncommissioned officer through the use of an explosive device, usually a fragmentation grenade. The growth in fragging incidents during the later stages of the Vietnam War has often been cited as a classic example of the disintegration of morale and discipline among U.S. troops. Sociologist Guenter Lewy, who in general was less critical of the U.S. effort in Vietnam than others, describes the "sharp increase" in fraggings beginning in 1969 as aimed at "intimidating or punishing persons in authority." He went on to say, "Enlisted men at times would seek to enforce the avoidance of combat, and fraggings were attempts to kill or injure those of their leaders who refused to go along with these practices."[8]

The source most commonly cited to support this argument is the testimony of senior Army officials before the Defense Subcommittee of the U.S. House Appropriations Committee in May 1971. The Army's own statistics showed the incidence of "actual and possible" assaults per 1,000 rising from 0.35 in 1969 to 0.91 in 1970 to 1.75 in 1971—a fivefold increase in two years.[9] While troubling, these statistics should be approached with caution. The same statistics show that "possible" assaults increased much faster than "actual" assaults, and that the category "Intended Victim Unknown" increased most rapidly of all. At the same time, actual deaths attributed to fragging actually dropped from thirty-seven in 1969 to twelve in 1971.[10]

Army Psychiatrist Thomas C. Bond conducted a study of twenty-eight soldiers convicted of fragging superiors in Vietnam. He found that most were assigned to support units, not combat units. The men were described as "apolitical." In fact, the vast majority had enlisted (only two of twenty-eight were draftees) and said they supported the war effort. Bond concluded that the men were not making a political statement, but represented a toxic combination of troubled individuals harboring a perceived personal slight from an officer or NCO, intoxicated on drugs or liquor, and having access to explosives.[11]

A study involving 28 soldiers out of 382 convicted of such behavior cannot be judged as conclusive, but it does strongly suggest a discipline problem not related to a systemic unwillingness to fight, and much more a reflection of individual issues. This is not to dismiss fragging as a serious problem, but to suggest that the resulting hysteria may have been an overreaction. Part of this may reflect the law of small numbers. Even at 1.75 per 1,000 at its peak in 1971, fraggings or possible fraggings did not take place in most company-size units, either at the front or the rear. In addition, a relatively small increase in numbers could lead to a large increase in percentages. Unfortunately, these statistics were cited so often that they created a perception of a spreading problem that in many ways was more harmful to discipline and morale than the acts themselves.

While fraggings were bad, they were perpetrated by and directed at a relatively small portion of servicemen in Vietnam. Not so with drugs, which were described as flourishing in epidemic proportions as the war dragged on. The combination of idle young men with money in their pockets and the wide availability of cheap drugs provided a fertile ground for drug use. As with the growing incidences of fraggings, it was the Army's own statistics that provided the most damning evidence. Unlike the incidences of fraggings, the law of small numbers clearly did not apply.

The Army's surveys of drug use showed a steady increase in the proportion of soldiers using marijuana, so that by mid-1971 nearly half the troops reported use over the last year.[12] While these numbers were disturbing, especially to an older generation who viewed marijuana as an addictive narcotic, they included anyone who admitted to smoking any marijuana at any time. So, not only were heavy users included, but also people who experimented and quit and people who lit up only when they were "off duty."[13]

Concern over marijuana was soon eclipsed by reports of an epidemic of heroin addiction, a drug much more addictive and potent than marijuana. By the time these reports had run their course, 1971 had become the year of the heroin addict. Senior Democratic leaders in Congress were the first elected officials to sound the alarm. Senator Thomas J. Dodd of Connecticut, a strong supporter of the Vietnam War, used his positions on the Senate Foreign Relations and Judiciary Committees to warn of what he saw as the threat of drug abuse in the military as early as 1966. As chair of the Senate Committee on Juvenile Delinquency, Dodd conducted highly publicized and highly sensational hearings on drug abuse in Vietnam in early 1970.[14] Democratic Senator Harold E. Hughes of Iowa, himself a recovering alcoholic and Vietnam War opponent, jumped into the fray in 1971, accusing the Nixon administration of "sleeping through a tidal wave."[15]

The opening alarm about heroin addiction came from a May 16, 1971, New York Times front-page story, "GI Heroin Addiction Epidemic in Vietnam." "The epidemic is seen by many here as the Army's last great tragedy in Vietnam," Alvin M.

Shuster wrote. He quoted an unnamed drug officer in the field: "Tens of thousands of soldiers are going back to the United States as walking time bombs."[16] Two weeks later, a special Congressional Committee co-chaired by Representatives Morgan T. Murphy (D-Illinois) and Representative Robert H. Steele (R-Connecticut) concluded that 10–15 percent of U.S. troops in South Vietnam had become addicted to heroin, or as many as 35,000 soldiers.[17] The report reiterated the walking time bomb argument. "The Vietnam War is truly coming home to haunt us," the report concluded. "The first wave of heroin is already on its way to our children in high school."[18] Other media outlets picked up on the story. *Newsweek* devoted its July 5 cover story to "The Heroin Plague: What Can Be Done?" It talked about the connection from "the back alleys at Long Binh and Saigon to middle American towns and neighborhoods."[19] The effect on public opinion was immediate. By June 1971 Americans cited drug addiction as the third most important issue facing the country, right after Vietnam and the economy. The number citing drugs as the top national problem had doubled from March to June.[20]

Not one to let an opportunity go by, President Nixon weighed in with a plan of his own. At a June 1, 1971, press conference, President Nixon, in what was described as a "well-prepared" statement, pledged to undertake a "national offensive" to deal with the country's drug problem, including "as many as 36,000" heroin addicts in Vietnam.[21] In following weeks the administration announced a series of measures to increase prevention, detection, and treatment of drug abuse among soldiers generally and heroin in particular. Within weeks this evolved into the "War on Drugs."

The 1971 heroin scare spread so quickly because elected officials on both sides of the war and both sides of the political spectrum could see benefit in sounding the alarm. In his 2009 book, *The Myth of the Addicted Army*, assistant history professor Jeremy Kuzmarov at the University of Tulsa documents how congressional Democrats used the drug epidemic to argue for an early termination of U.S. involvement in Vietnam, while the Nixon administration and its allies were able to pivot off this issue as yet further evidence of societal decay and the need to restore "law and order."[22]

Fortunately, an expansion of treatment and rehabilitation programs had bipartisan support, so there were benefits to addicted veterans who needed help to recover. But, the price was paid for by veterans who served honorably during this period, as they were also painted as walking time bombs in the media and elsewhere. For example, in early 1972 the Veterans Administration released a study conducted on their behalf by the Harris public opinion polling organization. Harris asked a sample of 1,985 Vietnam-era veterans about their perceptions of the incidence of drug use in the armed services (not just Vietnam). They asked the same questions in a survey of 1,601 households among the general public. The general public consistently perceived a higher incidence of drug use in the armed services than did veterans. This difference was particularly pronounced among young people eighteen to twenty-nine years old. Those of all ages who did not serve in the armed forces estimated a usage rate of 19 percent for heroin in the armed forces, while veterans of the armed forces estimated an average of 5 percent. "But the general phenomenon of the public being convinced that levels of drug usage are higher than veterans themselves in fact report is comparable to Harris surveys on rates of crime," Louis Harris concluded. "The more distant a person is from the actual scene, the worse they judge the situation to be."[23]

As public concern over GI drug abuse grew, so did questions as to who the ultimate suppliers might be. Allegations swirled around South Vietnamese government officials (both in the military and outside of it), as well as key U.S. governmental and nongovernmental allies in Laos, Cambodia, and Thailand.[24] These accusations clearly worried the White House. The president's advisers feared linking U.S. allies and U.S. government operatives (such as the CIA) to international drug trafficking would make the administration look bad and would undermine public support for Vietnamization. Donald Rumsfeld, special counselor to the president, went so far as to phone Representative Steele and ask him to moderate his tone to the media.[25] Before the end of July 1971, the administration and its allies in Congress began to sing a different tune. On July 26, Representative Steele, a former CIA analyst, said that he agreed with Dr. Jerome H. Jaffe, the president's special adviser on drug problems, who figured that only 4.5 percent of Vietnam GIs were hard-core heroin users. Steele attributed the difference to the beneficial effects of the sixty-day-old White House inspired initiatives.[26]

In fact, the much feared heroin epidemic never materialized. The February 25, 1980, edition of the Washington Post reported that two independent studies commissioned by the Veterans Administration found only 2.4 percent of veterans who returned from Vietnam in September 1971 were addicted in 1974.[27] Some of the improvement reflects the impact of upgraded detection and treatment efforts begun in the summer of 1971, but mostly it confirms that the crisis was overdramatized in the first place.

The rising racial tensions in the withdrawal Army are harder to quantify. While the disproportional ratio of black soldiers killed or wounded fell as the war went on, manifestations of racial division did not.[28] A sense of self-preservation blunted racial differences in front-line combat units, but the racial divide in rear areas grew as the war dragged on. Although the Army was late in addressing the issue, by 1971 it had begun the first tentative steps to bridging the racial divide through a variety of measures. It would take a number of years, but these efforts would put the Army in the forefront of a truly merit-based structure.[29]

With the incidence of fragging, drug abuse, racial divisions, and general malaise so much higher in the rear area support units, it is a wonder they were able to function at all. In mid-1971 freelance reporter Donald Kirk spent a month visiting units both in the field and in the rear in Military Region I. He found instances of combat refusals and drug use rare among combat units and their morale relatively good. But when he visited units in the rear, he sensed a much more threatening atmosphere permeated by talk of fragging, hard drugs, and racial conflict that he described as "bitter, desperate and almost dangerous."[30]

Although often derided by frontline soldiers as REMFs (rear echelon motherfuckers), these soldiers performed critical functions that allowed the units in close proximity to the enemy to function and survive. These support troops included ground crews who serviced the aircraft that provided fire support, delivered critical supplies, and evacuated the wounded. It not only included the surgeons who treated the wounded and the injured, but also the nurses, technicians, and orderlies who supported them. The rear echelon troops also included the heavy equipment operators, who maintained the transportation system, and the military police, who labored to maintain some sense of order. It included the signal personnel, who kept the communication lines open to the frontline troops, and the supply clerks and truck drivers, who kept the frontline troops supplied with food and ammunition. It included the finance clerks, who got the troops paid; the mail clerks, who kept them in touch with the world; and the personnel clerks, who made sure they made it to R&R and rotated home when they were supposed to. While various distractions were present in the so-called rear areas, enough of the troops did their jobs regularly so that the soldiers engaged with the enemy were able to accomplish their mission.

Perceptions of the performance of U.S. troops in this period were influenced, to at least some degree, by how they looked. Words like "ragged" or "unkempt" were often used to describe them, usually in tandem with "undisciplined" and "poorly motivated." Career soldiers like former Marine Colonel Robert Heinl and former USARV Commander General William Westmoreland, accustomed to the spit and polish of the Army before Vietnam, were particularly critical of the younger GIs. Westmoreland went so far as to never let himself be seen in public without freshly pressed fatigues and spit-shined boots.[31] Major General James Hollingsworth, Major General Wagstaff's successor as commander of the 3d Regional Assistance Command, complained in an April 1972 message to General William McCaffrey, USRV's deputy commander:

> It is very common to observe U.S. soldiers driving and riding in trucks along the roads and highways in the Long Binh–Bien Hoa–Saigon area who are a disgrace to the Army and to the United States.
>
> Seldom does one see such a soldier with a proper haircut wearing a complete and proper uniform. Frequently, they wear no headgear and are in their undershirts. Many times they are bare to the waist. Further, many of our soldiers wear defaced hats and jackets with unauthorized embroidered and

stenciled symbols and sayings, pins, buttons, and other items that give them a hippie like appearance.[32]

But the GIs of 1969–1972 didn't see themselves that way. While their civilian contemporaries sported uniforms of long hair, tie-dyed T-shirts, cut-off jeans, and sandals, U.S. ground troops were fond of long hair (by military standards), peace medallions, unusual headgear, and various slogans on helmets and uniforms. Many of their commanders in the field tolerated this to a large degree because they knew that how they looked and how well they fought were two different things.[33]

For example, the cover art of Jeremy Kuzmarov's *The Myth of the Addicted Army* features a photograph of five very unsoldierly looking GIs somewhere in the Vietnamese jungle. None of the five are in appropriate uniform. All have their shirts off. All are clearly unshaven. Two have on headbands, and another is wearing a North Vietnamese pith helmet. They aren't doing anything other than staring insolently at the camera. The picture is otherwise unidentified, but the association with possible drug use is crystal clear. Like many of the better known photographs of the Vietnam War, the full story behind this photograph is a little different than the perception.

In this particular case, the soldiers involved are from Delta Company 2/12th Cavalry, 1st Cavalry Division.[34] For the last week they had been clearing out a weapons cache in the fishhook region of the Cambodian border called Rock Island East. One kilometer long and 500 meters wide, it was the "single greatest trove" of the whole Cambodian Campaign.[35] By the time they were finished, these soldiers hauled or destroyed 326 tons of enemy ammunition and other supplies. The soldiers in the picture were unshaven because they had been out in the field for two weeks without the benefit of shaves, haircuts, or even a shower. Most likely they were shirtless because they were on break from a hot and sweaty work detail. By all accounts, D/2/12 and its sister units performed well in Cambodia in the spring of 1970.[36] Like all good soldiers, they looked dirty and unkempt because they were doing dirty work, not passing in review on a parade field.

According to Specialist Four Mark Jury, the Army photographer who took the picture, "The fact that they wear love beads and peace medallions doesn't mean they can't fight. The kids learn quickly that the best way to stay alive is to kill the guy trying to kill you. And in combat they're ferocious. But once the firefight is over, it's back to being peace and pot lovers. Often their opposition to the military has nothing to do with the moral aspects of Vietnam. It's just that they pick up a battered copy of *Life* magazine and see everybody else skinny-dipping at Woodstock, and that's a hell of a lot better than 'greasing gooks,' fighting malaria, and maybe going home in a plastic bag."[37]

CHAPTER EIGHTEEN

Follow Me

"Follow me!" barks the motto at the entrance to the U.S. Army Infantry School at Fort Benning, Georgia. This simple phrase and its corollary—"lead by example"—formed the bedrock of leadership doctrine for the entire generation of Army officers who served in Vietnam.[1] But by 1971 the perception of the troops they led and the country they served seemed to focus more on the growing slippage between principle and practice. Fueled by accusations of excess optimism, unimaginative tactics, scandals, and cover-ups, the Army Officer Corps represented, at least to some, a collection of self-serving, ticket-punching leaders who shouldn't be followed at all.[2] The officers and men of America's withdrawal Army of 1969–1972 faced a set of challenges unprecedented in the American military experience. Although the level of combat would be much less than for those who preceded them, they would be the first generation of American soldiers destined to fight a war they knew would not be won. Instead, they were to serve as the rearguard for a strategic withdrawal.

The stalemate in Korea a quarter of a century earlier was the most similar U.S. military experience, but by the time most U.S. soldiers had withdrawn from Korea, an armistice had been signed and regular enemy forces left South Korean territory. Although the Korean War was not popular when it finally ended, the debate over its legitimacy was nowhere near as intense as that which accompanied the Vietnam War. American armed forces in Korea were not combating drug abuse, racial tensions, and a war crimes scandal as they pulled out. The draft was not so unpopular it had to be replaced, and technology had not created the voracious appetite for pictures and sound from news personnel prowling the battlefield. During the withdrawal from Vietnam, U.S. commanders, from generals down to lieutenants and sergeants, had to keep their troops sufficiently motivated to engage a cunning and determined enemy, support an enigmatic ally, and stay away from the perils of drugs, crime, and boredom.

This environment also produced a mind-set where individual events could spark a symbolic resonance that extended far beyond the details of the events themselves. The May 1969 assault on Ap Bia Mountain, or "Hamburger Hill," and the November 1969 revelations about the My Lai massacre would still reverberate through the officer and enlisted ranks two years later. While the impact of these events—or, more appropriately, reactions to these events—are impossible to measure statistically, they are hard to ignore behaviorally. To many GIs they represented a common theme: if faced with a choice, the senior leadership of the Army would advance or protect themselves at the expense of their own men.

The Hamburger Hill controversy began with a decision by the senior leadership of the 101st Airborne Division in May 1969 to order a series of attacks against North Vietnamese soldiers dug in atop a heavily fortified mountain (Dong Ap Bia) in the A Shau Valley. Just two kilometers from the Laotian border, the mountain was believed to be the site of a significant enemy supply and transshipment point. The hill was finally captured, but only after twelve costly frontal assaults resulting in 70 GIs killed and 372 wounded. To the war-weary GIs charging up the hill and the reporters covering it, it felt like a meat grinder; hence the name Hamburger Hill.[3]

After Hamburger Hill was captured, the North Vietnamese disappeared back into the jungle. U.S. troops abandoned the hill and redeployed elsewhere. Within a month the North Vietnamese were back. The seemingly senseless operation provoked a storm of criticism back in the States. Critics charged the Army with mindlessly following the same strategy of attrition that had proved unsuccessful for more than four years. Senator Edward Kennedy (D-Massachusetts), the last surviving brother of President John Kennedy, was one of the most outspoken critics, but he was not alone.[4]

The commanders involved, including division commander Major General Melvin Zais, defended the operation. Zais maintained they had to keep the enemy off balance by taking him on wherever they found him. He also argued that bombing alone couldn't do the job and pointed to the destruction of a large cache of supplies that would limit enemy attacks in Military Region I for some time to come.[5] But coming at a time when public opinion had turned against the war, Hamburger Hill seemed to underscore the futility of large-scale frontal assaults. Rumors persisted throughout the Army that disgruntled GIs had put a price on the head of General Zais and others supposedly responsible for the assault.[6] The Nixon administration reportedly told General Abrams to back off such costly assaults in the future.[7]

Just as the Hamburger Hill controversy had begun to fade, a series of new, even more shocking revelations surfaced. In November 1969 stories began to appear in the press about the brutal murder of hundreds of unarmed women, children, and elderly people at the South Vietnamese village of My Lai in Quang Ngai Province. The atrocity by soldiers of the Americal Division took place in March 1968 but did not surface until the fall of 1969. The details of the horrific acts themselves and of the efforts of senior commanders of the Americal Division to cover it up dribbled out in explosive pieces over the next eighteen months. On

March 15, 1970, Lieutenant General William Peers, the senior Army official in charge of the investigation, submitted his findings to General Westmoreland. He summarized them as follows:

> The My Lai incident was a black mark in the annals of American military history. In analyzing the entire episode we found that the principal breakdown was in leadership. Failures occurred at every level within the chain of command, from individual non-commissioned officers, squad leaders to the command group of the division. It was an illegal operation in violation of regulations and of human rights, starting with the planning, continuing through the brutal, destructive acts of many of the men who were involved, and culminating in aborted efforts to investigate and, finally, the suppression of the truth.[8]

Although a number of soldiers up and down the chain of command were implicated, First Lieutenant William Calley, a platoon leader, turned out to be the only person convicted. He was found guilty by a military court-martial on March 28, 1971, after a heavily covered trial where the gruesome details of the event were meticulously laid out by Army prosecutors.[9] Calley's conviction managed to satisfy almost no one and stirred passions even further. (Calley was eventually pardoned, igniting yet another controversy.) Some, including many career military people, felt Calley and his entire chain of command should be punished severely for their actions, which were clearly against policy.[10] But a majority of the general public seemed to feel Calley was being a scapegoat for either the protection of his superiors or for just doing his job.[11]

For those soldiers still fighting in Vietnam, the outcome added yet another layer of confusion and ambiguity to an environment that was already frustrating enough in its own right. For example, in the aftermath of My Lai the Army confirmed that it expected its soldiers to recognize that they had not only the right but the duty to disobey an order that "a man of ordinary sense and understanding would know to be illegal."[12] This is not to imply the combat refusals that occurred at Pace in the fall of 1971 (or elsewhere during this period) involved either war crimes or illegal orders. But what it does say is the widespread knowledge of the controversies over both My Lai and Hamburger Hill eroded further the already frayed bond of trust between the leaders and the led in Vietnam at a time when it was needed most.

Army personnel policies in this period made things even worse. Enlisted men rotated home after twelve months, so all other things being equal, one-sixth of every unit was within one month of coming or going. Officers in command positions generally rotated in or out after only six months, meaning one-third of them were relatively new or were getting ready to depart at any one time. This policy broadened the number of officers with combat experience but played havoc with small unit cohesion.[13]

As troop withdrawals accelerated, the level of personnel turbulence increased. When a unit was withdrawn or sent home in this period, only the soldiers due to rotate home anyway left with the colors. The remainder—the unlucky majority—simply were reassigned to other units to finish out their tours. Both the Infantry and Artillery units at Pace had significant numbers of transplants from other units.[14] Thus, while the North Vietnamese were able to maintain extraordinary cohesion because their soldiers were in for the long haul, the Americans were in many ways an army of strangers. The siege of Firebase Pace provides an opportunity to examine at the ground level how leaders from generals down to sergeants coped with the issues described above, as well as the other issues associated with conducting a fighting withdrawal.

Major General Jack J. Wagstaff, sixty, commanded all U.S. forces in the Third Military Region. A twenty-nine-year Army career soldier, he reported directly to General Abrams and was the senior decision maker when it came to protecting Firebase Pace. Much like Abrams, he had a reputation as a straight-talking, action-oriented commander.[15] As senior U.S. Commander in the area around Saigon, it was Wagstaff's job to oversee the orderly withdrawal of U.S. troops and the upgrading of the capabilities of South Vietnamese troops. The activity in and around Firebase Pace and the South Vietnamese bases in the Krek–Tay Ninh highway would be his major hot spots during the fall of 1971. Consequently, his role would be to hold the enemy at bay, support the South Vietnamese troops fighting them, and protect the U.S. troops while they supported the South Vietnamese. In doing so, he had to decide how to protect Pace, when and how to evacuate Pace, and how to explain this to the press.

Protecting Pace was something Wagstaff clearly took seriously. He made several visits to Pace and a final visit to both Pace and Katum on September 22, 1971.[16] Reinforcements from the 1/12th Cavalry, including 4.2-inch mortars, arrived the next day. It turned out to be just in time. When the North Vietnamese offensive began on September 26, Pace had this extra level of protection. Wagstaff also saw to it that Pace had strong air support in terms of B-52s, tactical air, helicopter gunships, and resupply. In fact, the S-3 of 2/32d was told he had on call whatever he needed in the way of air support.[17] General Wagstaff also worked with his South Vietnamese counterpart, General Minh, to deploy additional South Vietnamese forces to the area.[18] Moving troops around was one thing; getting them to work together was another. Wagstaff had to intervene when his subordinates could not agree on what level of patrolling was appropriate to defend Pace, by establishing a framework in his messages of October 9 and 11.[19]

Evacuation of Pace sometime in the fall of 1971 was inevitable because 2/32d Field Artillery was due to rotate back to the States as part of the withdrawal program.[20] The decision on when and how to evacuate Pace was even more difficult because of the enemy action. In retrospect, the decision to pull out of Katum and Phu Dong in late September proved to be a good one. It allowed U.S. airpower to concentrate on protecting Pace, and the guns at Pace to concentrate on protecting the South Vietnamese at Krek. Getting safely out of Pace turned out to be more difficult. The decision was apparently made in mid-October after it was clear the enemy offensive had been halted.[21] The first choice was to leave by road, but Charlie Battery's vehicles were in no shape to move, and the road was still subject to ambush. In fact, an ARVN convoy was ambushed just south of Pace on October 10.[22]

Then the decision was made to depart by air, but that was postponed. It is not clear whether that decision was made because of concern over enemy anti-aircraft guns still in the area or lack of lift capability. In any event, the move was called off, which did not help morale on the ground. The aerial evacuation did finally proceed on the 22nd and was by and large successful. The guns were brought out two weeks later.

Once Richard Boyle broke the story of Bravo Company's refusal, Wagstaff and his immediate subordinates had the added challenge of managing a skeptical press corps. The normal tendency in cases like this is to hunker down and hope it blows over. Instead, Wagstaff and his subordinates made themselves available to reporters. They also did not appear to attempt to interfere with reporters' access to enlisted men and even made the members of Bravo Company available to the press at the Timbuktu base camp.[23]

Wagstaff's background served him well. Most general officers in this period graduated from West Point, which stressed engineering skills. Wagstaff received his commission through ROTC at the University of Oregon and went on to earn a law degree.[24] As a young lieutenant colonel in the mid-1950s he penned two pieces for the *Military Review* when it was considered a significant achievement for any Army officer to have just one article accepted by the Army's most prestigious professional journal. In his first piece, "The Army's Preparation for Atomic Warfare," Wagstaff reminded his readers that despite the current infatuation with so-called tactical nuclear weapons, the Army must also be ready to fight with only conventional weapons as well.[25] Five years later, the Pentagon came around to the same point of view in a doctrine known as "flexible response," which is still operational today.[26] His second article dealt with what he called "Politico-Military Policy." He argued, "Today [1955] the professional Army officer must have a general understanding of the political aspects of his military problems and vice versa. Such knowledge is important to officers of every rank and is absolutely essential to the conduct of intermediate and high level staff and command."[27]

Wagstaff would have the opportunity to practice what he preached. He clearly understood the various political forces at work in 1971 and was able to address them in a way that allowed him to accomplish his mission while looking out for the troops on the ground. In addition, he managed his press relations in a way that kept a minor incident at Firebase Pace from escalating into a major public relations catastrophe. The strategy Wagstaff and his subordinates used incorporated five fundamentals: respond quickly; make sure to frame what is known into a broader context; don't blame the troops; don't deny the obvious, but don't volunteer any additional information that may be embarrassing; and stay on message.

When Richard Boyle broke the story of Bravo Company's refusal, Wagstaff and his subordinates responded quickly. They praised the troops but did not volunteer information about the refusal of Delta Company, nor the issues with Charlie Battery's gun crews. Wagstaff, McCaffree, Dye, and the company commanders consistently delivered the same message: yes, the soldiers balked temporarily, but after discussions with their officers they agreed to complete their mission. Thus, this was not a big deal and no disciplinary action is necessary.

While General Wagstaff handled the situation at Pace with a reasonable degree of candor, he was much more circumspect when it came to describing any shortcomings on the part of his South Vietnamese counterparts (see discussion in Chapter 23). Wagstaff did not get back out to Pace after the siege began on September 26, most likely for security reasons, but he did leave a favorable impression on some of the enlisted men he met with.

Sergeant Donze of Charlie Battery recalls Major General Wagstaff's visit to Pace on September 22. "Is there anything you need?" Wagstaff asked a group of GIs just before he left.

"Beer and soda!" Donze blurted out.

"I'll take care of that," Wagstaff replied. The next day a resupply chopper brought out several cases of both.[28]

As the senior artillery commander at Pace, Lieutenant Colonel McCaffree had responsibility for its safety. He had been in command for only a little over one month before Fire Support Base Pace became the most threatened American outpost in all of South Vietnam. As the siege dragged on, his cannoneers became more and more skittish about manning the big guns while enemy mortars zeroed in on them. He had to deal with on-again, off-again orders to be prepared to evacuate Pace. He couldn't get the infantry assigned to protect Pace to do what he thought they should do, and after October 9 he had the press to contend with.

McCaffree finally addressed the morale and performance issues facing his gun crews by sending out a new leadership team on October 10.[29] He was able to safely evacuate his men by air on October 22. He also managed the press throughout the entire twenty-seven-day siege. He made sure higher headquarters knew when the press was around or when something they might find newsworthy was about to happen.[30] When he spoke to the press, he stayed on message with Wagstaff and the others. But when it came to defining an appropriate role for the infantry assigned to Pace, he clearly struggled.

McCaffree's interest in protecting his troops was certainly appropriate. What he expected the infantry to do as a result was not. This may have been a reflection of his lack of experience in a situation of this nature. He was only one month into his first Vietnam tour.

Normally the infantry were more exposed to enemy fire, and the relative casualty statistics reflected that. More than 500 troopers from the 1/12th Cavalry lost their lives in the eighty-two months the battalion served in Vietnam, a rate of six men a month on average.[31] By comparison, the 2/32d Field Artillery lost thirty-seven soldiers over a period of seventy-five months, or about one soldier every two months.[32] But at Firebase Pace, in September and October 1971, this relationship got turned on its head. Fortunately, no one from either unit was killed at Pace, but of the fifty-five men wounded in this period, thirty were from the artillery, compared to sixteen from the infantry.[33] This certainly explains why Charlie Battery's gunners and their officers were a little touchy about what they saw as a lack of support from the infantry.

To mount a major assault into the surrounding woods as McCaffree wanted would have meant death or injury to dozens of Lieutenant Colonel Tyson's Sky Troopers—at a time when enemy mortar fire was annoying and had wounded several but had not yet killed anyone. McCaffree's superiors at TRAC must have felt the same way, or they wouldn't have emphasized in their message of October 9 that "a certain amount of caution must be used."[34]

What came out of McCaffree's discussions with Captain Cronin that day bear the characteristics of an attempted compromise. Bravo Company would do something outside the perimeter, but it would be an ambush, not a frontal assault. What this would achieve, however, got lost somewhere in translation. It certainly would have surprised the North Vietnamese, but beyond that is still unclear. The plots from the antimortar radar at both Pace and Thien Ngon showed the mortars being fired from Cambodia about 1,000 yards to the west, but the ambush was sent to the east (see fig. 7.1). In addition, Pace's ground surveillance radar showed enemy movement in the woods around Pace that evening, but if that meant some sort of ground attack was imminent, the sixteen-man patrol would be more useful inside the perimeter than outside.[35] There is no way Pace could have spared men to rescue the sixteen-man patrol and defend the perimeter under those circumstances.

It is pretty clear the infantry involved (including their NCOs and possibly their junior officers) didn't think much of the idea either.[36] Sergeant Wernli remembers a discussion about moving against the anti-aircraft guns east of the base, which is more plausible, but he, Sergeant Demas, and Specialist French were legitimately concerned about the Claymores and what appeared to them as a less-than-satisfactory response from their commanders.[37] When the order came down, they balked, setting up the temporary standoff that Richard Boyle later dramatized as a mutiny.

The day after the incident, the 3d Cavalry brigade commander decided they needed to make some changes as well. Major Joseph Dye, who served as Battalion S-3 in the relative safety of the 1/12th base camp at FSB Timbuktu, was told by Brigadier General Jonathan D. Burton to grab his gear and hop on a helicopter for Fire Support Base Pace. He was informed he was now responsible for overseeing all of the infantry units providing security for Pace.[38] Sending field grade officers to an assignment this far out in the field was not standard protocol, but clearly his superiors felt this was not a standard situation. As Bravo Company was pulled out and replaced by Delta, they hoped Major Dye's more seasoned supervision would keep the base safe and the troops in line. Equally important, Dye would provide an experienced buffer between Colonel McCaffree and his staff and the infantry assigned to Pace. Dye found a hooch, moved in his gear, and stayed at Pace for the duration of the siege.[39]

The artillery officers found Dye to be condescending, but once he settled in at Pace, he proved to be a stabilizing influence.[40] In fact, one of the enlisted men credited Dye with keeping things calm and inspiring confidence at the beleaguered firebase. He could be seen telling the troops to make sure they stayed spread out, but to "take it easy, things weren't quite as bad as they seemed."[41]

Dye received his biggest test on the morning of October 13. Delta Company had replaced Bravo two days before, and now about twenty members of Delta Company told their commander, Captain Smith, they were not willing to go out on a daylight patrol to the wood line east of the base to protect incoming aircraft from enemy anti-aircraft fire. If helicopters could not land safely, needed supplies could not be carried in and medical emergencies could not be evacuated out. Dye's ability to convince these reluctant soldiers to go ahead with their mission was crucial to preventing a confrontation that could very easily escalate into an ugly incident.

At the critical moment, Dye offered to lead the patrol himself. Majors leading patrols was not standard operating procedure, but this was not a standard situation. Dye's willingness to share the risks with them proved to be the tipping point. The patrol went forward without further incident, and, in fact, Delta Company continued to run daylight patrols without incident for the remainder of their stay at Pace.[42]

This was not the only time in 1971 Vietnam that a field grade officer would make such a gesture to get his troops moving. Colonel Richard M. Meyer, commanding officer of the 1/77th Armor, did much the same thing when faced with a similar situation on Route 9 in March. He jumped into the lead tank and told his men to follow him.[43] They did. It is difficult to overestimate the power of such a dramatic gesture of leadership under these circumstances.

Three field artillery majors spent time at Pace during the twenty-seven-day siege—Major McCullum, Major Davis, and Major Garner. Clearly Colonel McCaffree put them there at one time or another to be his eyes and ears and to make sure things got done the way he felt they needed to be done. Other than the October 10 entry in the 23d Artillery Group log about the wholesale command changes at Pace, documentation about their performance is sparse. However, as described earlier, Major Davis recalls very clearly, as does Lieutenant Diggs, their instructions from Colonel McCaffree to go out to Pace and address the issue related to slow response times. They made a number of changes as a result.

"Major is the most worthless rank in the Army," or so goes the old saying. Captains command companies or batteries, lieutenant colonels command battalions, but majors? They just seem to get in the way. At Firebase Pace, however, senior commanders made good use of the majors on their staff. Most of the other soldiers (both infantry and artillery officers and enlisted men) had never before experienced anything like the siege of Pace. Even if the initial motivation on the part of Colonel McCaffree or General Burton was to get a leg up on who outranked who, the ultimate outcome of having more mature or experienced leadership at Pace helped stabilize operations there to the benefit of all concerned.

The other field grade officers involved in Pace's operations played an important but a less direct role. Colonel Stan Tyson, 1/12th Battalion commander, operated mostly out of Firebase Timbuktu during this period and had to look after a battalion spread over more than 100 miles, but his subordinates felt he supported them when needed.[44] Brigadier General Burton, Tyson's superior, faced the same problem, except he had five battalions spread out over Military Region III.[45] Both paid attention to what was going on at Pace and influenced unit assignments and missions, including the decision to send Major Dye.

General Burton did fly out to Pace during the later stages of the siege, which left a favorable impression on some of the enlisted men. Sergeant Mike Stevens of Delta Company remembers General Burton arriving at Pace in his own helicopter, bringing the mail with him. "General Burton was a great commanding general in my eyes, not just at Pace but since I joined the 1/12th Cav," Stevens wrote later. "He was often in the field with the troops, even sat down and had chow with me at another fire base. Got in the mud and made you feel he was one of you."[46]

Colonel Richard Hoffman, Colonel McCaffree's immediate commander, headed up the 23d Artillery Group, 2/32d's parent unit, which functioned as a cross between a brigade and a division headquarters. Clearly the 23d Group helped arrange for air strikes and other fire support, logistical support, and transportation. Colonel Hoffman did make one trip out to Pace during the siege, but many of the officers at Pace felt both Hoffman and 23d Group did not support them at the level they thought circumstances called for. They felt Colonel Hoffman was aloof and unfamiliar with the realities on the ground at Pace.[47] For example, Major Davis remembers the officer of the 23d Group sent out to oversee the evacuation of Pace was not an artillery but a medical officer. He didn't understand the difference between high explosive rounds (which needed to be fired off before Pace was evacuated so they couldn't be later remanufactured by the Vietcong or NVA) and smoke rounds, which carried little in the way of high explosives and could be safely abandoned.[48]

The performance of field grade officers during the Vietnam draw down was a mixed bag, but at Pace they managed to make the right decisions more often than the wrong ones. They accomplished their mission and, for the most part, protected the troops. At critical moments most of them led by example, often sharing the dangers with the troops they led. But the field grade officers were only part of the picture. The company grade officers (captains and lieutenants) and the noncommissioned officers (sergeants) were the ones on the ground with the troops who had to carry out these decisions and live with the consequences. How they performed would have a great deal of influence on the outcome of events on the ground.

CHAPTER NINETEEN

A Thousand Calleys?

The 1971 court-martial of First Lieutenant William Calley raised the issue of the qualifications and training of junior officers at this stage of the war. After revelations that Calley finished last in his class at Infantry Officer Candidate School at Fort Benning, critics claimed the rapid expansion of the Army to fight in Vietnam had forced a dilution in quality in the junior officer ranks that created "thousands" of Lieutenant Calleys.[1] No evidence other than Lieutenant Calley's conviction has ever been presented to support this. Clearly, the rapid expansion of the Army did result in large numbers of relatively inexperienced junior officers ending up in Vietnam, but the same thing happened when the Army expanded to fight World War II. In Korea, the Army and Marines had a number of experienced officers already in the Reserves.

Presumably the shortage of qualified junior officers in Vietnam came about because of widely available draft deferments for college graduates, and antiwar sentiment at elite universities robbed the Army and other services of the leadership skills of the "best and brightest" of American youth.[2] Ron Milam, a Vietnam veteran and assistant professor of military history at Texas Tech University, took a look at the leadership of junior Army officers in Vietnam in his 2009 book, *Not a Gentleman's War*. After reviewing after-action reports, oral histories, interviews, and other sources, Milam found that commissioning standards were not lowered and that the overwhelming majority of lieutenants who served in Vietnam performed their duties well. Milam speculates that much of the unjustified criticism of the leadership skills of lieutenants (most of whom went back to civilian life after returning home) came from field grade officers who stayed in the Army, and who wrote from a perspective of a generation removed from the soldiers of the Vietnam period. Milam explains:

> The infantry junior officers in Vietnam were grunts, like the men they led into battle. Consequently they tended to listen to the same music, cheat a little on the haircut regulations, look the other way when drugs were being used in the rear, and ignore the shaving and dress code in the boonies. This led field grade officers to develop a belief that lieutenants did not take their jobs seriously, even though in most cases they had to do so to stay alive.[3]

Colonel Richard Hoffman, commanding officer of the 23d Artillery Group (2/32d's parent unit) reflected the field grade officer's more traditional point of view in his January 1972 senior officer debriefing report. He did not accuse his junior officers of war crimes, but he did see them as poor leaders. This is what he wrote:

> (3) Discipline, law and order. There were many contributing factors which resulted in a low state of discipline. The following is a typical situation to be found during this period. First put a unit on an isolated firebase. Add a firebase commander, a captain or lieutenant, with less than three years service, little or none of it in a troop unit. Now give him section chiefs who are draftee E5's with less than two years service and essentially no leadership experience, who, furthermore, identify more with the plight of the enlisted man than with the responsibilities of being a non-commissioned officer. Now put in about five or ten heroin users and double that in marijuana users. Finally, give them no real identifiable combat mission. Here is a situation in which a young officer is faced with the dilemma of accepting sub-standard behavior and performance, or jeopardizing his physical well-being. The former is the easy way out, and I'm afraid that too many have accepted this compromise with principle which resulted in a general lowering of standards.[4]

During Hoffman's six-month tenure as commander of the 23d Group, three of the five artillery battalions assigned to him redeployed from Vietnam. The other two redeployed within ninety days after his departure. Charlie Battery 2/32d was the only firing battery of the fifteen to face sustained enemy contact during this period, so Hoffman had more than his share of bored soldiers and "short-time-itis" to deal with. Nevertheless, Hoffman did not spend a lot of time at Pace, and his sweeping indictment is not justified.[5] Ironically, he was relatively inexperienced himself—like all senior troop commanders in Vietnam, he spent only six months in his position because of Army rotation policies.

Six captains, all company or battery level commanders, spent time at Fire Support Base Pace during the twenty-seven-day siege—three each from the infantry and artillery. They were caught in the middle between their superiors, who wanted orders followed without embarrassment; junior officers and NCOs, who were largely inexperienced; and enlisted men, who were mostly draftees, distrustful of the Army and wary of unnecessary risks. Overlaying all this was a pretty strong disagreement between the infantry and artillery chains of command about how Pace should be defended, and hovering over that was an inquisitive stream of reporters, including, but not limited to, Richard Boyle.

All Army officers, including those of the Vietnam era, were expected to look out for the welfare of their men, but mission still came first. By 1971 protecting the troops' welfare took on added importance. The GIs knew the war was winding down. They knew what was expected of them, but not to the point of taking unnecessary risks. Most of their company grade officers, who were the closest to these young draftees in age and attitude, understood this and adapted accordingly.[6]

Life magazine reporter John Saar wrote about this phenomenon in an October 1970 piece entitled "You Just Can't Hand Out Orders." Saar described the time he spent out in the field with Alpha Company, 1/8th Cavalry, 1st Cavalry Division. Alpha Company had only 5 career soldiers out of a line strength of 118. The rest were all draftees. Their company commander, Captain Brian Utermahlen, a twenty-four-year-old 1968 West Point graduate, explained his leadership style as follows: "These guys are no longer blindly following puppets. They're thinkers and they want intelligent leadership. It's not a democracy, but they want to have a say. If I ran this company like an old time tyrant, I'd have a bunch of rebels. There are people in the company with more experience than I have, and if they think I'm doing something grossly wrong, I'm ready to listen."[7]

Like everything else, the troops had a name for it: "working it out." To traditionalists like Colonel Hoffman and many of his contemporaries, who came of age in a different time, working it out was a clear abdication of leadership. To Captain Utermahlen and his contemporaries facing reality on the ground, it represented what all good leaders do—adapt to the circumstances and get the job done.

Lee Reynolds, an enlisted man with the 25th Infantry Division, expressed the view held by many enlisted men in this period of the war:

> This leads me to something very important: the absence of blind obedience in Vietnam. In other wars, if a colonel or captain gave a bad order, you would have 100 or 200 or 1,000 troops just blindly obeying the order, like Gallipoli with its suicide charges. There was nothing like that in Vietnam. There were situations when you had mutinies and refusals. The kind of spin the media put on that was cowardice or lack of discipline or motivation, whatever negative connotation you want. These incidents were caused when some officer gave a stupid order. Because of the level of knowledge that was common among the troops, the men would refuse to carry out that order. That happened over and over again. They knew their jobs and refused to carry out stupid orders or suicidal orders just because some officer with doodads on his collar said so. There was a tremendous amount of bush wisdom and courage. I admired my fellow soldiers very much. I thought they were very fine people.[8]

Working it out was how Bravo Battery 2/35 Artillery approached the issue of perimeter security at Firebase Lanyard in late 1970. After it became clear the South Vietnamese unit assigned to the base was not particularly motivated, the officers convened a meeting of all the battery personnel at the base. They explained the situation and asked for volunteers to accompany them on daily patrols into the no-man's-land between the perimeter wire and the tree line about 300 meters away. The mission was to look for signs of enemy activity, such as digging, that might warn of preparations for an attack on the base, not to deliberately pick a fight with the North Vietnamese. Leaving the safety of the perimeter defenses meant some increased risk, particularly from mines and booby traps, they were told. But sitting behind the perimeter without knowing if the enemy was preparing an attack was an even greater risk.[9]

First a few hands went up, then everyone else volunteered. Each of the sections took turns providing half a dozen people for the daily patrols. Each of the three junior lieutenants in Bravo Battery took turns leading them. The activity continued without incident until a different ARVN Ranger unit moved into the area in January and commenced more aggressive patrolling.[10] Unlike the patrols that sparked the refusals at Pace in October, these patrols were in daylight, and no enemy troops were known to be in the immediate area. Nonetheless, had the artillerymen at Lanyard been ordered to conduct these patrols without any say in the matter, they may have balked as well.

The dynamics of working it out made their way to Firebase Pace in October. Captain Robert Cronin of Bravo Company faced the most well known case when some of his best and most experienced soldiers challenged his order for a night ambush. Cronin had considerable experience himself. He had been in Vietnam nearly a year before he took command, including time with both 2/7th Cavalry and the 173d Airborne Brigade.[11] Cronin took over command of Bravo Company when the previous commander was relieved. Some of the enlisted men felt Cronin was too aggressive, but others did not.[12] Even his critics gave him credit for looking after his troops by actions such as keeping them off trails and making them wear helmets and flak jackets.[13]

But the wisdom of a night ambush under these circumstances is certainly open to debate. How much of this was McCaffree's initiative and how much was Cronin's is still not clear.[14] But to Cronin's credit, he realized that disciplining these soldiers was not the answer. His willingness to accompany his men on a daylight patrol the next day turned out to be critical to getting his troops moving again.

Captain Kenneth Smith faced a similar challenge from Delta Company three days later when his men balked at a daylight patrol in the same area. According to Specialist Four Marling, Captain Smith initially would not agree to accompany the patrol.[15] Major Dye was brought in to work it out with the recalcitrant GIs. Major Dye did offer to accompany them. After discussing the matter, they moved out as planned, and no disciplinary action was taken. Smith did later join his troops on a mission to recover parts from one of the downed helicopters.[16]

Captain John Adams of Alpha Company was the most experienced company commander of the three. He was the most cautious when it came to taking patrols outside the perimeter, including resisting Colonel McCaffree's attempt to stage a night ambush west of the base. Alpha had not reported combat refusals in this period, but when Adams put together a patrol to attempt a rescue of the crew of the Huey shot down on September 30, he decided to lead the patrol himself. "I wouldn't ask my soldiers to do something I wouldn't do myself," he recalled later.[17]

Sorting out company level leadership roles in Charlie Battery during the September–October period is more complicated. Captain Timmons's evacuation due to a nonhostile injury occurred just as tensions at the base reached a critical point, so it is not clear how much of what transpired in the October 7–9 period reflects long-term concerns and how much reflects the confusion in a change of command of three battery commanders in four days.

As described previously, both Colonel McCaffree and the 23d Group had concerns about the timeliness of Charlie Battery's responses regarding both fire missions and reports of incoming. Major Davis's frustration with Charlie Battery's inability to complete a TOT mission he had ordered as battalion executive officer was described earlier. Colonel McCaffree was disappointed that junior officers at Pace didn't know how to do something as basic as a crater analysis.[18]

A critical moment on the deterioration of the relationship between the officers at Pace and their superiors occurred on or about October 5. McCaffree was at Pace on that day when the base took a barrage of incoming mortar fire.[19] McCaffree thought he saw something in the tree line that revealed the enemy's position. He instructed one of the eight-inch howitzer crews to engage it with direct fire. However, firing at that close of a target required the barrel to be lowered so far that the RPG screen (a six- to eight-foot-high cyclone fence) would be in the way. McCaffree wanted the screen taken down so the target could be properly engaged.[20] The battery executive officer and the section chief objected, explaining that the low elevation of the barrel would prevent the fuse from arming properly. In addition, they feared removal of the screen would invite the North Vietnamese to knock out the howitzer with RPG fire. First Lieutenant Alberg, the assistant executive officer, chimed in. "You must be fucking crazy," he told McCaffree. McCaffree felt they were being too defensive and ordered the fence taken down anyway, the barrel lowered, and the target engaged.[21]

McCaffree remembers the action silencing the mortar. Alberg and the enlisted men involved remember the round overshooting the target because the fuse failed to arm properly. The RPG screen did go back up without any enemy RPGs being fired at the gun position, but Colonel McCaffree was so infuriated by the incident that he eventually relieved the battery executive officer from his duties and replaced him with Lieutenant Diggs.[22]

Obviously, this is a case where the commander and his troops were not able to work it out. However, once Major Davis, Captain Ashley, Lieutenant Diggs, and Sergeant First Class Masters arrived on October 10, the conflict between Pace, 2/32d

Battalion Headquarters, and 23d Group seemed to have dissipated. What Lieutenant Diggs and Lieutenant Alberg both agreed on was the importance of leading by example, which meant them being out in the open with the gun crews.

In addition to Charlie Battery's executive officer, there must have been at least a dozen first and second lieutenants at Pace with either the artillery or the infantry units during the twenty-seven-day siege.[23] On the infantry side, lieutenants played a key role in patrolling the perimeter as platoon leaders. Lieutenant Shuler, whatever he may have thought of the wisdom of the October 9 night ambush, was willing to lead it and accompanied Captain Cronin on the patrol the next day. Specialist French remembers the example Lieutenant Shuler set by helping him disarm and collect the Claymores, something he knew Shuler didn't need to do.[24] A platoon leader from Delta Company led their first patrol on October 13 and Lieutenant Lee led one of the patrols that rescued the two Cobra pilots on October 12. And, of course, First Lieutenant Pace played a major leadership role in the defense of Firebase Lanyard against the enemy sapper attack on March 29.

In the Army chain of leadership, noncommissioned officers (sergeants usually) are the final link in the chain of command, and to many experts they are the most important, because they are supposed to make sure orders are carried out at the small unit level. But by the early 1970s many units in the field lacked the requisite number of experienced NCOs. By this stage of the war, many had done two or three tours in Vietnam and didn't want to go back.[25] Others served as advisers to the ARVN. Still others left the Army entirely. This left many units shorthanded, including those at Pace. It is impossible to quantify, but the lack of experience at the NCO level most likely contributed to a sense of distrust and rebelliousness in the lower enlisted ranks.

At the company level, the first sergeant was the most experienced noncommissioned officer. A veteran of many years of service (and usually multiple tours in Vietnam), he provided knowledge and stability as the company commander's right-hand man. The standard practice for most infantry companies in the field was to leave the first sergeant (and often the company executive officer) back at base camp to make sure needed supplies, equipment, and personnel got out to the field, and to make sure other administrative support functions were handled properly as well. This would be the case with the Cavalry units at Pace.[26] While a deployment of this nature made sense from an efficiency point of view, it did leave officers and NCOs without that experience in the field.

The next level of senior NCOs in a rifle company should be the platoon sergeants; while not as experienced as the first sergeant, they usually carried the rank of staff sergeant (E-6) and had significant experience. The Bravo Company roster for this period shows six individuals carrying the rank of staff sergeant assigned to Bravo's three platoons. However, four of these individuals had carried that rank for only eighteen months or less, meaning they were relatively new at their jobs.[27] There is very little evidence they participated in the platoon-level discussions of the merits of the night ambush on October 9 or the day patrols on October 10. One GI said they seemed to be inclined to remain under the radar and were not sure what to do.[28] Another commented that they seemed to turn over rather quickly.[29]

Significantly, a number of the more experienced enlisted men carrying the rank of sergeant (E-5) were very much involved. Many of them were short-timers but had been in the field for some time and had leadership positions in their respective platoons and squads. This included men like Sergeants Demas and Wernli, who normally took point or otherwise set a good example for the others.

Charlie Battery found itself in a better position. Their first sergeant, Rafael Santiago, hated it in the rear and stayed at Pace with the rest of Bravo Battery. One of his colleagues described him as a "soldier's soldier."[30] Two of the four gun section chiefs were staff sergeants with previous Vietnam experience.[31] In addition, the battery's mess sergeant stayed on at Pace, which benefited morale.[32]

Ironically, the biggest performance problem was the second senior enlisted man, the chief of firing battery (usually an E-7 or senior E-6). McCaffree replaced him on October 10 with Sergeant First Class Masters.[33] There is no written record as to why, but one of the section chiefs recalls hearing that he was relieved after leaving on R&R without approval.[34]

While looked down upon by Colonel Hoffman and some of the other career soldiers, graduates of the NCO Academy (also known as "Shake 'n' Bakes") filled important leadership positions as artillery section chiefs and infantry platoon sergeants and squad leaders. This includes soldiers like Sergeants Donze, Stevens, and Wernli. Many of their officers and fellow NCOs found their leadership to be an important part of what held units together under trying circumstances.[35]

The junior officers and noncommissioned officers at Pace and Lanyard came from different backgrounds but shared a common purpose. They knew the enemy was nearby, and they would have to stick together if they wanted to survive. To some of their senior officers they might have seemed inexperienced and too close to their men, but they knew what needed to be done. They knew that blindly following orders was not the road to salvation, and they were determined not to end up as victims.

In the end, the choices they made were the right ones. That is why the artillerymen at Lanyard decided to run their own short-range, daylight reconnaissance patrols in December 1970 and January 1971, even though no one told them to. They were not looking to pick a fight with the North Vietnamese if they didn't have to, but they were determined to be ready if the North Vietnamese chose to pick a fight with them. When the North Vietnamese did attack Lanyard at the end of March, the artillerymen and engineers unhesitatingly directly rushed to the perimeter to engage the enemy at close range before the camp could be overrun.

One of their number, Lieutenant Pace, chose to go even beyond that to give his own life to protect wounded comrades.

Five months later, when Firebase Pace came under attack, the artillerymen there continued working their guns despite suffering 60 percent casualties from incoming shrapnel. Three weeks later, when given a chance to leave as individuals, they told their commanding officers they chose to leave together or not at all.

The infantry units sent to protect Pace in September and October faced choices as well. For Alpha Company it meant saying no to a risky night operation, but yes to daylight patrols and a rescue mission to a downed helicopter. For Bravo Company a similar choice presented itself, except in this case the more experienced enlisted men took the lead in opposing the night patrol, but then turned around and patrolled the same area the next morning. It also meant challenging, in writing, and at some risk to themselves, the military and civilian hierarchy to confront the gap between their rhetoric and reality on the ground. The pattern repeated itself when Delta Company arrived and did what they needed to do, including revisiting the Huey crash site to make sure no remains were left behind. These may not have been the spit-shined, neatly groomed warriors envisioned by the Army's higher echelon, but in the end they did what all good soldiers needed to do. They fought on for each other even when everyone else no longer seemed to care.

Taken together, the incidents at Pace fall far short of a case of an Army lacking leadership. Despite multiple challenges, leaders down to the small unit level overcame these hurdles by appealing to self-interest in meeting a common threat and by taking pride in doing an important job no one else was willing to do. The glue that held this together was not the formal authority that comes from an insignia on a collar, but the moral authority that comes from saying, "follow me— this is so important I'm willing to put myself at risk, so you should too." Their reward was not a victory parade, or even much of a place in the history books. Instead, it was something even more valuable—the opportunity to get the job done and return home safely to make something of the rest of their lives.

The previous chapters have reviewed the performance of U.S. ground combat troops in Vietnam from the middle of 1970 to the end of 1971 to determine if the events at Pace were an anomaly or part of a pattern. This examination focused on the Military Region III, from Saigon to the border, and Military Region I, adjacent to Laos and Vietnam, because that is where U.S. ground troops were still engaged with the enemy.

In Military Region III almost all of the ground activity involved the five maneuver battalions of the 3d Brigade of the 1st Cavalry Division. That unit took a very aggressive posture regarding its defensive mission for the entire calendar year

1971. Despite distractions caused by conflicting messages from political leaders, withdrawal of supporting units, and growing drug abuse, these soldiers accomplished their mission without any reported refusals, other than those at Pace, and no other major mishaps.

The U.S. ground units stationed in Military Region I engaged the most direct combat in 1970–1971. It began with defense against enemy attacks on firebases Tomahawk and Ripcord in mid-1970 and culminated in the participation by U.S. ground troops in a supporting role for the South Vietnamese invasion of Laos in the first half of 1971. These troops faced issues similar to those in III Corps regarding combat refusals, drug abuse, and fraggings. But they also faced some of the most intense fighting of the Vietnam War. Two of the incidents most commonly associated with the breakdown of the U.S. Army in Vietnam—the combat refusal of 1/1st Cav on Route 9 and the failure to defend FSB Mary Ann occurred in Military Region I in the first part of 1971.

While both of these incidents were troubling for different reasons, they did not represent a pattern, but instead obscured the solid performance of most of the soldiers engaged with the enemy during this period. That includes Colonel Myers's actions in leading the 1/77th Armor down Route 9 by hopping in the lead tank himself. It includes the troops who successfully defended Tomahawk and Ripcord against intense enemy pressure. It also includes heavy artillery that fired in support of the ARVN from exposed firebases on the Laotian border, from the armored and mechanized infantry that kept Route 9 open despite constant enemy pressure, and the combat engineers who opened the road in the first place.

Perhaps the best explanation of why U.S. combat troops were able to perform the way they did comes from Colonel William Hauser, who commanded troops in Vietnam. "What kept them going, in spite of a pervasive sense that the war served no real purpose and that the country didn't care, was a combination of pride, mutual interest, and loyalty to good leadership."[36]

For the majority of troops who served combat support functions, the threat to their safety was less direct, the motivation less clear-cut. Consequently, the incidence of undesirable behavior regarding drugs, fraggings, and racial incidents was much higher. But in the end, the available evidence shows these units were able to hold it together long enough to accomplish their mission of supporting the frontline troops, no matter how inelegantly.

But U.S. troops were not the only players on the stage at this juncture. The South Vietnamese army was beginning to take over most of the fighting, the North Vietnamese army continued to fight on, and the press corps tried to keep the people back home informed about it all.

Aerial view headed north along Route 22. Pace is the large square on the upper left corner. Notice bomb craters along both sides of the road south of Pace. (Courtesy of Mark Crist)

Aerial view of Fire Base Pace sometime in late 1971 or early 1972 after the Americans have pulled out. The Cambodian border follows the stream that curves between the trees in the upper right-hand corner of the picture. The white spots are bomb craters. The craters in the trees west of Pace are the sites of suspected mortar positions. (Courtesy of Mark Crist)

FSB Pace under construction by U.S. army engineers in the spring of 1971. Pace was designed to be a "model" firebase, meaning dry and easier to defend than Lanyard. (Courtesy Tom Colaiezzi)

Aerial shot of Pace in July 1971. Construction is continuing, but the four emplacements for the artillery of Charlie Battery can be clearly seen. (Courtesy of the National Archives)

ARVN convoy speeds north along Highway 22 toward Cambodia in January 1971. This road was the only land route to Lanyard and Pace from the supply bases in the rear and a favorite target for NVA ambushes. (Photo by the author)

A CH 54 Flying Crane hovering over Pace. Note the tower for the CSR III ground radar to the right. (Courtesy of J. Paul White)

Huey landing at Pace. GIs are sitting on the floor with the doors open so they can make a quick exit upon landing. (Courtesy of J. Paul White)

A wounded soldier is rushed to a medical evacuation helicopter at FSB Pace in October 1971. The helicopter is hovering about four feet off the ground in order to make a quick exit in the event of incoming. (Photo used with permission of AP/Wide World Photos)

Funeral service for South Vietnamese soldiers killed at Pace. Three of the coffins belong to Kit Carson scouts (former North Vietnamese soldiers who defected from the North Vietnamese Army and served as scouts). They were killed by incoming mortars at Pace in early October. One died instantly. The other two succumbed to wounds. (Courtesy J. Paul White)

Tracker dog and handler flown out to Pace on October 21 to assist in finding remains of Huey crew shot down on September 30. 175mm gun to the right has been pulled off line because of damage from enemy mortar fire. (Courtesy of J. Paul White)

Members of Delta Company at site of September 30 Huey crash south of FSB Pace. All four crew members died in the crash. This patrol took place on October 21 in order to recover remains and any sensitive equipment. (Courtesy of Mike Stevens)

Site of the October 13 crash of a Cobra gunship just east of FSB Pace. Both pilots survived and were rescued by elements of Delta Company. The ship was a total loss. This patrol took place on October 17. (Courtesy Mike Stevens)

Crew firing a 175mm cannon at FSB Lanyard in the spring of 1971. This gun along with the rest of C Battery moved to Pace in May. (Courtesy of Tom Colaiezzi)

A powder charge being loaded into the breech of a 175 mm cannon at FSB Lanyard. Charge is sufficient to propel a 142-pound projectile up to 20 miles when fired. (Courtesy of Tom Colaiezzi)

Crew firing an 8-inch howitzer at FSB Lanyard. The Cambodian border is on the other side of the trees in the background. (Courtesy of Tom Colaiezzi)

The 8-inch howitzer "Canned Heat" at FSB Lanyard. Gun crews often named their pieces beginning with at least one letter consistent with the battery designation. For example, guns or howitzers from C Battery would all have names that begin with C. "Canned Heat" moved to Pace with the rest of Charlie Battery in May 1971, where it stayed through the siege in October. (Courtesy of Tom Colaiezzi)

Direct fire from an 8-inch howitzer round hits near a suspected enemy position in the trees about 300 meters west of FSB Pace. (Courtesy of J. Paul White)

B-52 strike in the woods west of Pace, most likely 600–1,000 meters away on the Cambodian side of the border. (Courtesy of J. Paul White)

Quad Fifty machine guns similar to the four located at FSB Pace for perimeter defense. This particular unit is operating in support of U.S. Marines near Khe Sanh in 1968. (Courtesy of the National Archives)

Twin 40mm Duster at FSB Lanyard in January 1971. Note the road wheels are nearly covered by the mud endemic to the base. (Photo by the author)

155mm self-propelled howitzer firing from Lanyard into Cambodia in December 1970. Note that the crew had some degree of protection because of the enclosed turret, while crews working the 8-inch howitzers and 175mm cannons did not. By the time Pace was occupied in May 1971, these 155mm howitzers had been redeployed back to the United States and were not replaced. (Photo by the author)

TV crew filming at FSB Pace sometime in mid-October. Correspondent is most likely Walter Lord from NBC. (Courtesy of J. Paul White)

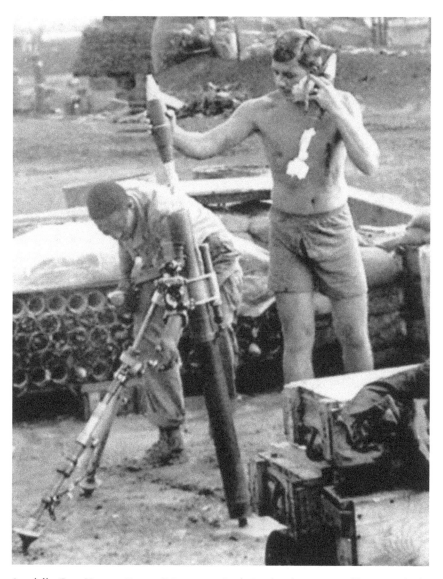

Specialist Four Harmon Young, E Company 1/12th Cavalry, drops a round into a 4.2-inch mortar at FSB Pace in October 1971. The mission came so quickly he didn't have time to wipe the shaving cream off his face or chest. Sergeant First Class Cecil Pittman is the man ducking down. (Used with permission from the *Stars and Stripes*. Copyright 1971, 2010, *Stars and Stripes*)

First Lieutenant Gary Lynn Pace. FSB Pace was named for him in recognition of his heroism in defending FSB Lanyard against an enemy sapper attack the night of March 29–30. Lt. Pace was posthumously awarded the Silver Star. (Courtesy of Steve Pace)

Members of Bravo Company hold an impromptu press conference at FSB Timbuktu on October 13, 1971. Lt. Shuler is on the far left. (Copyright Dieter Ludwig. Used with permission)

Anchor Harry Reasoner reporting on FSB Pace, ABC Evening News, October 19, 1971. FSB Pace was featured on all three network news broadcasts that week. (Copyright ABC News. Used with permission)

Where Pace was located in 1971 is now an empty field. Rt. 22, in the foreground, has been paved in this 2006 photo. (Courtesy of Paul Marling)

Jack Ryals at the site of FSB Lanyard in 2008. Watch tower in the background is at the approximate location of the watch tower at Lanyard thirty-seven years earlier, about 300 meters from the Cambodian border. (Courtesy Jack Ryals)

PART THREE

The Press

CHAPTER TWENTY

Richard Boyle vs. the Powers That Be

One casualty of Vietnam turned out to be the relationship between the officials conducting the war and the press that covered it. As the conflict dragged on, news organizations increasingly believed many official statements to be either unjustifiably optimistic or downright deceitful. Conversely, many U.S. officials in Vietnam and their counterparts in Washington believed the press was lazy and biased against them.[1] The events at FSB Pace in the fall of 1971 were widely reported, both in print and broadcast media, and as such provide a rare opportunity to examine this controversy.

Any such analysis needs to begin with Richard Boyle, the person who first broke the story. Boyle was not a mainstream journalist, but his background at that point certainly fit the profile of what the military command would describe as someone with an agenda to embarrass them. He was kicked out of Vietnam earlier by the Saigon government for his alleged participation in an antiwar protest. He'd worked for *Overseas Weekly*, an independent tabloid that was a favorite among lower-ranking enlisted men because it took delight in exposing the shortcomings of senior officers.[2] Now he was associated with *Ramparts Magazine*, a San Francisco–based publication that specialized in antiestablishment politics. Was it even possible for a person with such an agenda to objectively report on what was going down in the complex and emotionally charged environment that was FSB Pace in October 1971?

The story Boyle wrote for *Le Monde* never appeared in English, nor was it ever printed in the United States. But Boyle wrote a detailed account in *Flower of the Dragon*, published by Ramparts Press in 1972.[3] Comparing that version with what was reported elsewhere at the time, now unclassified official documents and eyewitness accounts, it is possible to determine whether Richard Boyle reported what he saw or, as an instigator or provocateur, made something out of nothing.

The fundamentals of the story—the tactical situation, names, dates, location of the refusal, and the petition—all check out with other sources. In fact, Boyle provides some useful insight of his own. Except for incorrectly placing the North Vietnamese mortars northeast instead of northwest of the base, his description of the dilemmas facing Captain Cronin, Lieutenant Colonel McCaffree, and the other senior American commanders responsible for the security of Firebase Pace was right on target:

Cronin was facing a tactical, possibly a political dilemma. The North Vietnamese had built an extensive underground bunker complex inside the tree line along the Cambodian border, on Pace's northeastern side. From these bunkers, NVA gunners would quickly set up a mortar tube or rocket launcher, fire, and duck back into their tunnels. Within seconds the Americans would pour out machine-gun fire, followed by artillery and even air strikes; but by then the gunner would have jumped into his gopher hole and scurried through an underground tunnel, emerging about fifty meters away.[4]

Boyle went on to say:

All the artillery and air fire the Americans poured on the North Vietnamese seemed useless. The battlefield technology developed by the Americans, representing billions of dollars—electronically controlled B-52s, Spooky gunships which pour out enough machine-gun bullets in a few seconds to fill up a football field, and all the other gadgets—seemed useless against a few men with a mortar who could pop up at will, drop a few rounds, and duck back into the safety of their tunnel with virtual impunity. The electronic battlefield, the pride of the American military establishment, was being thwarted by troops using the same kinds of mortars used in the First World War. Cronin knew it, his superiors knew it, and his troops knew it.[5]

It is true that the U.S. troops at Pace were frustrated that all the firepower applied at Pace did not seem to knock out the mortars. But whether they saw it as "useless" was an entirely different matter. In fact, many of the men felt the firepower, despite its limitations, kept the enemy at bay. But Boyle was on a roll. Here's what he said next:

Cronin was very candid: the artillery commander wanted more protection, he told me, and somebody had to go out and get those North Vietnamese rocket and mortar tubes. I had seen at Ben Het and Bu Prang that it's suicide to sit back and let the enemy pound your positions until there is nothing left but shattered flesh and mud. Dien Bien Phu proved this to the French.[6]

Again Boyle starts out with a truthful statement. McCaffree, the artillery commander, did want more protection.[7] Invoking the cataclysm of Dien Bien Phu, where the defenders were cut off with no support, was a bit of a stretch, but it did perfectly set up Boyle's punch line:

Somebody had to go out and get those North Vietnamese bunkers, or within a day, maybe two, the enemy mortar and rocket positions would multiply faster than the rats that were also fighting the Americans for domination of Firebase Pace. When the North Vietnamese had enough fire-power to knock out the camp's big guns, they would rain a deadly barrage of fire on the Americans, covering a sapper attack. And that would be it.[8]

Boyle had now placed the Americans at Pace on the edge of the abyss. It makes for dramatic reading, but it does not reflect the situation on the ground or the events of October 9. The mortar and rocket positions had not multiplied, but instead remained relatively constant. The heavy guns were not critical to the defense of Pace—that role was filled by the grunts, the Quad Fifties, the ARVN artillery at Pace and Thien Ngon, and U.S. air support. And, if the North Vietnamese did launch a ground assault under the cover of a mortar barrage, that would not be "it" in the sense of an inevitable defeat. It did mean, however, that the grunts and artillerymen at Pace would have to defend themselves, just as American GIs had a hundred times at a hundred isolated firebases over the past six years, including Lanyard just six months earlier.

While Boyle's description of the tactical situation is melodramatic, it does capture to a large degree the challenges facing the defenders of Firebase Pace. But then he launched into hyperbole when he described the actions of Bravo Company on the evening of October 9 as a mutiny. "Mutiny" is one of the most emotion-laden terms in the military lexicon. Richard Boyle used the term three times in describing the events of October 9–10 in *Flower of the Dragon*. In fact, his chapter on the episode is titled "Mutiny." The Uniform Code of Military Justice, which governs the conduct of all U.S. service personnel, regardless of branch, defines a mutiny as any person "with intent to usurp or override lawful military authority, refuses in concert with another person to obey orders or otherwise do his duty or create violence or disturbance is guilty of mutiny."[9]

The definition is a broad one and clearly some discretion is delegated to unit commanders. Many of the facts in this case are not in dispute. Six members of Bravo Company did, at least initially, refuse an order to conduct a night ambush. There were six of them, so technically they acted in concert to disobey a lawful order, but the entire chain of command in this case, from company commander to commanding general, agree the order was rescinded. So technically there could be no mutiny because there was no order. But more important than technicalities were the other circumstances in the case. Taken to the extreme, two soldiers griping about an order are potential mutineers. That is why the language about intent to usurp or override lawful military authority is important. There was no violence or threat of violence, no overthrow of authority, and no pattern of refusal in Bravo Company other than this one incident.

One way to judge the appropriateness of word choice is to see how other news organizations handled the story. When the Associated Press (AP) ran its story on the incident on October 11, it said the soldiers "balked" at a night ambush, but it also quoted Colonel McCaffree as saying the men had not refused the order because it was rescinded, and they all went out on patrol the next day as ordered.[10] Boyle's response was to accuse the AP of conspiring with the U.S. Command to "cover up the facts."[11]

Boyle went on to say that the United Press International (UPI) version was much more accurate in describing what happened.[12] UPI did in fact include quotations from the GIs involved explaining why they took this action and AP didn't. But, UPI also steered clear of the term "mutiny," saying the soldiers "refused" to go out on patrol.[13] A bylined story by Craig R. Whitney in the New York Times the same day said the soldiers "balked for a time."[14]

So three independent news organizations came to a similar conclusion on their choice of words, and "mutiny" was not among them. It is likely these news organizations viewed the term "mutiny" in the context of its typical use. Webster's Dictionary defines a mutiny as "a revolt against and, often, forcible resistance to constituted authority; esp. rebellion of soldiers or sailors against their officers."[15] Again, there was resistance to a specific order, but there is no evidence that force was ever used or even threatened in this case. Nor is there any evidence of a continuing effort by anyone in Bravo Company to undermine military authority in this period.

Boyle didn't stop there. Instead, he made a series of allegations of conspiracies on the basis of little or no evidence. For example, Boyle accused the Army multiple times of a conspiracy to deny GIs were even at Pace.[16] As pointed out previously, a CBS film crew visited Pace and filed a film report that CBS broadcast on July 15.[17] When Pace and other border outposts came under fire in September, the AP reported it and the New York Times printed it on September 26.[18] Then, on September 29, the AP reported the redeployment of U.S. troops to reinforce Pace and other firebases on the Cambodian border. This account made it onto the front page of the Washington Post the next morning.[19]

Pacific Stars and Stripes, the military's own newspaper, began reporting on U.S. troops being under fire at Pace as early as September 30, nine days before Boyle arrived.[20] On October 4, Stars and Stripes published a photograph of a wounded soldier being rushed to a medical evacuation helicopter at Pace, along with a story that U.S. artillery and infantrymen were at Pace and thirty of them had been wounded since the siege started on September 25.[21] Then, on the morning of October 9, the morning Boyle arrived at Pace, the Pacific edition of Stars and Stripes carried a feature from Pace identifying soldiers specifically from the 2/32d Artillery and the First Air Cavalry Division.[22]

Perhaps the most compelling evidence of the weakness of Boyle's argument was his own description of how he got there. If the Army was really intent on keeping the activity at Pace under wraps, how could they allow an unaccredited journalist, who'd already been kicked out of the country once, to hitch a ride on a Vietnamese army helicopter, walk unaccompanied into Pace, talk freely with enlisted men, then leave unchallenged with a petition and tape recording?

Boyle goes even further with this conspiracy angle to argue the mail was being censored.[23] In fact, there were problems with mail delivery. On November 6, 1971, Major General Adamson, assistant chief of staff to the personnel officer for all of MACV, sent an unclassified message to commanders of all four regions (including General Wagstaff) acknowledging numerous complaints about deterioration of mail service throughout Vietnam due to manpower shortages caused by troop withdrawals and pledging to take steps to correct it.[24]

Boyle concluded his description of his trip to Pace with an assertion of an unwritten understanding between Bravo Company GIs and the North Vietnamese in the tree line: "The men agreed and passed the word to other platoons: nobody fires unless fired upon. As of about 1100 hours on October 10, 1971, 1st Cav Division declared their own private cease fire with the North Vietnamese. For the first time since they got to Pace, it was all quiet on the Cambodian front."[25]

Eleven hundred hours on October 10, 1971, was not the first time there was a lull in firing at Pace. Pace averaged five or six mortar attacks daily at random intervals, sometimes separated by a number of hours. None of the Bravo Company GIs who were at Pace that day can validate Boyle's description of a "private" cease fire on the tenth or any other day. In fact, some of them laughed at the suggestion.[26]

The 2/32d Artillery's daily logs show that at 1355 hours on October 10, North Vietnamese gunners fired five mortar rounds inside the perimeter and two rockets outside. Just before 1800 hours, a second barrage of five to six rounds landed inside the berm. An hour later, sentries reported AK-47 fire from the east.[27] Fortunately, no one was hurt, but the war was clearly on. The next day Pace took another ten rounds of incoming, including the ones that knocked out two guns and injured five GIs.[28]

The final question that needs to be asked is whether Boyle instigated or provoked the events he later reported on. The available evidence suggests not. The differences over the U.S. Infantry's obligation to protect Firebase Pace started with Alpha Company and the artillery command structure long before Boyle got there. The decision to refuse the order to go out on night ambush started with 3d Platoon. The idea to send the letter to Senator Kennedy started with 2d Platoon. Even forty years later, members of Bravo Company remain firmly convinced they were justified in objecting to the night ambush, even if they have differing views about Boyle.[29]

Having said that, it is pretty clear that Richard Boyle didn't serve as a calming influence. He reportedly told Bravo Company GIs, "The lifers don't care about you," and "The South Vietnamese won't protect you."[30] He was also the means by which Bravo's refusal came to the attention of the national news media, but it would be a misreading of the intensity of feelings on the part of GIs at Pace to attribute this story and what flowed from it primarily to Richard Boyle.

Based on what can be determined by other credible sources, some of Richard Boyle's account of what happened at Pace on October 9 and 10, 1971, can be verified. Some members of Bravo Company 1/12th Cavalry did refuse, at least initially, an order to conduct a night ambush. Most of the company supported the refusal and signed a letter saying so. It was an embarrassment for the Army. But there is also a credible body of evidence that clearly contradicts Boyle's claim of a mutiny, his claim of a cover-up, and his claim of a grunt-inspired truce. After the controversy died down, U.S. troops were withdrawn from Pace, the South Vietnamese took their place, and the war continued on.

CHAPTER TWENTY-ONE

The Press and the White House

In the fall of 1971, Americans got almost all of their news about the Vietnam War from three sources: the daily newspaper, one of three national news magazines, and one of three national TV networks. There was no Internet, no cable news networks, or cell phones, iPods, Blackberries, YouTube, or Twitter. This concentration of the perceived power to influence public opinion gave partisans both for the war and against it ample opportunity to argue why the American people were being denied the truth, at least as they saw it.

The year 1971 was a particularly combative time between the U.S. media and the U.S. government over coverage of the war. It began with conflicting perspectives over the reporting of the American-supported invasion of Laos (Lam Son 719), then escalated over the summer into legal battles over the publication of the so-called Pentagon Papers. In the fall, controversy continued over allegations of rigging the South Vietnamese presidential election. In between, print and broadcast media regularly ran stories about alleged atrocities against civilians, drug abuse among soldiers, fraggings against officers, racial tension between soldiers, and corruption in both the U.S. and South Vietnamese military.[1] In this environment it is difficult to imagine how a complex, emotionally charged issue like the combat refusals at Fire Support Base Pace could be treated fairly. Did the press reports accurately describe what happened, or did press reports reflect bias based on news organizations' editorial positions on the war?

Sixty-two million Americans read over 1,700 daily newspapers in 1971.[2] For war coverage, most newspapers depended on feeds from the three major wire services: the Associated Press, Reuters, and United Press International. Each of these three wire services had their own Vietnam bureau. Since they served a variety of clients, they tended to steer to the middle of the political spectrum, but occasionally they delved into controversial issues. As discussed previously, both AP and UPI approached the Pace refusals cautiously, with UPI being a little more likely to report on the views of the GIs themselves, instead of just official spokesmen.[3] In addition to the wire services, major dailies such as the *New York Times* and the *Washington Post* had Saigon bureaus. They could and did initiate coverage that was picked up elsewhere in print or on television. Many of them did their own reporting on the incidents at Fire Support Base Pace.

The *New York Times* viewed itself as the upholder of high journalistic standards in this period.[4] Viewed as arrogant and insulated by its critics, it did support the largest team of reporters in Vietnam and devoted the most newspaper space to news about the war. For example, between September 27, 1971, and October 24, 1971, the Times ran fourteen different news articles in which Fire Support Base Pace was mentioned.[5] Of these fourteen accounts in the Times, twelve were Associated Press versions; the other two carried bylines.[6] By comparison, the Chicago Tribune, which was probably more typical of other large dailies, ran only five.[7]

The first bylined report appeared in the New York Times in the October 12 edition. The 500-word, page-3 piece by Craig R. Whitney carried the headline "Army Says Some GIs Balked Briefly at Patrol." It followed the AP story pretty closely, except that Whitney specifically mentioned Boyle and that the GIs' refusal was based on the "defensive" nature of their mission. It also included a denial from an Army spokesman that U.S. forces were operating in Cambodia and closed with a reference to the first combat refusal by GIs of the Americal Division in an August 1969 incident.[8] The Times relied on wire service accounts for the remaining three weeks, until October 23. At that point, Fox Butterworth's 450-word story, "US Troops Leave Cambodian Border," described the details of the evacuation of Fire Support Base Pace. Butterworth included a reference to the first refusal by Bravo Company, but not the second refusal by Delta.[9]

Lining up a distant second behind the New York Times in terms of daily newspaper influence at that time stood the Washington Post. Although it lacked the tradition and national scope of the Times, the Post had significant resources of its own and a special niche as the flagship newspaper of the nation's capital. The Post ran seven articles mentioning Firebase Pace between October 2 and October 25, 1971.[10] Four of these were AP versions, one was the UPI story on the second refusal, two were bylined, and another was a small 200-word, un-bylined description of Senator Kennedy's request for the Pentagon investigation. That account ran on page A4 of the October 16 edition and included references to Boyle and to the petition signed by sixty-five GIs.[11]

The following weeks, the Washington Post's treatment of the events at Pace started to diverge significantly from that of the New York Times. On October 22, the Post ran the UPI version on Delta Company's temporary refusal on October 13 on page A19 with a six-column headline, "Second Refusal to Patrol at Firebase Revealed."[12] The New York Times didn't carry any story at all.

On October 23, the Post ran a front-page analysis by Saigon Bureau Chief Peter A. Jay on the evacuation of Firebase Pace, including a photograph of the base at night. The 1,000-word piece reviewed the entire episode—the mission of the soldiers there, both refusals and subsequent patrols, and the decision to withdraw. Jay included extensive quotations from both the recalcitrant GIs and their officers. "The troubles at Pace had come to symbolize, in a small way, the unpleasant dilemma confronting those few American Officers and men still on a ground combat role in South Vietnam," Jay observed. "With the war grinding to a halt, said the men of Bravo Company—the recalcitrant unit at Pace—there was no point in taking unnecessary risks."[13]

Two days later, on October 25, the *Post* featured yet a second front-page story from Peter A. Jay. "Combat Refusals Called Rare: Pace Incident 'Overblown,'" read the headline. This 600-word account featured an interview with General Wagstaff, who Jay described as "an officer with a reputation for candor." Wagstaff maintained there really was no refusal because in both cases the troops did eventually go out on patrol.[14]

David Halberstam wrote in his book, *The Powers That Be*, that *Washington Post* editors were miffed that the *New York Times* scooped them on the Pentagon Papers release that summer and were trying to play catch-up.[15] Consequently, they may have decided to give these events more play simply because the *Times* didn't. On the other hand, Jay, who was Saigon bureau chief at the time, recalls no special interest or inquiries from his editors that prompted a ratcheting up in coverage and felt himself that the story was relatively routine.[16] The two front-page pieces ran on a Saturday and Monday, so it is also possible it was just a slow news day, rather than some conscious attempt to turn the story into a major news event. Ironically, Richard Boyle singled out the *Washington Post* as one of the participants in what he claimed was the conspiracy to cover up the actions at Pace, but there is absolutely no evidence to support that assertion.[17]

The *Chicago Tribune* provides a good baseline to compare the *Times* and *Post* coverage. The *Tribune* was published in the Midwest, not the East Coast, and it editorially supported President Nixon's war policies, while the *New York Times* and *Washington Post* did not. The *Tribune* ran five articles mentioning Pace during this period. Four were wire service stories in the interior of the paper, which meant the editors thought the news value was only moderate.[18] Interestingly enough, the *Tribune* was one of the few papers to run the UPI version of the first refusal (the version Richard Boyle preferred), along with the AP version.[19] Donald Kirk's article, "Find Viet Vets Feel Rejected, Deceived," on October 31, 1971, represented the *Tribune*'s only bylined story mentioning Pace. That piece included a quotation from a recently returned GI who served with the 11th Armored Cavalry unit that extracted B Battery from Katum. He said he supported the GIs at Pace who balked at the order.[20]

Stars and Stripes, the Defense Department's sponsored daily newspaper, also reported extensively on the border battles, including the events at Pace. *Stars and Stripes* describes itself as the "hometown newspaper of the US military" and can trace its roots back to the Civil War, where it began as a one-page newsletter designed to keep Union soldiers informed about the war's progress. The Pacific Edition, which was the version distributed to the troops in Vietnam, has published continuously since 1945 and claimed a distribution in Vietnam of 125,000 at the height of the U.S. buildup in the late 1960s.[21]

GIs in the rear areas paid a dime for the tabloid-sized daily. Troops in the field, including those at Pace, received theirs free of charge. It usually came in with the U.S. Mail daily resupply helicopter. *Stars and Stripes* ran sixteen articles mentioning Pace between September 28 and October 24, 1971. Most were based on wire service copy. This included a version of the AP account on the first refusal and the UPI story on the second refusal.[22] *Stars and Stripes* also ran its own feature by Private First Class Ken Schultz from FSB Timbuktu quoting Bravo Company GIs complaining the patrol was an offensive not defensive act and quoting Captain Cronin and Lieutenant Shuler defending the idea of the night patrol but denying disobedience of the direct order.[23]

Although *Stars and Stripes* tried to walk a middle line between those who wanted it to operate as an independent news outlet and those who wanted it to be more protective of the Army's image, the GIs at Pace seemed inclined to draw their own conclusions. For example, Sergeant Michael Donze remembered how he and the men in his section compared the counts of incoming rounds reported in *Stars and Stripes* every morning with what they had seen the day before. They felt the reported number of incoming rounds (which came from official Army sources) was always undercounted.[24]

Looking at the newspaper coverage of the events at Pace that fall, it is difficult to make a case that the coverage was inaccurate, inflammatory, or biased. The refusals were described accurately, and efforts were made to put the events in context. Nowhere was there any pattern of bias that related news coverage to the newspaper's editorial position on the Vietnam War. The *New York Times*, clearly the most outspoken editorially, was very low key in its coverage and never even reported on the second refusal. The *Washington Post* got more animated at the end of the siege, but its Saigon bureau did the most of anyone to put these events in context. The *Chicago Tribune*, which supported the president editorially, was the only paper of the three to run the UPI version of the first refusal, which contained more criticism of the president's policies. Even when *Stars and Stripes* reported on the events at Pace, they gave the enlisted men involved an opportunity to express their objections.

During the Vietnam War, the national news magazines played a unique role in reporting on the war. Unlike the television networks and newspapers, they did not operate against the immediacy of a daily deadline; hence, they concentrated on what one scholar has described as "a summary and synthesis of the previous week's events."[25] Three major magazines—*Time*, *Newsweek*, and *U.S. News and World Report*—regularly covered the Vietnam War during this period. They claimed 38 million readers—fewer than newspaper readers, but proportionally more of their subscribers were well-educated opinion leaders.[26] *U.S. News* did not find the events at Pace to be significant enough to merit attention; however, *Time* and *Newsweek* did. Both did one article appearing the last week of October after the first combat refusal had been reported in the newspapers and on TV. *Time* called it "A Question of Protection" in its October 25, 1971, issue. The short (200-word) unsigned article focused on what *Time* described as the "I don't want to be the last man shot" syndrome.[27]

Correspondent Nicholas C. Proffitt did an in-depth analysis for the October 25 issue of *Newsweek* in an 800-word piece titled "Soldiers Who Refuse to Die." Proffitt had an interesting background. The son of a career Army sergeant, he enlisted in the Army himself upon graduation from high school in 1961. He was admitted to West Point but dropped out after one semester. Proffitt completed his three-year military obligation serving as a member of the honor guard at Arlington National Cemetery. He graduated from the University of Arizona with a journalism degree in 1968, then joined *Newsweek*'s Los Angeles bureau. He moved on to the Saigon bureau in 1970 and ended up being Saigon bureau chief in 1971.[28]

Proffitt's account differs significantly from Boyle's. First, Proffitt reported that all three platoon leaders told Cronin the day before that a night ambush was a bad idea.[29] The next day, they went out anyway. This is significant because it supports the conclusion that the refusal by Bravo Company GIs that evening was more a case of a veteran unit of good soldiers balking at a specific order than evidence of some overall breakdown of order and discipline or a political statement. As mentioned previously, Captain Cronin disputes that version, but Lieutenant Coreno supports Proffitt's account.[30] Cronin also disputes Proffitt's description regarding his offer to take point and his promise to not press charges if the individuals involved went out the next day.[31] At least three witnesses support Cronin's statement that he participated in the patrol but did not take point. Recollections differ on whether the troops involved were threatened with court-martial, promised they wouldn't be court-martialed, or if the issue even came up.[32]

Proffitt devotes quite a bit of effort to discussing Richard Boyle's role in the incident. It becomes clear very quickly that Proffitt is not an admirer of Boyle, whom he refers to as a "radical journalist" and a one-time employee of "sensation-seeking *Overseas Weekly*." Proffitt goes on to describe Boyle as having "peddled" his account to Agence France-Presse, which produced what Proffitt describes as a "dramatic rendition of the incident, labeling it as a mutiny." As a final coup de grâce, he quotes unnamed Pentagon officials referring to Boyle's work as "scavenger journalism."[33] In the end, Proffitt comes down pretty much where *Time* was. "The incident at Pace will soon be forgotten," he concludes. "Yet it is not without significance. For an increasing number of GIs, there is a feeling of being forgotten men."[34]

Proffitt is no longer alive, but it is possible to determine where he got his information about events at Pace. Like any good reporter, Proffitt constantly cultivated his own sources. One of those turned out to be former Army enlisted man Richard Brummett. Brummett, like Proffitt, came from a military family. His unusual story began in 1967 when he dropped out of seminary training to volunteer for Vietnam. Originally assigned to the 1st Infantry Division near Saigon, Brummett was subsequently transferred to the newly constituted 1/1st Cavalry Squadron in I Corps in January 1968. He served as a loader in a tank crew. He rotated home and was honorably discharged in July 1968.[35]

One of his fellow soldiers called him the "conscience of the cav," because of his concerns about the effects of the war on soldiers and civilians alike.[36] "I'll never get this country [Vietnam] out of my soul," he would later write. So after telling his parents he was going to Europe, he returned to Vietnam as a credentialed photographer in the summer of 1970. He returned again in August 1971.[37] While on this second visit, Brummett heard about the fighting in the Cambodian border region northwest of Tay Ninh, so he found his way to Fire Support Base Pace. He ended up staying in one of the bunkers with GIs of the 2d Platoon of Bravo Company, 1/12th Cavalry at the same time Richard Boyle arrived and the night ambush aborted.[38]

Pace was a "keep your head down kind of place," Brummett remembered. He did manage to catch a tiny fragment of shrapnel from an RPG that detonated in the chain-link fence surrounding one of the bunkers. When Brummett returned from Pace, he sought out Newsweek's Proffitt, whom he knew well (in fact, Newsweek had helped him get his press credentials), and told him what he had seen, which was at odds with Boyle's report. Proffitt used Brummett's account, along with his interviews of Bravo Company GIs at Firebase Timbuktu, to develop his account debunking Boyle's mutiny story.[39] Editorially, both Time and Newsweek were opposed to the conduct of the war at this point. U.S. News and World Report was supportive. Clearly, U.S. News didn't consider Pace a very significant story. Time did, but only a little. On balance the Proffitt account was probably the most nuanced in terms of point of view. Proffitt, who was clearly most sympathetic to the GIs, which would not endear him to the military brass, was also the most critical of Richard Boyle. Newsweek and the Washington Post shared the same ownership at this time, but the editorial operations were separate. Both the Newsweek and the Washington Post wrap-up stories on Pace were similar in that they represented the best writing about what was or was not going on at Pace and how it fit into a larger context.

By 1971 most informed observers had declared television the most powerful news medium, with a particularly strong impact on public perception regarding the Vietnam War. Much of that thinking has since been disputed, yet the role of TV coverage is still significant, if not for any other reason than key decision makers at the time believed it to be significant.[40] A reported 48 million people watched the evening news on any given night on ABC, CBS, or NBC.[41] Thus, the events at Fire Support Base Pace, which generated twelve separate reports on all three TV networks in October 1971, provides an opportunity to compare TV coverage among the three networks, between the TV networks and the print media, and between the media accounts and reality on the ground.

The television audience first learned of Bravo Company's October 9 refusal on the ABC and CBS evening news broadcasts on the evening of October 11, one day before the stories appeared in the nation's newspapers. Both reports involved the anchors (Harry Reasoner for ABC and Walter Cronkite for CBS) reading copy similar to the AP report, with a map of Vietnam in the background. Both lasted just short of one minute. ABC placed it first in the broadcast; CBS placed it second, indicating they thought it was a significant story.[42]

Both ABC and CBS came back the following day to describe the transfer of Bravo Company from Pace to Timbuktu. Again, the reports involved the anchors reading wire copy, but the time devoted to the story was decreased, and its sequencing dropped in the broadcasts. NBC did not mention the incident in either of its two broadcasts.[43]

October 13 featured two pieces that attempted to address the incident in greater depth. ABC sent reporter Ron Miller to Firebase Timbuktu, where he interviewed, on camera, four members of B Company, including Specialist Four Al Grana, who explained why they refused to go on patrol. This segment went on for three minutes and was placed third that evening.[44] CBS did not run anything that evening, but NBC jumped in for the first time with a commentary from coanchor David Brinkley. He labeled the mission "senseless and suicidal," and went on to say, "Being the last American killed in Vietnam is not a distinction worth having." He closed by agreeing with Republican Senator Hugh Scott of Pennsylvania that "the sooner we get the hell out of there, the better."[45]

The saga of Firebase Pace then took a six-day hiatus from the network news until October 19. On that day, both CBS and NBC (but not ABC) reported on the accidental killing of eighteen South Vietnamese soldiers near Pace by a friendly air strike. NBC added a ninety-second segment featuring a stand-up by reporter Arthur Lord about the day-to-day lives of the GIs at Pace.[46] The final stories on Pace aired on October 22. All three networks, ABC, CBS, and NBC, reported Pace was being evacuated, and the departing soldiers celebrated by drinking whiskey and Kool-Aid. The average length of the three segments was twenty seconds.[47]

In the end, television coverage was very similar to what appeared in print. In fact, the majority of the accounts in this period involved the anchor reading copy very similar to wire service versions. The term "mutiny" was never used. Only two reports lasted longer than a minute. CBS, who had the largest army of correspondents on the ground in Vietnam, took the most limited approach, offering nothing more than reading wire service copy on four segments totaling no more than ninety seconds, although they had done a longer story about Pace in July.[48]

ABC was first out of the box with a major treatment that included interviews with members of Bravo Company at Timbuktu on October 13, but then their interest tapered off. Perhaps they felt there was less of a story there than they first thought. Lieutenant Colonel Stan Tyson, commanding officer of the 1/12th Cavalry, Bravo Company's parent unit, recalls ABC's Ron Miller telling him the whole thing "fell apart," meaning there was no real story there.[49] NBC joined the party late, not reporting anything until David Brinkley's commentary on October 13. Four days later they sent correspondent Arthur Lord out to Pace, where he did a two-minute stand-up. On the afternoon of October 17, Major General Wagstaff sent an update on the situation at Pace to General Abrams. In that message he mentioned that correspondent Art Lord and an NBC film crew were at the base. According to Wagstaff, Lord told the TRAC information officer, "I have never seen a finer bunch of soldiers—morale was high and that is the way I intend to tell it."[50] Lord's report ran on the evening of October 19 and presented a positive description of the day-to-day lives of the GIs at Pace. He didn't mention either refusal. All three networks reported briefly on Pace's evacuation on October 22 and never mentioned Pace again.

What about bias? In the eyes of the Nixon administration, CBS coverage was consistently the most biased against them.[51] But in this case, CBS gave the events the least play. ABC gave it the most attention initially and was regarded as the network news operation least unfriendly to the Nixon administration. NBC ran a stinging commentary from David Brinkley but a positive story from Arthur Lord. Even the most cynical of conspiracy theorists would be hard pressed to see a pattern of bias here.

The Nixon White House did monitor press coverage closely, including accounts of the Vietnam War. White House staffer Pat Buchanan prepared a daily summary of newspaper, news magazine, and network news reports for the president's review. Items were grouped by subject area, and a daily summary could easily total twenty typewritten pages. President Nixon would often write comments in the margin—sometimes just expressing an opinion on the coverage, sometimes directing his staff to do something. These reports are now on file at the Nixon Library in Loma Linda, California. They show the White House did follow press coverage about Pace, beginning with the first reports on October 12, 1971. The entry for that day reads as follows:

ABC led with a report, noted by the other nets, that 5 GIs balked at going out on a patrol but before the issue could come to a head the patrol was canceled. Their commander said the men redeemed themselves by going out on patrol the next morning. EMK called for an immediate investigation: "Any refusal by GIs to engage in combat is a cause of extremely serious concern . . . the events—demand . . . a full exploration by the Admin." The Senator also expressed concern that the incident took place on the Cambodian border in light of Church-Cooper.[52]

The underlining above appears to be the president's. EMK is Senator Edward M. Kennedy. Church-Cooper is the amendment banning reintroduction of U.S. ground troops into Cambodia. The summaries about Pace appear fairly regularly through the end of the siege of October, including Nicholas Proffitt's story in *Newsweek*, but no additional comments are noted.[53]

A cynic might say the lack of a reaction of the Nixon White House proves the press conspired with the Army to play down the significance of the events at Pace. However, there is absolutely no evidence to support this. More likely, the White House had other priorities in October 1971, including upcoming trips to Russia and China, the battle with Senate Democrats over a Supreme Court nominee, leaks from the State Department, and what columnists Evan and Novak would say about him in their forthcoming book—all of which received margin notes from Nixon to his staff directing them to follow up.

What the Nixon administration liked or didn't like is probably not the most appropriate test of fairness. In his official history of the U.S. Army and the media in Vietnam, William M. Hammond described the press coverage of Pace as an example of "even handed" reporting, except for Boyle's mutiny charge.[54] Based on a careful examination of print and electronic reports from a range of media outlets, it appears, in this case, that Hammond's conclusion is correct. Despite all the controversy in 1971, the press was able to relay to the American public a reasonably balanced account of what was going on at this remote border outpost.

However, the press was less successful at being able to describe to its readers and viewers what the real mission was of the remaining ground troops. The confusion surfaced early in 1971 and grew throughout the year. As described previously, Secretary Laird followed President Nixon's January 1971 statement that the end of the U.S. combat role was "in sight" by issuing a confusing set of statements of his own referring to a midsummer date.[55] The drama repeated itself after the August press conference in which President Nixon asserted that U.S. troops were now in "defensive positions." Secretary Laird followed up quickly to explain what the president really meant, and that tortured explanation is what provoked Specialist White's letter.[56]

But the mother of all clarifications came in mid-September, just five days before the North Vietnamese surrounded Firebase Pace and threatened the whole border area. On September 21, 1971, *Pacific Stars and Stripes* carried a UPI report on Secretary Laird's efforts to debunk speculation that U.S. forces would terminate its ground combat role entirely, assuming only advisory and air support roles after June 30, 1972. Laird's message was a mixed one, saying these reports were "speculation," but that any such announcements regarding a change of mission would be made by the president, perhaps as early as November. Laird then went on to declare that "Phase I of the Vietnamization program, which dealt with the turning over of ground responsibility to the forces of Vietnam, has been virtually completed." Phase II would be completing the takeover of artillery and logistical operations (which was rumored to be coming in June). Phase III would be to put American troops in a purely advisory role, which they had been in before the big buildup in 1965.[57]

UPI even tried to help the secretary by pointing out that "the Pentagon Chief [Laird] is known to be anxious to avoid making optimistic predictions like those which came back to haunt the Johnson Administration." The wire service went on to quote "Pentagon officials," confirming that U.S. troops were engaged in "active defense," meaning that they "patrol wide areas around many military installations, but they no longer conduct the long search and destroy missions which dominated the war for years." The report closed with the reminder that the U.S. weekly death toll had averaged between 14 and 18 since August 4, compared with more than 500 during the Tet Offensive.[58]

It is easy to see why GIs at Pace, or any other outpost where the enemy was active, might be confused about what their mission really was or wasn't after reading this. In less than 500 words UPI used at least ten different word combinations to describe U.S. operations, including the following:

"assume only advisory and air support roles"
"formally ending offensive combat activities"
"ground responsibility virtually completed"
"moved into defensive positions"
"artillery and support operations"
"active defense"
"protect remaining US positions"
"patrol wide areas around many military installations"
"no longer conduct the long search and destroy missions"[59]

The culprit here is not UPI, which was attempting to define policy in a constructive way, but the efforts of the administration to have it both ways when it came to explaining its goals. The senior civilian leaders—President Nixon, National Security Advisor Kissinger, and Defense Secretary Laird—often disagreed; but in this case, they agreed strongly that they wanted to head off any moves in Congress to set a fixed withdrawal date or cut off aid to South Vietnam. Consequently, they wanted to announce that U.S. troops were out of ground combat as soon as possible.[60]

General Abrams and other senior military leaders felt strongly that they needed the flexibility to mount preemptive operations against the enemy in order to protect both U.S. and South Vietnamese troops. They also worried that if these ground actions produced casualties, as they most surely would, it could create a credibility problem after declaring U.S. troops were out of ground combat.[61]

According to the Army's official history, the outcome was an agreement among all the principals to use the term "dynamic defense" or "active defense."[62] While "active defense" gave the White House what it wanted to show, the success of Vietnamization, it also gave senior commanders the flexibility to pursue the enemy however they felt it appropriate, running the gamut from a night ambush 500 meters from Firebase Pace to the pursuit of the 33d NVA Regiment all across the northeast corner of Military Region III. But it left the troops in the field and their junior officers holding the bag with no choice but to work things out as best they could.

CHAPTER TWENTY-TWO

The Press and the M-Word

In addition to the refusals at Firebase Pace, three combat-refusal incidents are most often cited as evidence of mutinous behavior by American combat troops in Vietnam. These are a refusal by soldiers of the Americal Division to assault a bunker complex south of Da Nang in August 1969; a refusal of a company of the 1st Air Cavalry Division to walk down a road on the Cambodian border northwest of Saigon in April 1970; and the refusal of a cavalry unit of the Americal Division to advance down Highway 9 near the Laotian border in March 1971 (see fig. 22.1). In fact, Richard Heinl cited these three incidents as examples in his June 1971 piece "Collapse of the Armed Forces" in Armed Forces Journal.[1] How the press covered these three incidents compared to how they covered the refusals at Pace tells us something about the relationship between the press, the commanders, the troops, and the events on the ground as the war slowly wound down.

The August 26, 1969, incident involving members of Alpha Company, 3/31st Infantry of the Americal Division was the first documented case of a combat refusal during the Vietnam War and, as such, received quite a bit of attention. The basic facts are not in dispute. In five days of heavy fighting against dug-in Vietnamese regulars in the Song Chang Valley, between one-half and one-third of the exhausted company was killed or wounded. Their commander, a second lieutenant who had been in Vietnam less than a month, radioed back to battalion headquarters that his men were tired, thirsty, hungry, and scared, and that five refused to move down the hill to assault an enemy bunker. The frustrated acting company commander (2nd Lieutenant Eugene Shurtz) had this exchange with his battalion commander (Lieutenant Colonel Robert Bacon) on a field telephone:

> Shurtz: I am sorry, sir, but my men refused to go. . . . We cannot move out.
> Bacon: Repeat that, please. Have you told them what it means to disobey orders under fire?
> Shurtz: I think they understand, but some of them simply had enough—they are broken. There are boys here who have only 90 days left in Viet Nam. They want to go home in one piece. The situation is psychic here.[2]

Colonel Bacon sent out his executive officer and a senior NCO with orders to get the reluctant soldiers moving, which they did. No charges were filed, but the unfortunate lieutenant was replaced by a more senior captain and reassigned to a desk job. AP photographer Horst Faas happened to be in battalion headquarters

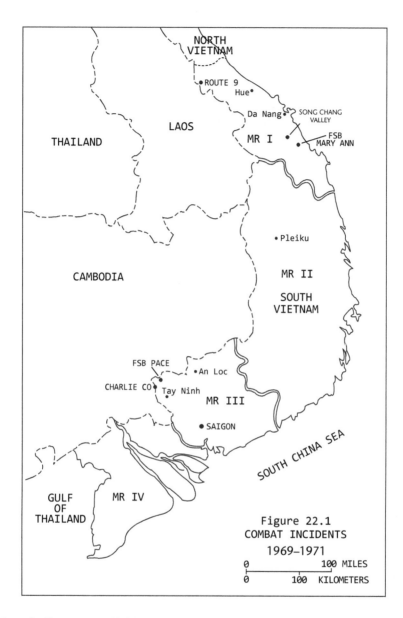

Figure 22.1
COMBAT INCIDENTS
1969–1971

when the lieutenant called in. He jotted down the conversation and turned it over to colleague Peter Arnett, who after confirming the events with battalion head-quarters filed the story with the AP.[3] The *New York Times* printed the account on page 1 in its August 26 edition.[4] It followed with another piece on August 27 that the young lieutenant had been relieved.[5] That same day (August 27), all three net-works ran segments on Lieutenant Shurtz's dismissal. The average length of the story, which involved the anchor reading text in the studio, was less than thirty seconds.[6]

The next day (August 28), the *Times* ran a page 2 description of Lieutenant Shurtz's visit to his old unit.[7] Then, as additional information became available, the nature of the coverage began to change. The *Times* sent reporter James Sterba out to the field to talk to soldiers about the refusal. In a front-page analysis titled "G.I.'s in Battle Area Shrug Off the Story of Balky Company A," Sterba reported that several of the GIs and Marines had told him that they had witnessed similar incidents, in which scared soldiers griped about heading back into combat but after a pep talk went in anyway. "Why the men of Company A refused to fight seemed simple to those interviewed," Sterba observed. "None of these explanations concerned fighting for lost causes, fighting for no apparent reason, antiwar sentiment, troop withdrawals or the Paris peace talks."[8]

Then the following day the *Times* ran an AP dispatch quoting Lieutenant Shurtz saying that only five men had actually refused the order, not the whole company, although it also reported other GIs saying the whole company supported the five reluctant soldiers.[9] In the days following the initial AP report, all three TV networks sent correspondents out to the field to talk to the troops. Richard Threlkeld did a long lead item for the CBS *Evening News* on August 28, in which he talked to both officers and enlisted men who told him essentially what Sterba reported— this was not some sort of political statement or mutiny but a temporary refusal on the part of some tired and scared GIs.[10] ABC ran a similar but shorter story that same night.[11] NBC followed the next day.[12]

After a week of intense press coverage, it looked like the controversy was beginning to finally wind down. Then, on August 27, respected *New York Times* columnist James "Scotty" Reston jumped into the fray with a 1,000-word opinion piece titled "A Whiff of Mutiny in Vietnam." Reston wrote, "In every American war there have been isolated incidents of mutiny among the troops. It is the tragic human pattern. There is a breaking point where discipline, duty and even loyalty to men at your side are overwhelmed by fear and death and a paralyzing feeling of the senselessness of the whole bloody operation. And we are now getting a glimpse of it in Vietnam. . . . For the more the President says he's for peace, the more troops he withdraws from Vietnam and Thailand, the more he concedes that Southeast Asia is not really vital to the security of the United States, the harder it is to ask for the lives of the men of Company A."[13]

New York Times reporter James Sterba took a differing view in his report written from the field at Landing Zone West four days later. He argued this incident was more of an aberration, more like a family squabble that somehow got out into the neighborhood, as opposed to some sort of political statement.[14]

Time magazine weighed in with its own point of view in a long, unsigned statement in its September 5 edition. *Time*, which by that point had editorially turned critical of the war, now turned critical of Arnett's reporting and Reston's "Whiff of Mutiny" comments. "Neither man (Faas or Arnett) . . . saw or spoke to anyone at Alpha first hand; no reporter did until week's end," *Time* said. "Their basic account held up, but their report that 'nearly all the soldiers of A Company broke' was plainly exaggerated. The Army insisted that the incident was not unusual and certainly did not amount to a 'whiff of mutiny,' as *New York Times* columnist James Reston called it."[15] While the *New York Times* and the national TV networks viewed this story as a big deal, not everyone shared their view. The *Washington Post* didn't report on it at all; nor did the *Chicago Tribune*, *Newsweek*, or *U.S. News*.

Reporting Alpha Company's refusal presented a major challenge to both *Stars and Stripes* and the Armed Forces Radio and Television Networks (AFVN). It helped spark a major disagreement over the proper role of the military in-house news organizations. Tensions between the news staff and their superiors had been building for some time when Specialist Five Michael Maxwell, a news editor at AFVN, went public with allegations that his superiors had ordered him not to use commercial television reports on the incident.[16]

The controversy ratcheted up another notch when word leaked out that Army Colonel James Campbell, the newly assigned editor in chief of *Pacific Stars and Stripes*, branded the newspaper the "Hanoi Herald" for what he described as "treason" in its coverage of the incident.[17] The dispute dragged on through early 1970 until it was resolved by MACV. In a classic bureaucratic move, Colonel Campbell, the flashpoint of the controversy, was quietly reassigned. But according to Army historian William Hammond, *Stars and Stripes* and AFVN were quietly told to frame their stories more positively.[18]

Alpha Company's refusal in the Song Chang Valley would be the first combat refusal story, but not the last. In the spring of 1970, veteran CBS correspondent Jack Laurence wanted to get out into the field to show viewers what it was like for the grunts on the ground as the war wound down. With support of the Army brass, he attached himself to a unit of the 1st Cavalry Division operating in the jungles of War Zone C near the Cambodian border, not far from where Firebase Pace would be built a year later. It would be a 1970 version of an embedded correspondent. He'd been out in the field with Charlie Company, 2/7th Cavalry for a week and had already filed a very positive report about the affection and respect the men of Charlie Company had for their commanding officer, Captain Robert Jackson.[19]

However, Jackson had a heart condition and had to be sent back to the States. Captain Al Rice succeeded him and had been in command for less than a week. While out on patrol they received an order from higher headquarters to change direction and follow a dirt road for a helicopter extraction for an unexplained reason. Charlie Company's point squad, who were veteran soldiers, told their platoon leader, who told Captain Rice, that Captain Jackson had taught them to cut their own trail rather than take the road in order to avoid ambush. Rice replied that orders were orders and they needed to move out. The entire platoon refused while CBS cameras captured the back and forth on film, including sound.[20]

Finally, a new order came back to advance down the road a short distance for a helicopter extraction, which the company reluctantly agreed to do. After returning to the relative safety of their base camp, some of the enlisted men teed off on Captain Rice, referring to his order as "a suicide walk."

"Was there a rebellion today?' Laurence asked Specialist Four Grady Lee.

"You might call it that. Back in the world they call it rebellion. Here it's just downright refusal. We had the whole company—CO says OK, we're going to walk through it and the whole company says no, negative. We've heard too many companies; too many battalions want to walk the road. They get blown away."[21]

After Laurence returned from the field, concerned Army officers, including Brigade Commander Colonel William Oches, called him and his crew in for a conference. They asked Laurence what he planned to report. He said he would describe it as a rebellion. They objected and also shared with him the reason for the move: A B-52 strike had been called into that area to head off an attack against friendly troops. They couldn't share that information with Captain Rice at the time because Charlie Company did not have an encrypted radio. Laurence confirmed what Oches told him and added that explanation to the story, which ran on the CBS Evening News on April 9.[22]

The AP produced its own account of the incident about a week later. They quoted Lieutenant Colonel Robert Drudik, the deputy brigade commander, who was in contact with both the troops on the ground and the B-52s when the events took place. Drudik praised the troops for questioning the order. "Thank God we've got young men who question," he said. "The young men in the Army today aren't dummies, they are not automatons. They think." Stars and Stripes ran the AP version in its April 16 edition.[23]

After that, interest seemed to be dying down. None of the other networks or newspapers picked it up. No charges were filed, and Charlie Company headed back out to the field. Then, Newsweek ran a small, nonbylined summary in its April 20 issue, focusing on the refusal.[24] Apparently this was too much for the Army. They told Laurence his permission to travel with Charlie Company was withdrawn because it was "hard for morale."[25] CBS protested all the way to the Pentagon, but to no avail. Three weeks later U.S. forces assaulted into Cambodia. John Laurence grabbed one of the first helicopters out and found himself with Charlie Company 2/7th Cavalry at LZ X-Ray. It turned out that Charlie Company was leading the assault into the Fishhook area in hopes of finding COSVN. Laurence also found that Charlie Company GIs and Captain Rice had come to understand and respect each other.[26] Laurence later acknowledged the word "rebellion" was probably inappropriate.[27] In fairness to Laurence, the overall approach was balanced and supportive of both the GIs and their commanders. In the divisive climate of the early 1970s, it drew a certain amount of interest because it had been captured so well on film.[28]

The last combat refusal widely reported prior to Pace occurred on March 22, 1971, on Route 9 near the Laotian border. The AP quoted U.S. military spokesmen as saying a company commander was relieved of duty when two platoons of troopers (about fifty-three men) from Bravo Troop, 1st Squadron/1st Cavalry of the American Division refused to advance down the highway to recover sensitive equipment from a downed helicopter. This is the same incident described in chapter 16. Unlike previous refusals, these GIs did not agree to go out later. They were replaced by another unit that finished the job. No action was taken against any of the fifty-three GIs who refused to go. This caused a fair deal of controversy within the Army. Some officers felt the company commander, Captain Carlos Poveda, was by all accounts a good officer who was made a scapegoat by his superiors.[29]

Of the three incidents, this one probably came the closest to a breakdown, but it received fairly muted press attention. The *New York Times* did run an account on page 1, but half of it was a rehash of the August 1969 refusal.[30] *Time* ran a small piece. CBS and ABC each gave it twenty seconds on the evening news on March 22.[31] NBC News and the *Washington Post* didn't report on it at all. *Stars and Stripes* ran the AP account of the incident, which quoted Brigadier General John Hill, commander of the Task Force, who acknowledged the incident happened but argued it should not be "blown out of proportion."[32]

The role of the press in a free society in wartime is always a matter of contention. This would be especially true in Vietnam where the press had unprecedented access to military operations and where the war itself would be long and controversial. And, next to war crime allegations, nothing is more emotionally charged than reports of combat refusals, rebellion, or mutiny, as the case may be. Comparing the press reports of the refusals at Pace in October 1971 with the refusals that preceded it reveals a number of similarities that identify the challenges facing both the press and the military command structure.

First, it confirms the wisdom of the warning that the first reports from the battlefield are usually incorrect, or at least incomplete. At Pace, the initial account from Richard Boyle about a mutiny was clearly exaggerated. The first dispatches from Song Chang Valley in 1969 were incomplete. The refusal involved five men, not the whole company, although the whole company appeared to support them. On the Cambodian border in 1970, John Laurence did not find out until a day later that the order to move along the road was prompted by an impending B-52 strike. But, in all three cases, the mainstream press worked to correct the record and present this additional information to readers or viewers. For the most part, the press was careful about word choice, using "balked" or "refused" to describe the actions of the soldiers involved, instead of a more emotionally loaded term like "mutiny." In the one case, where John Laurence used the term "rebellion," he acknowledged later he had made a mistake.

In all these cases, reporters happened to be there when the events occurred. There is no evidence that they fomented rebellion or anything else. In all four cases the reports included both sides of the story, often buttressed by additional on-site work. Despite allegations of a pack mentality, different news organizations used their own judgment to decide what to report or what not to report. The *New York Times* gave major play to the refusal by Alpha Company in 1969. The *Washington Post* and *Chicago Tribune* did not. Even the *Times* columnists Jim Reston and James Sterba took opposing viewpoints. CBS gave play to John Laurence's 1970 story, but the other two networks and the daily newspapers did not. The *New York Times* decided the second refusal at Pace in 1971 was not worth reporting. The *Washington Post* thought otherwise. *Time* thought the 1971 incident on Route 9 was worth reporting; *Newsweek* did not.

To professional military people conditioned to close ranks once the higher ups make a command decision, these deviations from the party line must have appeared insane. But, in nongovernment-run news organizations at that time, differences of opinion were valued as a source of strength. It is also clear that as the war dragged on, the significance of combat refusals as a news item declined. The reports of Alpha Company's refusal in 1969 generated the largest number of lead stories of the group. By the time Bravo Troop balked on Route 9, it was barely news. When the Pace story broke six months later, the mainstream media who investigated the story spent more time explaining what it wasn't (a mutiny), than what it was.

The two exceptions to this rule were Richard Boyle and Robert Heinl. Boyle and Heinl couldn't be more different in background or perspective. Boyle, in his mid-twenties, worked for *Ramparts*, an icon of the political left. Heinl, a retired Marine officer, wrote for the *Detroit News*. Yet both sensationalized these stories. The flaws in Boyle's approach have been discussed. Heinl's slant is equally obvious. For example, he wrote that "an entire company of the 196th Light Infantry Brigade publicly sat down on the battlefield."[33] In fact, five men temporarily refused to move on a bunker complex after days of heavy fighting where they lost a third of their comrades and most of their leaders. Although the rest of the company did support the reticent five, they all moved out together to soldier on an hour later.

Heinl described the 1970 road incident with John Laurence as follows: "Later that year, another rifle company from the famed 1st Air Cavalry Division flatly refused—on CBS TV—to advance down a dangerous trail."[34] What Heinl failed to mention was that neither Charlie Company nor its commanding officer knew why they had been ordered down the trail. Nor did he let his readers know that Charlie 2/7th Cavalry had an excellent combat record (which Laurence captured on film) both before and after the incident.

Regarding the Route 9 incident, Heinl wrote: "The issue of 'combat refusal,' an official euphemism for disobedience of orders to fight—the soldier's gravest crime—has only recently been again precipitated on the frontier of Laos by Troop B, 1st Cavalry's mass refusal to recapture their Captain's command vehicle containing communication gear, codes and other secret operations orders."[35] What Heinl failed to point out in this case was that these same soldiers had risked their lives to rescue their commanding officer from his damaged vehicle minutes before.

"Publicly sat down on the battlefield . . . flatly refused . . . mass refusal." Heinl's choice of words here painted a picture of a massive breakdown of discipline and order. That was, of course, his point. But his point was wrong. Stringing together three separate incidents involving maybe 300–400 soldiers, nineteen months apart, does not stand on its own, especially when other legitimate news organizations did a much more balanced job of describing these incidents at the time they occurred.

Although not a combat refusal, the March 1971 attack on Fire Support Base Mary Ann provides another opportunity to view how the press treated bad news. The report on the attack did make the front page of both the *New York Times* and *Washington Post*.[36] Both accounts were similar in that they quoted Army sources that thirty-three Americans were killed and seventy-six wounded; the largest toll for a single attack in nearly a year. The *Chicago Tribune* ran an AP version on page 6 the next day, but was the only newspaper of the three to mention that Army officers conceded the base was taken by surprise.[37] All three TV networks carried short segments on the attack on their evening newscasts.[38] The next day all three had reporters out in the field who described how carelessness and overconfidence contributed to the success of the enemy attack.[39] *Stars and Stripes* sent its own reporter to Chu Lai to cover the story. He reported on the large number of GIs killed and wounded but made no mention of reported laxness among the defenders.[40]

Once again *Newsweek*'s Nicholas Proffitt provided one of the most insightful accounts. After talking with survivors of the attack, Proffitt explained how the defenders' unpreparedness contributed to the tragedy at Mary Ann.[41] But, he also debunked allegations that this happened because most of the soldiers on the base, including the perimeter guards, were high at the time of the attack.

By all accounts, press coverage in this case was fair and complete. It didn't whitewash the lack of vigilance on the part of the officers and enlisted men at Mary Ann, but it didn't slip into hysteria and speculation. That would come later from some historians who should have known better. Supporters of the war criticized the press in this period for focusing only on negative events as "news."

But the record does not support this. As documented previously, a number of reporters went out of their way to get out to the field and issue positive reports on the activities of American GIs. They also reported favorably on the progress of Vietnamization. For example, in May 1971 Iver Peterson of the New York Times visited U.S. commanders and their troops in all four military regions of Vietnam to asses the impact of Vietnamization on the security of the remaining U.S. troops. "Pullout Is Not Seen as Threat to G.I.'s in Field" read the headline in the June 1, 1971, New York Times. Peterson concluded that the danger to U.S. soldiers in the field had not increased, despite a 70 percent reduction in troop strength over the previous two years.[42]

When it came to drug abuse, the 1971 press coverage was much less balanced and much more sensationalized. As discussed earlier, some of the coverage described an epidemic that turned out to be significantly exaggerated. However, it is also fair to point out that most of what the press reported in this period came from public officials who were presumed to be in a position to know. This included the president himself, as well as members of his staff, congressional leaders of both parties, and various experts.[43] Although the problem they described was a real one, its exaggeration politically benefited incumbent officials who wanted to show concerned voters they were on top of this problem and were determined to solve it. The big losers in this mini drama were the thousands of GIs who did their duty only to return home under a cloud of suspicion—not because of who they were or what they did, but because they were stereotyped as drug addicts.

This is not to say the U.S. Army in Vietnam wasn't showing the strain of a long and unpopular war. For every incident reported, there were many others that were not. But if these three or four examples of combat refusal are the best the Army's critics can come up with to prove that combat units out in the field were close to mutiny or collapse, their case is not a very compelling one. Perhaps the ultimate irony here is that while the reporting of John Sterba, John Laurence, Nicholas Proffitt, and Peter Jay have stood the test of time since 1971, the inflammatory words from the pens of Richard Boyle and Robert Heinl have generated the most attention.

Clearly, the conflict between the press's desire to report what they saw and the military's concern about the impact of "negative" stories on morale was never really resolved. Perhaps the best description of the conflict comes from William Hammond:

> The Saigon correspondents clearly sympathized with the military services' attempts to solve their problems, but they were aware that an army without discipline lacked the means of survival and remained constantly on the alert for the worst. The military, in turn, resented the attention. As had Campbell with his allusions to the "Hanoi Herald," they put loyalty to the institution

they served first and refused to believe that the situation was as bad as some news reports made it seem. The press had already demonstrated, however, that the best reporters, by virtue of their many contacts, sometimes had a better grasp of the war's unmanageable human element than the policy makers supposedly in control.[44]

The press's focus on drug abuse notwithstanding, it is fair to say that, on balance, the press contributed more than it took away. For the most part, both the print and broadcast media presented a balanced picture of what was going on and endeavored to put these confusing events in an appropriate context. In some cases, individual reporters put themselves in harm's way along with the troops in order to help the folks back home better understand what the soldiers sent to Vietnam in their name faced on a day-to-day basis.

PART FOUR

The Bigger Picture

CHAPTER TWENTY-THREE

South Vietnamese Allies

Although the fate of the 200 American GIs at Pace may have attracted the most attention in the U.S. media, 20,000 South Vietnamese troops operating in the Cambodian border area also heavily influenced the outcome on the ground. Pace was somewhat unusual in this regard because it represented one of the few cases where American ground troops were very dependent on South Vietnamese ground troops while under enemy attack. This provides some revealing insights as to how the South Vietnamese soldiered on and how their American allies responded.

As part of the Nixon administration's plan to disengage from Vietnam, the South Vietnamese forces took over a large share of the fighting. The withdrawal of U.S. troops began in mid-1969 and was completed with the signing of the Paris Peace Accords in early 1973. This means the efforts to defend Fire Support Base Pace in September and October 1971 took place about two-thirds of the way through this process.

The effort to Vietnamize the war in Military Region III began in earnest in early 1969. The region's senior U.S. commander, Lieutenant General Julian J. Ewell, replicated a program he developed when he commanded the U.S. 9th division in 1968, except on a wider scale. He wanted to pair every major ARVN unit with an American counterpart. They would jointly operate in the same area as part of a buddy system. For example, the ARVN Airborne would be paired with the U.S. 1st Cavalry Division, the ARVN 25th Division would be paired with the U.S. 25th Division, and so on.[1]

Ewell's counterpart, Lieutenant General Do Cao Tri, who himself had just assumed command of ARVN III Corps in August 1968, liked the idea. Ewell and Tri jointly kicked off the program in July under the name of Dong Tien (Forward Together). As a first step, they moved both Vietnamese and American units away from Saigon, where they'd been since Tet, and toward enemy base areas on the Vietnam-Cambodian border.[2] The first real test of Dong Tien came ten months later, when both U.S. and South Vietnamese troops were given the go-ahead signal to attack across the border into Cambodia.

Despite the hyperbole about capturing COSVN, the primary military objective of the 1970 invasion into Cambodian sanctuaries by U.S. and South Vietnamese troops was to disrupt the North Vietnamese logistical infrastructure. This would hopefully set back the enemy long enough to buy time to withdraw the remaining American ground troops north and northwest of Saigon while building up the capability of the South Vietnamese units taking their place. The window opened by this action was supposed to be from six to eighteen months.[3]

MACV declared the Cambodian operation a success because it expelled, at least temporarily, the North Vietnamese from their Cambodian sanctuaries. Both U.S. and independent observers thought the South Vietnamese generally fought well; however, they were still dogged by systemic weaknesses that would haunt them until the end of the war. While elite troops such as the ARVN Airborne, Rangers, and Armored Cavalry met or exceeded expectations, the line infantry units did not. Shortcomings included weak leadership at the division level and over dependence on U.S. airpower instead of their organic artillery.[4]

Shortly after the Cambodian operation ended in June 1970, the withdrawal of American troops from the area between Saigon and the Cambodian border accelerated. The Army's 1st Infantry Division had already departed prior to the invasion. Now they were joined by the 25th Division, two-thirds of the 1st Cavalry Division, and a laundry list of support units, all of whom were gone by the spring of 1971.[5] That meant by the fall of 1971, when Pace came under attack, only five maneuver battalions (or about 5,000 Americans) remained to protect U.S. installations in the Third Military Region, compared to thirty-two maneuver battalions eighteen months earlier.

South Vietnamese army units had been upgraded in this interim with better weapons and intensified training so they could take the place of the departed Americans. This included the ARVN 5th, 18th, and 25th Divisions, all of whom were previously assigned to the border areas protecting Saigon and its populous environs.[6] One of the first tasks of the upgraded ARVN came in the now-vacated enemy sanctuaries in southwestern Cambodia. U.S. ground troops were no longer allowed into Cambodia, although they could provide air and artillery support from bases on the South Vietnamese side of the border. U.S. and South Vietnamese planners agreed the mission of the upgraded South Vietnamese ground troops would be to keep the Communist forces out of their historic border area base camps so they could not infiltrate back into the more populous areas of South Vietnam.[7]

The border areas remained relatively quiet for the first six months after the spring 1970 Cambodian incursion. But by January 1971, the MACV saw the enemy was returning to its border sanctuaries and agreed it was time to take advantage of the remaining dry season and go on the offensive. Approximately 10,000 South Vietnamese troops, including armor and mechanized infantry supported by U.S. air and artillery, blitzed across the border to drive the enemy even farther away.[8] The operation called "Toan Thong (Total Victory) 1/71," consisted of two phases. The first was aimed at clearing the remaining North Vietnamese forces out of their bases in the Chup Rubber Plantation about ten miles deep into Cambodia and eighty miles northwest of Saigon. The second phase involved a drive into the Dambe Valley about 40 miles deeper into Cambodia in order to destroy enemy bases there and capture the Cambodian town of Kratie (see fig. 23.1).

On January 31, 1971, the lead forces charged north along Highway 22 from their assembly area at Thien Ngon. Supported by U.S. heavy and medium artillery from Firebase Lanyard, they drove northwest into Cambodia along Highway 7. The South Vietnamese troops advanced confidently under the leadership of General Tri, one of their most aggressive and respected commanders. By February 22, the first phase had been successfully completed. Attention then turned to Kratie and the Dambe Valley just forty miles away.[9]

The next day, February 23, General Tri was killed in a helicopter crash, an event that would have a profound impact on this operation and the border battles to follow. The charge into Cambodia stopped dead for a week as shaken U.S. and South Vietnamese commanders pondered what to do.[10] Normally a successor would be expected to be elevated into command from one of the fallen leader's key subordinates. But U.S. advisers and their Vietnamese counterparts considered all three of Tri's division commanders unsuited to the job.[11] Tri himself had never done much to groom a successor in the event something happened to him.[12] Eventually, the South Vietnamese Command named Lieutenant General Nguyen Minh to succeed General Tri.

Minh began his military career in 1950 serving as an airborne officer with the Vietnamese forces, fighting alongside the French against the Viet Minh. He steadily worked his way up the chain of command, leading the 21st ARVN Division in 1965. The senior American commander in the area described him as "very temperamental and has frequently requested relief when under stress" and recommended his removal.[13] Instead, he was promoted in 1968 to command of the coveted Capital Military District surrounding Saigon, in large part because of his close ties to President Thieu.[14] Now Minh commanded the entire Military Region III, the area that included Saigon, as well as the Cambodian border region to the north and west. One historian described this assignment as "the most important South Vietnamese field command of the war."[15] Minh's initial instinct upon assuming command was caution. He decided to order a withdrawal.[16]

Sensing an opportunity, the North Vietnamese struck back. Elements of the 7th and 9th NVA Divisions sprang a series of ambushes, decimating Minh's retreating columns. The South Vietnamese reportedly lost 1,000 men in a single day.[17] Finally, after shedding a great deal of blood, and under protective cover from U.S. helicopter gunships and B-52s, the thinned out column crossed back across the south border by mid-March. Fortunately for General Minh, this debacle did not receive a lot of attention in the U.S. press. At that moment they were distracted by an even bigger story, the ARVN's retreat from Laos.

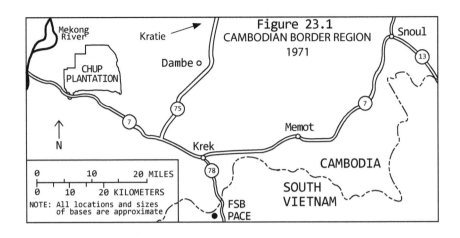

Figure 23.1
CAMBODIAN BORDER REGION
1971

The North Vietnamese weren't about to let up. In late June 1971, almost a year to the day that the U.S. Cambodian invasion ended, North Vietnamese regulars from the 5th and 7th NVA Divisions attacked the South Vietnamese firebases protecting Snoul, the Cambodian rubber plantation town they'd lost to American troops in May 1970. While working over the firebases with mortars and rockets, they also cut off the road (Highway 13) that served as Snoul's only land supply line.[18]

The South Vietnamese decided to mount a relief effort and sent an armored column north from Katum along Highway 13. Meanwhile, the South Vietnamese forces at Snoul were supposed to break out to the south and meet the relief column halfway. But the relief column from Katum ran into enemy resistance and stalled short of its objective. The retreating column moving south from Snoul did reach its first day's objective, only to be attacked by a strong enemy force just before dark. The South Vietnamese soldiers panicked, turning the retreat into a rout. Stragglers trickled into Vietnam over the next several days, having abandoned most of their vehicles and heavy equipment.[19]

Unlike the Dambe debacle, which went largely unreported, the American press jumped all over this one. South Vietnamese army spokesmen tried to spin the action as a "realignment," but no one was buying it. The AP filed a report describing the South Vietnamese forces at Snoul as in retreat and "badly battered."[20] On June 27 the *New York Times* followed up with a bylined story reporting South Vietnamese casualties in the operation were nearly 2,000 dead, wounded, and missing, four times greater than what the Saigon government was admitting. The same article claimed the Communists were in control of three-fourths of the Cambodian countryside and quoted Cambodian officials complaining the South Vietnamese were not doing enough to stop the enemy from overrunning their country.[21]

Criticism of the South Vietnamese performance at Dambe and Snoul was not limited to the press. Major General Wagstaff, senior U.S. Commander in Military Region III, characterized the Snoul battle as a "debacle" for the South Vietnamese Army in a confidential report.[22] General Donn Starry, who commanded a U.S. Armored task force in the 1970 Cambodian operation, labeled these operations a "disaster" in a postwar analysis.[23]

The significance of these two defeats in Cambodia cannot be underestimated. In February 1971 Defense Secretary Laird pointed out the South Vietnamese offensive in Cambodia "involves more forces on both sides" than the much more highly publicized operations in Laos going on at the same time.[24] Now in July, after twenty-four months of Vietnamization, South Vietnamese troops had suffered setbacks in Laos and Cambodia. They could not afford yet another.

This was the situation when the Allied Command learned in September that the North Vietnamese were on the move against another isolated string of outposts on the Cambodian border, including Fire Support Base Pace. Whether on his own or as a result of prodding from his U.S. advisers, General Minh had apparently learned his lesson from the retreats at Dambe and Snoul. This time, the South Vietnamese decided to stand and fight. Minh moved quickly to bring in reinforcements in the form of the ARVN Airborne Division.[25] The ARVN Airborne was regarded as one of the elite units of the South Vietnamese Army. Despite its name, it did not normally arrive on the battlefield by parachuting from airplanes. Instead, it was designed to be highly mobile by use of helicopters. As such, it served, along with the South Vietnamese Marines, as the Strategic Reserve for the entire South Vietnamese Army. The training of South Vietnamese Airborne troops dated back to the days of the French. In 1968 several separate battalions were consolidated into an Airborne Division. Their ranks were filled with the pick of the best soldiers South Vietnam could muster. Their leadership, training, and equipment were regarded as first rate.[26]

The ARVN Airborne Division had played a major role in the invasion into Laos in the spring of 1971. As the offensive bogged down against strong North Vietnamese resistance, U.S. officers began to express concern about the division's leadership and its willingness to fight. In a controversial decision, President Thieu pulled the Airborne Division out of the Laotian offensive to reduce casualties and preserve its fighting power. Critics charged that the real motive was to preserve the Airborne's other mission—protection against a possible coup.[27] By the fall, the Airborne Division's losses of both men and equipment in Laos had been replaced.

On September 26, the North Vietnamese initiated their attacks in the border area, including on Firebase Alpha in Cambodia, which protected the ARVN positions near Krek. They also attacked Pace, Thien Ngon, and Hung Dao, which defended Route 22, the main supply line from Vietnam to the forces at Krek (see fig. 6.1). These tactics were very similar to the Dambe and Snoul battles earlier that year. The next day (September 27), Minh airlifted a two-battalion Airborne Task Force to reinforce his positions around Krek. By September 29, a second 1,200 man Airborne Brigade arrived in Tay Ninh with orders to sweep north up Highway 22 to the border. By October 2 they were joined by yet another Airborne Brigade air assaulted into the areas east and west of Hung Dao.

Assisted by U.S. B-52 strikes, U.S. and South Vietnamese tactical air strikes, helicopter gunships, and artillery, the South Vietnamese column broke the siege of Hung Dao on October 4 and continued to move north to Thien Ngon. Farther north, the siege of Firebase Alpha was broken by October 5.[28] MACV reported the North Vietnamese began pulling back their forces in early October, and by October 22, the last enemy units had withdrawn. Allied forces claimed 2,581 enemy killed in this operation and a loss of 198 South Vietnamese killed and 1,194 wounded.[29]

On October 26, 1971, General Wagstaff gave General Abrams what he described as his personal appraisal of the operation in a secret message:

2. (S) Personal appraisal: My assessment of the situation remains unchanged since my last report. Since 26 September, US air power and artillery have been the decisive factor. The ARVN continue to play a passive role, with the exception of the air-borne units, who have displayed certain aggressiveness. By far the greatest number of casualties have been inflected by our B-52's, TAC air, and gunships, with the ARVN operations limited to bomb damage assessments after an area has been cleared by our fire power. It is my belief that, without US air power, the ARVN would have inflicted negligible damage on the enemy, may have lost at least FSB Alpha, and would probably have evacuated all advance bases in Cambodia.[30]

On November 1 Wagstaff sent a second message with a more detailed analysis. This time he emphasized "US helicopter support, particularly in the helilift of ammunition and supplies, was instrumental in averting disaster in the early stages of the campaign." He also pointed out, "there is little question the massive use of air power provided by the 7th US Air Force and VNAF (Vietnamese Air Force) prevented a catastrophe for ARVN forces in the area." He then concluded on an optimistic note, observing, "Most important of all, the ARVN success in defeating the enemy has resulted in a new sense of confidence which extends from the troop level to the highest level of command."[31]

At the end of his tenure as commander of TRAC, in December 1971, General Wagstaff submitted a confidential debriefing report to his superiors in Saigon. This debriefing provided an assessment of the performance of the ARVN in the Krek-Pace Campaign, as well as the Snoul battle three months earlier. "The former

(Snoul) can only be considered a defeat for the ARVN while the latter (Krek) was an impressive victory," he concluded, but this time he was a little more positive about the South Vietnamese.[32] He praised them for their decision to quickly reinforce at Krek and Pace, for their effective use of superior firepower, and the excellent performance of the ARVN Airborne and the Third Armored Brigade that supported them.[33]

Wagstaff's assessment of the ARVN Airborne was confirmed by other Americans on the ground at Pace. Captain Ray Rhodes, who took over as senior adviser to the ARVN 6th Airborne Battalion at Pace when his predecessor was wounded, praised his troops as "the finest soldiers I ever served with—bar none."[34] For example, one of the Airborne's platoons took a direct hit from a 500-pound bomb dropped on them by mistake. Eighteen were killed and seven wounded. Two days later, another mistake killed three South Vietnamese paratroopers and wounded five.[35] Such a blow would have caused most units to unravel, but in Captain Rhodes's words, the ARVN Airborne soldiered on "gallantly."[36]

While the Airborne's prowess was generally recognized, the record of the 3d Armored Brigade was less obvious. Richard Boyle criticized them for staying close to the road and not leaving their base camps during the two days he was at Pace.[37] This criticism is probably not justified since the role of the 3d Armored Brigade was to secure the road, not charge into the jungle looking for North Vietnamese. With thousands of troops in the area, the South Vietnamese clearly had the capability to sweep the area if they chose to do so. However, documents declassified since the end of the war show pretty clearly that both the U.S. and South Vietnamese commands were most concerned about enemy concentrations around FSB Alpha in Cambodia and in the area between Thien Ngon and Hung Dao; hence, they concentrated their forces there.[38] The Allied response was influenced by intelligence that Pace was only a sideshow and the enemy's real prime target was Firebase Alpha on the Cambodian side of the border, two and a half miles east of Krek. On October 14, South Vietnamese forces captured the political officer of the NVA 141st Regiment of the 7th NVA Division. He confirmed that the primary role of the 141st and 209th Regiments was to ambush convoys on Highway 22.[39] It just didn't make sense militarily to go after a relatively small number of troops dug in around Pace when the more immediate danger lay north and south.

What was not mentioned in General Wagstaff's debriefing, but what was also critical to the defense of Firebase Pace, were the ARVN artillery units. Their light and medium howitzers provided close-in protection to Pace that Charlie Battery's heavy guns could not provide. This included 155mm and 105mm howitzers at Thien Ngon that responded regularly to suspected enemy mortar locations throughout the twenty-seven-day siege.[40] In addition, ARVN Airborne 105mm howitzers were eventually moved to Pace itself to provide additional defense.

From what little exists in the Army's official records, it appears that the South Vietnamese artillery fire was both timely and accurate. There were no reports of friendly fire incidents or accidents on the guns.

If relative casualties are one way of measuring who was doing the fighting, the results are pretty clear. On October 13, General Wagstaff submitted a report to General Abrams listing the following comparison of casualties for the entire operation to date (see table 23.1).[41]

On October 19, Colonel McCaffree submitted a report to 23d Group that verified the same pattern. He reported that between October 11 and 18, U.S. forces at Pace suffered five wounded and none killed. By comparison, South Vietnamese forces in the same area suffered six killed and fifty-two wounded.[42] So, if the goal was to turn over the majority of the fighting to the South Vietnamese, that goal was being met. The story, unfortunately, does not end there.

One of the dilemmas facing an army seeking to develop specialized elite units is the impact they make on other units of the same army. While units such as the ARVN Airborne can be effective far in excess of their numbers, they also siphon off good soldiers who would be natural leaders in regular line units, particularly the ARVN infantry divisions. All armies face this dilemma. The South Vietnamese Army was no exception. So while the allied effort benefited greatly from the presence of 4,500 elite paratroopers in the Krek-Pace area, it was also adversely affected by continuing performance problems in many of its other line units. This was a problem that plagued the ARVN for the remainder of the war.[43]

For example, the ARVN 25th Infantry Division was originally tasked with securing Firebase Pace and other South Vietnamese positions in the border area. As previously noted, the ARVN 25th Infantry Division did not have a sterling reputation to begin with.[44] The division did nothing to enhance that reputation in this campaign. They are conspicuously absent from General Wagstaff's list of kudos, even though they had several thousand troops in the area. It is pretty clear why. On October 1 Colonel McCaffree sent a message to his superiors complaining about lack of support from the 25th Division.[45] In an October 13 secret message to General Abrams, General Wagstaff himself referred to two battalions of the 25th Division's 50th Regiment (which comprised two-thirds of the regiment's strength) as "combat ineffective" and noted their regimental commander recommended they both be relieved.[46] The U.S. soldiers at Pace noticed the same thing. Both officers and enlisted men recall watching every morning an undisciplined ARVN unit (probably from the ARVN 25th Division), head south down Route 22 only to return late in the afternoon looking beat up and dragging their wounded with them. The next morning the cycle would repeat itself again.[47] Perhaps this is the same unit an unnamed ARVN sergeant at Pace referred to when he told a Time magazine reporter, "We are not strong enough. Every time we move out, we get our asses kicked off."[48]

Table 23.1. U.S. and South Vietnamese Casualties, Tay Ninh Border Area, September 26–October 13, 1971

	United States	South Vietnam
Killed in action	3	150
Wounded in action	40	963
Missing in action	3	42

Note: These figures show three Americans killed in this period even though four Americans died when the Huey gunship was shot down near Pace on September 29. It's possible these men were listed as missing until their deaths were confirmed when a patrol from Pace reached the crash site on October 21.

U.S. commanders on the ground also lacked confidence in the ARVN Ranger units tasked with providing security around U.S. firebases before the siege of Pace began in September. Known as "Border Rangers," these units consisted of Cambodian mercenaries incorporated into ARVN during the second half of 1970. As such, they were different from the ARVN Rangers who formed part of the Strategic Reserve.[49] The Strategic Reserve Rangers were regarded as decent soldiers at this point. The Border Rangers were not.

As described in chapter 3, dissatisfaction with the lack of activity of the Border Rangers assigned to Lanyard provoked one of the artillery batteries assigned there to run their own patrols.[50] A battery commander at Firebase Katum in the same time period described the Border Rangers there as "worthless."[51] Another officer complained to his superiors that the Border Rangers at his location were "the worst of any unit so far," because they "just wander around the area" instead of guarding the base.[52]

Concerns about the capability of the ARVN senior leadership continued to trouble senior U.S. commanders. Their American counterparts worried that too much was based on loyalty to President Thieu and too little on their performance on the field.[53] The loss of the aggressive General Tri in February was a major blow, but a high performing organization would have found someone to pick up the mantle. Instead, the South Vietnamese government promoted General Minh.

Major General George S. Eckhardt, who had worked with Minh in the Delta, recommended his dismissal as a division commandeer in 1967, noting he was "very temperamental" under stress.[54] Lieutenant General Michael S. Davidson, Wagstaff's predecessor as senior American commander in Military Region III, described Minh as "burned out" and "desperate."[55] Wagstaff himself described Minh as "over worked" and "highly emotional," his decisions "colored largely by his sensing of the moment."[56]

After winning kudos for his decision in September 1971, Minh returned to his erratic pattern of behavior in October. In a bizarre press briefing on October 6, Minh volunteered to reporters that he "told a lie" when he said his troops killed

4,000 North Vietnamese. He admitted the correct number was more like 450, but justified himself by saying he did it to raise the morale of his own troops and to demoralize the North Vietnamese. He also admitted he told his battalion commander that ARVN Airborne were going all the way to the Chup and Mimot Rubber Plantations in Cambodia, but "that was a lie, too."[57]

Then, two weeks later he came back with a claim that his forces had killed 2,200 of the 4,000–5,000 North Vietnamese 7th Division in a four-week period. He claimed half were confirmed by body count and another 1,100 confirmed by "aerial observers." He then declared Hanoi had been set back at least six months.[58]

General Wagstaff had concerns over General Minh's numbers. In an October 23 message to General Abrams he complained, "Attempts at detailed reconciliation have, essentially, been counterproductive." The fundamental difference lay in the reported number of NVA killed in action. Wagstaff's numbers showed 1,344; Minh's were 78 percent higher at 2,399. In a classic case of bureaucratic rationalization, Wagstaff explained: "While there is a general feeling that the ARVN KBA estimates are likely inflated, there is also recognition that perhaps our figures are much too low. We are hereafter reporting one set of figures—those reported to us by ARVN. We will continue to work closely with the III Corps staff and do our best to keep casualty data reasonable."[59]

In late November, Minh commenced a second offensive with 25,000 troops directed against North Vietnamese staging areas in Cambodia. The thirty-nine-day drive ended on December 30 after it was clear the North Vietnamese had pulled deeper into Cambodia. Minh in turn pulled his troops back into South Vietnam, but only after claiming he had killed another 1,336 North Vietnamese. Skeptics observed that since only 195 weapons were captured, the figures might be inflated.[60]

An equally stubborn challenge proved to be how well the South Vietnamese learned the American style of waging war. While the North Vietnamese seemed to be able to master the art of defeating the enemy by outlasting him, the Vietnamizing South Vietnamese seemed to be becoming more and more dependent on burying their enemy under a torrent of firepower. Civilian critics were already raising the issue of whether or not the South Vietnamese were becoming too much like the Americans, but without the American's resource base.[61]

In this regard, General Wagstaff's confidential analysis of the Krek-Pace Campaign is particularly revealing. As part of his report, Wagstaff presented a table describing the integrated fire plan he defined as mandatory for success as one of the principal differences between failure at Snoul and success at Krek. The entry is repeated in its entirety below:

> Concurrent with the ground maneuver, an integrated fire support plan was executed. Initially, fire support was directed toward relieving the pressure

around friendly firebases. Unit locations and anti-aircraft positions were carefully targeted. Next, the enemy's reserve positions and supply areas were attacked, and finally, routes of resupply were interdicted. The magnitude of fire power utilized in the Krek Battle is shown by the following statistics:

B-52 Strikes 89
USAF Fighter Sorties (Day) 743
USAF Fighter Sorties (All Weather) 413
VNAF Fighter Sorties (Day) 1,398
US Helicopter Gunship Sorties 3,699
ARVN Artillery (Rounds) 153,960
US Heavy Artillery (Rounds) 4,800[62]

Although the South Vietnamese were successful in this case, Wagstaff's analysis itself points out the fundamental contradiction in U.S. strategy. To be successful the South Vietnamese had to become better at the American way of war. But the better they got at it, the more unsustainable it would be over the long run. A little over thirteen months after this report was written, five of the seven weapons systems listed would be gone from Vietnam under the terms of the Paris Peace Accords. What would be left, VNAF Fighter Sorties (Day) and ARVN Artillery, would still be significant in number and would be equal to much of what the North Vietnamese had, but would be much less than what the South Vietnamese had learned to depend on. Wagstaff concluded his report by saying "the short-term outlook for keeping the enemy divisions out of MR 3 is good; however, the long term prospects are not clear and will depend to a large extent on the results of the current III Corps cross border operations and results of the war within Cambodia."[63]

If Minh was listening to Wagstaff in September, he was back to being super cautious in December. Despite a great deal of fanfare about a successful thirty-nine-day drive against Cambodian sanctuaries in November and December, the North Vietnamese remained dug in to their bases in the seventy-five-square-mile Chup Rubber Plantation.[64] The AP reported the South Vietnamese had been searching the southern boundary of the plantation, while the North Vietnamese were dug in along the northern boundary.[65] Nevertheless, Minh declared victory and pulled all his troops back across the border.[66] The Airborne troops would be redeployed to the Central Highlands, leaving the 25th Division in charge of border security in that area. The North Vietnamese would be able to continue to build up their base areas relatively unmolested.[67]

At the end of 1971, Vietnamization was now three-fourths complete in terms of time allotted. Both U.S. and South Vietnamese commanders could point to some successes. Another 150,000 U.S. troops had been withdrawn over the last twelve months, including 40,000 from Military Region III. South Vietnamese troops stepped forward to fill the gap without a major breakdown. The ARVN ended the year with a hard-fought victory against an NVA offensive in the border area around Krek and Pace. Some of their troops, particularly from the Airborne Division, fought extremely well.

But there were troubling patterns emerging as well. While some troops stepped up, others didn't. Including the November–December campaign, the ARVN spent a year trying to clear the North Vietnamese out of their base camps along Route 7 in Cambodia and failed, despite massive U.S. logistical and air support. In two cases (Dambe and Snoul), they had to beat a hasty and disorderly retreat. A similar effort to destroy enemy logistical networks in Laos that spring fell short of expectations despite the commitment of Saigon's best troops. Continued fundamental performance problems remained in terms of leadership, combined arms coordination, and fire support.[68]

Army Secretary Stanley R. Resor struck a note of caution when he visited Vietnam in a ten-day fact-finding tour in May 1971. At a Saigon Press conference at the end of his trip he pointed out that half of all U.S. servicemen in Vietnam two years earlier had been withdrawn, including 65 percent of all combat troops. He also warned that "while progress to date has been encouraging, a difficult period lies ahead," because of the continued pullout of U.S. troops. This meant the South Vietnamese would have to step up their efforts. The South Vietnamese "are making appreciable progress," he concluded, "but time is running out, so that I would hope that (Vietnamization) progress can continue to accelerate."[69]

In a September message to General Abrams, General Wagstaff described the overall situation as follows: "As a recap, the security situation at present appears to be a stand off, with neither side having gained a marked advantage since Vietnamization of the conflict began."[70] With the Americans pulling out, this stalemate could deteriorate significantly for the South Vietnamese if they could not step up their efforts. But to fully understand the success or failure of Vietnamization in this period, it is also instructive to look at the North Vietnamese forces to see how they coped with the challenges facing them.

CHAPTER TWENTY-FOUR

North Vietnamese Enemies

The units designated the 5th, 7th, and 9th Divisions formed the core of the Communist forces who fought the American and South Vietnamese forces in Military Region III from 1965 through 1972. Prior to 1965 most of the Communist forces in this area had been local Vietcong guerrillas supplemented by a handful of cadre infiltrated from the north. But beginning in 1965, the North Vietnamese significantly increased the infiltration of regular soldiers into South Vietnam. In addition, local VC battalions and regiments were formed into large groups called NLF (National Liberation Front) Divisions. Two of these, the 5th and 7th Divisions, were established north and northwest of Saigon and were eventually joined by the 9th Division.[1] Over the next five years they battled regularly with U.S. and South Vietnamese troops, and by 1971 they were filled with North Vietnamese draftees infiltrated from the north down the Ho Chi Minh Trail. For all practical purposes, they were manned, equipped, and operated as conventional units of the NVA.[2]

Through a combination of captured documents and prisoners of war, Generals Wagstaff and Minh were able to confirm the objectives of the enemy offensive in September–October 1971, which were to attack and defeat ARVN forces in the Krek/Thien Ngon area and force a withdrawal from Cambodia. The major effort was focused on firebases Alpha and Hung Dao so that ARVN forces could be attacked as they withdrew. Success in this regard would embarrass the Saigon government on the eve of the October 3 presidential election and disrupt ARVN dry season campaign plans.[3]

Five regiments from the 5th and 7th Divisions participated in the fall 1971 offensive in the Krek-Pace border area. By mid-October, allied intelligence was able to identify each regiment, its approximate location, and its role. The E-6 and 147th Regiments of the 5th Division were responsible for isolating Firebase Alpha on the Cambodian side of the border near Krek. The 141st and 209th Regiments of the 7th Division were initially deployed along Highway 22 from Firebase Pace to Hung Dao with the mission of ambushing convoys leaving Alpha or relieving Alpha—a strategy very similar to the one successfully used against the South Vietnamese at Dambe in February and Snoul in June. The 165th Regiment of the 7th Division hid in the woods west of Pace and served as the division reserve.[4] After it became clear the offensive would not succeed as planned, the 209th Regiment remained behind as the rear guard to cover the withdrawal.[5] Since the 209th

Regiment had the most intense interactions with U.S. forces at Pace, it is appropriate to look at them first.

The 209th Regiment was not originally assigned to the NLF 7th Division. Instead, it can trace its origins to the Viet Minh fight against the French, where it participated in the 1954 battle of Dien Bien Phu. In early 1968, it departed North Vietnam and infiltrated to the central highlands, where it eventually joined the North Vietnamese 1st Division. Its first major engagement was the attack on Fire Support Base 14, a U.S. Army position about thirty kilometers west-northwest of Kontum. Using flamethrowers, the 209th almost overran the base on the night of March 26. They captured one artillery piece but were eventually driven out in a counterattack. After-action reports described the enemy as "exceptionally well equipped," as well as "healthy and well fed."[6]

The unit infiltrated farther south and ended up participating in the fighting along the Cambodian border in 1969–1970, where it was assigned to the 7th Division. Along with the rest of the 7th Division, the 209th fled deeper into Cambodia in response to the Spring 1970 allied offensive, but by the fall of 1971 had worked its way back to the border area. After the North Vietnamese Election Day offensive petered out, the 209th was assigned the task of harassing and delaying would-be pursuers as a rearguard—a task it approached with skill and tenacity.

Even though its soldiers were armed with weapons no more sophisticated than 82mm mortars, fifty-one caliber machine guns, and occasional rockets, they were able to hold on against an array of allied hardware, including 105mm, 155mm, and 8-inch artillery, Quad Fifty machine guns, helicopter gun ships, AC130 Spectre gunships, tactical air and regular B-52 strikes aided by ground sensors, infrared, ground surveillance radar, countermortar radar, and aerial observers. They fired more than 800 mortar rounds at Pace and a similar number at Thien Ngon. They succeeded in knocking out a 175mm long-range gun and wounded over fifty Americans and at least an equal number of South Vietnamese soldiers.[7]

On October 19, 1971, a South Vietnamese army long-range reconnaissance patrol ambushed a small party of North Vietnamese couriers near the Cambodian border southwest of Pace. The South Vietnamese recovered records belonging to the personnel section of the headquarters of the 209th Regiment that provided insight into the organization, strength, and fighting capabilities of this unit. These documents revealed a participating strength of 1,343, plus 33 in an attached artillery element and 114 in an anti-aircraft element, or about 1,500 soldiers in all—a number consistent with earlier intelligence estimates.[8] Most of the mischief directed at Pace came from the mortars of the 33-man artillery element and the machine guns of the 114-man anti-aircraft element, while the infantry tangled with the South Vietnamese Airborne, Ranger, Armored, and Infantry units in the area, who probably greatly outnumbered them.

The South Vietnamese claimed a victory in the end, having moved quickly to block the enemy offensive. Their troops fought well, protecting Alpha and Hung Dao and forcing two divisions of enemy troops deep into Cambodia, thus avoiding a major embarrassment before the presidential elections on October 3. They also protected FSB Pace sufficiently to avoid a debacle like Mary Ann. After it was all over, the 209th retreated into Cambodia, leaving the South Vietnamese Army in control of the battlefield.

Yet the North Vietnamese could claim that, despite massive American firepower, they were able to accomplish the following:

- Knock out one of two remaining 175mm long-range cannons supporting South Vietnamese forces in Cambodia
- Wound 100 south Vietnamese and American soldiers at Pace (forcing almost half of them into hospitals) with low risk, stand-off mortar attacks
- Down at least three armed helicopters, killing a crew of one
- Cut off all overland supplies to Firebase Pace, forcing resupply by air
- Attract an enormous concentration of resources and firepower that could have been used elsewhere
- Force a hasty U.S. withdrawal from a strategic outpost

All of these points are self-evident, except possibly the last one regarding the timing of the evacuation of Pace. When the time came to leave Pace, the Army maintained it was a "routine" step in the phased withdrawal of American troops from direct combat roles. While it is true that Pace was scheduled to eventually be evacuated, the available evidence shows that date was hastened. The 2/32d Field Artillery Battalion was scheduled to depart Vietnam on January 22, 1972, as part of MACV's withdrawal plan. The U.S. Command's standard practice was to keep units in the field as long as possible to leverage firepower.[9] For example, when B Battery 2/35th Artillery was pulled out of Firebase Lanyard on February 5, 1971, it needed only five weeks to prepare for redeployment, which occurred on March 13 of that year.[10] Had Charlie Battery 2/32d followed the same schedule, it could have stayed at Pace through early December, which also would have more closely corresponded with South Vietnamese plans to wrap up their Cambodian offensive.

Other information, including documents declassified since the war, point to a hasty withdrawal:

- Intelligence reports indicate the enemy buildup in northwest Tay Ninh Province initially caught the allies by surprise and was regarded as quite serious at the time.[11]
- In a secret message to General Abrams on October 12, General Wagstaff said, "General Minh understands our political requirements for pulling out of Pace."[12]

- The AP reported on October 23 that the evacuation of Pace took place ten days "ahead of schedule." Although the story did not specifically identify the source of this information, it appeared to be MACV.[13]
- Abandoning guns in the face of the enemy is not something the Army would normally do, even though the guns were later recovered.[14]

But what the 209th Regiment was able to accomplish at Pace had a price tag in the blood and lives of the North Vietnamese soldiers involved. The documents captured by South Vietnamese patrols referred to earlier also included casualty figures. They revealed combat losses of thirty-one killed in action and sixty-one wounded in action, or about 6 percent of regimental strength in the sixteen-day period from September 26 to October 12. This averages out to about two killed and four wounded a day—significant losses but certainly not catastrophic given the amount of firepower employed against them.[15]

This also says something about the enemy's skill in avoiding B-52 strikes. Records show over forty-seven strikes in this area between September 26 and October 12.[16] If one of these had come close, the loss totals would have been much higher. But it appears the law of averages may have caught up with the North Vietnamese as the siege went on. For example, South Vietnamese soldiers reported finding fifty-three dead North Vietnamese killed in an air strike south of Pace on October 23.[17] Anecdotal evidence from U.S. troops on the ground and from the air also tends to confirm significant enemy losses from air and artillery. For example, one of Charlie Battery's section chiefs recalled, "The ARVN Rangers reported the smell of bodies so bad in the jungle that it was months before they could go back to cutting trees. Body parts were found in trees and were laying all over the ground around the FSB and for several thousand meters south of the base where the B-52 strikes landed."[18]

Captain John LeVesque, the S-3 of the 2/32d Artillery recalled finding a burial site southwest of Pace that held 250 bodies. He was flying in a helicopter on a reconnaissance flight shortly after Pace had been evacuated when he and the pilots were overcome by an "unbelievable stench." They dropped down to check it out and discovered what appeared to be a trench filled with bodies and parts of bodies that had been dragged there by the North Vietnamese as a common burial ground.[19] The daily unit logs include much of the same. Aerial observers reported seeing bodies and body parts hanging from trees south of Pace.[20]

In his final debriefing on the battle, Major General Wagstaff reported 2,500 enemy killed out of an attacking force of approximately 10,000, or about 25 percent.[21] If the 250 bodies Captain LeVesque found in a mass grave and the 53 bodies found by the South Vietnamese on October 23 were all from the 209th Regiment, that would suggest at least 20 percent of the unit's strength were killed in this campaign (303 divided by 1,500), which is close to the 25 percent proportion Wagstaff reported. However, both the 141st and 165th NVA regiments also operated in that area, so if the bodies came from those units, then the percentage killed would be much less.

Less than six months later, allied intelligence identified all the units involved in this campaign as refreshed, renewed, back up to strength, and back on the offensive.[22] This suggests either enormous powers of renewal on the part of the North Vietnamese or exaggerated claims of enemy dead on the part of the Americans and South Vietnamese. The veracity of body counts has been an area of intense debate both during and after the war.[23] It is hard to believe the North Vietnamese could consistently experience the level of losses the allies claimed and still function. As described in the proceeding chapter, General Wagstaff and his staff felt the South Vietnamese body count claims were clearly exaggerated. In any event, it is clear that even if the North Vietnamese took heavy losses in this campaign and others they were able to come back for more in a relatively short period of time.

That resiliency can be seen most clearly in the combat record of the 271st Regiment. The persistence of the 271st Regiment of the 9th Division stands as a classic example of the North Vietnamese ability to soldier on despite dreadful losses. The 271st Regiment did not participate in the Krek-Pace battles in September and October 1971, but it had a long history of operating in the Cambodian border area. U.S. intelligence sources identified the 271st as the "oldest VC regiment in War Zone Three." Originally activated in War Zone C in July 1961 at battalion strength, it grew to regimental strength by July 1963. By 1965 it had become part of the newly organized NLF 9th Division.[24]

The 271st's first known encounter with U.S. troops occurred in November 1965 when one of its battalions charged a position held by the 2/2d Infantry of the U.S. 1st Division near the town of Bau Bang / Lai Khe. According to one account, the assault failed as U.S. machine guns "cut great holes in the ranks of running, crawling and staggering Viet Cong infantry." U.S. sources report the three regiments of the 9th Division lost 198 soldiers killed in action in that operation.[25] The 271st and its sister regiments from the 9th Division continued to skirmish with the Big Red One in and around Loc Ninh for the next six months. On June 30 the 271st tried to spring an ambush on the First Division's 1/4th Cavalry on Highway 13. It turned into a disaster, with the regiment losing 270 men killed in a single action.[26]

During the remainder of 1966 and early 1967, the 271st tried to protect its traditional base areas in War Zones C and D as American forces grew more numerous and more aggressive. This phase of the war reached a climax on the afternoon of April 1, 1967, during the final phases of Operation Junction City. The 271st regiment mounted a massive infantry assault against the 1st Infantry Division's 1/26th Infantry Battalion at LZ George in War Zone C. The American forces responded with massed artillery and air strikes, pounding their assailants with 15,000 rounds of artillery and 100 tons of high explosives and napalm delivered from the air. When it was all over, U.S. forces counted 609 enemy bodies, or about 40 percent of the regiment's total strength. "In this particular attack, I think . . . when you get belly to belly with a large VC force, they are not sufficiently flexible to react especially intelligently," boasted the U.S. commander, Lieutenant Colonel Al Haig Junior.[27] As if to underscore Colonel Haig's point, the 271st Regiment lost another 196 men in June in what was described as a "savage three hour battle" with the U.S. 1st Infantry Division in War Zone D, forty-three miles north of Saigon.[28]

But four months later, the battered 271st Regiment finally turned the table on their pursuers. Operating in War Zone D's Long Nguyen Secret Zone, about forty-five miles north of Saigon, they sprang a deadly ambush on the "Black Lions" of the 1st Division's 2/28th Infantry, commanded by Lieutenant Colonel Terry Allen Jr., son of World War II hero and First Division Commander Terry Allen Sr. Before the day ended, Terry Allen Jr. fell along with sixty of his troopers. Almost everyone else in the company suffered wounds of some sort, in what would be one of the First Division's darkest moments in Vietnam. This ambush and the controversy surrounding it was described in vivid detail thirty-four years later by David Maraniss in They Marched into Sunlight.[29]

The success of the 271st did not go unnoticed by MACV. In a confidential study issued in December 1967, two reviewers described the 271st as a unit with "a reputation for being especially adept at conducting double play ambushes against an exposed force and against the reaction force sent out to assist. This classical enemy ambush emphasized one of the most difficult problems facing the US in its war against the Viet Cong." The authors went on to ask, "How do you bring superior firepower to support friendlies in jungle areas which are suddenly hit from enemy positions only a few meters away?"[30]

After the ambush of Terry Allen's Black Lions, the 271st moved back into Cambodia for rest and resupply. They emerged at midnight New Year's Day 1968 to attack Fire Support Base Burt on the Vietnamese/Cambodian border. This time they clashed with elements of the 25th Infantry "Tropic Lightning" Division. In what was described as "savage and desperate" fighting, the Vietcong were repulsed under a hail of bombs and bullets, including 1,500 mortar and artillery rounds and 200,000 rounds of small arms. When daylight came, more than 400 enemy bodies were counted.[31] The defenders of this base included a young enlisted man named Oliver Stone. His recollections of this attack would form the basis of the climactic ending scenes in the movie Platoon twenty years later.

The 271st Regiment then moved south to participate in the 1968 Tet Offensive. Its mission was to assist in the attack on the Tan Son Nhut Airbase in Saigon. In the early morning hours of January 31, Vietcong and North Vietnamese soldiers of the 271st captured the Vinatexco textile factory and moved onto the runways at Tan Son Nhut. Their timing could not have been worse. The 3/4th Cav of the 25th Division arrived at the same time, having made a hurried road march from twenty-five kilometers away in what was later known as the "3/4 horse midnight ride." The tanks and APCs of 3/4th Cavalry slammed into the 271st Regiment while they were in the open. The battle went on for most of the day. When it was over, 300 enemy dead were left behind on the battlefield.[32] The Tet Offensive failed militarily at Tan Son Nhut, just as it did across South Vietnam. By the time it was finished, U.S. intelligence estimated the 271st had lost 600 men, or over 40 percent of its pre-Tet strength. It rated the division as no longer combat effective.[33] As if to prove otherwise, the Communist Command pushed their forces to renew the offensive as soon as possible in Tet II in June. The U.S. Command reported the depleted ranks of VC regiments like the 271st were now made up of 80–90 percent North Vietnamese draftees infiltrated from the north.[34]

In September 1968, the 271st Regiment resurfaced for the Battle of Tay Ninh. Their mission was to attack the heavily fortified Special Forces camp at Thien Ngon, north of Tay Ninh. The assault was repulsed, costing the regiment another 157 killed.[35] By April 1969 the 271st was back again, attacking a 25th Infantry Division firebase, Frontier City, forty-five miles west of Saigon near the Cambodian border. U.S. forces reported only one man wounded, while killing 213 enemy soldiers. News reports said U.S. commanders were "unable to explain why the enemy continues to attack," even though they had lost more than 700 men in half a dozen such assaults in recent weeks.[36]

On November 4, 1969, they attacked again. This time it was Fire Support Base Ike on the Cambodian border, manned by units of the 1st Air Cavalry Division. The attack was repulsed with the loss of sixty-three North Vietnamese soldiers killed in the assault. Gunships chased the survivors fleeing into the jungle after daybreak, killing an additional seventy or so. "Man, it was just like a turkey shoot," exclaimed one pilot.[37]

The 1st Air Cavalry was having a great deal of success in pushing back to the border the North Vietnamese and whatever Vietcong remained, so early in April 1970 the 9th NVA Division participated in a series of retaliatory attacks on First Cavalry Division border firebases. The 271st drew the assignment of attacking FSB Illingsworth about six miles east of where FSB Pace would be a year later. The attack was repulsed with an estimated body count of sixty-five. But U.S. casualties were twenty-four U.S. soldiers killed and fifty-four wounded.[38]

A month later, U.S. and South Vietnamese forces charged across the Cambodian border. Rather than stand and fight, the 271st regiment and other North Vietnamese units hurriedly evacuated deeper into Cambodia, leaving base camps and stockpiles behind. By January 1971 elements of the 271st Regiment were identified in the woods west of Lanyard, but by and large they avoided confrontations with U.S. forces.[39] However, they continued to clash with South Vietnamese forces in Cambodia.

The pattern here is clear. The 271st Regiment suffered significant losses over an extended period of time. Even if body counts were inflated 50 percent, the regiment was theoretically wiped out two or three times between 1965 and 1972. Yet it and the other regiments fought on. Understanding how and why reveals a lot about how the North Vietnamese were able to prevail in the end.

The skillful use of camouflage and concealment underpinned much of their success. Hiding from the enemy has not been a major tenet of the American way of war in the last sixty years, because the United States has always enjoyed air and firepower superiority. But, in order to survive, both the VC and NVA needed to develop these skills. As described in chapter 2, the North Vietnamese were able to either build or rebuild a seventy-meter-long bunker complex between Lanyard and Thien Ngon and stage ambushes along Highway 22 less than ninety days after this border area had been "cleaned out" and secured by thousands of U.S. and South Vietnamese troops in May 1970.[40] More than a year later General Abrams complained that "some of the bunkers along Highway 22 appear to have been constructed several months prior to the beginning of the operation during which time Highway 22 was in constant use."[41]

The North Vietnamese knew concealment alone was not sufficient. The troops had to be willing to carry the fight to the enemy at the appropriate time in sufficient strength to carry the day. So how the North Vietnamese were able to replenish their diminished ranks and keep them fighting was equally important. The U.S. Command knew at the time that replacing losses in VC units with infiltration from the north was part of the strategy from at least 1965 on. These replacements also needed to be trained, fed, equipped, transported to their new units, and supplied. Finally, they needed to be motivated to risk their lives far from home to do battle with a determined and sophisticated enemy.

Army Colonel William Darryl Henderson tackled this topic in a study of cohesion in the North Vietnamese, U.S., Soviet, and Israeli armies, published by the National Defense University Press in 1985. Henderson, who had served as a rifle company commander in Vietnam, observed that the North Vietnamese Army "endured the most concentrated firepower ever directed against an army for seven continuous years." He explained that the attention the North Vietnamese paid to what he called "development of the human element" created "one of the most cohesive armies ever fielded."[42] Henderson identified the three-man cell common to both the Chinese and North Vietnamese armies as the key building block to a cohesive force. Each cell or unit is part of three like cells or units, which in turn are part of three larger units. "The three-man military cell with proper leadership became the strength upon which the extraordinary endurance of both armies was based. This is especially significant in the case of the North

Vietnamese Army (NVA) since it was required to operate widely dispersed under the conditions of extreme hardship and stress often described as characteristic of future battlefields," Henderson concluded.[43]

After the 1970 Cambodian invasion, the North Vietnamese were able to disperse yet remain cohesive enough to beat back three separate attempts by South Vietnamese forces to destroy their Cambodian sanctuaries north of Route 7 at Dambe, Snoul, and Krek. They were able to do this at a time when the South Vietnamese army had been supposedly upgraded as part of Vietnamization, yet still supported by massive amounts of U.S. fire support. Buoyed by a sense of confidence that they were in fact the ones getting stronger in 1971, the North Vietnamese command decided that 1972 would be the right time to go for broke and win the war. This would lock North and South Vietnamese troops in an intense struggle that would dwarf anything that happened before.

CHAPTER TWENTY-FIVE

Vietnamese Verdun

Beginning in January 1972, the Allied Command began to pick up intelligence of significant activity along the Ho Chi Minh Trail; however, there was not uniform agreement about what this meant. What U.S. and South Vietnamese planners didn't know was that the North Vietnamese had already made a decision to go for broke in 1972 and attempt to win the war in one massive countrywide offensive.[1] On March 30, 1972 (Holy Thursday in the Christian calendar), the so-called Easter Offensive began with massive attacks by regular North Vietnamese troops supported by tanks and artillery—first against South Vietnamese forces in the northern part of South Vietnam along the demilitarized zone. Over the next four days, the entire length of Vietnam erupted along the Laotian and Cambodian borders as North Vietnamese regulars surged forward.[2]

On April 2, two regiments of North Vietnamese soldiers (the 24th and 271st), supported by tanks and heavy artillery, struck across the border from their Cambodian sanctuaries into Tay Ninh Province. The NVA 24th Regiment attacked the ARVN 25th Division outpost at Firebase Lac Long where Route 22 crossed the Cambodian border, near the now-abandoned Fire Support Base Lanyard I (see fig. 25.1). The assault began at 0245 with a 600-round mortar and rocket barrage. An infantry assault followed, supported by the U.S.-built M41 tanks. By 0420 the tactical operations center had been overrun. Friendly losses were estimated at 50 killed and 100 wounded, including the battalion commander and his executive officer among the slain.[3]

Fearful their other border outposts, including Pace, could not be protected, General Minh ordered a general withdrawal back to Tay Ninh. This played right into the hands of the North Vietnamese as the 271st Regiment sprung a ferocious ambush of a retreating column on Highway 22, just south of Thien Ngon. The South Vietnamese lost almost all of their guns and vehicles. By the time a relief column arrived the next day, the enemy had disappeared. The attack had been a feint.[4]

Three days later, the North Vietnamese main forces overran the border town of Loc Ninh, eighty miles north of Saigon. Once again supported by tanks and heavy artillery, they headed straight for the provincial capital at An Loc, fifteen miles to the south. What followed turned out to be one of the most dramatic sieges of the Vietnam War. Surrounded and outnumbered by a larger enemy force, the small

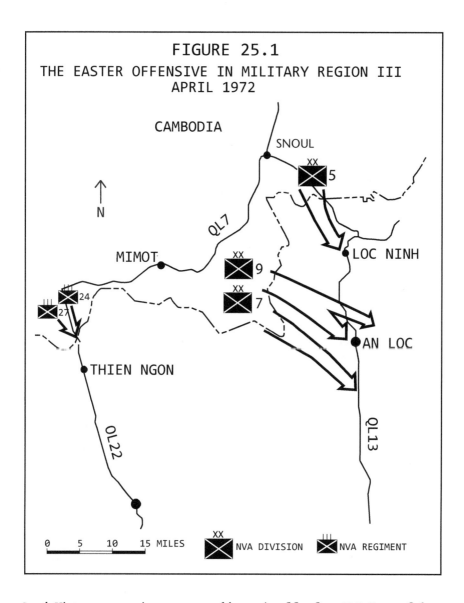

FIGURE 25.1
THE EASTER OFFENSIVE IN MILITARY REGION III
APRIL 1972

CAMBODIA

SNOUL

N

QL7

MIMOT

LOC NINH

THIEN NGON

AN LOC

QL22

QL13

0   5   10   15 MILES

NVA DIVISION   NVA REGIMENT

South Vietnamese garrison, supported by a rain of fire from U.S. B-52s, fighter bombers, and helicopter gunships, held on for seventy grim days.[5]

The Siege of An Loc involved the 5th, 7th, and 9th NVA divisions, as well as other troops. On the South Vietnamese side, ARVN Airborne and Rangers, as well as the 5th and 21st Infantry Divisions and Regional and Popular Forces participated. The North Vietnamese attack on An Loc reached a critical point on May 11–12, when NVA soldiers closed in on a key command center. Staying close to their South Vietnamese enemy to avoid B-52 strikes, the durable 271st Regiment of the 9th Division advanced to within striking distance of what one observer called "the verge of a major victory," the command bunker of the battered ARVN 5th Infantry Division.[6] But, in one of those seemingly random decisions that shape the outcome of close struggles, the 271st attacked to the northeast instead of the southeast. They captured their objective, a provincial public works building, which turned out to be meaningless.

The Allied Command recognized the risk and hurriedly redeployed an ARVN airborne battalion from another part of the perimeter. Since they realized the North Vietnamese were too close to call in B-52 strikes, AC-130 Spectre gunships and A-37 tactical aircraft were called in to rake the North Vietnamese positions. This fierce battle went on for another four days.[7]

At one point MACV was so concerned about whether the South Vietnamese could hold at An Loc they developed a contingency plan to use the few remaining U.S. ground troops as a blocking force. They hoped these ground troops could hold the North Vietnamese just long enough to evacuate by sea thousands of U.S. support personnel still in Saigon and Long Binh. Lieutenant Colonel Stan Tyson's 1/12th Sky Troopers, along with the two other remaining battalions of the 1st Cavalry's 3d Brigade (Separate), were told to be prepared to move out on short notice to stop the North Vietnamese surging south down Route 13. The 2/8th Cavalry would head north on a "movement to contact," while the brigade's remaining two battalions would form a defense line south of the Dong Nai River. In other words, the 2/8th would sacrifice itself to buy time for the others.[8]

The 1/12th would be assigned a seventeen-kilometer sector (a little more than eight miles) to defend with 600 men in what was described as a "mobile defense." Normally a mobile defense would be supported by reserves in the rear, except at this point there were no reserves because the 3d Brigade *was* the reserve.[9] If all went according to plan, 1/12th, 1/7th, and whatever remained of 2/8th would be airlifted out after the evacuation of Long Binh and Saigon was complete. If things didn't go as well as planned, survivors were expected to reassemble at preselected rally points and retreat overland forty-five miles to the Vung Tau Peninsula to be evacuated by sea.[10]

If this contingency plan had become a reality, it would have had explosive political consequences back in the United States. The volatile mix of televised images of friendly forces in a humiliating retreat, the grim reality of more American boys coming home in body bags, and the posturing accompanying the impending 1972 presidential primaries would have fueled unrestrained political warfare. President Nixon's critics would have tied this catastrophe directly to his failed Vietnamization program. Not ones to allow their opponents to gain an advantage, the Nixon White House would have struck first, blaming this catastrophe on a "stab in the back" of America's soldiers by antiwar opponents. The ensuing rancor would have even further divided the country for decades.

In the end, the ARVN held. The 271st NVA Regiment and the remaining North Vietnamese troops retreated back to their base camps in Cambodia. The South Vietnamese had suffered heavily (5,400 casualties, including 2,300 killed or missing), but the North Vietnamese suffered more. U.S. sources estimated 10,000 North Vietnamese soldiers killed out of a total of 50,000 engaged.[11]

The impact of U.S. firepower on the North Vietnamese concentrated around An Loc had to be devastating. If U.S. estimates of 10,000 North Vietnamese soldiers killed out of 50,000 engaged are correct, the proportion of 20 percent of the engaged forces killed or missing rivals the level of slaughter seen among German and French forces at Verdun, the legendary World War I battle considered the benchmark of military carnage.[12] At Verdun, it took seven months to achieve this toll—at An Loc, it happened in three months.

President Thieu and President Nixon were quick to claim success. "The Binh Long victory is not a victory over Communist North Vietnam only," Thieu declared. "The Binh Long victory is a victory of the Free World over the theory of peoples war [and the] revolutionary war of world communism."[13] General Alexander Haig, now President Nixon's chief military aid, was even more effusive. After a brief visit to South Vietnam, he declared, "In terms relative to ARVN, the NVA are now extremely weak. Although they continue to infiltrate replacements, the quality of their infantry has declined sharply and ARVN is no longer intimidated by their armor. Many recently captured NVA are young and inexperienced with reports that some have only had rudimentary training. . . . Saigon has been given a new lease on life."[14]

While it is true the South Vietnamese army fought the North Vietnamese without assistance of U.S. ground combat units, the South Vietnamese "victory" at An Loc still raised issues about their performance hauntingly similar to the issues involved with the successful defense of Krek and Pace six months earlier. The elite Ranger and Airborne units fought well, and in this case, territorial units (Regional Forces and Popular Forces) did too.[15] But the regular ARVN Infantry Divisions did not, and their leaders again came under fire from American commanders for lapses in leadership.

Major General James Hollingsworth, General Wagstaff's successor as U.S. commander of TRAC, described General Hung, commander of the ARVN 5th Infantry Division, as having "choked" and "didn't do anything."[16] He also criticized the regimental commanders. "There was no control. There was no supervision; there was no command emphasis to get out into the crew positions."[17]

Even though some individual soldiers and small units demonstrated grit and heroism, many others did not. James H. Willbanks, who served as adviser to the South Vietnamese at An Loc, later wrote that the officers of the ARVN 5th Division "apparently lacked sufficient control and discipline" to prevent looting, and in other cases demonstrated cowardice under fire.[18] The ARVN 21st Infantry

Division found itself bogged down when ordered to relieve An Loc from the south.[19] Both division commanders were relieved after the battle.[20]

General Minh's leadership came into question once again. The ability of the North Vietnamese to amass the amount of manpower, supplies, and equipment that close to the border had to raise doubts as to what the South Vietnamese troops under Minh's command had accomplished in Cambodia in November and December 1971. The thirty-nine-day offensive against enemy sanctuaries involved 20,000 troops. After declaring victory, Minh then proceeded to pull all his troops back across the border and wait.[21] This was completely contrary to the aggressive strategy suggested by General Wagstaff and practiced by General Tri before his death.[22]

Senior U.S. advisers, including General James F. Hollingsworth, senior U.S. commander for Military Region III, tried to have Minh removed. In fact, Ambassador Ellsworth Bunker described Minh as a problem "we have had . . . for a long time."[23] Finally, after personal intervention from both Ambassador Bunker and General Abrams with President Thieu, Minh was replaced in August 1973.[24]

Lieutenant General Du Quoc Dong, commander of the well-regarded ARVN Airborne Division, 1964–1972, was chosen to take Minh's place. If anyone expected Dong to be the South Vietnamese equivalent of Maxwell Taylor or Matthew Ridgway, they would be sorely disappointed. Dong rarely visited the field because his skill was not as a troop leader but as a political operative unquestionably loyal to President Thieu. His U.S. advisers found him unimpressive, highly resistant to advice, and a "problem child." In fact, he'd been removed as commander of the Airborne Division just a year before.[25]

The constant shuffling of President Thieu's political allies from one key command slot to another enraged his American advisers and raised serious questions in their minds about the ability of the South Vietnamese military leadership to prevail, not only in Military Region III but also across the country.[26] The experience at An Loc was replicated across South Vietnam that spring. In both Military Regions I and II, the North Vietnamese initially made strong advances. Some South Vietnamese units performed well. Many others did not. In the end, the North Vietnamese offensive was halted, though barely, through a combination of North Vietnamese mistakes, the courage of South Vietnamese units that did stand, the heroic efforts of American advisers, and massive application of U.S. firepower from the air. But the margin was a narrow one, and serious weaknesses in ARVN senior leadership remained.[27]

The strength of North Vietnamese units at the start of the Easter Offensive once again showed the North Vietnamese had extraordinary powers of renewal. For example, the 209th Regiment of the NVA 7th Division had the strength of 1,466 in October 1971, according to documents captured on October 12.[28] U.S.

and South Vietnamese forces claimed killing 2,500 NVA out of the 10,000 NVA involved in the Krek-Pace border battles. Separate figures by regiment are not available, but if the 209th had suffered proportionally that means it would have lost about one-quarter of its strength, or about 375 killed and at least an equal number wounded, which is certainly possible given that the 209th stayed behind as a rear guard. But on the eve of the Easter Offensive, U.S. intelligence estimates showed a roster strength of the 209th back up to 1,500, which meant whatever losses the 209th endured in September–November were fully made up before the April offensive just five months later.[29] And the 209th Regiment did more than just show up; it played a major role in what would be called the Battle of Tau O Bridge. The 209th's mission was to block Highway 13 so that the embattled ARVN's in An Loc couldn't break out and the relief column couldn't break through. Its soldiers endured U.S. B-52 strikes and tactical air strikes, continuous shelling, and repeated ground assaults by ARVN infantry and armor. Yet they held their ground for thirty-eight days of continuous fighting.[30]

The 209th's sister regiments of the 7th Division also rebuilt themselves after the Pace battles in October to fight in the Easter Offensive. The 165th Regiment played a key role in the battle of Benchmark 75, where over five days they endured eight B-52 strikes, 142 tactical air strikes, and 30,000 rounds of incoming artillery.[31] The 141st Regiment led the attack on Firebase Tan Kai.[32]

As mentioned previously, the 271st Regiment of the NVA 9th Division did not participate in the Krek-Pace battle, but it did battle ARVN forces in Cambodia all during 1971. They started the Easter Offensive with a reported strength of 2,000 men. After overrunning Pace and ambushing a column from the ARVN 25th Division, they joined the fighting at An Loc and played a critical role in the May 11–12 attacks on the city itself.[33]

Their powers of recuperation notwithstanding, the North Vietnamese leadership committed a number of strategic, tactical, and operational errors that contributed to their defeat at An Loc. These included a failure to concentrate their forces on just one or two objectives instead of spreading them across all three military regions; poor coordination of tanks and infantry, so the enemy could pick them off separately and individually; and closing the escape route to the south, so the South Vietnamese had no choice but to stand and fight. A bad case of overconfidence, fed by the ARVN's poor showing in Lam Son 719 a year earlier, contributed to the North Vietnamese failure.[34]

But the most significant similarity between the successful defense of An Loc in the spring of 1972 and the successful defense of the Krek-Pace border area in the Fall of 1971 revolved around the successful use of integrated and proliferate U.S. firepower, particularly from the air. The massing of infantry and armor by the North Vietnamese outside of An Loc proved to be a target-rich environment for U.S. forces on a scale unprecedented in the Vietnam War. U.S. documents show 5,700 air strike sorties in Military Region III in April alone, or better than 190 a day. This includes U.S. and South Vietnamese air force tactical fighter bombers, Spooky and Spectre gunships, and B-52s. Over 700 B-52 strikes were flown in April and May alone in support of South Vietnamese forces defending An Loc.[35]

Unlike the Krek-Pace border battles where the heaviest fighting took place in Cambodia, the fighting at An Loc was almost completely on South Vietnamese territory. This meant U.S. advisers could stay on the ground with their units. The advisers performed a multitude of critical functions in this battle. The most obvious was the coordination of all this massive airborne firepower so that the bombs and rockets would land on enemy troops and not friendly troops. This is something the South Vietnamese had not yet mastered. U.S. advisers also provided intelligence on friendly troops to U.S. commanders, and their very presence lifted the morale of friendly troops and the civilian population. They also served as a critical backup for South Vietnamese ground commanders who were killed or incapable of leading.[36] General Donald McGiffert called the advisers "the glue that kept them (the ARVN) together."[37] However, as at Krek, the dependence on U.S. advisers and U.S. airpower would be a double-edged sword for the South Vietnamese. A year later, all U.S. advisers and all U.S. airpower would be gone, and the South Vietnamese would be on their own.

Some have argued that the collapse of the South Vietnamese Army in the spring of 1975 was not a foregone conclusion, and, in fact, the war had been won when U.S. aid was abruptly cut off by Congress. This argument is made most forcefully by Lewis Sorley in *A Better War: The Unexamined Tragedy of America's Last Years in Vietnam*. "There came a time when the war was won," Sorley begins. "The fighting wasn't over, but the war was won. This achievement can probably best be dated in late 1970, after the Cambodian incursion in the spring of the year."[38] Sorley then goes on to single out Military Region III as a shining example of victory. His support is a letter from General Michael S. Davidson, Major General Wagstaff's predecessor as senior U.S. commander of Military Region III. The letter says in part: "It is fair to say that by the winter of 1970–1971 the VC had virtually been exterminated, and the NVA, which had endeavored to go buy time with division size units, had been driven across the border into Cambodia."[39]

First, it is important to draw a distinction between a "victory" over the Vietcong insurgency and a "victory" over the North Vietnamese regular army. Most historians agree that the Vietcong insurgency had been severely diminished by 1971.[40] They would also concur that the North Vietnamese had been *temporarily* pushed out of South Vietnam by the 1970 Cambodian cross border offensive. But 50,000 battle hardened troops hovering in base camps just a few miles across the border is not the sign of a defeated enemy and without a defeated enemy there can be no victory.

As previously described, South Vietnamese units, strongly backed by American air power and logistical support, were not able to keep the "defeated" enemy from returning to their traditional base areas in 1971 and from mounting a massive offensive (that was nearly successful) in the spring of 1972. In short, it is hard to see how one successful defensive campaign (Krek-Pace in October), one nonevent (November–December shadow boxing near the Chup Rubber Plantation), and two embarrassing defeats (Dambe in March and Snoul in June) are evidence of a South Vietnamese "victory" in 1970–1971 by any definition. The 1970 Cambodian operation in Military Region III was successful in that it bought time for further U.S. troop withdrawals, which on its own is not insignificant, but was hardly the victory Sorley would like it to be.

General Wagstaff, the U.S. commander on the ground in Military Region III, certainly wasn't about to declare victory. He described the situation as a "stand off."[41] General Donn A. Starry reached a similar conclusion in a 1978 monograph: "The year 1971 was not successful to either side; it ended with the Viet Cong and North Vietnamese as strong, if not stronger, than the South Vietnamese."[42]

The North Vietnamese were back on the march ninety days after the 1971 Cambodian campaign ended in December of that year. They routed the South Vietnamese forces protecting Pace and Thien Ngon the first day of the 1972 Easter Offensive. South Vietnamese soldiers fought well enough to stop a massive North Vietnamese effort to capture An Loc, but the margin was a narrow one and required massive amounts of American assistance in terms of firepower and leadership. After An Loc and the Easter Offensive, the United States could declare Vietnamization a success and go home. The South Vietnamese, left with an impressive but unsustainable force structure, would grow weaker by the day. And even with massive American aid in 1972–1973, the South Vietnamese were never able to recapture any territory in Military Region III. The South Vietnamese did recapture Quang Tri in Military Region I in September 1972, but in Military Region III, Loc Ninh, Thien Ngon, Pace, and Lac Long remained under enemy control for the remainder of the war.[43]

The North Vietnamese, having learned a bloody lesson at An Loc and elsewhere in the spring of 1972, would set about to deliberately correct their shortcomings and in doing so, would get stronger every day. In the spring of 1975 they would strike again. The South Vietnamese military would collapse with surprising speed.

Retired Army Lieutenant General Phillip B. Davidson, the former intelligence chief for MACV and no relation to Michael S. Davidson, took a much different view from Sorley or Michael Davidson. In his 1988 history of the war, Phillip Davidson observed:

Nor did any knowledgeable individual delude himself that the RVNAF (Republic of Vietnam Armed Forces) could withstand a major NVA offensive. True ENHANCE and ENHANCE PLUS had loaded the RVNAF with equipment, but it soon became apparent that the United States had given South Vietnam airplanes they couldn't fly, ships they couldn't man, and tanks and other equipment they couldn't maintain. Even more fundamental, little or no progress had been made curing the basic flaws in the South Vietnamese government and its armed forces.[44]

The basic flaws in the South Vietnamese government Phillip Davidson refers to were never really addressed in General Thieu's reign because they were so deeply enmeshed in the way the Thieu government did its business and stayed in power. They didn't change and weren't going to change, no matter what the Americans wanted because change of that magnitude would threaten the government's very existence as much, or more, than the Communists did.

The assumption underlying the "victory" strategy Sorley advocates was the belief that the United States could and should forcefully intervene should the North Vietnamese violate the Paris Peace Accords. Clearly, it is highly unlikely that by 1972 the American public or the military would have supported the commitment of U.S. ground troops. In fact, it's not likely the troops would have been willing either. While ground troops did rise to the challenge of fulfilling their defensive mission in support of Vietnamization, could they have done so again if ordered to? When President Nixon ordered the Cambodian offensive in the spring of 1970, most of the troops involved responded positively because they saw it as a chance to hit back at the enemy who directly threatened them. A year later, U.S. troops rose to the challenge of supporting the South Vietnamese operation into Laos, although the level of enthusiasm was not high. By the time the Pace-Krek battles took place in the fall of 1971, U.S. troops at Pace again rose to the challenge but openly questioned the distinction between "offensive" and "defensive" patrolling.

Sorley makes the seductive argument that ground troops were not necessary. If only financial, logistical, and air support had been continued, the South Vietnamese would have been strong enough to prevail.[45] But this argument fails on two levels. First, just unleashing the B-52s and other aircraft, similar to the response to the 1972 Easter Offensive, overlooks the critical role played by U.S. advisers in coordinating these attacks on the ground and in shoring up leadership deficiencies in the South Vietnamese chain of command. If air power alone could have turned the tide of this war, there would have been no need to send in ground troops in 1965.

Second, the United States was no longer in a position strategically to commit such a large portion of its military strength, even without ground troops, to a war that meant less and less to the nation's security needs. By 1971 U.S. military planners, both in uniform and not, were speaking out publicly about the sorry state of U.S. forces in Europe, the Middle East, and other parts of Asia.[46] Defense Secretary Melvin Laird understood this better than anyone. Although criticized by some for his support of an aggressive troop withdrawal, Laird was no closet pacifist. He had supported U.S. involvement in Vietnam as a congressman, but as secretary of defense, he had to worry about the well-being of the whole U.S. force structure. Early in his tenure as secretary of defense he recognized that continued involvement in Vietnam seriously downgraded the ability of U.S. forces to respond elsewhere.[47]

In order to build up U.S. capacity in Vietnam to respond to the 1972 Easter Offensive, President Nixon and his lieutenants had to strip U.S. forces elsewhere—not only of aircraft and pilots but also of ground crews, air traffic controllers, security refueling capability, and logistical support. In fact, Secretary Laird opposed this dramatic redirection of resources because of his fears of the impact on the readiness of U.S. forces in other potential trouble spots.[48] This was not idle speculation. For example, in 1973 U.S. forces worldwide were put on alert in response to the Arab-Israeli Six Day War.[49]

As it was, the Air Force and Navy paid a high price for the rapid shift of planes and ships to Vietnam in the spring of 1972. Sailors and airmen were redeployed despite previous leave and training commitments. Maintenance schedules were disrupted. Spare parts were used up. Wear and tear on equipment and personnel exceeded guidelines. By the middle of 1972, all U.S. draftees were gone from Vietnam, but unrest among Air Force and Navy personnel, who were volunteers, not draftees, manifested itself in a series of incidents. This included disturbances on the carriers *Kitty Hawk* and *Constellation* and the fleet oiler *Hassayampa*.[50] "The U.S. military would cope with the material and personal costs of this deployment for a decade," concluded Air Force historian Stephen P. Randolph.[51]

The what ifs in history provide an opportunity to debate and, hopefully, better understand the great decisions of history. But based on what is now known about conditions on the ground in Military Region III and elsewhere in South Vietnam in 1971–1972, it is hard to picture a happy ending of an independent South Vietnam capable of defending itself without massive American aid and military support, and that support was not forthcoming. The activities on the South Vietnam–Cambodian border during the crucial years of Vietnamization foreshadowed a difficult road ahead. The South Vietnamese armed forces fought well at times, and the North Vietnamese failed at times. But the pattern that emerged shows clearly that the North Vietnamese were a little tougher, a lot more resourceful, and much more focused on what they needed to do once the Americans and their B-52s were gone.

CHAPTER TWENTY-SIX

Pace as History

The work of military historians to date reflects a marked lack of interest in the events at and around Firebase Pace in the fall of 1971. The first military histories to cover the war on the ground emerged from the U.S. Army's military monograph series. Major General David Ott's *Field Artillery 1954–1973*, published in 1975, is regarded as the classic account of American artillery forces in the Vietnam War and the firebases they occupied. Nowhere in the 253-page volume is Firebase Pace mentioned, except when it fell to the Communists in the 1972 Easter Offensive.[1] Two subsequent commercially published ventures describing artillery in the Vietnam War made no mention at all of Pace: Bantam Books' *The Illustrated History of Artillery in the Vietnam War*, published in 1987, and Osprey Publishing's *Vietnam Firebases 1965–73*, published in 2007.

Pace fared no better in the more general military histories published since the war's end. It did not make it at all into retired Lieutenant General Phillip B. Davidson's 837-page opus, *Vietnam at War* (1988). Nor was it recognized in either of Shelby Stanton's works—*The Rise and Fall of an American Army: U.S. Ground Forces in Vietnam, 1965–1973* (1985) or *Anatomy of a Division: The 1st Cav in Vietnam* (1987). More general histories were equally silent, including Stanley Karnow's 750-page *Vietnam, A History* (1983) or Boston Publishing's multivolume series, *The Vietnam Experience* (1981–1988). Even the Army itself found no reason to address Pace from a military perspective, giving it no mention in either *MACV: The Joint Command in the Years of Withdrawal, 1968–1973* (2007) or *Advice and Support: The Final Years, 1965–1973* (1988). What attention Pace did receive from military historians was the distinction of being overrun in the first day of the Easter Offensive in Military Region III. Dale Andrade and James Willbanks devoted a couple of paragraphs to these events in *Trial by Fire: The 1972 Easter Offensive, America's Last Vietnam Battle* and *The Battle of An Loc*, respectively.[2]

While the military operations in and around Pace in September and October of 1971 didn't generate much interest, the combat refusals did. Richard Boyle's overdramatic account in *Flower of the Dragon* was first in what would be a sequence of similar descriptions.[3] David Cortright, a former Army enlisted man, picked up Boyle's theme in his 1975 book, *Soldiers in Revolt: GI Resistance during the Vietnam War*. Cortright based his version on Boyle's but was also careful to point out that Boyle's description "becomes uncertain," because "independent observers say Boyle in fact set up the mutiny and subsequent protest." He credits Nicholas

Proffitt's October 27, 1971, *Newsweek* piece. But Cortright also places his treatment of the events at Pace in a section labeled "The Quasi-Mutiny," which he begins by stating that "mutiny is a potent and evocative term, but it accurately describes what in fact took place frequently among American soldiers in Vietnam. . . . The latter stages of the Vietnam War produced no fewer than ten major incidents of mutiny," of which he includes Pace as one.[4]

Myra MacPherson upped the ante in 1984 with *Long Time Passing: Vietnam and the Haunted Generation.* Citing Cortright as her source, she describes the incidents at Pace as an "insurrection."[5] Ten years later, in his 1995 biography of filmmaker Oliver Stone, James Riordan identifies Stone's associate, Richard Boyle, as the man who "secretly returned" to Vietnam and "broke the story of the mutiny at Fire Support Base Pace."[6]

Gerald Nicosia went even further six years later in 2001's *Home to War: A History of the Vietnam Veteran's Movement.* He characterized the events at Pace in this way: "The year 1971 had seen the rise of large-scale mutinies among enlisted men. In October, almost the whole of Bravo Company, First Cav, at Firebase Pace on the Cambodian border, had refused to continue night patrols. Several senators and congressmen had called for an investigation, but the infantrymen refused to budge."[7] So, in the first thirty years following the event, Pace had escalated from a "quasi mutiny," to an "insurrection," to a "mutiny," to a "large-scale mutiny" in five-year increments. But not everyone writing about the Army's problems in this period chose such inflammatory language.

Army Lieutenant Colonel William L. Hauser became the first author to write about Fire Support Base Pace after Boyle. Hauser devoted 700 words to the Pace "incident" in his 1973 volume, *America's Army in Crisis: A Study in Civil-Military Relations.* Under the heading "Discipline in Vietnam," Hauser concluded the following:

> Probably the most unfortunate aspect of the Firebase Pace affair . . . was the impression created that something extraordinary had happened. In fact, even a cursory reading of military history shows that refusals are not rare in war, and the conflict is unusual that lacks at least one full-fledged mutiny. Such moments in combat, when the discipline of individuals or even whole units is overcome by the powerful instinct of self-preservation, are the ultimate challenge to leadership. The incidents described above, however, were scarcely more than demurrals at what appeared to be ill-considered orders.[8]

Hauser cited Nicholas Proffitt's October 25, 1971, *Newsweek* article as his principal source. Robert Jay Lifton, writing on antiwar sentiment of GIs in 1973, described the incidents at Pace as "refusal to follow combat orders," not a mutiny.[9] Richard Moser, discussing GI dissent in Vietnam in *The New Winter Soldiers: GI and Veteran Dissent during the Vietnam Era* (1996), described the refusal at Pace as follows: "Combat refusals were complicated events in which good soldiers hesitated or chose not to court death for questionable goals or risky battle tactics." He listed his documentation as Richard Boyle's *Flower of the Dragon* and an October 12, 1971, wire service story in the *Chicago Tribune*.[10]

In 1995 the Army's Center for Military History weighed in with its version in William M. Hammond's *Public Affairs: The Military and the Media, 1968–1973*, part of its Army in Vietnam Series. Hammond's 350-word essay in the section devoted to combat refusals is the only complete statement on the issue in any official history. He focuses primarily on the press coverage, which Hammond finds was handled in "an even handed manner," except for Boyle's characterization as a "so-called mutiny."[11]

Perhaps it is a reflection on the complexity and divisions on the Vietnam War that so many alternative realities could flow from the same source material. The growth of the Internet in the late 1990s provided yet another medium for differing realities to play out. On the one hand, it provided a forum for veterans, including those who had been at Pace, to memorialize their experiences. Foremost among them were veterans of the 2/32d Field Artillery in their Web site, http://www.proudamericans.homestead.com. The site contains not only summaries of the ORLL reports from every quarter of the 2/32d's stay in Vietnam, but it also includes reminiscences from Pace veterans. Tom Colaiezzi's 700-word essay, "How FSB Pace was Named," and Paul Cibolski's "The Battle for Fire Support Base Pace" are the two most detailed. Colaiezzi was a fire direction officer who was with Lieutenant Pace the night he was killed. Staff Sergeant Cibolski was a section chief on one of Pace's 175mm guns. Soldiers from other units have posted items as well. The Vietnam Helicopter Pilots Association includes the incident report on the crash of Warrant Officer Stansbury's helicopter on their Web site. Paul Marling, a former medic with Delta Company 1/12th Cavalry, published his 2,800-word account of a reunion with families of the downed helicopter at the Usenet group alt.war.vietnam (accessible through Google Groups). The Virtual Wall provides testimonials to Gary Lynn Pace and to Warrant Officer Stansbury's helicopter crew.

The Internet also provided an opportunity for those with dissenting opinions to express themselves, especially if they wanted to characterize events at Pace as a mutiny. A Google search for "Firebase Pace" or "Fire Support Base Pace" will generate forty to fifty unduplicated entries, of which 90–95 percent refer to Richard Boyle or his account.[12] The remaining are references to news stories or Web sites of individual veterans.

Pace's role as an icon of the antiwar movement also played a prominent role in the 2005 David Zeigler documentary, *Sir! No Sir!*, an award-winning film that claimed to tell "the suppressed story of the GI movement to end the war in Vietnam." The five-minute segment on Fire Support Base Pace begins with a dramatic reading by veteran actor Ed Asner of Robert Heinl's "The Collapse of the Armed Forces." An interview with Richard Boyle follows, augmented by still photographs and excerpts from the audiotapes he made on October 9–10, 1971. Boyle does not use the word "mutiny," but he repeats his claim that the Army denied these soldiers were there and that the refusal was some sort of turning point in the war.[13]

The confusion over Fire Support Base Pace's role in history is best represented by Michael P. Kelly's 2002 *Where We Were in Vietnam*. Kelly pulled together an exhaustive list of more than 10,000 entries describing firebases, landing zones, airfields, base camps, and other installations in Vietnam and surrounding areas. For each facility or firebase, he included a location (including map coordinates), who occupied the base, when it was occupied, and any significant events that transpired there. Fire Support Base Pace is included. This is what it says: "Approx 3 KM S Cambodia, 4 KM NW Thien Ngon AF, 27 KM WSW Katum and 34 KM NNW Tay Ninh. Apparently built sometime between 70–72? Apparently a mutiny of some sort here at one time? Tay Ninh pr, III Corps."[14]

The refusals at Pace were part of what transpired there, but they were not mutinies in the most common understanding of the word, and they were not the only activity of significance involving the GIs who fought there. It is unlikely Mr. Kelly, himself a combat veteran who was badly wounded in Vietnam, would intentionally do anything to reflect poorly on his fellow veterans. More likely, he repeated or remembered something he had heard or seen from the writings of Richard Boyle, or Myra MacPherson, or Gerald Nicosia, all of whom perpetuated alternative interpretations to advance a certain point of view. But the perpetuation of the myth of Pace solely as an icon of rebellion or insurrections demeans the sacrifice of the young men who served their country honorably in a time of incredible turmoil. This is especially true of the five young men who gave their lives defending Pace and the other fifty who spilled blood there.

The varying interpretations of the refusals at Pace since the war ended replicates itself in interpretations of the other combat refusals as well. Cortright enumerates what he calls ten instances of mutiny in his book *Soldiers in Revolt*. He includes, in addition to Pace, what he calls "the first reported incidence of mass mutiny in Vietnam," in describing Alpha Company's refusal in the Song Chang Valley in 1969. He refers to Charlie Company's 1970 War Zone C refusal as "another mutiny." B Troop's 1971 refusal on Route 9 is described as "one of the most significant and widely publicized mutinies of the war." For good measure, Cortright lists another six incidents.[15] MacPherson and Moser dutifully follow suit.

Alternative interpretations began as early as 1973. After reviewing B Troop's episode on Route 9, as well as at Pace, Lieutenant Colonel William Hauser concluded: "What makes headlines in an unpopular war would hardly make back-page news in a conflict with public support. In any case, the Army's reaction to such breaches of battle discipline as did occur was generally a healthy one of forgive, forget and get on with the job."[16]

Keith William Nolan reached a similar conclusion in his 1986 book, *Into Laos: The Story of Dewey Canyon II / Lam Son 719, Vietnam 1971*, which included the B Troop episode on Route 9. "And yet, most combat units continued to function," Nolan wrote.[17] He elaborated on this point in *Sappers in the Wire: The Life and Death of Firebase Mary Ann*: "And yet, however reluctantly, there were still soldiers like those in the 1–46th Infantry out fighting the war. Their hardships should be recognized. Perret [historian Geoffrey Perret] got it right when he wrote that these troops who 'had faith in nothing much, least of all men like Johnson and Nixon,' still 'served their country a lot better than it served them.'"[18]

David Axe picked up on the same theme in an October 2005 article he wrote for *Vietnam* magazine. Axe defended the actions of Alpha Company 3/21st Infantry, the unit involved in the temporary refusal in the Song Chang Valley in August 1969. Axe included material from Alpha Company's battalion commander, Lieutenant Colonel Robert Bacon, defending the performance of his soldiers that day.[19]

It is important to point out that in all four refusals, the immediate objectives of the military mission were accomplished. The Americal Division secured the Song Chang Valley, at least temporarily, in its 1969 summer offensive. The 1st Air Cavalry Division pushed the North Vietnamese across the border, at least temporarily, in the 1970 spring offensive in War Zone C. The Americal Division, 101st Airborne, and 1/5th Mechanized held Route 9 open, at least temporarily, for retreating South Vietnamese troops in the spring of 1971. And, in the fall of 1971, units of the 1st Cavalry Division's 3d Brigade and the 2/32d Field Artillery protected the Cambodian border and held off the North Vietnamese until the spring.

Yet the controversy (and confusion) surrounding these events continues. For example, William Thomas Allison, a respected historian, wrote about Charlie Company 2/7th Cavalry's April 1970 refusal to walk down a trail near the Cambodian border in his carefully documented book, *Military Justice in Vietnam: The Rule of Law in an American War*. According to Allison, this was an example of the "disintegration of US forces in Vietnam," because "in one of the more memorable television news reports from the war a rifle company refused to patrol a known dangerous trail right in front of Columbia broadcasting [CBS] cameras. Americans at home got to see a combat refusal first hand."[20] Allison's account came out in 2007, well after both J. D. Coleman's 1991 account and John Laurence's 2002 account, explaining how this incident reflected the actions of a good veteran unit dealing with confusion over a change in command and an impending B-52 strike rather than a breakdown in discipline.[21]

These dueling realities extended beyond just combat refusals. The same pattern manifests itself in historians' overall treatment of the 1970–1971 withdrawal period. Some, most notably Keith William Nolan, Phillip B. Davidson, and William Hammond, tried to present a more balanced view of the challenges facing the Army on the ground in Vietnam in this period. Others did not.

Treatment of the attack on Firebase Mary Ann by military historians is a classic example. By the mid-1980s, the debacle at Mary Ann had assumed almost mythical proportions. Shelby Stanton teed off first in his 1985 book, *The Rise and Fall of an American Army: U.S. Ground Forces in Vietnam, 1965–1973*. Stanton wrote, "They [VC] roamed through the firebase, destroying one 155mm howitzer and damaging another, throwing satchel charges in the command bunker, knifing Americans in their sleeping bags and wrecking communications equipment. They killed and wounded nearly half the 250 soldiers there, who only got ten in exchange because they were cringing in their bunkers."[22]

A year later, Keith William Nolan described the defenders of Mary Ann as "a mob."[23] In 1989 Geoffrey Perret chimed in with *A Country Made by War*, in which he described the defenders of Fire Base Mary Ann as "too drunk, too stoned, too lazy and too undisciplined to mount a proper perimeter defense. The enemy simply walked in and took the fire base."[24]

Ten years later Nolan decided to examine this incident in more detail in *Sappers in the Wire: The Life and Death of Fire Support Base Mary Ann*. Taking the first comprehensive look at this incident since it occurred a quarter of a century earlier, Nolan reviewed official reports and interviewed dozens of survivors. He concluded this about Mary Ann:

Unfortunately, we historians got it wrong. I do not mean to whitewash what happened at Firebase Mary Ann with such a remark, for the incident was a tragic disaster with much to teach today's soldiers about vigilance. What I do mean to say is that commentary which tars the 1–46th Infantry as a "mob," as I put it at first glance, is grossly exaggerated. Most of the draftees on Mary Ann had already proven themselves in combat. My comment about "waning" action was far off the mark when it came to this particular area of operations.

While some men may have been "cringing in their bunkers" during the sapper attack, much of the inaction was typical of any surprise attack in which a unit's officers are almost instantly killed or wounded. Leaderless troops were reluctant to start blasting away at shadows in the dark, unable to distinguish friend from foe. I found no evidence of sappers "knifing Americans in their sleeping bags." There was panic and confusion that night, but there were also men like "Doc" Vogelsang, a conscientious objector turned medic, who ran unarmed through the smoke and flames to treat the wounded . . . and Lieutenant McGee, who went down in hand-to-hand combat . . . and Tom Schneider, who although wounded three times, took up a back-to-back position outside his bunker with his buddy, "Shorty" Rivero, and helped kill four sappers . . . and Bill Meek, who got two more despite his own injuries . . . and David Tarnay, who stayed on the radio in the command bunker despite the fact that it was blowing up and burning down around his head. The actions of these men and others have never been recorded in any book, and it is my purpose to finally describe in minute-by-minute detail exactly what happened that infamous night. The men who were killed or maimed for life on that hill deserve as much.[25]

The contemporary press accounts, based on partial information and written against a short deadline, by and large did not sensationalize the story. The three historians cited above (Stanton, Perret, and Nolan) all had the luxury of writing well after the event. All three had reputations of being fairly knowledgeable about military matters and were generally supportive of the GIs on the ground. Yet in this case they saw the event through their own filters of what the 1971 Army was about. Undoubtedly, the 1/46th Infantry's association with the Americal Division didn't help. That unit already had a low reputation because of its association with the 1968 My Lai Massacre, which included a cover-up involving the division's entire chain of command. But My Lai had happened more than three years earlier. None of the soldiers at Mary Ann had anything to do with My Lai. Nonetheless, Keith William Nolan was the only one of the three historians listed above to try to set the record straight.

Mary Ann was an embarrassment because its defenders let their guard down when they shouldn't have. And those soldiers paid a terrible price in dead and wounded for their mistake. In its own way, Mary Ann is an extreme example of how anecdote and symbolism can overpower a more complex reality. Yet for those trying to make a political point, the temptation was to leverage the Army's troubles as yet more evidence for a specific point of view. For those on the political left, the Army's problems were further evidence of what a bad decision it was to go to war in the first place and why withdrawals should have been accelerated. For example, in *Army in Revolt*, David Cortright argued that in "recounting this seemingly endless tale of woes we tend to lose sight of what was actually happening in the ranks. Underlying the various statistics and measures of unrest was an Army on the verge of collapse, crippled by a virtual 'general strike' among a sizable minority of its enlisted people."[26]

For the other side of the political spectrum, focusing on the woes of the withdrawal Army provided an opportunity to argue that—after being stabbed in the back by critics at home—the soldiers' lack of motivation cost us the war, not a failed strategy or bad decisions at the higher levels. For example, General Bruce Palmer argued the following:

Performance continued to be of a high quality until the 1969–70 period, when dissent at home began to be reflected in troop attitudes and conduct in Vietnam. From 1969 until the last U.S. combat troops left in August 1972, a decline in performance set in; the discovery of widespread drug use in Vietnam in the spring of 1970 signaled that more morale and disciplinary troubles lay ahead. The so-called "fraggings" of leaders that began in 1969–70 were literally murderous indicators of poor morale and became a matter of deep concern.

Extremely adverse environmental conditions and very trying circumstances contributed to this decline in performance. Particularly galling to our forces in the field were the widely publicized statements of highly placed U.S. officials, including senators, against American involvement. Such statements were perceived to support the enemy and badly damaged the morale of our troops.[27]

What gave these sweeping generalizations of decay resonance was an underlying ring of credibility. The people making the charges were not politicians but people of substance. Bruce Palmer was a retired Army general who commanded II Field Force in Vietnam. Robert Heinl was a retired Marine colonel. David Cortright was a former Army enlisted man who skillfully, but somewhat selectively, used the Pentagon's own numbers to make his case.

There was a problem with drugs and fraggings. Motivation did become more difficult as the war wound down. People in the lower ranks were more willing to challenge authority. But what these analyses share is a theme of victimization—of both officers and enlisted men who were too confused, too weak, too strung out, or too mindless to take charge of their own destiny, or even to defend themselves, especially in the picture Heinl painted. What these analyses overlook is how both officers and enlisted men, regardless of how they felt about the war, struggled but managed to hold it together without much help from anywhere else. Thrown together by a common sense of danger, they banded together to overcome their environment, get the job done, and return safely home. A close examination of even the most notorious combat refusals in this period shows the ability of these men to soldier on. They showed it at FSB Pace, they showed it elsewhere in III Corps, and they showed it in the other military regions of Vietnam.

CHAPTER TWENTY-SEVEN

Lessons Learned?

In 2005 former Defense Secretary Melvin R. Laird contributed an article for *Foreign Affairs* on the lessons of Vietnam based on his experience during the withdrawal period of 1969–1972.[1] His writing focused on providing advice that might be applicable to the Iraq War, then in its third year. But Laird's lessons learned also stand on their own as a useful way to look back at America's disengagement from Vietnam. As the senior civilian leader of the military in that period, Laird had to balance realities on the ground in Vietnam with the Byzantine realities of politics in Washington and the Nixon White House. As one of the few senior U.S. decision makers (along with General Abrams) to touch Vietnam and emerge with his reputation largely intact, he deserves at least the presumption of some degree of credibility. Thus, Secretary Laird's lessons learned is a good place to look back at these key decisions, with a special emphasis on their relationship to reality on the ground on the Cambodian border and elsewhere in Vietnam from 1970 to 1972.

1. *Getting Out Is Harder than Getting In.*—"It's a helluva lot easier to get into a war than it is to get out of one." Reportedly these words were former Secretary Laird's parting advice to newly installed Defense Secretary Donald Rumsfeld in February 2001.[2] Laird was clearly speaking from his own experience in the painful withdrawal from Vietnam. Once a military commitment is made and soldiers start dying and suffering grievous injuries, the degree of flexibility remaining for any country's political leaders have decreases enormously. A blood debt has been incurred, and leaders owe it to the soldiers in harm's way, and to their family and loved ones, to make sure those sacrifices are not in vain. This obligation is present whether the original decision to go to war was good or not and whether conditions do or do not change.

The Nixon administration expressed this by describing its objective as "peace with honor." This meant turning the war over to the South Vietnamese, negotiating with the North Vietnamese, and securing the return of American prisoners of war while conducting a phased withdrawal of U.S. troops.[3] At the time the Paris Peace Accords were signed in January 1973, this appeared to have been accomplished successfully. But a little over two years later, South Vietnam collapsed with surprising speed. Historians, politicians, analysts, and academics have since debated whether the war ended in peace with honor or something much less, which brings out the next point.

2. *Defining Success Is Almost as Difficult as Achieving Success.*—Laird argues that his efforts in Nixon's first term were a success because the United States was able to withdraw its forces from Vietnam while building up South Vietnam's ability to defend itself. Requiring our allies to achieve a certain "standard of competence" is something Laird argues has to be a major building block of an exit strategy.[4] But this is much easier said than done.

The U.S. Command in Vietnam did collect information on the effectiveness of South Vietnamese military forces as part of a system called SEER (System for Evaluating the Effectiveness of RVNAF [Republic of Vietnam Armed Forces]), but the system struggled with its own set of credibility problems, proving again the challenge of defining success.[5] The U.S. Command also developed a measuring system for pacification called HES (Hamlet Evaluation System) that Sorley and others are fond of quoting as measures of success.[6] HES and SEER were both well intentioned but suffered from the same flaws. In a military culture, soldiers in general, and officers in particular, are expected to do what is necessary to accomplish their mission. "Can do" is the operative phrase, and excuses are not welcome. This does not mean that the uniformed military personnel filling out these forms were being intentionally dishonest, but the stakes were so high that the advisers and others feeding information into the systems felt they had no choice but to report success because failure was not an option.[7]

We also now know that the withdrawal was accomplished without a major catastrophe while U.S. troops remained in Vietnam, although U.S. forces endured an embarrassment at Mary Ann, as did the South Vietnamese forces at Snoul and Dambe. So, in that sense it was a success, but at the cost of the lives of 11,000 servicemen in that time period (mid-1969–mid-1972), or about 20 percent of the total U.S. losses in Vietnam.[8]

Secretary Laird argues with some degree of persuasiveness that his model of Vietnamization worked: the troops were pulled out, the draft was ended, and South Vietnam did not collapse (at least not immediately). In addition, President Nixon got reelected in 1972 in what could be argued was, at least in large part, a referendum on his handling of the Vietnam War.[9] The problem with this line of argument is that it does not account for the collapse of the South Vietnamese government twenty-seven months later. Laird counters that the defeat of the South Vietnamese in 1975 wasn't the fault of the Nixon administration policy or peace treaty. He argues that they were overcome because "Congress snatched defeat from the jaws by cutting off funding for our ally in 1975."[10] This is essentially the same argument Lewis Sorley made, except Sorley declared victory at the end of 1970, and he put at least part of the blame for defeat on the Nixon administration's negotiation of the Paris Peace Accords.[11]

As discussed previously, the conditions on the ground in the Krek–Snoul–Tay Ninh border area from the end of 1970 through the 1972 Easter Offensive at

An Loc do not coincide with the rosy picture of a defeated enemy or a victorious ARVN as portrayed by either Laird or Sorley. Historian James Willbanks provided a different definition of success in *Abandoning Vietnam: How America Left and South Vietnam Lost Its War*. He argues that if success meant pulling out U.S. troops while avoiding an immediate catastrophe, then Vietnamization was a success. If the goal was to get U.S. troops out and leave behind a stable, viable government able to defend itself against the North Vietnamese, it was not.[12]

That seems to be as fair an assessment as any. Because of the way the war ended with the collapse of South Vietnam in 1975, Secretary Laird and General Abrams have never gotten the credit they deserve for successfully extracting U.S. troops under fire. This includes the 1971 battles around Fire Support Base Pace, which could have turned out very differently. The debacle at Fire Support Base Mary Ann six months earlier stood out because, fortunately, it was the exception rather than the rule.

But the fighting between South Vietnamese and North Vietnamese troops along the Cambodian and Laotian borders in 1971 and 1972 revealed fundamental weaknesses in the South Vietnamese army that would have made it very difficult to argue that South Vietnam could have survived much longer than it did without a reescalation of the war. What it also does is raise questions about timing. Was the problem a failure to stay the course, as Laird argues, or something more fundamental?

3. *Timing Is Everything.*—Once a decision is made to withdraw from combat, the next decision is how fast. It is probably the most difficult decision because the danger of making a wrong decision is high. If withdrawal happens too precipitously and the effort collapses, then it appears the sacrifice was in vain. If the withdrawal is too slow or indigenous forces don't step up, the public gets restless and additional sacrifice appears to be in vain. While guiding the U.S. withdrawal from Vietnam, Secretary Laird was attacked by critics on the left for moving too slowly and critics on the right for moving too quickly. The flip answer would be, then, that he must be doing something right, but that really begs the question. Unfortunately, there is no simple template to measure how fast is too fast or how slow is too slow. What is clear in hindsight is that the withdrawal of ground troops took thirty-eight months, from July 1, 1969, to August 30, 1972, compared with forty-nine months for build-up, from March 1965 to a peak in April 1969.[13]

The timing question Laird does not address involves the relative pluses and minuses of a fixed withdrawal date. Opponents of a fixed withdrawal date argue that such a measure would limit needed flexibility to adapt to conditions on the ground and would also benefit the enemy by letting him know our ultimate plans. With the Vietnam War having ended so long ago, we now have the benefit of hindsight to evaluate this argument. While the historical record shows that Washington gave some flexibility to MACV in Saigon over troop withdrawals, the timeline was driven by Washington, and Washington was driven by the date of November 7, 1972, when President Nixon would stand for reelection based on the success of his Vietnamization program.

When it came to keeping the North Vietnamese off balance, the argument is even more specious. Any North Vietnamese fifth grader could do the math that would answer this question: if you start with 543,000 troops in a country and withdraw them at a rate of 10,000 a month, how long would it take to get to a residual number of 50,000? If you upped the rate to 12,000, how long would it take? Not only that, but U.S. planners had to share information with South Vietnamese planners so ARVN would be ready to take over. As we suspected then, and know now, the North Vietnamese had deeply penetrated the South Vietnamese command structure and already knew everything the ARVN knew.[14] So, the elaborate charade of a secret withdrawal date didn't keep anyone in the dark except for the American public.

It is instructive to know now what we only could have guessed then, which is what a weak lever the withdrawal schedule was on the North Vietnamese. For nearly three years, from 1969 to mid-1972, when there were enough U.S. troops in Vietnam to presumably exert "leverage," negotiations went nowhere. Only in October of 1972, after the failure of the spring offensive and after U.S. ground troops were gone, were the United States and North Vietnam able to "negotiate" an end to the war.[15]

4. *Allies Are Not Always Friends.*—History is replete with examples of military alliances where managing the relationship with one's allies is almost as difficult as managing the war against one's enemies. During World War II, even though the United States and Great Britain shared a common heritage and common enemy, squabbling among the commanders required constant attention. Add the Russians to that mix, and coalition warfare featured a high degree of distrust. In Korea, U.S. commanders had a constant challenge in keeping South Korean President Syngman Rhee on the same page.

Vietnam would turn out to be no different. The most obvious rupture occurred when the South Vietnamese government in October 1972 balked at signing the terms of the Paris Peace Accords. Some analysts argue the United States ended up bombing the North to get the South back to the conference table.[16] These larger strategic issues aside, the fighting around Fire Support Base Pace in late 1971 showed how complex that relationship could be in its own right. South Vietnamese troops, particularly airborne units from the Strategic Reserve, played a significant role in protecting the beleaguered base. Their availability depended in turn on General Wagstaff's success in convincing General Minh to overcome his innate sense of caution to make the commitment, but what if he hadn't? General Wagstaff would have then faced the unpleasant choice of leaving U.S. troops in an exposed position where they could have suffered significant losses, or trying to extract these troops under enemy fire, which would have been equally dangerous.

The larger question this raises is more difficult to resolve. At this stage, the United States was fighting for peace with honor. That meant getting U.S. troops out while giving the South Vietnamese a chance to determine their own destiny. It also meant recognizing the South Vietnamese government as something more than a puppet, which in turn meant allowing this supposedly independent government to do what it needed to do, even if at times it worked against U.S. interests, because to do otherwise would undercut the claims of independence. Consequently, for some period of time (almost two years) the U.S. Command had to work with General Minh, even though they felt he was not up to the job, because of Minh's close ties to the Saigon government, specifically President Thieu.[17]

Arnold Isaacs covered the Vietnam War for the *Baltimore Sun*. Writing about the collapse of Vietnam eight years after the fall of Saigon, he described the dilemmas facing U.S. policy as follows:

> In South Vietnam, during Thieu's years, a fatal passivity ran from the president's office to the village street. Among all but a tiny handful of Vietnamese, the Americans were deemed responsible for Vietnam's fate. Neither in the leadership nor in the population at large—except for the Communists—was there any conviction that the future could be grasped in their own hands. But the Americans, imprisoned in their own faulty doctrines and their ignorance of Vietnamese realities, never found a way to influence the ruling system either. Through the entire war, power in South Vietnam was used only for the personal ends of those who held it.
>
> In fact, just as the Thieu regime seemed to combine the worst effects of democracy and dictatorship, the Americans seemed to reap all the disadvantages of both intervention and nonintervention in Vietnamese affairs. The U.S. could not really dictate events, certainly where the personal interests of members of the Vietnamese power structure were concerned. But the Americans did often make Vietnamese decisions meaningless. The sheer weight of the U.S. presence overwhelmed the Vietnamese capacity for organization and leadership, so the result of the alliance in the end was a kind of paralysis.[18]

One alternative would have been to let the Saigon government make its own mistakes and learn the hard way. But as long as U.S. troops were involved, the Nixon administration could not afford to take the risk politically of a string of South Vietnamese failures. So the United States could intervene with overwhelming firepower, like it did at Krek or An Loc, or pretend the defeat didn't happen (like at Dambe or Snoul). Either way, it did not leave South Vietnamese allies fully capable of defending themselves or as a society fully capable of governing itself.

In his *Foreign Affairs* article, Laird calls the U.S. effort in Vietnam "a success story—albeit a costly one—in nation building, even though the democracy we sought halfheartedly to build failed."[19] It is difficult to understand how Vietnam's failed democracy can be labeled a success at the same time. It may be that Secretary Laird himself struggled with how to put the best face on what he knew was a failure.

Laird's biographer, Dale Van Atta, reports that Laird privately thought the Thieu government's rigged election in October 1971 actually undercut Vietnamization and refused to be photographed with Thieu as a result.[20] The ultimate irony of the Krek-Pace campaign was that it started because the North Vietnamese were trying to embarrass the Thieu government just before the October 3, 1971, presidential election. The North Vietnamese failed in this case, but the South Vietnamese government embarrassed itself anyway by running a rigged election that involved intimidating opponents and shutting down dissenting newspapers, which undermined its credibility at home and the credibility of its American allies.[21]

In the fall of 1971, President Nixon sent California governor Ronald Reagan to Vietnam as his personal envoy to show his support for President Thieu. At an October 15 press conference, Governor Reagan responded to the critics of the recent South Vietnamese presidential election. He congratulated President Thieu on his October 3 victory, which he described as "a referendum." Reagan went on to compare President Thieu's victory to George Washington's first presidential campaign, in which the first president of the United States also ran unopposed.[22]

While the Nixon administration had a valid point in saying the success of representative democracy in the fifteen-year-old Republic of Vietnam cannot be measured by the same standards of the almost two-hundred-year-old political system in the United States, the comparison with George Washington is a telling one. Washington succeeded as a leader because he put the country's interests ahead of his own. He identified and supported strong subordinates as both president and commander in chief. He developed a winning strategy to defeat a better armed foe. And he did this all while maintaining public support and working through difficulties with a cantankerous Congress. President Thieu was not able to do any of this. This meant when the end came in 1975 the Thieu government had nowhere to turn.

5. *Know Your Enemy.*—Former Defense Secretaries Robert McNamara and Melvin Laird don't agree on a lot, but the one thing they do seem to agree on is that we really blew it in terms of understanding the Vietnamese, particularly the Vietnamese the United States ended up fighting against.[23] Viewing Vietnam Communists through Cold War lenses marked Ho Chi Minh and his followers as Communists (which they were) but overlooked their appeal as Vietnam nationalists. What is equally as troubling is how little was known then and now about what made the North Vietnamese army tick, and how they could take the pounding unleashed on them and still manage to prevail. During World War II, the U.S. Army produced a detailed handbook on both German and Japanese forces. Similar documents were produced on Chinese and Russian forces during the Cold War.[24] And

although a great deal of material about the North Vietnamese army was captured, presented, and analyzed, very little exists in print about how that army prevailed, even after years of declassification. There is no wartime handbook on North Vietnamese and Vietcong forces, nor is there much on individual units.

For example, a search for the history of the 209th and 271st NVA Regiments would turn up nothing. The Military History Division of MACV did a handful of regimental profiles, including one on the 271st sister regiment, the 273d.[25] But only a few of these were completed, and all seem to end in June–December 1969, well before Vietnamization got under way. As a result, mythology and half-truths tended to dominate U.S. Command's thinking about its North Vietnamese enemies, as opposed to a hardheaded assessment of strengths to avoid and weaknesses to exploit.

Lewis Sorley quotes General Abrams as observing, "Enemy staying power is his most effective battlefield characteristic. It is based first on his complete disregard for expenditure of resources, both men and material, and second on discipline through fear, intimidation and brutality."[26] While North Vietnam was very much a police state that did employ fear, intimidation, and brutality, this characterization doesn't explain how North Vietnamese units were still able to accomplish their mission far from home, dispersed in small groups. An army held together solely by fear could not function in that way for extended periods of time, because as soon as it dispersed its soldiers would disappear. While the North Vietnamese had a desertion problem, as did the South Vietnamese, the North Vietnamese were able to motivate enough of their soldiers long enough to prevail.

Senior American policy makers were never able to fully anticipate North Vietnamese moves because they also never fully understood the motivation of the senior leadership in Hanoi. Arnold Isaacs described the North Vietnamese approach to peace "negotiations" this way: After feeling they were betrayed by negotiated "settlements" in 1946 and again in 1954, the leadership in Hanoi were determined to avoid what they saw as another Munich in settling for anything less than total victory.[27]

The Johnson administration tried a negotiated settlement anyway and failed. The Nixon administration at first threatened reescalation in 1969 and failed.[28] Negotiations succeeded only after the United States initiated a unilateral withdrawal and agreed to allow North Vietnamese forces to remain in South Vietnam. In exchange, the North Vietnamese dropped their demand that the Thieu government be replaced, thereby setting the stage for a decent interval between the departure of U.S. troops and the fall of the South Vietnamese government.[29] It was the best the administration could do given the situation on the ground and at home, but it was not a victory.

Laird seemed to recognize this to a greater degree than many of his colleagues by defining what he calls the "asymmetry of stakes," meaning victory was "everything to North Vietnam and nothing to the average American."[30] Consequently, the North Vietnamese were willing to pay any price and bear any burden to prevail. The American public was not. What Laird's argument overlooks is that the South Vietnamese were not willing, either.

The ultimate irony here is that the North Vietnamese, who existed in a closed society, and who Lyndon Johnson once referred to as a "piddling piss ant country," were better able to understand their enemies and what motivated them than the U.S. government, with a vast intelligence network and technological resources, was able to understand North Vietnam.

6. *A Little Candor Goes a Long Way.*—When a society asks soldiers to risk their lives, it has an obligation to let those soldiers and their loved ones know what they are fighting for and what dangers they face. During the Vietnam draw down of 1969–1972, primary responsibility for translating administration policy objectives into reality on the ground rested with the secretary of defense. As a former Navy officer in World War II and congressman during the Vietnam buildup, Laird had the requisite experience for this difficult task. In his *Foreign Affairs* piece he stressed the importance of candor in describing the continued operations involving American soldiers.[31]

The historical record for the most part supports the secretary's commitment to greater candor. For example, Laird opposed what he felt was excessive secrecy regarding the bombing of Laos and Cambodia in 1969.[32] He also argued, although unsuccessfully, for a more credible accounting of the results of the Cambodian operation in 1970.[33] The one significant exception is the tortured series of statements he made in 1971 about the evolving combat role of U.S. troops. His biographer claims Laird did this to keep pressure on President Nixon to maintain the pace of withdrawal.[34] The historical record does not support this interpretation. The Army's own official history reveals the Nixon administration's aversion to the term "combat" led to the choice of "active defense" to describe the mission of the remaining U.S. combat troops. The purpose of this language was to head off imposition of a fixed withdrawal date by the war's opponents in Congress.[35] While it is true that both combat operations and casualties declined steadily throughout 1971, U.S. combat troops who remained in Military Regions I and III were still out in the field looking for enemy forces well into 1972.[36]

Politicians and journalists thrive on the nuances of words and phrases. To soldiers whose lives are immediately at risk, nuances are meaningless. A soldier being shot at considers himself in combat whether it is labeled active defense, patrolling, protecting an installation, or a support operation, on the ground or in the air.

Specialist Four Derek Paul, a twenty-one-year-old draftee from Munster Indiana, and a member of the Bravo Company 1/12th Cavalry at Pace, summed up his frustration in a letter home to his parents: "I felt I had to speak out against something that was wrong. Constantly one reads in the paper we have relinquished our combat role to the ARVNS. Then what am I doing in the bush fighting. I'm tired of our leaders telling people that we're not out here. That means I'm nothing and I don't exist."[37]

While Secretary Laird deserves credit for keeping more Americans from dying in Vietnam by pushing the troop withdrawals forward, his deliberate ambiguous messages about their mission contributed to the sense of cynicism and distrust among the troops who remained. They soldiered on at Pace and elsewhere with very little public recognition of the dangers they faced, in part because of the words he chose.

7. *Some of the Most Significant Costs Are Hidden.*—Secretary Laird rightfully pointed out that the greatest cost of war is human suffering. He also pointed out that even limited wars can't be run on the cheap. He also correctly highlighted the disastrous consequences on the U.S. military of President Johnson's political decision to use draftees to expand the Army instead of trained reservists and National Guard units.[38] But what he should have acknowledged in his *Foreign Affairs* piece was the terrible toll the Vietnam War took on the U.S. military, particularly in terms of operational readiness, self-esteem, and public support. It would literally take nearly two decades to recover.[39]

8. *All Wars Are Not the Same.*—Historians and policy makers both study previous decisions to learn from the mistakes of others and hopefully not repeat them. Unfortunately, the misapplied lesson of one war can shape another in unintended ways. For example, the American decision to take a stand against Communism in Vietnam was driven, at least in part, by a desire to avoid the road to war paved by the Allied Powers trying to appease Hitler and the Nazis in 1938. The problem was that the Vietnamese Communists, though determined to take over South Vietnam by force and run it as a police state, were not identical to Hitler and the Nazis. As a result, the United States and its allies may have missed a chance to co-opt Ho Chi Minh and his followers in the period following World War II in a way that was more beneficial and less costly than what eventually transpired.

During the Korean War, the United States found it could stop numerically superior Chinese Communists' mass infantry assaults by massed firepower, particularly artillery, until the Chinese finally had enough and agreed to an armistice.[40] The Army "learned" from this experience and tried fifteen years later to adapt to Vietnam these lessons with a much less satisfactory outcome.

Secretary Laird and Lewis Sorley argue that the United States really "won" in Vietnam and that the lesson is to stay the course in the face of adversity. But this argument overlooks the lesson about the limits of one nation, even with overwhelming wealth and firepower, to ensure its allies are successful if the allies are not up to the job.

Secretary Laird's lessons learned piece on Vietnam is still a useful starting point to assess what was learned from that conflict. While Laird's insights as an insider contribute to our understanding of these issues, his vested role in defending these policies limits him as well. For example, one critical question Laird hints at but doesn't really address is the inherent limits on the use of force in these circumstances. Why after half a million ground troops, twenty-five years of effort (since 1950), and tons of explosives did the United States fail to get either the North Vietnamese or the South Vietnamese governments to respond in a way the United States wanted? Perhaps Arnold Isaacs summed it up best when he said, "What the United States really lacked in Vietnam was not persistence but understanding."[41]

Former Secretary Laird was not the only participant to draw broader conclusions from the Vietnam experience. Army General Colin Powell spent two tours in Vietnam as a young infantry officer prior to becoming Army chief of staff. In 1992 he wrote an article for *Foreign Affairs* discussing his perspectives.[42] He did not argue that the outcome in Vietnam would have been better if the United States had just stuck it out longer. What he did argue was this:

> When a "fire" starts that might require committing armed forces, we need to evaluate the circumstances. Relevant questions include: Is the political objective we seek to achieve important, clearly defined and understood? Have all other nonviolent policy means failed? Will military force achieve the objective? At what cost? Have the gains and risks been analyzed? How might the situation that we seek to alter, once it is altered by force, develop further and what might be the consequences?[43]

What later became known as the "Powell Doctrine" would itself be tested over time. But one thing is clear: if the right questions aren't asked going in, they become that much harder to address when the time comes to get out.

When measured against what we now know about the end of the conflict in Vietnam, Secretary Laird's analysis of *Lessons Learned* stands up well in many cases but falls short in others. What he does best is describe the obstacles he had to overcome in extracting 540,000 troops while hostilities continued and how he did so without a major military or political catastrophe while the troops were still there. What he failed to do is candidly address how fundamental weaknesses in civilian and military leadership in the Saigon government contributed to the eventual collapse of South Vietnam. He also bears some responsibility for failing to fully and clearly explain to the American people the degree to which U.S. troops still on the ground in 1971–1972 would need to continue to conduct combat operations so that disengagement could proceed. The debate over the lessons of Vietnam is likely to go on for some time. The more important set of issues going forward are not just about what happened there, but how we will summon the wisdom to better understand how these lessons may apply to the conflicts that follow.

CHAPTER TWENTY-EIGHT

Conclusions
A Difficult End to a Long War

Most veterans would like to think of their military service in terms of commitment to a greater good—often for very high stakes. For those soldiers who stormed the beaches at Normandy, liberated Seoul, or even jumped off helicopters into the Ia Drang Valley, the connection between their own actions and what they were fighting for was crystal clear. But, for most soldiers, life isn't that dramatic. They serve instead at obscure, forgotten places; sometimes in harm's way, sometimes not. Fire Support Bases Pace and Lanyard were among those obscure places.

At first glance, what stands out is its seeming insignificance. In the end, neither the MACV nor the South Vietnamese found Pace or Lanyard to be a piece of real estate worth fighting for. Even the North Vietnamese, who ended up with it in the end, captured it as part of a feint while their main focus was elsewhere. Despite the drama over combat refusals, this story received less than fifteen minutes of air time on all three networks combined, over the entire length of Pace's existence. In the years since, military historians have overlooked it entirely. What notoriety it did receive came from antiwar groups rooted in the false premise of a reported mutiny there.

Because of the way the Vietnam War was fought, the turmoil at home while it was fought, and the tragic way in which it finally came to an end, Vietnam Veterans never received the recognition they had earned—especially those who held things together during the final stages of withdrawal. But that does not mean the sacrifices they made were any less worthy than the sacrifices of those who came before or after them. It is tempting to conclude that these soldiers risked their lives, and in some cases gave their lives, for nothing because the war ultimately ended badly for the United States and its South Vietnamese allies. But that conclusion overlooks what all good soldiers understand. Very few of the American soldiers at Pace or Lanyard wanted to be there. Most of them were draftees or short-term volunteers. What they fought for in the end was not the viability of a political regime or a certain strategy. What these soldiers risked their lives for was the one thing they knew trumped all other considerations—and that was each other. What that means for the families and loved ones who survived them is that the men who gave their lives there were heroes in every sense of the word.

The events at these two firebases told us a lot about why soldiers fight, how commanders lead, and the role of a free press in a democratic society at war. In doing so, they reflected the stresses and strains on America's soldiers as the country tried to extract itself from a long and difficult conflict. It showed how good soldiers can and will fight when properly led. It showed how good leaders can lead by example, even under the most challenging conditions, and it showed how an independent press can sort out fact from fiction in even the most confusing circumstances.

On a broader level, Pace and Lanyard remained obscure because of what did *not* happen there. The sapper attack on Lanyard occurred just one day after the assault on Mary Ann. The outcome was very different. At Lanyard the North Vietnamese sappers were repulsed without being able to inflict heavy casualties on the defenders. It is difficult to imagine what the precise impact on troop morale in Vietnam or public opinion in the United States would have been if Lanyard had suffered the same fate as Mary Ann, but it would not have been good.

The same is true at Pace. The North Vietnamese had pulled the same bait-and-switch ambushes successfully twice before in the preceding nine months, first at Dambe, then at Snoul. It is now clear that they wanted to do the same at Firebase Alpha just on the other side of the Cambodian border near Krek. If they had succeeded, and the South Vietnamese forces had been routed as they had before, the chaos would have spilled south down Route 22, sweeping over both Pace and Thien Ngon, pulling U.S. ground forces into the fighting. The ugly scenario that occurred in the midst of the already controversial South Vietnamese presidential elections would have played out in parallel with unfavorable news coverage from all over the world. If temporary combat refusals had escalated into full-blown mutinies and been thrown into this mix, the outcome would have been even more destabilizing to the shaky Saigon government.

Critics could argue that by doing their duty the soldiers of the withdrawal Army simply prolonged the war but didn't change the inevitable outcome—a South Vietnamese defeat. This in turn meant three and a half more years of war and hundreds of thousands more casualties on both sides. But this line of argument ignores the unintended consequences of a South Vietnamese collapse in late 1971 or early 1972, instead of April 1975. Despite the war's tragic end in 1975, it did allow for the orderly, if painful, withdrawal of U.S. troops. However difficult that was, the United States did disengage. We know now, in the years that followed, that the Army was able to rebuild itself into an all-volunteer force. This effort was led by young officers like Colin Powell and Norman Schwarzkopf, who applied what they learned in Vietnam and provided the leadership needed to move forward. Many other veterans either stayed in the military or returned to civilian life to lead productive lives and raise families. And, after a slow start, the rest of the country reached out a helping hand to the veterans who had difficulty adjusting because of physical and psychological wounds.

We know now the dominoes did not fall. In fact, the Tigers of Southeast Asia (including Vietnam) have edged their countries forward into more market-driven economies. We also now know that differences over Vietnam did not derail détente between the United States and the Soviet Union, and the United States and the People's Republic of China. Nor did the loss of South Vietnam alter the eventual outcome of the Cold War. And we now know that after the Vietnam War the United States managed to keep itself out of foreign quagmires for a quarter of a century while it and the rest of the world enjoyed a period of relative peace and prosperity.

Nothing in this outcome obviates the suffering of the South Vietnamese, who opposed the forced unification of their country or the suffering of Laotians and Cambodians as well. Some were executed, many were sent to reeducation camps, others perished while trying to escape. But it's hard to imagine in retrospect how the outcome would have been different. The South Vietnamese government was too dependent on the United States to stand on its own. And by 1975 the United States could no longer afford to prop up the South Vietnamese government at the expense of its other worldwide commitments or the needs of its own people at home.

The year 1971 turned out to be a difficult year for the Army in Vietnam. The end of America's ground combat role was clearly in sight, yet some units remained in harm's way. Populated with draftees, short-term volunteers, and a sprinkling of career soldiers, the Army struggled with sagging morale, fickle allies, and a determined enemy. Back in the rear, discipline problems, fragging, racial tension, and drug abuse made the front lines look placid by comparison.

"Don't mean nothin'" seemed to be the catchphrase of the day. But it did mean something, and the troops that had to rose to the occasion. They looked out for each other, sacrificed for each other, and, in the end, protected the interests of their country. The way out ended up not being as honorable as it should have been. Too many were left behind. But get out they did, in a way that let the country renew itself and move on. History will be the final judge. And it will show that while their countrymen were divided and distracted, they held it together and soldiered on.

Epilogue

The veterans of Pace and Lanyard returned home to a reception that was sometimes hostile and often indifferent. Some struggled with posttraumatic stress, others with medical issues related to exposure to Agent Orange. Nevertheless, they moved on to raise families and contribute to society in many different ways. Here are some of them:

Captain Jack Adams (A/1/12 Cav) earned a bachelor's degree and an MBA, and he attended the Army's Command and General Staff College. He spent thirty-two years in the Army in a number of senior command and staff positions. He retired as a colonel and now lives with his wife in North Carolina. He has two grown children.

Staff Sergeant Roger Atkin (C 2/32 FA) completed a degree in social studies after leaving the Army. He never taught history, as he planned, but instead became a successful construction contractor. He and his family now live in Virginia.

Lieutenant Wayne Alberg (C/2/32 FA) stayed in the Army and served in both Germany and the continental United States. He retired as a major in 1990. He has worked since then in the private sector and lives in Virginia. He has two daughters.

Captain Richard Ashley (C/2/32 FA) served as a member of the faculty at the U.S. Military Academy at West Point and as a professor of military science at Berkeley. He retired from the Army as a colonel and is a training manager for East Tennessee State University.

Sergeant Steve Belt (71st ADA) remained in the Army and earned a commission as an infantry officer in 1972. He retired from the Army in 1990, taught for awhile, and is now living in North Carolina.

Sergeant Morris Bloomer (B/1/12 Cav) returned to his previous employer after leaving the Army and is currently living in Indiana.

Richard Boyle returned to Southeast Asia to cover the occupation of Cambodia by the Khmer Rouge. He then moved on to Nicaragua and El Salvador to cover the war there. He met Oliver Stone and ended up being the inspiration for the character played by James Woods in Stone's film *Salvador.* An antiwar activist, he played a major role in the movie Sir! No Sir!, in which he discusses his version of the events at FSB Pace. He is currently living in California.

Richard Brummett returned to Vietnam again in 1972. He was hit by shrapnel fragments during the Easter Offensive near Don Ha. He was with the 1/1 Cavalry when they conducted their last patrol before standing down in March of that year. Brummett retired from the U.S. Postal Service in 2005, after spending sixteen years as a small-town postmaster. He visited Vietnam twice after the war, once in 2004 and again in 2006. He helped to finish Keith William Nolan's final book, *Search and Destroy*, after Nolan's untimely death in 2009.

Staff Sergeant Paul Cibolski (C/2/32 FA) stayed in the Army and retired in 1986 as a first sergeant. He and his wife now live in Kentucky.

Lieutenant Tom Colaiezzi (C/2/32 FA) was medevaced in April 1971 after being hit by shrapnel from an ARVN 105. After three months in the hospital he was discharged. He took a job with the IRS in 1973 and retired in 2006 as a senior manager. He also went back to school and earned a master's degree in taxation and still teaches part time. He and his wife live in Pennsylvania.

Specialist Four Tim Colgan (557 Engineers) went to college after leaving the Army and earned an accounting degree. Tim also earned a pilot's license and owns a corporate jet service business in Wisconsin.

Lieutenant Rich Coreno (B1/12 Cav) stayed in the Army after returning to the States, but he left after ten years of service as a captain. He took a civilian personnel job at Fort Benning, where he still works as a human resources specialist.

Specialist Four Greg Cowles (D/1/12 Cav) left the Army and spent time as a miner in Butte, Montana. He lost his job when the mine shut down, and he eventually moved to Texas.

Specialist Four Marc Crane (C/2/32 FA) has worked in construction since he left the Army. He married a woman he met by mail. They've been married for thirty-eight years. He has three sons and a daughter and ten grandchildren. He lives in Missouri.

Specialist Five Mark Crist (11 ACR) made the Army a career, eventually going to flight school and flying the Huey and UH-60 Blackhawk. He retired as a chief warrant officer in 1988 and now lives in Texas.

Captain Robert Cronin (B/1/12 Cav) stayed in the Army for thirty years and retired as a colonel. He commanded an infantry battalion and participated in Operation Just Cause (Panama). Now lives in Pennsylvania.

Major Russell Davis (HQ 2/32d FA) attended the Command and General Staff School at Fort Leavenworth. He retired from the Army in 1986 with the rank of colonel and now lives in Florida.

Sergeant Nick Demas (B/1/12 Cav) served as a purchasing agent and plant manager after leaving the Army. He is retired and lives in Michigan.

Specialist Four Bill Denton (B and E/1/12th Cav) stayed in touch with many of the members of Bravo Company after returning home and is regarded as the company's unofficial historian. Bill is living in Arkansas.

Lieutenant Mark Diggs (C/2/32/FA) resigned his commission when hearing loss precluded his staying with combat arms; however, before he left the Army he took a number of computer courses. He became a software entrepreneur and is the founder, CEO, and chairman of Litmus, a software company. He lives in Arkansas.

Captain Tom Dombrowsky (HQ 1/12 Cav) served as an assistant professor of military science at Johns Hopkins University in Baltimore as well as with U.S. forces in Germany.

Sergeant Michael Donze (C/2/32 FA) earned a college degree after leaving the Army. He retired after thirty-five years and lives in Minnesota.

Major Joe Dye (HQ 1/12 Cav) spent time as an ROTC instructor, attended Command and General Staff School, commanded an infantry battalion, and served as a corps operations officer before retiring as a colonel in 1987. He lives in rural Oregon.

Specialist Four Danny Farmer (B/1/12 Cav) entered the construction business after leaving the Army and now lives in Ohio.

Specialist Four Ernie French (B/1/12 Cav) worked for an oil company for thirty years. He is retired and lives in Illinois.

Major Keith Garner (HQ 2/32 FA) eventually became a tactics instructor, then deputy director of the tactics department at the Army Command and General Staff College at Fort Leavenworth, Kansas. He retired from the Army in 1980 and returned to Texas, where he worked as a safety engineer until he retired in 2008.

Specialist Four Al Grana (B/1/12 Cav) left the Army at the end of his Vietnam tour and went back to college to finish his degree. He taught English as a second language and is now retired and living in California.

Captain Peter Hanson (B/2/35 FA) left the Army after his enlistment ended to become an commercial banker. He is now living in Connecticut.

Private Caesar Hastings (B/1/12 Cav) worked for General Motors for thirty-two years after leaving the Army. He now lives in Tennessee.

Private First Class Levell Hinton (C/2/32 FA) went to work for Ford Motor Company after returning from Vietnam, and he raised a family. He retired from Ford in 2002 and lives in Missouri.

Peter A. Jay worked for the Washington Post until late 1973, when he bought a weekly paper near his home in Maryland. He sold that in 1988. Now works full time running his family's 260-acre farm, which he says he enjoys "enormously."

PFC Steve Lonchase (E/1 12 Cav) returned to New Mexico after leaving the Army. He teaches and coaches sports at a local school.

Captain Gerald LeVesque (HQ 2/32 FA) left the Army after completing his tour in Vietnam. Since leaving the Army he has worked in finance and insurance in the private sector. He and his wife live in California.

Lieutenant Colonel Robert McCaffree (HQ 2/32 FA) was promoted to colonel and later became comptroller of Fort Sill. He is retired and lives with his wife near Fort Sill, Oklahoma.

Private First Class William McCormick (C/2/32 FA) left the Army when he returned from Vietnam but decided to reenlist for Germany four years later. He retired in 1996 after serving a total of twenty years. He earned a bachelor's degree in criminal justice and a master's degree in human relations. He now works as a civil service employee at Fort Sill, Oklahoma, and resides in nearby Lawton.

Specialist Four Mike McNamara (B/1/12 Cav) traveled after leaving the Army. He eventually moved to Florida, where he has run or owned a number of businesses in real estate and construction.

Specialist Four Paul Marling (D/1/12 Cav), after completing his military obligation, returned to his job with the mentally retarded and developmentally disabled for the State of New York. He earned degrees in nursing and health care administration, and retired in 2005. In 2006 he returned to Vietnam and visited both the site of Firebase Pace and of the Huey gunship crash nearby. He has maintained contact with the families of three of the four crew members who perished in that crash.

Specialist Four Mark Maxfield (C 2/32 FA) left the Army in 1972 and has held a steady job and raised a family.

Captain Ross Nagy (C/2/32 FA) earned a master's degree in information systems. He remained in the Army, where he served a variety of assignments, including battalion commander and XO VII Corps Artillery. He retired as a colonel. After retirement from the Army he worked for the Red Cross in disaster recovery and for the State of Vermont as deputy director of emergency management.

Sergeant Bruce Oestrich (C/2/32 FA) left the Army in 1972 and took a job with John Deere making diesel engines and earth-moving equipment. He retired in 2002 and lives in Iowa.

Lieutenant Gary Lynn Pace (31st Engineers) was honored on April 22, 2010, along with twenty-seven other Clemson University alumni who gave their lives in Vietnam. Clemson University dedicated the Scroll of Honor Memorial to the members of the Clemson family, who "have given the ultimate sacrifice to their country."

Specialist Four Derek Paul (B/1/12 Cav) and his wife live in Minnesota. He describes himself as still distrustful of higher authority as a result of his experiences in Vietnam.

Nicholas Proffitt worked for Newsweek until 1981. His novel Gardens of Stone was made into a movie in 1987. He died of cancer in 2006, at age sixty-three.

Captain Ray Rhodes (Adviser 6th ARVN Airborne) sponsored his Vietnamese counterpart in the States when the soldier escaped from Vietnam in 1975. Rhodes retired from the Army as a colonel and is now international security manager for a Texas energy firm.

Lieutenant Jack Ryals (B/2/35 FA) started a successful clothing store after leaving the Army in 1971. He is now involved in commercial real estate and economic development in Florida. He and his wife have three sons, one of whom served with the 3/7th Cav as it led the charge to Baghdad during Operation Iraqi Freedom.

Lieutenant Ron Shuler (B/1/12 Cav) stayed in the army and eventually attained the rank of lieutenant colonel. He passed away in 1999.

Sergeant Michael Stevens (D/1/12 Cav) returned to college to complete a bachelor's degree in community development and regional planning. After not being able to find work in his field, he continued his education and earned an associate degree in commercial photography. He then established Stevens Photographics, a commercial/industrial studio. However, he found his real passion was wine. After studying at various venues in Philadelphia and New York City, he is now a certified wine sommelier. He has one daughter, who is in graduate school.

Captain Tom Timmons (C/2/32 FA) stayed in the Army and retired as a lieutenant colonel in 1989. He is living in Arizona.

Specialist Four Reuben Topinka (B/1/12/Cav) returned to civilian life, where he had several different jobs but settled into data entry. He and his wife are now living in Illinois.

Major William Tozer (HQ 3d BDE) served as a casualty notification officer after leaving Vietnam, an experience that affected him deeply. He retired from the Army as a lieutenant colonel in 1981 and is now living in Idaho.

Lieutenant Colonel Stan Tyson (HQ 1/12 Cav) attended the Army War College at Carlisle Barracks, Pennsylvania, and commanded the 3rd Bde, 1st Infantry Division in Germany. He retired from the Army in 1975.

Major General Jack J. Wagstaff (HQ TRAC) served as chief of the military advisory group to the German government before retiring from the Army in 1975. He died of cancer in 1998 at his home in Virginia and is buried in Arlington National Cemetery. He is survived by his wife and two children.

Sergeant Walt Wernli (B/1/12 Cav) returned to his job at Dow Chemical, where he worked for thirty-three years in various research and development positions. He and his wife have two daughters. He retired from Dow in 2001 and spends most of his time managing two cattle ranches in Texas.

Specialist Four Paul White (D/1/12 Cav) played trumpet in the Winston Salem Symphony Orchestra after returning from Vietnam. He also spent a year as band director of the Goldsboro, North Carolina, City School System. He lives in North Carolina with his family. He has been a certified financial planner since 1987.

FSB Pace and FSB Lanyard are now empty fields. Route 22 is now a two-lane paved road. In 1986 the Dog's Head was declared a protected area by the Vietnamese government to commemorate "its historical importance during the Second Indochina (Vietnamese-American) War." In 2002 it was officially designated a national park and bird sanctuary.

Appendix A

Order of Battle MR III—U.S. Forces, Fall 1971

23d Artillery Group
    2/32 Field Artillery
    5/42 Field Artillery
    187th Assault Helicopter
3d Brigade, 1st Air Cavalry Division (Separate)
Cavalry
    2/5 Cavalry
    1/7 Cavalry
    2/8 Cavalry
    1/12 Cavalry
    2/11 Armored Cavalry
Artillery
    1/21st Field Artillery
    F/26 Field Artillery
    F/77 Aerial Rocket Artillery
    F/79 Aerial Rocket Artillery
Aviation
    229 Aviation
    362 Assault Helicopter Co.
    Troop F/9 Cavalry

Source: Headquarters, 3d Brigade (Separate), 1st Air Cavalry Division (Airmobile), ORLL, period ending October 31, 1971, NARA, B-1; Headquarters, 23d Artillery Group, ORLL, period ending October 31, 1971, 6.

Appendix B

Order of Battle MR III—North and South Vietnamese Forces

SOUTH VIETNAMESE TROOPS, FALL 1971

Infantry Divisions

5, 18, 25

Ranger Groups

3, 5, 6, Border

Armor

15 and 18 Regiments

Source: MG Jack Wagstaff, *Debriefing Report*, May 27, 1971–December 15, 1971, 101, CMH, appendix B.

NORTH VIETNAMESE TROOPS AS OF OCTOBER 1, 1971

5th Division

E-6 and 174 Regiments

7th Division

141, 165, 209 Regiments

9th Division

95C, 271, 272 Regiments

Other

88, 101, 203, 204, 205 Regiments

Source: Headquarters II FFORCEV, *ORLL*, period ending April 30, 1971, NARA, 84; Headquarters, 3d Brigade (September), 1st Cavalry Division, *Operation Katum After Action Report*, September 27–October 20, 1971, Annex B (Intelligence), B-1.

Appendix C

Inspector General's Report, October 11, 1971

72-55

SUMMARY OF INVESTIGATION/INQUIRY/INSPECTION

1. UNIT: 3d Brigade, 1st Cavalry Brigade

2. LOCATION: Bien Hoa

3. DATE: 11 October 1971

4. ALLEGATION/PURPOSE: Alleged combat refusal by members of Company B, 1st Battalion, 12th Cavalry and the state of morale and welfare of the men in that unit.

5. SOURCE: Oral directive from the Deputy Brigade Commander, 3d Brigade, 1st Cavalry Division.

6. FINDINGS: a. There was not a combat refusal on 9 or 10 October 1971 by members of Company B, 1st Battalion, 12th Cavalry.

    b. The welfare of the company is good considering their location.

    c. The morale of the men in the company is fair.

7. IG ACTION: None

8. UNIT ACTION: Unknown

9. ADDITIONAL ACTION: Unknown

10. FOLLOW-UP: Unknown

DISPOSITION FORM

For use of this form, see AR 340-15; the proponent agency is The Adjutant General's Office.

REFERENCE OR OFFICE SYMBOL	SUBJECT
AVDAIG	Report of Investigation Concerning Alleged Combat Refusal in B Company, 1st Bn, 12th Cavalry

TO   Commanding General   FROM Inspector General   DATE 12 Oct 71   CMT 1

1. The report of investigation concerning the alleged combat refusal by members of B/1/12 is enclosed (TAB A).

2. Recommend that:

    a. The report of investigation be approved.

    b. The case be closed.

1 Incl
as

                        William S. Tozer
                        WILLIAM S. TOZER
                        MAJ, IG
                        Inspector General

AVDACG

TO Inspector General FROM Commanding General DATE   CMT 2

Approved *JRB*

See Me _____

1 Incl
nc

                        Jonathan R. Burton
                        JONATHAN R. BURTON
                        Brigadier General, USA
                        Commanding

DA FORM **2496** REPLACES DD FORM 96, EXISTING SUPPLIES OF WHICH WILL BE
1 FEB 62   ISSUED AND USED UNTIL 1 FEB 63 UNLESS SOONER EXHAUSTED.

AVDAIG   12 October 1971

SUBJECT: Report of Investigation Concerning Alleged Combat
          Refusal in B Company, 1st Battalion, 12th Cavalry

TO: Commanding General
          3rd Brigade (Separate)
          1st Cavalry Division (Airmobile)
          APO San Francisco 96490

   I. AUTHORITY

       1. This investigation was conducted on 11 October
1971 at Fire Base Pace pursuant to an oral directive from the
Deputy Commanding Officer of the 3rd Brigade (Separate), 1st
Cavalry Division (Airmobile).

   II. MATTERS INVESTIGATED

       2. This investigation was concerned with:

           a. An alleged combat refusal by members of
B/1/12.

           b. The state of morale and welfare of the men
of B/1/12.

   III. BACKGROUND

       3. B Company, 1st Battalion, 12th Cavalry arrived
at Fire Base Pace on 7 October. Their mission was to provide
fire base security, and they were placed under the operational
control of 2nd Battalion, 32nd Artillery which is commanded
by LTC McCaffery.

   IV. EVIDENCE

       4. CPT Cronin, the company commander, in the pre-
sence of LT Shuler, the platoon leader of the platoon
involved, COL Spence, the DCO-B, and the Inspector General,
related the following sequence of events in unsworn testimony. He, CPT Cronin, on the afternoon of 9 October directed
LT Shuler to organize and prepare a 15-man patrol to depart

the fire base at 2130 hours for a night ambush operation.
At 1800 hours, LT Shuler informed CPT Cronin that it was
likely that 5 of the men selected for the patrol would refuse
to go. CPT Cronin gave this information to LTC McCaffery,
who gave instructions to continue with the patrol as scheduled.
CPT Cronin and LT Shuler formulated the steps to be taken in
the event of a combat refusal and continued preparations for
the patrol. At 2120 hours an ARVN Liaison Officer came to CPT
Cronin with the information that the planned patrol area was
already occupied by ARVN troops. CPT Cronin consulted LTC
McCaffery and the patrol was cancelled. The following afternoon at 1430 hours, a platoon of 41 men, including the 15 men
who were originally scheduled to go the previous evening,
left the fire base on a reconnaissance operation and proceeded
towards the same general area scheduled to be occupied the
previous evening. Enroute to the objective area, the patrol
discovered and dismantled an automatic claymore ambush which
apparently had been set up by a friendly unit. In consideration of the possibility that there were other automatic
ambushes in the area, CPT Cronin ordered the patrol to return
to the fire base.

5. My conversation with CPT Cronin was followed
by a group conversation with approximately 15 enlisted members of the company. Their version of the events of 9 and
10 October corroborated CPT Cronin's story.

6. I asked for a show of hands of the men who would
have gone on the night patrol if it had not been cancelled
and if they had been given a direct order to go. No one
raised his hand. I then directed the same question to three
different individuals of the group. One said that he would
have gone, one said he didn't know and the third indicated
that he would not have gone and he was prepared to suffer
the consequences.

7. CPT Cronin said that after the night patrol had
been cancelled, he interviewed the five men who indicated they
would not go. Three stated to him that they would have gone
in compliance with a direct order to do so from him and the
other two stated that they would not have gone.

8. Approximately 85 of the men in B Company are
scheduled to return to the states in less than 60 days. They
can naturally think of places they would rather be than Fire
Base Pace. They get hot food whenever incoming does not close
down the mess hall, the rest of the time they must eat
C-rations. They have received mail once in the last four

2

days. There appeared to be adequate protective cover and
their living areas were as neat and comfortable as the rain,
mud and enemy would allow.

9. One man of the company was lightly wounded by
shrapnel on the 9th of October. Because of poor weather
and lack of need for immediate evacuation, the decision was
made not to risk a Medevac. Some of the men interpreted
this to be a lack of support.

10. On the afternoon of 10 October, several of the
men observed a helicopter pilot who had received a serious
wound in his leg. This upset them.

11. CPT Cronin stated that the morale of his company
was good. I talked with one enlisted man who stated that it
was OK and another who stated that morale was so low that
they didn't have any.

12. The enlisted men I talked with seemed intelligent, alert, concerned, in good health and willing to discuss the matter openly. When I talked with them collectively,
they were considerably more defiant than when I had private
conversations with them.

13. In response to questions by me, the men revealed
that they had written a letter to Senator Kennedy asking, in
effect, why, if the United States has assumed a defensive
posture in Vietnam, is there such a place as Fire Base Pace
and why should they have to go out on offensive operations
to defend it. It was estimated by one of the men who signed
it to have contained 65 to 75 signatures.

V. CONCLUSIONS

14. There was not a combat refusal on 9 or 10 October
1971 by members of B Company.

15. The welfare of the Company is good considering
their location.

16. The morale of the men in B Company is fair.

VI. RECOMMENDATIONS

17. It is recommended that:

3

|FOR OFFICIAL USE ONLY|

a. This report be approved.

b. The case be closed.

WILLIAM S. TOZER
Major, IG

4

Appendix D

Fact Sheet, Fire Support Base Pace Incident, October 22, 1971

DEPARTMENT OF THE ARMY
OFFICE OF THE CHIEF OF STAFF

22 Oct 71

_ General Westmoreland

_ General Palmer

_ MG Bennett

2 MG Bennett   22 OCT 1971

1 COL Cooper

3 LTC Giles

_ FILE

BJECT: WH Fact Sheet

---

1. Attached is a fact sheet
regarding Fire Support Base Pace
incidents. This fact sheet was
requested by the White House
thru OSD.

2. Recommend this fact sheet
be provided per request and that
copies also be provided OSA, LTC
Coffey, BG Dunn, BG Sumner, and
MG Karhohs.

APPROVED

SEE ME

DEPARTMENT OF THE ARMY
OFFICE OF THE DEPUTY CHIEF OF STAFF FOR PERSONNEL
WASHINGTON, D.C. 20310

2 2 OCT 1971

MEMORANDUM FOR: CHIEF OF STAFF, UNITED STATES ARMY

ATTN: WHITE HOUSE LIAISON OFFICER

SUBJECT: White House Fact Sheet

1. In accordance with request from your office on 21 October 1971 the attached White House Fact Sheet is submitted for transmittal to the White House.

2. This memorandum has been coordinated with the Chief of Information, The Judge Advocate General, and the Chief of Legislative Liaison.

WALTER T. KERWIN, JR.
Lieutenant General, GS
Deputy Chief of Staff
for Personnel

FACT SHEET

Fire Support Base Pace Incidents

Recent allegations by news media concerning soldiers refusing to
accompany their unit on patrols on two separate instances in the vicinity
of Fire Support Base Pace, Republic of Vietnam, have been investigated.

With regard to the first instance, the base commander of FSB Pace, a
U.S. heavy artillery base, had directed that the company commander of
B Company, 1/12 Cavalry, 3d Brigade (Separate), 1st Cavalry Division,
which provides infantry security for the base, conduct an ambush patrol
on the night of 9 October 1971. In keeping with normal procedures, the
platoon which had been selected for the mission began preparation for the
operation.

Five members of the platoon were in their bunker preparing their gear
for the mission when a reporter came into the bunker and engaged the group
in conversation. In the course of this conversation, the men said that
they were scheduled for a patrol but that they were not going. That
evening as the platoon was about to form up for the patrol, the liaison
officer from the major Army of the Republic of Vietnam (ARVN) unit in the
area came to FSB Pace to coordinate the ARVN operations for the evening.
It was revealed at that time that the ARVN unit had scheduled an operation
in approximately the same area designated for the B Company ambush patrol
and were already in position. After receiving this information, the base
commander canceled the platoon operation.

The events surrounding this action did not involve a refusal to obey
an order. No disciplinary action was taken against the men involved and
none is contemplated.

The next day the company commander of B Company directed that the same
platoon participate in a daylight patrol with the company around the fire
base and in the same general area for which the operation had been planned
the previous night. The patrol was conducted and all members of the
platoon, including the five soldiers who originally talked to the reporter,
participated.

By reason of the publicity resulting from this event and the possible
harm it could do to company morale, the Commanding General, Third Regional
Assistance Command, deployed the company to another operational area.
The infantry security mission at FSB Pace was assumed by another company
from the 3d Brigade.

The second incident involved the replacement company, D Company,
1/12 Cavalry, 3d Brigade (Separate), 1st Cavalry Division.

The company arrived at FSB Pace on 12 October 1971. Almost immediately upon landing, Major Dye and a significant portion of the company performed heroically in attempting to rescue crew members of a nearby downed helicopter gunship.

On 13 October 1971, the 3d Platoon, D Company, was scheduled for a 1030 hours daylight patrol. At 0930, members of the 2d Squad, 3d Platoon, told their platoon leader that they did not want to go on patrol. They similarly informed their company commander upon his arrival on the scene. After discussion between squad members and the company commander, the Base Defense Commander, Major Dye, talked to the men and explained that the patrol mission was to screen the tree line where the gunship was downed the previous day, and to provide security for incoming aircraft. All members of the platoon, including those who stated they did not wish to go on patrol, did in fact, go on patrol within 30 minutes after discussion with Major Dye. Major Dye states that he did not have to talk the men out of refusing to go on patrol. He states that once the men fully understood the mission, they unhesitatingly walked off the base on patrol.

The 3d Platoon and all other platoons of the company went on all scheduled patrols between 13 October and 22 October, the day that all US troops were withdrawn from FSB Pace. There were approximately 6 patrols made during that period.

There were no combat refusals. Consequently, there are no grounds for disciplinary action.

The underlying cause of the incidents was the fact that the men had talked themselves into a negative frame of mind. Once the soldiers understood their mission, no further incidents arose.

2

Appendix E

Letter from Senator Kennedy to SP4 Al Grana, October 18, 1971

EDWARD M. KENNEDY
MASSACHUSETTS

United States Senate
WASHINGTON, D.C. 20510

October 18, 1971

Specialist 4 Albert Grana
Bravo Company
1st Bn, 12th Cav
1st Cavalry Division
APO San Francisco 96490

Dear Mr. Grana:

Many thanks for the letter signed by you and your 64 colleagues in Bravo Company, expressing some feelings and problems of American troops remaining in Vietnam.

Press accounts of recent events at Pace have told of your and your colleagues courage and bravery under fire, and because of your sense of responsibleness in carrying out your duty, your eloquent letter should be a cause of deep and sympathetic concern to all Americans.

I have taken the liberty of forwarding your letter to the Secretary of Defense, and have requested his comments on the activities of American troops along the Cambodia-Laos border and on recent events at Fire Base Pace.

Again, many thanks for getting in touch with me. Be assured the situation of you and your associates has not gone unnoticed among many in the Congress and millions of your fellow citizens.

Best wishes.

Sincerely,

Edward M. Kennedy

Appendix F

Letter from MG Donnelly Bolton to SP4 John P. White

Specialist Four John P. White
Co B, 1/12 Cav, 1st Cav Division
APO San Francisco 95498

Dear Specialist White:

On behalf of Secretary Laird, I am replying to your letter of 15 September 1971 concerning a 3 September 1971 *Stars and Stripes* article covering the Secretary's remarks to the Washington Press Corps.

On Wednesday, 1 September 1971, Secretary Laird stated to the press: "We have transferred the combat responsibility in Vietnam on the ground as we have completed Phase I of the Vietnamization Program. We are (now) defending the forces which are in Phase II."

When Secretary Laird's remarks are taken in this context, it becomes clear that US forces remaining in Vietnam have not stopped fighting but have changed to a defensive role. And I must agree with you. This is certainly not "relinquishing all combat roles to the South Vietnamese." I am sure Mr. Laird did not intend to leave this impression.

A soldier knows that an effective defense requires frequent aggressive patrols to find and neutralize enemy forces and firing positions that threaten his position. A commander in a defensive situation must find the enemy and know his movements to properly counter hostile actions. This may require limited-range offensive type operations. Nevertheless, in contrast to the "search and destroy" operations of the late 1960's, our current overall force posture cannot be termed offensive.

Two other points are worthy of mention. First, every effort continues to be made to keep the American public informed. However, primarily because we are not currently engaged in large scale operations, similar to those conducted earlier in Cambodia, the news media [unintelligible] relegated the combat in Vietnam to the back pages of the newspapers and short clips on television. The American public thus sees the present conflict as basically a Vietnamese war with the United States forces providing logistical support and some limited combat support. Also, at times military terminology has understandably caused some confusion. In any case, the American public is not being misled. The second point I would like to stress is that every effort is being made to bring the Vietnam conflict to a just and honorable conclusion. The reduction of United States forces in Vietnam is directly related to the continuing progress of the Vietnamization program. As Secretary Laird stated in the article you referred to in your letter, we are on schedule and even ahead of schedule in all areas in Phase II of Vietnamization. Thus, you will continue to see a decline in US troop strength in Vietnam.

Specialist White, I hope this letter will be helpful to you in understanding the intent of Secretary Laird's remarks as well as reassure you that the Vietnam conflict continues to be of primary concern here in Washington.

Sincerely,

DONNELLY BOLTON
Major General, GS
Director of Operations

Appendix G

Valorous Unit Award for Extraordinary Heroism to the
2/32d Field Artillery and Attached Units, July 3, 1972

THE VALOROUS UNIT AWARD
FOR EXTRAORDINARY HEROISM
IS AWARDED TO THE
2D BATTALION, 32D FIELD ARTILLERY
AND ASSIGNED AND ATTACHED UNITS
INCLUDING
Company A, 1ST BATTALION, 12TH CAVALRY
Company B, 1ST BATTALION, 12TH CAVALRY
Company C, 1ST BATTALION, 12TH CAVALRY
Company D, 1ST BATTALION, 12TH CAVALRY

The 2D BATTALION, 32D FIELD ARTILLERY and its assigned and attached units distinguished themselves through extraordinary heroism while engaged in military operations during the period 23 September 1971 through 25 October 1971 in Tay Ninh Province, Republic of Vietnam. While providing heavy artillery support to the ARVN III Corps and the Tay Ninh Provincial Forces, the battalion firebases, along with deployed ARVN forces in the area of operations, were attacked by elements of three NVA divisions. Although hit by withering fire from all locations, the members of the battalion delivered accurate and devastating fire on the enemy forces despite numerous casualties suffered among themselves. The units gave unstinting support to all ARVN forces in the III Corps and in Tay Ninh Province. The selfless, heroic action of this battalion was responsible for numerous enemy casualties during the period and was the most notable and concrete example of American support to the ARVN forces in the region. The extraordinary heroism and devotion to duty displayed by the members of the 2D BATTALION, 32d FIELD ARTILLERY and assigned and attached units are in keeping with the highest traditions of the military service and reflect great credit upon themselves, their units, and the United States Army.

General Orders No. 1484
United States Army, Vietnam
3 July 1972

Confirmed by:
General Orders No. 5
Headquarters, Department of the Army
26 April 1985

[Home] [Up]

Notes

ABBREVIATIONS

ACR	Armored Cavalry Regiment
ADA	Air Defense Artillery
AP	Associated Press
ARVN ABN	South Vietnamese Airborne
AXO	Assistant Executive Officer
BC	Battery Commander
BTRY	Battery
CAV	Cavalry
CO	Commanding Officer
E	E-mail Interview
FA	Field Artillery
FDC	Fire Direction Center
FDO	Fire Direction Officer
IG	Inspector General
L	Letter Interview Response
P	Phone Interview
S-2	Intelligence Officer
S-3	Operations Officer
XO	Executive Officer

CHAPTER 1. WINDING DOWN

1. Comptroller, Secretary of Defense, "Vietnam War Deaths by Month, 1966–1971," http://members.aol.com/forcountry/kiamonth.htm (accessed January 13, 2004).

2. Graham A. Cosmas, *MACV: The Joint Command in the Years of Withdrawal, 1968–1973* (Washington, DC: CMH, 2007), 178.

3. Andrew J. Glass, "Defense Report: Draftees Shoulder Burden of Fighting and Dying in Vietnam," *National Journal*, August 15, 1970, 1747–1755.

4. "The Troubled Army in Vietnam," *Newsweek*, January 11, 1971, 37.

5. Max Frankel, "President Terms Cuba Off Limits for Soviet Subs," *New York Times*, January 5, 1971, 1.

6. John L. Hess, "End of G.I. Combat Foreseen by Laird," *New York Times*, January 7, 1971, 1.

7. Alvin Shuster, "Laird Expects Wider Pullout of Troops," *New York Times*, January 12, 1971, 3.

8. Reuters, "U.S. Command Finds Nothing for a Report," *New York Times*, January 10, 1971, 2.

9. Benjamin Weller, "U.S. May Pull Out 20,000 Saigon-Area Troops," *New York Times*, January 10, 1971, 3.

10. UPI, "4th Negro G.I. Held in Vietnam Slaying," *New York Times*, January 13, 1971, 6.

11. UPI, "Blast Hurts 27 G.I.'s during Vietnam Riot," *New York Times*, January 12, 1971, 8.

12. Peter A. Jay, "Laird Calls War Trend Heartening," *Washington Post*, January 12, 1971, A-15.

13. Louis Harris, "The Harris Survey: Support for Nixon on War Drops to 34%," *Washington Post*, March 13, 1971, A7.

14. "Incident on Route 9," *Time*, April 5, 1971, 25.

15. Iver Peterson, "Foe Kills 33 GI's, Wounds 76 in Raid South of Danang," *New York Times*, March 29, 1971, 1.

16. William M. Hammond, *Public Affairs: The Military and the Media, 1968–1973* (Washington, DC: CMH, 1995), 505–510.

17. UPI, "Colonel Says Every Large Combat Unit in Vietnam Has a My Lai," *New York Times*, May 25, 1971, 13.

18. AP, "Pentagon Reveals Rise in 'Fraggings,'" *New York Times*, April 21, 1971, 9.

19. "John Kerry's Testimony . . . and the Anguish of a Veteran," *Washington Post*, April, 25, 1971, 38.

20. AP, "30 U.S. Soldiers Killed in Attacks on Vietnam Bases," *New York Times*, May 22, 1971, 1.

21. Iver Peterson, "Enemy Saboteurs Invade U.S. Base and Blow Up Fuel," *New York Times*, May 25, 1971, 1.

22. Felix Belair, "House Unit Cites Rise in G.I. Drug Use," *New York Times*, May 26, 1971, 14.

23. Colonel Robert D. Heinl Jr., "The Collapse of the Armed Forces," *Armed Forces Journal*, June 7, 1971 (TTVVA #2131805053), 1.

24. Ibid., 4.

25. Neil Sheehan, "Vietnam Archive: Pentagon Study Traces 3 Decades of Growing Involvement," *New York Times*, June 13, 1971, 1.

26. B. Drummond Ayers, "Army Is Shaken by Crises in Morale and Discipline," *New York Times*, September 5, 1971, 1.

27. Rowland Evans and Robert Novak, "Last GI's in Bitter Mood," *Washington Post*, September 17, 1971, A27.

28. Haynes Johnson and George C. Wilson, "The Army: Its Problems Are America's," (Last in a Series), *Washington Post*, September 20, 1971, A12.

29. One of the first references to the Four U's appeared in a May 6, 1970, dispatch from *Washington Post* reporter Jack Foisic, who observed the letters scribbled on the helmets of GIs from the 4th Infantry Division as they unloaded from helicopters into Landing Zone Fox on the Cambodian border (Jack Foisic, "Reds' Stiff Fight Upsite GI Drive," *Washington Post*, May 8, 1970, A22).

30. For a good explanation of the origins of "It Don't Mean Nothin'," see Christian G. Appy, *Working Class War: American Soldiers and Vietnam* (Chapel Hill: University of North Carolina Press, 1993), 208.

CHAPTER 2. PROUD AMERICANS

1. "Vietnam 1963 to 1971," 1–14, and "Honor roll for the 2/32 Artillery," 1–4, *Proud Americans*, http://proudamericans.homestead.com/history.html/ (accessed July 5, 2008).

2. "Lineage and Honors," *Proud Americans*, http://proudamericans.homestead.com/history.html/ (accessed July 5, 2008).

3. David Ott, *Field Artillery, 1954–1973* (Washington, DC: Department of the Army, 1975), 39–55.

4. Shelby M. Stanton, *Vietnam Order of Battle* (Washington, DC: U.S. News Books, 1981), 278.

5. Ibid.

6. By 1971 various improvements had extended tube life to 1,200 rounds (interview with Paul Cibolski, SSG, Section Chief, M, 11/8/09, P, November 10, 2009; all information concerning e-mail, fax, phone, and letter interviews used for this book are in my possession).

7. Ott, *Field Artillery*, 39–49.

8. Stanton, *Vietnam Order of Battle*, 51.

9. Ibid., 278.

10. Ibid.

11. "Vietnam 1963 to 1971," 4.

12. Bernard W. Rogers, *Cedar Falls—Junction City: A Turning Point* (Washington, DC: Department of the Army, 1974), 83, 86, and William LeGro, "Draft of the Big Red One, Chapter 4" (TTVVA Item #3370164001), 5.

13. Rogers, *Cedar Falls*, 87.

14. Ibid., 149–153.

15. Phillip B. Davidson, *Vietnam at War* (New York: Oxford University Press, 1991), 529, and Graham A. Cosmas, *MACV: The Joint Command in the Years of Withdrawal, 1968–1973* (Washington, DC: CMH, 2007), 141–144.

16. Cosmas, *MACV*, 103–104.

17. John M. Shaw, *The Cambodian Campaign: The 1970 Offensive and America's Vietnam War* (Lawrence: University Press of Kansas, 2005), 16–17.

18. Ibid., 18–22; Shelby L. Stanton, *Anatomy of a Division: The 1st Cav in Vietnam* (New York: Warner Books, 1989), 153–154.

19. J. D. Coleman, *Incursion: From America's Choke Hold on the NVA Lifelines to the Sacking of the Cambodian Sanctuaries* (New York: St. Martin's Press, 1991), 191–198.

20. Ibid., 205–206.

21. Ibid., 207–208.

22. "Honor roll for the 2/32 Artillery," 1–4.

23. Davidson, *Vietnam at War*, 625–626; Cosmas, *MACV*, 297–302.

24. Headquarters, 2/32d Artillery, ORLL, period ending July 31, 1970, NARA, 3–4.

25. Shaw, *The Cambodian Campaign*, 158, table 2.

26. Davidson, *Vietnam at War*, 627–629; Cosmas, *MACV*, 297–302.

27. Stanton, *Vietnam Order of Battle*, 334. The major part of the U.S. 25th Infantry Division departed as part of Increment V (October–December 1970). The bulk of the First Air Cavalry departed as part of Increment VI (January–April 1971).

28. Ott, *Field Artillery*, 214, 218–219.

29. Headquarters, II Field Force Vietnam, ORLL, period ending July 31, 1970, 53, Enclosure 11.

30. Headquarters, 2/32d Artillery, 4.

31. William E. LeGro, *Vietnam from Cease Fire to Capitulation* (Washington, DC: CMH, 1981), 36; James P. Harrison, *The Endless War: Fifty Years of Struggle in Vietnam* (New York: Free Press, 1982), 225.

32. Ott, *Field Artillery*, 11–17.

33. Ibid., 46–47.

34. Interview with G. John LeVesque, CPT, S-3, 2/32 FA, P, March 26, 2009; interview with Peter Hanson, CPT, BC, B BTRY, P, April 29, 2010; interview with Thomas H. Timmons, CPT, BC, C BTRY, P, May 3, 2009; interview with Jack Ryals, 1LT, FDC, B BTRY, P, July 22, 2010; interview with Roger Atkin, SSG, Section Chief, E, March 22, 2010.

35. Headquarters, 2/32d Artillery, 4.

36. Headquarters, 1/27th Field Artillery, June 27, 1970, and June 29, 1970, 1.

37. Ibid., June 27, 1971, 1.

38. Ibid., June 29, 1970, 1.

39. Headquarters, 23d Artillery Group, ORLL, period ending July 31, 1970, NARA, 2–3.

40. SP4 Frank Morris, "Enemy Wilts under Tanker Pressure," *Tropic Lightning News*, August 24, 1970, 1, and "Vietnam Diary of SP 5 Stephen L. (Andy) Anderson," http://25thaviation.org/scrapbook/id988htm (accessed October 7, 2010).

41. Stanton, *Vietnam Order of Battle*, 81.

42. Headquarters, 2/35th Artillery, ORLL, period ending April 30, 1971, NARA, 1.

43. Ibid., 4.

44. Headquarters, 23d Artillery Group, ORLL, period ending October 31, 1970, NARA, 7.

45. Headquarters, 2/35th Artillery, daily staff journal, May 30, 1970, NARA, 1.

46. Interviews with Hanson and Ryals.

47. Headquarters, 2/23d Artillery, daily staff journal, January 2, 1971, 1.

48. Ibid., January 10, 1971, 1.

49. Headquarters, 2/35th Artillery, ORLL, period ending April 30, 1971, 1.

50. President Nixon had announced that all U.S. troops would be out of Cambodia by June 30, 1970.

51. Lanyard plots 300 meters inside of South Vietnam on military maps of the era. Lieutenant Jack Ryals visited Vietnam in October 2007 and drove out to Lanyard. The site is still on the Vietnamese side of the border (Ryals interview).

52. Headquarters, 31st Engineer Battalion, ORLL, period ending April 30, 1971, NARA, 9.

53. Headquarters, Second Field Force, ORLL, period ending April 30, 1971, NARA, 53.

CHAPTER 3. SAPPERS IN THE WIRE

1. Steve Pace, "My Brother—My Hero," *The Wall*, http://www.thewall-usa.com/cgi-bin/search5.cgi.1 (accessed March 27, 2003); Interview with Steven Pace, brother of Gary Pace, P, March 18, 2010.

2. Interview with Tom Colaiezzi, 1LT FDO, C BTRY, E, May 9, 2009.

3. Steve Pace interview.

4. Interview with Tim Colgan, SP4, Equipment Operator, 557 Engineers, P, January 11, 2010.

5. Headquarters, 2/32d Artillery, daily staff journal, March 22, 1971, NARA, 2, and March 23, 1971, 1.

6. Colaiezzi interview; interview with Ross Nagy, CPT, BC, C BTRY, E, January 16, 2010.

7. Headquarters, 2/32d Artillery, March 30, 1971, 3; Tom Colaiezzi, "How FSB Pace Was Named," *Proud Americans*, http://proudamericans.homestead.com/stories.html (accessed February 14, 2009); Nagy interview.

8. Headquarters, 2/32d Artillery, March 30, 1971, NARA, 2; Colaiezzi interview.

9. Ibid.

10. Ibid.; Clemson University Alumni Association, "Gary L. Pace," http://CUAlumni.clemson.edu./Pace.aspx?pid=1706 (accessed August 10, 2010) 1, 4.

11. SP5 Albert Gore, "Alert Engineers Repulse VC in Hand-to-Hand Fighting," *Pacific Stars and Stripes*, April 28, 1971, 23. Specialist Gore would go on to serve as vice president of the United States, 1993–2001.

12. Headquarters, 2/32d Artillery, March 30, 1971, 2; Colaiezzi interview.

13. Colgan interview.

14. Pace, "My Brother—My Hero."

15. Headquarters, 2/32d Artillery, May 4, 1971, NARA, 2.

16. Ibid., May 14, 1971, 1.

17. Headquarters, 2/32d Artillery, ORLL, period ending October 31, 1971, NARA, 3.

18. Headquarters, 2/32d Artillery, daily staff journal, May 23, 1971, 1.

19. Ibid., May 28, 1971, 2.

20. Nagy interview; interview with Mark Diggs, 1LT, XO, C BTRY, E, February 5, 2009; interview with Roger Atkin, SSG, Section Chief, C BTRY, E, March 22, 2010.

21. "Vietnam War," CBS News, July 15, 1971 (Record #217981 VTNA).

22. Ibid.

23. Ibid.

24. Special to the *New York Times*, "Transcript of the President's News Conference on Foreign and Domestic Matters," *New York Times*, August 5, 1971, 16.

CHAPTER 4. BAD OMEN

1. Headquarters, 2/32d Field Artillery, daily staff journal, September 22, 1971, NARA, 1.

2. "Jack J. Wagstaff, Major General US Army," *Arlington Cemetery*, http://www.arlingtoncemetery.net/wagstaff.htm (accessed July 14, 2008).

3. General Wagstaff passed away in 1998, so he was not available to be interviewed. However, what he was thinking at this time can be reconstructed from an extensive debriefing report he filed when he completed his tour in December 1971 and other documents, all of which are cited below.

4. Headquarters, Third Brigade (Separate), First Cavalry Division (Airmobile), *Operation Katum after Action Report*, October 7, 1971, Annex B (Intelligence), B-1.

5. Ibid., Operations Map, A-2-D-1.

6. The drawing of Firebase Pace was developed from a 1971 aerial photograph from Company B, 31st Engineer Battalion, completed July 19, 1971, NARA, #111-CC-81146 and additional information provided by Bruce Oester.

7. Shelby Stanton, *Vietnam Order of Battle* (Washington, DC: U.S. News Books, 1981), 278.

8. Headquarters, 31st Engineer Battalion, ORLL for period ending October 31, 1971, NARA, 5.

9. Headquarters, 2/32d Artillery, September 21, 2001, 1.

10. Ibid., September 22, 2001, 1.

11. Stanton, *Vietnam Order of Battle*, 73.

12. "A Question of Protection," *Time*, October 25, 1971, 38.

13. Larry A. Niksch, "Vietnamization: The Program and Its Problems," Congressional Research Service, January 5, 1972 (TTVVA, Item 2131901010), 75.

14. Jeffrey J. Clarke, *Advice and Support: The Final Years* (Washington, DC: Center of Military History, 1988), 451.

15. *MACV, 1971 Command History*, Vol. 1 (TTVVA Item 1070702011), fig. IV-14.

16. Clarke, *Advice and Support*, 361–390.

17. Ibid., 418–425.

18. Craig R. Whitney, "Saigon's Cambodia Drive in Confusion after Death of Its Colorful Commander," *New York Times*, March 2, 1971, 3.

19. MG Jack J. Wagstaff, "Debriefing Report," May 23–December 15, 1971, CMH, 7–8.

20. Headquarters, 2/32d Artillery, September 8, 1971, 1.

21. David Fulgham and Terrence Maitland, *South Vietnam on Trial, Mid 1970 to 1972* (Boston: Boston Publishing, 1984), 61.

22. Clarke, *Advice and Support*, 411.

CHAPTER 5. SKY TROOPERS

1. S2/S3 Sections 1/12th Cavalry, daily staff journal, September 23, 1971, Daily Report/Jim Bowie Report, NARA, 1.

2. Operations Section, 23d Artillery Group, daily staff journal, September 23, 1971, NARA, 3.

3. "Charger History," 12th Cavalry Regiment Association, http://12cav.us/112CAV_01F0608_P04.htm (accessed January 6, 2010), 1.

4. "Vietnam War," 1st Cavalry Division Association, http://www.first-team.US/journals /12th regmt12-ndxus.html (accessed July 22, 2008), 1–8.

5. Shelby Stanton, *Vietnam Order of Battle* (Washington, DC: U.S. News Books, 1981), 71–73.

6. Headquarters, 3rd Brigade (Separate), 1st Cavalry Division, ORLL, period ending October 31, 1971, NARA, 12–13.

7. S2/S3 Sections 1/12th Cavalry, daily staff journal, September 23, 1971, NARA, 2.

8. Operations Section, 23d Artillery Group, September 24, 1971, 1.

9. Interview with Jack Adams, CPT, CO A Co, P, April 6, 2010.

10. AP, "Foe Hits 11 Allied Bases along Cambodian Border," *New York Times*, September 27, 1971, 1.

11. Operations Section, 23d Artillery Group, September 26, 1971, 3.

12. Headquarters, 2/32d Artillery, September 28, 1971, 1. Of the total of twenty-one, nine were infantry, eight were artillery, three were Quad Fifties, and one was combat engineer.

13. S2/S3 Sections 1/12th Cavalry, September 28, 1971, 2.

14. Operations Section, 23d Artillery Group, September 26, 1971, 3.

15. Ibid., September 27, 1971, 4. Although these were NLF divisions in name, they were manned by North Vietnamese regulars and operated as units of the North Vietnamese Army.

16. Headquarters, 2/32d Artillery, September 27, 1971, 2. It is tempting to dismiss this as the product of someone with an overactive imagination. In fact, the North Vietnamese did employ tanks in this area six months later as part of the Easter Offensive.

17. Ibid.

18. Clifford Gessell, "Camp Thien Ngon," *The Red Dragon*, http://cliffordgessell.blogsdpot.com/2008/05/camp-thien-ngon.html, 1–3 (accessed July 24, 2008).

19. S2/S3 Sections 1/12th Cavalry, September 27, 1971, 1.

20. Operations Section, 23d Artillery Group, daily staff journal, September 29, 1971, 2.

21. Interview with Thomas H. Timmons, CPT, BC, C BTRY, P, May 3, 2009.

22. Ibid.; interview with Michael Donze, SGT, Section Chief, P, April 20, 2010; interview with Paul Cibolski, SSG, Section Chief, M, 11/8/09, P, November 10, 2009.

CHAPTER 6. ARVNs, BUFFs, AND OTHER FRIENDS
1. AP, "U.S. Forces Support Saigon Border Drive," *Washington Post*, September 30, 1971, A1.
2. S&S Vietnam Bureau, "B-52s Hit Reds Near Cambodian Border," *Stars and Stripes*, October 1, 1971, 6.
3. MAJ A.J.C. Lavalle, ed., *Airpower and the 1972 Spring Invasion*, USAF Southeast Asia Monograph Series, vol. 2, monograph 3 (Washington, DC: Government Printing Office, 1976), 13, 103.
4. AP, "Highway Is Objective," *New York Times*, September 30, 1971, 1.
5. PFC Ken Schulte, "Mortars, B-52's Enliven Bunker Life," *Pacific Stars and Stripes*, October 9, 1971, 6.
6. AP, "Saigon Troops Lift Enemy Siege of Firebase along Border Area," *Washington Post*, October 2, 1971, A16.
7. Interviews with Robert J. McCaffree, LTC, CO, 2/32 FA, P, December 15, 2008; G. John LeVesque, CPT, S-3, 2/32 FA, P, March 26, 2009; and Mark Diggs, 1LT, XO, C BTRY, E, February 5, 2009.
8. Edgar C. Doleman Jr., *Tools of War* (Boston: Boston Publishing, 1985), 148–149.
9. Headquarters, 2/32d Artillery, daily staff journal, September 30, 1971, NARA, 1.
10. McCaffree interview.
11. AP, "Saigon Troops Lift Enemy Siege of Firebase along Border Area," *Washington Post*, October 2, 1971, A16.
12. Headquarters, 2/32d Artillery, September 30, 1971, 1.
13. LeVesque interview; LTC McCaffree to COL Hoffman, "Artillery Sitrep for Period 171800–181800 Oct 71," NARA, 1.
14. S2/S3 Sections 1/12th Cavalry, daily staff journal, September 28, 1971, NARA, 2; Headquarters, 2/32d Artillery, daily staff journal, October 2, 1971, NARA, 2; and Headquarters, 23d Artillery Group, daily staff journal, September 26, 1971, NARA, 2.
15. Vietnam Helicopter Pilots Association, "Helicopter UH-1C65–09458," *Fly Army*, http://www.flyarmy.org/incident/71093010.HTM (accessed December 20, 2005), 1–2.
16. Department of the Army, Headquarters, 1st Aviation Brigade, "Award of the Distinguished Flying Cross (Posthumous)," Special Orders No. 7134, November 10, 1971 (document courtesy of Paul Marling).
17. Paul Cibolski, "The Battle for Fire Support Base Pace," *Proud Americans*, http://www.proudamericans.homstead.com (accessed February 14, 2009); interview with Jack Adams, CPT, CO A Co, P, April 6, 2010; interview with Steve Belt, SGT, Section Chief, D/71st ADA, E, July 28, 2009.
18. Headquarters, Third Regional Assistance Command, daily staff journal, October 1, 1971, NARA, 2–3.
19. Headquarters, 2/32d Field Artillery, October 1, 1971, 1.
20. Ibid., October 3, 1971, 2.
21. Alvin Shuster, "Saigon Reports Thieu Capturing 90% of the Vote," *New York Times*, October 4, 1971, 4.
22. Headquarters, 3d Brigade, 1st Air Cavalry Division, *Operation Katum After Action Report*, October 6, 1971, A-3-1 to A-3-2 (author's collection).

23. Operations Section, 23d Artillery Group, October 2, 1971, 2.

24. UPI and S&S Vietnam Bureau, "Weather, Jets Help Viets Blunt NVA Offensive," *Stars and Stripes*, October 3, 1971, 6.

CHAPTER 7. INCOMING

1. Interview with Robert J. McCaffree, LTC, CO, 2/32 FA, P, December 15, 2008.

2. "Vietnam 1971," *Proud Americans*, http://proudamericans.homestead.com/files/vietnam/_1963_1971_1.htm (accessed July 5, 2008), 11.

3. McCaffree interview.

4. Headquarters, 2/32d Field Artillery, daily staff journal, October 3, 1971, NARA, 1.

5. Headquarters, Department of the Army, FM 6–40, "Fire Commands and the Execution," *Field Artillery Cannon Gunnery* (Washington, DC: Government Printing Office, 1969), 4–19 through 4–27.

6. "VC Weapons," *Sky Soldier*, http://www.skysoldier17.com/VC_weapons.htm (accessed May 10, 2009), 5–6.

7. Interview with Steve Belt, SGT, Section Chief, D/71st ADA, E, July 28, 2009.

8. Interview with Paul Cibolski, SSG, Section Chief, M, C BTRY, 11/8/09, P, November 10, 2009.

9. Interview with Thomas H. Timmons, CPT, BC, C BTRY, P, May 3, 2009; interview with Mark Diggs, 1LT, XO, C BTRY, E, February 5, 2009; interview with Mark Maxfield, SP4 Btry Recorder, C BTRY, E, January 8, 2009.

10. Diggs interview; Cibolski interview.

11. Timmons interview; interview with Al Grana, SP4, Infantry, B Co, P, December 29, 2009.

12. J. D. Coleman, *Incursion* (New York: St. Martin's Press, 1991), 205.

13. CO 2/32d Artillery to CO 23d Artillery Group, "Report on Pace," October 18, 1971, NARA, 2; Cibolski interview; Interview with Wayne Alberg, ICT, AXO, C BTRY, June 25, 2009.

14. "VC Weapons," 3.

15. McCaffree interview; interview with Russell Davis, MAJ, XO, 2/32 FA, E, June 28, 2010; and interview with Michael Donze, SGT, Section Chief, P, April 20, 2010; Alberg interview.

16. CO 2/32 to CO 23d Group, "Situation Report Updated," October 1, 1971, NARA, 1–2.

17. Headquarters, 2/32d Artillery, October 1, 1971, 1.

18. Ibid., October 3, 1971, 2.

19. CO 2/32 to CO 23d Group, "Situation Update No. 2," October 4, 1971, NARA, 1.

20. Thomas G. Bryant, Gerald B. Morse, Leslie M. Novak, and John C. Henry, "Tactical Radars for Ground Surveillance," *Lincoln Laboratory Journal* 12, no. 2 (2000): 342–343.

21. Headquarters, 2/32d Artillery, ORLL, period ending April 30, 1971, NARA, 4.

22. McCaffree interview.

23. Diggs interview.

24. CO 2/32d to CO 23d Group, "Situation Update No. 2," October 4, 1971, NARA, 1.

25. CO 2/32d to CO 23d Group, "Situation Update," October 9, 1971, NARA, 1.

26. Interview with Stan W. Tyson, LTC CO, 1/12 CAV, E, March 6, 2009.

27. Interview with Jack Adams, CPT, CO A Co, P, April 6, 2010.

28. Ibid.

29. S2/S3 Sections 1/12th Cavalry, daily staff journal, September 29, 1971, NARA, 2.

30. S2/S3 Sections 1/12th Cavalry, October 5, 1971, October 1, 6, 1971, 2.

31. S2/S3 Sections 1/12th Cavalry, Daily reports (Jim Bowie Report), September 25–October 7, 1971, NARA. These one-page reports are completed daily and track the location of every platoon-sized unit in the battalion. Presumably Battalion, or more likely Brigade, shifted these units around to meet the more immediate threat.

32. Adams interview.

33. S2/S3 Sections 1/12th Cavalry, October 5, 1971, 1, and October 6, 1971, 2.

34. Headquarters, 2/32d Artillery, daily staff journal, October 5, 1971, NARA, 1.

35. Operations Section, 23d Group, October 5, 1971, NARA, 2.

36. McCaffree interview.

37. Headquarters, 2/32d Artillery, October 6, 1971, 1, and Operations Section, 23d Group, October 6, 1971, 1.

38. CO 2/32d Artillery to CO 23d Group, "Situation Update," October 6, 1971, 1.

39. Ibid.

40. Ibid., 1, 2.

41. Ibid., 3.

42. CO 2/32d Artillery to CO 23d Group, "Artillery Sitrep," October 6, 1971, NARA, 1.

43. AP, "Saigon's Forces Said to Rout Foe," New York Times, October 6, 1971, 15.

44. SP5 Steve Montiel, "Troop Shift Surprised Reds—Gen.," Pacific Stars and Stripes, October 8, 1971, 6.

45. AP, "Fresh Enemy Unit in a Border Clash," New York Times, October 9, 1971, 9.

46. Headquarters, 2/32d Artillery, daily staff journal, October 5, 1971–October 8, 1971, NARA.

47. Ibid., October 8, 1971, 2, and Operations Section, 23d Artillery Group, October 8, 1971, 2.

CHAPTER 8. CONFUSION ON THE GROUND

1. Interview with Al Grana, SP4, Infantry, B Co, P, December 29, 2009.

2. Ibid.

3. Ibid.

4. Ibid.

5. Operations Section, 23d Artillery Group, daily staff journal, October 9, 1971, NARA, 1.

6. Headquarters, 2/32d Artillery, daily staff journal, October 9, 1971, NARA, 1.

7. Ibid.

8. Headquarters, Third Regional Assistance Command, daily staff journal, October 9, 1971, NARA, 4.

9. CO 2/32d to CO 23d Artillery Group, "Situation Update," October 9, 1971, NARA, 1–2.

10. Interview with Robert Cronin, CPT, CO Bravo Co, May 1, 2009, and November 26, 2010.

11. Ibid.

12. Interview with Rich Coreno, 1ST LT, Platoon Leader, B Co, E, November 9, 2009, and October 3, 2010. Sergeant Wernli also recalls the mission being first offered to Second Platoon. Interview with Walt Wernli, SGT, Squad Leader, B Co, E, April 14, 2010.

13. Coreno interview; Grana interview.

14. Grana interview.

15. Coreno interview.

16. Cronin interview.

17. Operations Section, 23d Group, 1–3.

18. Ibid., 2

19. Ibid.

20. Interview with Nick Demas, SGT, Infantry, B Co, P, March 1, 2010; interview with Ernest French, SP4, Infantry, B Co, P, April 8, 2010; Wernli interview.

21. Ibid.; interview with Paul Cibolski, SSG, Section Chief, C BTRY, M, 11/8/09, P, November 10, 2009; interview with Caesar Hastings, PVT, Infantry, B Co, P, March 30, 2009.

22. French interview; Demas interview.

23. Operations Section, 23d Artillery Group, October 9, 1971, 3.

24. Ibid.

25. SP4 Al Grana to the author, September 20, 2009, 3.

26. Operations Section, 23d Artillery Group, 2.

27. Headquarters, 2/32d Artillery, 2.

28. Cronin interview.

29. CO 2/32d Artillery to CO 23d Artillery Group, 3.

30. Ibid.

31. Ibid.

32. Grana interview.

CHAPTER 9. WELCOME TO PRIME TIME

1. Richard Boyle, *Flower of the Dragon: The Breakdown of the U.S. Army in Vietnam* (San Francisco: Ramparts Press, 1972), 22.

2. Interview with Richard Boyle, Author, P, December 22, 2009.

3. Boyle, *Flower of the Dragon*, 61.

4. Boyle interview; Boyle, *Flower of the Dragon*, 180.

5. Boyle interview.

6. Boyle, *Flower of the Dragon*, 224.

7. Ibid., 226–228.

8. Interview with Al Grana SP4, Infantry, B Co, P, December 29, 2009.

9. Copy of original letter courtesy of SP4 Mike McNamara.

10. Boyle interview; interview with Mike McNamara, SP4, Infantry, B Co, E, November 14, 2009.

11. Copy of original letter.

12. Boyle, *Flower of the Dragon*, 229.

13. Ibid., 260–262; Boyle interview.

14. Nicholas Proffitt, "Soldiers Who Refuse to Die," *Newsweek*, October 25, 1971, 67. A number of GIs at Pace dispute Boyle's account. This is discussed in greater detail in Chapter 20.

15. "Vietnam/Patrol Refusal," *ABC Evening News*, October 11, 1971, VTNA #12809, and "Vietnam/Troops," *CBS News*, October 11, 1971, VTNA #213222.

16. Craig R. Whitney, "Army Says Some GI's Balked Briefly at Patrol," *New York Times*, October 12, 1971, 3; AP, "5 U.S. Troops Balk at Vietnam Patrol," *Washington Post*, October 12, 1971, A14; UPI, "Refuse Patrol Duty," *Chicago Tribune*, October 11, 1971, 10; S&S Vietnam Bureau, "5 FB Pace GI's Balk at Night Patrol," October 13, 1971, 6.

17. AP, "Border Bases Hit; Troops That Balked Sent to New Base," *Washington Post*, October 13, 1971, A17.

18. "Vietnam/Rebellion," *ABC Evening News*, October 12, 1971, VTNA #12835; "Vietnam/Reluctant Co," *CBS Evening News*, October 12, 1971, VTNA #213253.

19. AP, "Border Bases Hit: Troops That Balked Sent to New Base," *Washington Post*, October 13, 1971, A17.

20. Proffitt, "Soldiers Who Refuse to Die," 68.

21. Ibid.

22. "Vietnam/Fighting/Reluctant Company," *ABC Evening News*, October 13, 1971, VTNA #12849.

23. Boyle, *Flower of the Dragon*, 265–266; "Kennedy Asks Probe of GI Plea," *Washington Post*, October 16, 1971, A4.

24. Boyle, *Flower of the Dragon*, 266.

25. Ibid., 265.

CHAPTER 10. UNDER NEW MANAGEMENT

1. Operations Section, 23d Artillery Group, daily staff journal, October 9, 10, 1971, NARA, 1; interview with Nick Demas, SGT, Infantry, B Co, P, March 1, 2010.

2. Ibid., October 10, 1971.

3. Headquarters, 2/32d Artillery, daily staff journal, October 10, 1971, NARA, 1.

4. Interview with Robert Cronin, CPT, CO, B Co, E, May 1, 2009.

5. Demas interview; interview with Ernest French, SP4, Infantry, B Co, P, April 8, 2010, and July 18, 2010; interview with Walt Wernli, SGT, Squad Leader, B Co, E, April 10, 2010, and August 17, 2010.

6. Wernli interview.

7. Recollections also differ on how many men finally joined the patrol, but about a dozen seems to be the best estimate.

8. Wernli interview.

9. "M18 Claymore," *FAS Military Analysis Network*, http://www.fas.org/man/dod-1011/sys/land/m18-claymore.htm (accessed July 23, 2010), 1.

10. Demas interview; French interview.

11. French interview.

12. Demas and French interviews.

13. Wernli and Cronin interviews.

14. Cronin interview.

15. Interview with Mark Diggs, 1LT, XO, C BTRY, E, February 5, 2009.

16. Ibid.

17. Ibid.

18. Ibid. The helicopter had to refuel because the pilots mistakenly headed to Firebase Mace instead of Pace before getting on the correct course.

19. Ibid.

20. Ibid.

21. Operations Section, 23d Artillery Group, October 10, 1971, 2.

22. Diggs interview

23. Ibid.

24. David E. Ott, *Field Artillery, 1954–1973 (Vietnam Studies)* (Washington, DC: Department of the Army, 1975), 61.

25. Diggs interview.

26. Interview with Russell Davis, MAJ, XO/2/32, E, June 28, 2010.

27. Ibid.

28. Ibid.

29. Interview with Joseph E. Dye, MAJ S-3, L, January 13, 2009.

30. Ibid.

31. Ibid.

32. Edgar C. Doleman Jr., *Tools of War (The Vietnam Experience)* (Boston: Boston Publishing, 1985), 4.

33. Ott, *Field Artillery*, 108–110.

34. LTC McCaffree does not recall the exchange with Major Dye regarding the ARVN 105's, but other sources confirm the differences between the infantry and artillery chains of command at Pace, including interviews with Thomas H. Timmons, CPT, BC, C BTRY, P, May 3, 2009; G. John LeVesque, CPT, S-3, P, March 26, 2009; Diggs interview; Dye interview.

35. Headquarters, Third Regional Assistance Command, daily staff journal, October 2, 1971, NARA, 10. Photographs taken at the time confirm the presence of the ARVN 105s.

36. AP, "S Viets Open Key Road, Resupply Cambodia Base," *Pacific Stars and Stripes*, October 11, 1971, 6.

37. Operations Section, 23d Artillery Group, October 11, 1971, 2.

38. Headquarters, 2/32d Artillery, October 11, 1971, 1.

39. William S. Tozer, Major, IG, "Report of Investigation Concerning Alleged Combat Refusal in B Company, 1st Battalion, 12th Cavalry," October 12, 1971, NARA, 2.

40. Ibid.

41. Interview with William Tozer, MAJ, IG, 3d Bde, 1st CAV, E, October 5, 2009.

42. Operations Section, 23d Artillery Group, October 11, 1971, 3; Headquarters, 2/32d Artillery, October 11, 1971, 2–3; interview with Paul Cibolski, SSG, Section Chief, C BTRY, M, 11/8/09, P, November 10, 2009.

43. S2/S3 Sections 1/12th Cavalry, daily staff journal, October 11, 1971, NARA, 4.

CHAPTER 11. LEAVE NO ONE BEHIND

1. S2/S3 Sections 1/12th Cavalry, daily staff journal, October 12, 1971 NARA, 3.

2. Interview with Paul Marling, SP4, Medic, D Co, E, February 24, 2009.

3. Ibid.

4. Headquarters, 2/32d Artillery, daily staff journal, October 12, 1971 NARA, 1; Marling interview.

5. "Cobra Crashes Near Pace." This document has no date or other identifying information, but appears to be either a unit newsletter or an article from *Stars and Stripes*, and is consistent with other source material (document courtesy of Paul Marling). "Rickenbacker, Ernest W.," *Fly Army*, http://www.flyarmy.org/DAT/datR/D05570.htm (accessed June 28, 2010).

6. Marling interview.

7. Ibid.

8. Ibid.

9. Interview with Michael Stevens, SGT, Infantry, D Co, E, September 4, 2010.

10. Ibid.

11. Operations Section, 23d Artillery Group, daily staff journal, October 12, 1971, NARA, 3.

12. Ibid., October 11, 1971, 3; Headquarters, 2/32d Artillery, October 12, 1971, 1.

13. Major William G. Tozer, IG, "Report of Investigation Concerning Alleged Combat Refusal in B Company, 1st Bn, 12th Cavalry," October 12, 1971, NARA, 3.

14. Interview with Robert Cronin, CPT, CO Bravo Co 1/12th CAV, E, May 1, 2009.

15. Headquarters, 2/32d Artillery, October 13, 1971, NARA, 1.

16. Don Davis, "GI's Refuse to Go on Patrol in Second Incident at Base"; *Pacific Stars and Stripes*, October 23, 1971, 6; Lt. General Walter T. Kerwin, "Fact Sheet: Fire Support Base Pace Incidents," October 22, 1971, CMH, 2; interview with Greg Cowles, SP4, Medic, D Co, P, August 31, 2009.

17. Stevens interview.

18. Don Davis, "GI's Refuse to Go on Patrol in Second Incident at Base"; Lt. General Walter T. Kerwin, "Fact Sheet: Fire Support Base Pace Incidents"; Cowles interview.

19. Davis, "GI's Refuse to Go on Patrol."

20. Ibid.

21. Headquarters, 2/32d Artillery, October 13, 1971, 1.

22. Operations Section, 23d Artillery Group, October 12, 1971, 3.

23. Ibid., October 14, 1971, 1.

24. Ibid., October 15, 1971, 1.

25. S2/S3 Sections 1/12th Cavalry, October 13, 1971, 2.

26. Ibid., October 15, 1971, 1.

27. Operations Section, 23d Artillery Group, October 18, 1971, 2.

28. Message from CO 2/32d Artillery to CO 23d Artillery Group, "Report on Pace," October 18, 1971 NARA, 1–2.

29. Stevens interview.

30. Operations Section, 23d Artillery Group, October 19, 1971, 1.

31. Message from CO 2/32d Artillery to CO 23d Artillery Group, October 18, 1971, 1.

32. AP, "Cambodian Border Is Raided by B-52's," *New York Times*, October 17, 1971, 2.

33. AP, "Sharp Fighting Breaks Out Near Cambodia Line," *New York Times*, October 19, 1971, 3.

34. AP, "U.S. Bombs Kill 18 in Saigon Unit," *New York Times*, October 20, 1971, 16.

35. Arthur Lord, "Fire Base Pace," NBC *Evening News*, October 19, 1971, VTNA #454342.

36. Ibid.

37. Operations Section, 23d Artillery Group, October 15, 1971, 1.

38. Headquarters, 2/32d Artillery, October 17, 1971, 1.

39. S2/S3 Sections 1/12th Cavalry, October 21, 1971, 1; Marling interview.

40. Marling interview.

41. Ibid.

CHAPTER 12. WHISKEY AND KOOL-AID

1. Interview with Michael Donze, SGT, Section Chief, C BTRY, P, April 20, 2010.

2. Ibid.

3. David Ott, *Field Artillery, 1954–1973* (Washington, DC: Department of the Army, 1975), 136.

4. Donze interview.

5. Operations Section, 23d Artillery Group, daily staff journal, October 21, 1971, NARA, 2.

6. Donze interview.

7. Headquarters, 3d Brigade, 1st Cavalry Division, ORLL, period ending October 31, 1971, NARA, 43.

8. Operations Section, 23d Artillery Group, October 21, 1971, NARA, 1.

9. Interview with Mark Diggs, 1LT, XO, C BTRY, E, February 5, 2009.

10. Headquarters, 2/32d Artillery, daily staff journal, October 22, 1971, NARA, 1.

11. "Vietnam / Fire Base Pace," CBS Evening News, October 22, 1971, VTNA #454416; interview with Wayne Alberg, 1LT AXO, C BTRY, P, June 25, 2009.

12. MG Wagstaff to GEN Abrams, "HOA 2041," October 22, 1971, CMH, 2.

13. Interview with Russell Davis, MAJ, XO/2/32, E, June 28, 2010; interview with Richard C. Ashley, CPT, BC, C BTRY, E, January 21, 2009; Diggs interview.

14. Operations Section, 23d Artillery Group, October 22, 1971, 2.

15. Ibid., 3.

16. AP, "2 GI's Left Behind at Isolated Base Consider It a 'Holiday'," Los Angeles Times, October 24, 1971, 1.

17. Interview with Steve Belt, SGT, Section Chief, D/71st ADA, E, July 28, 2009.

18. Interview with Ray Rhodes, CPT, Adviser, 6th ARVN ABN, E, October 24, 2009.

19. UPI, "GI's Turn Over to S. Viets Last Exposed U.S. Firebase," Chicago Tribune, October 23, 1971, A13.

20. Senator Edward M. Kennedy to SP4 Al Grana, October 18, 1971 (courtesy of Al Grana). See appendix E for a copy of this letter.

21. Walter T. Kerwin Jr., "White House Fact Sheet: Fire Support Base Pace Incidents," Memorandum for Chief of Staff, United States Army, October 22, 1971, CMH, 2 (see appendix D for report).

22. UPI, "Second Refusal to Patrol at Firebase Revealed," Washington Post, October 22, 1971, A-1; "GI's Refuse to Go on Patrol in Second Incident at Base," Pacific Stars and Stripes, October 23, 1971, 6.

23. "Fire Support Base Pace," October 22, 1971, VTNA, http://tvnews.vanderbilt.edu/diglib-fulldisplay.pl?SID (accessed May 9, 2008); Fox Butterfield, "U.S. Troops Leave Cambodian Border," New York Times, October 23, 1971, 2; Peter A. Jay, "U.S. Troops Removed from Vietnam Firebase," Washington Post, October 23, 1971, 1.

24. Richard Boyle, Flower of the Dragon (San Francisco: Ramparts Press, 1972), 266–267.

25. Ibid., 267; interview with Richard Boyle, Author, P, December 22, 2009.

26. Ibid.

27. AP, "S. Viets Claim 6-Month Hanoi Setback," Washington Post, October 24, 1971, 33.

28. Ibid.

29. "Vietnam 1971," Proud Americans, http://proudamericans.homestead.com/files/vietnam_1963_1971_1.htm (accessed July 5, 2008), 13.

30. Belt interview.

31. Interview with Keith Garner, MAJ, S-3, E, January 20, 2010.

32. Headquarters, 2/32d Artillery, October 3, 1971, 1.

33. Ibid., October 1, 1971, 1.

34. Jessee Edwards, "My Best Friend," The Wall, http://thewall-usa.com/guest.asp?recid=21179 (accessed January 3, 2010), 1.

35. Fox Butterfield, "Saigon Force Put at 5,000 in Drive," *New York Times*, November 23, 1971, 15.

36. AP, "Chup, in Cambodia, Seized, Saigon Says," *New York Times*, December 15, 1971, 3.

37. AP, "Saigon Ends Cambodia Drive," *New York Times*, December 31, 1971, 4.

38. Rhodes interview.

39. Shelby L. Stanton, *Vietnam Order of Battle* (Washington, DC: U.S. News Books, 1981), 103.

40. Ibid., 131.

41. Dale Andrade, *Trial by Fire* (New York: Hippocrene Books, 1995), 42.

CHAPTER 13. THE GRUNTS

1. Brian G. Hutton, director, *Kelly's Heroes*, Metro Golden Mayer, 1970 (Burbank, CA: Warner Home Video, 2000).

2. Robert L. Heinl Jr., "The Collapse of the Armed Forces," *Armed Forces Journal*, June 7, 1971, 1 (TTVA #2131805053).

3. David Fulgham and Terrence Maitland, *South Vietnam on Trial* (Boston: Boston Publishing, 1984), 25.

4. Stephen E. Ambrose, *Band of Brothers* (New York: Simon & Schuster, 2001), 234–235.

5. Walter G. Hermer, *United States Army in the Korean War: Truce Tent and Fighting Front* (Washington, DC: CMH, 1966), 351.

6. Heinl, "The Collapse of the Armed Forces," 2.

7. Peter A. Jay, "Combat Refusals Called Rare," *Washington Post*, October 25, 1971, A12.

8. Myra MacPherson, *Long Time Passing: Vietnam and the Haunted Generation* (New York: Doubleday & Co., 1984), 343.

9. David Cortright, *Soldiers in Revolt* (Chicago: Haymarket Books, 2005), 23–25.

10. Headquarters, 23d Artillery Group, ORLL, period ending October 31, 1971, NARA, 3; Operations Section, 23d Artillery Group, daily staff journal, October 22, 1971, 2.

11. From News Dispatches, "Desertions among GI's Near Record High," *Washington Post*, August 11, 1971, A1 (emphasis added).

12. Headquarters, 3d Brigade, First Cavalry Division, ORLL, period ending October 31, 1971, NARA, "Tab K: Provost Marshal Activities," K-1.

13. Interview with Steve Lonchase, PFC, E/1/12, P, July 6, 2010.

14. Ibid.

15. Headquarters, 1/12th Cavalry, daily staff journal, September 23, 1971, and September 24, 1971, NARA, "Daily Reports."

16. S2/S3 Sections, Headquarters, 3d Brigade, 1st Cavalry Division, daily staff journal, September 29, 1971, 2; October 5, 1971, 1; October 6, 1971, 2, NARA.

17. See note 16 above; interview with Jack Adams, CPT, CO, A Co, P, April 6 2010.

18. David Ott, *Field Artillery 1954–1973* (Washington, DC: Department of the Army, 1975), 73.

19. Jay, "Combat Refusals Called Rare."

20. Headquarters, 2/32d Artillery, daily staff journal, October 9, 1971, NARA, 1.

21. Interview with Nick Demas, SGT, Infantry, B Co, P, March 1, 2010; interview with Walt Wernli, SGT, Squad Leader, B Co, E, April 14, 2010; interview with Ernest French, SP4, Infantry, B Co, P, April 8, 2010.

22. Interview with Paul Cibolski, SSG, Section Chief, C BTRY, M, 11/8/09, P, November 10, 2009.

23. Headquarters, 3d Brigade, 1st Cavalry Division, ORLL, period ending October 31, 1971, 8–13.

24. MAJ William S. Tozer, "Report of Investigation Concerning Alleged Combat Refusal in B Company, 1st Bn, 12th Cavalry," October 12, 1971, NARA, 3.

25. Ibid.

26. Ibid.

27. Ibid., 2.

28. Interview with Rich Coreno, 1LT, Platoon Leader, B Co, E, November 9, 2009.

29. Tozer, "Report of Investigation," 3.

30. Ibid.

31. Interview with Joe Reiger, SP4, RTO, B Co, E, March 16, 2010; interview with Al Grana, SP4, Infantry, B Co, P, December 29, 2009; interview with Mike McNamara, SP4, Infantry, B Co, E, November 14, 2009; interview with Derek Paul, S4, Infantry, B Co, P, January 28, 2010.

32. Grana interview.

33. S2/S3 Sections, daily staff journal, October 15, 1971, 2.

34. Terrence Smith, "Troop Withdrawals: Combat Role May End but Casualties Will Not," *New York Times*, January 10, 1971, E4.

35. AP, "GI Combat Role in Vietnam Nearly Ended—Laird," *Pacific Stars and Stripes*, August 6, 1971, 5.

36. Ibid.

37. PFC Ken Schultz, "Ambush Patrol 'Wasn't Our Job,' B Co. GIs Say," *Pacific Stars and Stripes*, October 15, 1971, 6.

38. McNamara interview; Paul interview; interview with Caesar Hastings, PVT, Infantry, B Co, P, March 30, 2009.

39. The veracity of Boyle's report is the subject of chapter 20, "Boyle vs. the Powers That Be."

40. This letter is included in appendix F.

41. Interview with Paul White, SP4, RTO, D Co, E, November 21, 2009.

42. UPI, "Laird: More Viet Cuts Due in Mid-November," *Pacific Stars and Stripes*, September 3, 1971, 24.

43. Donald Kirk, "Viet Vets Feel Rejected, Deceived," *Chicago Tribune*, October 31, 1971, 1.

44. Ibid., 2.

45. For an excellent discussion of the conflicting opinions of GIs about the war, see Christian Appy, *Working Class War* (Chapel Hill: University of North Carolina Press, 1993), 300.

46. Interview with Wayne Alberg, 1LT AXO, C BTRY, P, June 25, 2009.

47. John Laurence, *The Cat from Hue: A Vietnam War Story* (New York: Public Affairs Books, 2002), 798.

48. Grana interview.

49. Ibid.; McNamara interview; Paul interview; interview with Reuben Topinka, SP4, Infantry, B Co, P, November 8, 2009.

50. Headquarters, 3d Brigade, First Cavalry Division, ORLL, period ending October 31, 1971, 13.

51. Don Davis, "GI's Refuse to Go on Patrol in Second Incident at Base," *Pacific Stars and Stripes*, October 23, 1971, 6; interview with Michael Stevens, SGT, Infantry, D Co, E, October 27, 2010.

52. Headquarters, 2/32d Artillery, daily staff journal, October 19, 1971, 1.

53. Ibid., October 17, 1971, 1–2.

54. S2/S3 Sections, 1/12th Cavalry, daily staff journal, October 24, 1971, 1.

55. Headquarters, 3d Brigade, 1st Cavalry Division, ORLL, period ending October 31, 1971, 13.

56. Laurence, *The Cat from Hue*, 798.

57. Davis, "GI's Refuse to Go Out on Patrol," 6.

58. Ron Miller, "Vietnam /Reluctant Company," *ABC Evening News*, October 13, 1971, VTNA #12894.

59. Interview with Robert Cronin, CPT, CO, B Co, E, May 1, 2009.

60. Interview with Stan Tyson, LTC, CO, 1/12 CAV, E, March 26, 2009.

61. See, for example, Robert K. Brigham, *ARVN: Life and Death in the South Vietnamese Army* (Lawrence: University Press of Kansas, 2006), 45–47.

62. Ambrose, *Band of Brothers*, 289.

63. Frank Gabrenya, "Grunt Work," *Columbus Dispatch*, August 6, 2006, C1, C4.

CHAPTER 14. ARTILLERY AND OTHER COMBAT SUPPORT TROOPS

1. Headquarters, II Field Force Vietnam, ORLL, period ending April 30, 1971, NARA, 6.

2. Headquarters, 23d Artillery Group, ORLL, period ending October 31, 1971, NARA, 3.

3. William M. Hammond, *Public Affairs: The Military and the Media, 1968–1973* (Washington, DC. CMII, 1995), 182.

4. Ronald H. Spector, *After Tet* (New York: Vintage Books, 1993), 278.

5. Hammond, *Public Affairs*, 392.

6. Interview with Peter Hanson, CPT, BC, B BTRY, P, April 29, 2010; interview with Thomas H. Timmons, CPT, BC, C BTRY, P, May 3, 2009; interview with Mark Diggs, 1LT, XO, C BTRY, E, February 5, 2009; interview with Roger Atkin, SSG, Section Chief, C BTRY, E, March 22, 2010; interview with Michael Donze, SGT, Section Chief, C BTRY, P, April 20, 2010; interview with Tim Colgan, SP4, Equipment Operator, 557 Engineers, P, January 11, 2010; and interview with Mark Maxfield, SP4, Battery Recorder, C BTRY, E, January 8, 2009.

7. Headquarters, 2/32d Artillery, ORLL, period ending April 30, 1971, NARA, 2.

8. Ibid.

9. Ibid., period ending October 31, 1971, 2.

10. Operations Section, 23d Artillery Group, ORLL, period ending October 31, 1970, NARA, 16–17.

11. AP, "Senate Study Finds Drug Abuse by G.I.'s a Rarity in Combat," *New York Times*, April 21, 1971, 10.

12. Headquarters, 2/32d Artillery, ORLL, period ending April 30, 1971, 2.

13. Headquarters, 2/32d Artillery, *Consolidated Staff Journal*, March 30, 1971, NARA, 2; interview with Tom Colaiezzi, 1LT FDO, C BTRY, E, May 9, 2009.

14. William Thomas Allison, *Military Justice in Vietnam* (Lawrence: University Press of Kansas, 2006), 68.

15. Myra MacPherson, *Long Time Passing: Vietnam and the Haunted Generation* (New York: Doubleday & Co., 1984), 24–25.

16. Army-wide trends for both courts-martial and Article 15s are addressed in chapter 17, but the figures for the 2/32d demonstrate the difficulty in making sweeping generalizations. While it is clear this artillery battalion struggled with increased drug abuse and other

disciplinary issues during the draw-down period, it is also clear it was not overwhelmed by them.

17. MG David Ott, Field Artillery, 1954–1973 (Washington, DC: Department of the Army, 1975), 173–179.

18. C.D.B. Bryan, Friendly Fire (New York: Bantam Books, 1977).

19. Interview with Russell Davis, MAJ, XO/2/32, E, June 28, 2010; Diggs interview; Maxfield interview.

20. Headquarters, 2/32d Artillery, ORLL, period ending October 31, 1971, NARA, 6.

21. Interview with Wayne Alberg, 1LT AXO, C BTRY, P, June 25, 2009.

22. Davis, Diggs, and Alberg interviews.

23. Operations Section, 23d Artillery Group, daily staff journal, October 9, 1971, 2; October 10, 1971, 2.

24. Interview with Richard C. Ashley, CPT, BC, C BTRY, E, January 21, 2009; interview with Paul Cibolski, SSG, Section Chief, C BTRY, M, 11/8/09, P, November 10, 2009; Timmons interview; Diggs interview; Alberg interview; Donze interview.

25. CO 2/32d Artillery to CO 23d Group, "Artillery Sit Rep," October 8, 1971, NARA, 3.

26. CPT Timmons left on October 7, CPT Ashley arrived on October 10. In the period between, CPT Craig H. Stoudnor served as interim battery commander.

27. Robert Pisor, The End of the Line: The Siege of Khe Sanh (New York: Ballantine Books, 1983), 194–195.

28. CO 2/32d Artillery to CO 23d Artillery Group, "Report on Pace," October 18, 1971, NARA, 1–2.

29. CO 2/32d Artillery to CO 23d Group, "Situation Update," October 6, 1971, NARA, 2; interview with Mark Crane, SP4, Commo Section, C BTRY, P, March 10, 2010.

30. CO 2/32d Artillery to CO 23d Group, "Report on Pace," October 18, 1971, 1–2.

31. Interview with Jack Adams, CPT, CO A Co, P, April 6, 2010; interview with Al Grana, SP4, Infantry, B Co, P, December 29, 2009; interview with Derek Paul, SP4, Infantry, B Co, P, January 28, 2010.

32. AP, "Pentagon Reveals Rise in 'Fraggings,'" New York Times, April 21, 1971, 9.

33. Operations Section, 23d Artillery Group, daily staff journal, September 25, 1971, 2.

34. Hammond, 174–182.

35. Interview with Levell Hinton, PFC, FDC, C BTRY, P, June 23, 2010.

36. Ibid.; interview William McCormick, SP4, C BTRY, P, June 21, 2010.

37. Operations Section, 23d Artillery Group, October 22, 1971, 2.

38. Interview with Steve Belt, SGT, Section Chief, D/71st ADA, E, July 28, 2009.

39. Diggs interview.

40. SP4 Clayton Kinkade, "Keeping Pace with Teamwork," Army Reporter, November 29, 1971, 6–7; courtesy of CPT Ashley.

41. Interview with Ray Rhodes, CPT, Adviser, 6th ARVN ABN, E, October 24, 2009.

42. Boyle, 217.

43. Headquarters, 2/35th Artillery, daily staff journal, January 19, 1971, 4.

44. SSG Cibolski interview; SGT Donze interview.

45. CPT Rhodes interview.

46. Phillip B. Davidson, Vietnam at War (New York: Oxford University Press, 1988), 663.

47. Ibid.

48. John Prados, Vietnam: The History of an Unwinnable War, 1945–1975 (Lawrence: University Press of Kansas, 2009), 278.

49. Interview with Stan W. Tyson, LTC CO, E, March 6, 2009.

50. Headquarters, 2/32d Artillery, ORLL, period ending October 31, 1971, NARA, 8.

51. Interview with Robert J. McCaffree, LTC, CO, P, December 15, 2008.

52. LTC Robert J. McCaffree, "Commendation for Fire Support Base Pace," October 17, 1971; courtesy of SP4 Paul White.

53. Ibid.

54. "Valorous Unit Award, General Orders No. 1484 United States Army, Vietnam, 3 July 1972," 12th Cavalry Regiment Association, http://www.12th cav.us/112_ Cav_VUC_Tay _Ninh.htm (accessed May 11, 2006).

55. "Lineage and Honors," Proud Americans," http:/proudamericans, homestead.com/ files/History 32.htm (accessed July 4, 2009); "1st Battalion, 12th Cavalry Regiment Unit Decorations," 12th Cavalry Regiment Association, http://www.12th cav.US/112_unit_decorations_ list.htm (accessed July 4, 2009).

56. CO 2/32d Artillery to CO 23d Artillery Group, "Report on Pace," October 18, 1971, NARA, 2.

CHAPTER 15. BEYOND PACE

1. Shelby L. Stanton, The Rise and Fall of an American Army (New York: Ballantine Books, 2003), 356; David Fulgham and Terrance Maitland, The Vietnam Experience: South Vietnam on Trial, Mid 1970 to 1972 (Boston: Boston Publishing, 1984), 22–24.

2. Shelby L. Stanton, Vietnam Order of Battle (Washington, DC: U.S. News Books, 1981), 73.

3. Stanton, The Rise and Fall of an American Army, 354–357; Fulgham and Maitland, The Vietnam Experience, 16; Phillip B. Davidson, Vietnam at War: The History, 1946–1975 (New York: Oxford University Press, 1991), 661–663.

4. Headquarters, 3rd Brigade, 1st Air Cavalry Division, ORLL, period ending October 31, 1971, NARA, 1.

5. Ibid.

6. Ibid., enclosures, D-1–D-6, I-1, N-1.

7. Headquarters, 1st Cavalry Division, ORLL, period ending April 30, 1970, NARA 34, 01–04.

8. Stanton, The Rise and Fall of an American Army, 356.

9. Fulgham and Maitland, The Vietnam Experience, 24.

10. "Indochina: There's Still a War On," Time, January 24, 1972, 22.

11. Ibid.

12. AP, "US Patrol Ambushed," New York Times, January 4, 1972, 5.

13. AP, "Mortar Fire Wounds 18 GI's at Base 20 Miles from Saigon," New York Times, January 8, 1972, 4.

14. Reuters, "A Vietcong Attack 6 Miles from Saigon Is Reported," New York Times, January 11, 1972, 3.

15. AP, "10 GI's Wounded in Several Clashes East of Capital," New York Times, January 29, 1972, 10.

16. "Indochina: There's Still a War On," 23.

17. Gloria Emerson, "'Grunts' Wonder When Their Fighting Became Defensive," *New York Times*, January 22, 1972, 9.

18. Stanton, *Vietnam Order of Battle*, 131.

19. "Mark Fredrick Biagini," The Vietnam Veterans Memorial, http://thewall-usa.com/info.asp?recid=3885 (accessed November 17, 2009).

20. Stanton, *Vietnam Order of Battle*, 88.

21. Headquarters, 173d Airborne Brigade, ORLL, period November 1, 1970–April 30, 1971, NARA, 1.

22. Iver Peterson, "Pullout Is Not Seen as Threat to G.I.'s in Field," *New York Times*, June 1, 1971, 5.

23. Headquarters, 173d Airborne Brigade, 3–4, enclosures D, E, F.

24. Ibid., 260, 376–380; Stanton, *Vietnam Order of Battle*, 260, 376–380.

25. Fulgham and Maitland, *The Vietnam Experience*, 21–22.

26. Ibid.

27. Stanton, *Rise and Fall of an American Army*, 342–343.

28. Ibid., 343.

29. Keith W. Nolan, *Ripcord* (Novato, CA: Presidio Press, 2000), 404; Samuel Zaffiri, *Hamburger Hill: The Brutal Battle for Dong Ap Bia, May 11–20, 1969* (San Francisco: Presidio Press, 1988), 272.

30. Nolan, *Ripcord*, 403.

CHAPTER 16. SOLDIERING ON IN MR I

1. General Donn A. Starry, *Mounted Combat in Vietnam* (Washington, DC: Department of the Army, 1978), 187; Keith William Nolan, *Into Laos: The Story of Dewey Canyon II/Lam Son 719, Vietnam 1971* (Navato, CA: Presidio Press, 1988), 41–42, 66.

2. Graham A. Cosmas, *MACV: The Joint Command in the Years of Withdrawal, 1968–1973* (Washington, DC: CMH, 2007), 325.

3. Congressional Quarterly, "Congress and the Nation, Vol. III, 1969–1972" (Washington, DC: Congressional Quarterly Service, 2006), 912–913; William M. Hammond, *The Military and the Media, 1968–1973* (Washington, DC: CMH, 1995), 403–404.

4. Cosmas, *MACV*, 329–331.

5. Ibid., 332–335.

6. Nolan, *Into Laos*, 289.

7. Ibid., 302, 342.

8. Ibid., 298.

9. Ibid., 299.

10. Ibid., 300.

11. "Incident on Route Nine," *Time*, April 5, 1971, 25.

12. Nolan, *Into Laos*, 304–305.

13. Ibid., 307.

14. Ibid., 290.

15. "Counteroffensive, Phase VII (07/01/70—6/30/71)," 2d Battalion 94th Artillery, Six Year History, http://www.2ndbattalion94thartillery.com/chas/II2.htm (accessed November 13, 2009).

16. Nolan, *Into Laos*, 309–310.

17. Ibid., 315–316.

18. Ibid., 336.

19. Cosmas, MACV, 339.

20. Hammond, *The Military and the Media*, 379–380.

21. Nolan, *Into Laos*, 290.

22. Ibid., 57.

23. Ibid., 213.

24. Ibid., 43.

25. John Prados, *Vietnam: The History of an Unwinnable War, 1945–1975* (Lawrence: University Press of Kansas, 2009), 417–418.

26. Cosmas, MACV, 335.

27. Phillip B. Davidson, *Vietnam at War* (New York: Oxford University Press, 1988), 552.

28. Hammond, *The Military and the Media*, 505.

29. Ibid., 506.

30. Ibid.

31. Ibid., 507–508.

32. Ibid., 251; Keith William Nolan, *Sappers in the Wire: The Life and Death of Firebase Mary Ann* (College Station: Texas A&M University Press, 1995), 200.

33. Nolan, *Into Laos*, 255.

34. Ibid., 334–336.

35. Headquarters, 2/32d Artillery, *Consolidated Staff Journal*, March 30, 1971, NARA, 2; interview with Tom Colaiezzi, 2LT FDO, E, May 9, 2009.

36. Nolan, *Sappers in the Wire*, 9, 30–31.

37. Ibid., 116.

38. Nicholas Proffitt, "The Hell at Mary Ann," *Newsweek*, April 12, 1971, 45.

39. Ibid.

40. Shelby Stanton, *Vietnam Order of Battle* (Washington, DC: U.S. News Books, 1981), 77.

41. Headquarters, 101st Airborne Division, *Combat Operations After Action Report*, Operation Op Ord 13–70, November 3, 1971, NARA, 3–5, 14.

42. Headquarters, 23d Infantry Division, ORLL, period ending October 15, 1971, NARA, 38, 41, 46.

43. AP, "U.S. Patrol Reports 3 Killed in Ambush in Hills at Da Nang," *New York Times*, August 1, 1971, 6.

44. "5 Americans Killed by Mine in Vietnam," *New York Times*, August 6, 1971, 5.

45. Craig R. Whitney, "5 G.I.'s Are Killed in Enemy Attack," *New York Times*, August 22, 1971, 4.

46. AP, "U.S. War Deaths Drop to 10, Lowest for a Week in 6 Years," *New York Times*, August 27, 1971, 3.

47. Stanton, *Vietnam Order of Battle*, 88, 144.

48. Dale Andrade, *Trial by Fire* (New York: Hippocrene Books, 1995), 544–545.

CHAPTER 17. REMFs, FRAGGERS, DOPERS, SLACKERS, AND OTHER LOSERS

1. The ratio of combat to support troops in Vietnam has been the subject of some controversy. One of the better analyses was done by Shelby Stanton in his history of the

First Air Cavalry, *Anatomy of a Division: The 1st Cav in Vietnam* (New York: Warner Books, 1989), 190–194. He examined in detail personnel summaries for the entire division prior to its advance into Cambodia in May 1970. He found that about 80 percent of the soldiers assigned to the maneuver battalions were actually deployed in the field. However, when the entire division's manpower (about 20,000) was factored in, only about one-third of the division's manpower was actually in the field. Adjusting for the incidence of maneuver battalions and support troops throughout the entire theater, including Air Force and Navy personnel, it is clear that no more than 20–25 percent of the troops were engaged in direct combat missions on any given day.

    2. The ratios calculated are based on courts-martial statistics and troop levels derived from George S. Prugh, *Law of War: Vietnam, 1964–1973* (Washington, DC: Department of the Army, 1975), appendix K; Graham A. Cosmas, *MACV: The Joint Command in the Years of Withdrawal, 1968–1973* (Washington: CMH, 2007), "Table—U.S. Troop Redeployments," 178.

    3. U.S. House of Representatives, Committee on Appropriations, Subcommittee on Department of Defense, DOD Appropriations for 1972, Hearings, 92d Cong., 1st sess., pt. 9, May 17, 1971–September 23, 1971, 586.

    4. Ibid.; Prugh, *Law of War*, appendix K; Cosmas, *MACV*, 778.

    5. Ibid.

    6. "Desertions among GI's Near High," *Washington Post*, August 11, 1971, A1.

    7. William M. Hammond, *Public Affairs: The Military and the Media, 1968–1973* (Washington, DC: CMH, 1995), 382.

    8. Guenter Lewy, *America in Vietnam* (New York: Oxford University Press, 1980), 155.

    9. U.S. House of Representatives, Committee on Appropriations, Subcommittee on Department of Defense, DOD Appropriations for 1972, Hearings, 92d Cong., 1st sess., pt. 9, May 17, 1971–September 23, 1971, 585.

    10. Ibid.

    11. Thomas C. Bond, "The Why of Fragging," *American Journal of Psychiatry* 133, no. 11 (November 1976): 1328–1330.

    12. Hammond, *Public Affairs*, 186.

    13. Ibid.

    14. Jeremy Kuzmarov, *The Myth of the Addicted Army* (Amherst: University of Massachusetts Press, 2009), 48–51.

    15. Ibid., 51.

    16. Alvin M. Shuster, "G.I. Heroin Addiction Epidemic in Vietnam," *New York Times*, May 16, 1971, 20.

    17. Felix Belair Jr., "House Unit Cites Rise in G.I. Drug Abuse," *New York Times*, May 26, 1971, 14.

    18. Kuzmarov, *The Myth of the Addicted Army*, 52.

    19. "The Heroin Plague: What Can Be Done?" *Newsweek*, July 5, 1971, 27.

    20. "Poll Finds Drugs No. 3 Issue in U.S.," *New York Times*, June 17, 1971, 29.

    21. James M. Naughten, "President Gives 'Highest Priority' to Drug Problem," *New York Times*, June 2, 1971, 1.

    22. Kuzmarov, *The Myth of the Addicted Army*, 95–112.

    23. Louis Harris, "Drugs, Military," *Washington Post*, February 21, 1972, E1.

24. Kuzmarov, *The Myth of the Addicted Army*, 75–88.

25. Ibid., 52–53.

26. "G.I. Use of Heroin Is Reported Cut," *New York Times*, July 27, 1971, 9; Kuzmarov, *The Myth of the Addicted Army*, 51.

27. Spencer Rich, "Fears of Narcotics Wave among Vets Exaggerated," *Washington Post*, February 25, 1980, A3.

28. Lewy, *America in Vietnam*, 154–155.

29. Cosmas, *MACV*, 234–236.

30. Donald Kirk, "Who Wants to Be the Last American Killed in Vietnam?" *New York Times Magazine*, September 19, 1971, SM 9–66.

31. Ron Milam, *Not a Gentleman's War* (Chapel Hill: University of North Carolina Press, 2009), 166–167.

32. Hammond, *Public Affairs*, 371.

33. Gloria Emerson, "G.I.'s Now Wear a Lot the Army Didn't Issue," *New York Times*, August 28, 1970, 51.

34. Samuel Lipsman and Edward Doyle, *Fighting for Time, 1969–1970* (Boston: Boston Publishing, 1983), 93–94, 188.

35. John M. Shaw, *The Cambodian Campaign: The 1970 Offensive and America's Vietnam War* (Lawrence: University Press of Kansas, 2005), 102.

36. Stanton, *Anatomy of a Division*, 178, 187, 194; J. D. Coleman, *Incursion: From America's Choke Hold on the NVA Lifelines to the Sacking of the Cambodian Sanctuaries* (New York: St. Martin's Paperbacks, 1991), 268–271.

37. Keith William Nolan, *Into Laos: The Story of Dewey Canyon II/Lam Son 719, Vietnam 1971* (Novato, CA: Presidio Press, 1986), 24.

CHAPTER 18. FOLLOW ME

1. See, for example, Ron Milam, *Not a Gentleman's War: An Inside View of Junior Officers in the Vietnam War* (Chapel Hill: University of North Carolina Press, 2009), 43–44.

2. See, for example, "Crisis in Command," in *The Vietnam Experience: South Vietnam on Trial, Mid 1970 to 1972*, ed. David Fulgham and Terrance Maitland (Boston: Boston Publishing, 1984), 34–49; and Eric Bergerud, *Red Thunder Tropic Lightning* (Boulder, CO: Westerico Press, 1993), 290–315.

3. William M. Hammond, *Public Affairs: The Military and the Media, 1968–1973* (Washington, DC: CMH, 1995), 85–86.

4. Ibid., 86–87.

5. Ibid.; Samuel Zaffiri, *Hamburger Hill: The Brutal Battle for Dong Ap Bia, May 11–20, 1969* (San Francisco: Presidio Press, 1988), 273–280.

6. Samuel Lipsman and Edward Doyle, *The Vietnam Experience, Fighting for Time (1969-70)* (Boston: Boston Publishing, 1983), 101.

7. Graham A. Cosmas, *MACV: The Joint Command in the Years of Withdrawal, 1968–1973* (Washington, DC: CMH, 2007), 252–253.

8. Fulgham and Maitland, *South Vietnam on Trial*, 38.

9. Hammond, *Public Affairs*, 220–260.

10. Ibid., 255.

11. Ibid., 254.

12. Fred P. Graham, "War Crimes Conviction Raises Series of Legal Conflicts for Foot Soldiers," *New York Times*, May 31, 1971, 18.

13. Fulgham and Maitland, *The Vietnam Experience*, 44–45.

14. Interview with Paul Cibolski, SSG, Section Chief, C BTRY, M, 11/8/09, P, November 10, 2009; interview with Bruce Oestrich, SGT Commo Chief, C BTRY, P, November 18, 2008; interview with Al Grana, SP4, Infantry, B Co, P, December 29, 2009.

15. Peter A. Jay, "Combat Refusals Called Rare," *Washington Post*, October 25, 1971, A1.

16. Headquarters, 2/32d Artillery, daily staff journal, September 22, 1971, NARA, 1.

17. Interview with G. John LeVesque, CPT, S-3, 2/32 FA, P, March 26, 2009.

18. MG Jack J. Wagstaff, *Debriefing Report*, May 27, 1971–December 15, 1971, CMH, 11.

19. Headquarters, TRAC, daily staff journal, October 9, 1971, NARA, 4; Headquarters, 2/32d Artillery, October 11, 1971, 1.

20. Gen Abrams to MG Wagstaff et al., "Increment Ten Redeployments," November 2, 1971, Abrams Papers, Military Heritage Center, Carlisle, PA, 4.

21. Wagstaff to Gen Abrams, "NOA 1993," October 13, 1971, OCMH, 2.

22. Headquarters, TRAC, daily staff journal, October 10, 1971, 9.

23. Hammond, *Public Affairs*, 380.

24. "Jack J. Wagstaff," *Arlington Cemetery*, http://www.arlingtoncemetery.net/wagstaff .htm (accessed July 14, 2008).

25. Jack J. Wagstaff, "The Army's Preparation for Atomic Warfare," *Military Review* 35, no. 2 (May 1955): 6.

26. John B. Wilson, *Maneuver and Firepower* (Washington, DC: CMH, 1998), 291.

27. Jack J. Wagstaff, "Your Place in Politico-Military Policy," *Military Review* 35, no. 8 (November 1955): 47.

28. Interview with Michael Donze, SGT, Section Chief, C BTRY, P, April 20, 2010.

29. Operations Section, 23d Artillery Group, daily staff journal, October 10, 1971, NARA, 2.

30. Ibid., October 9, 1971, 3; October 12, 1971, 1.

31. "Project Sky Trooper, 1st Battalion, 12th Cavalry—Vietnam," 12th *Cavalry Regiment Association*, http://lcda.org/boh_vn_1-12_cav.htm (accessed August 25, 2008), 1–9.

32. "Honor roll for 2/32 Field Artillery," *Proud Americans*, http://proudamericans.homestead .com/Honor_roll~ie4.html/ (accessed July 5, 2008), 1–4.

33. Operations Section, 23d Artillery Group, daily staff journal, October 22, 1971, NARA, 2.

34. Headquarters, TRAC, daily staff journal, October 9, 1971, 4.

35. Operations Section, 23d Artillery Group, daily staff journal, October 10, 1971, 3.

36. Nicholas Proffitt reported that all three platoon leaders expressed concerns about the wisdom of this mission. Captain Cronin does not recall any of them raising objections. Lieutenant Coreno recalls that they did.

37. Interview with Nick Demas, SGT, Infantry, B Co, P, March 1, 2010; interview with Ernest French, SP4, Infantry, P, April 8, 2010; interview with Walter Wernli, SGT, Squad Leader, E, April 10, 2010.

38. S2/S3 Sections 1/12th Cavalry, daily staff journal, October 11, 1971, NARA, 4; interview with Joseph E. Dye, MAJ S-3, 1/12 CAV, L, January 13, 2009; interview with Stan W. Tyson, LTC CO, 1/12 CAV, E, March 6, 2009.

39. Dye interview.

40. Interview with Mark Diggs, 1LT, XO, E, February 5, 2009, Dye interview.

41. Grana interview.

42. LTG Walter J. Kerwin Jr., "Fact Sheet: Fire Support Base Pace Incidents," memorandum for chief of staff, U.S. Army, October 22, 1971, CMH, 2.

43. Keith W. Nolan, *Into Laos: The Story of Dewey Canyon II/Lam Son 719, Vietnam 1971* (Navato, CA: Presidio Press, 1988), 304–305.

44 Interview with Jack Adams, CPT, CO A Co, P, April 2, 2010; interview with Robert Cronin, CPT, B Co, E, May 1, 2009.

45. Headquarters, 3d Brigade (Separate), 1st Cavalry Division, ORLL, period ending October 31, 1971, NARA, 1.

46. Stevens interview.

47. Interview with Russell Davis, MAJ, XO/2/32, E, June 28, 2010; interview with Wayne Alberg, 1LT AXO, C BTRY, P, June 25, 2009; Diggs interview.

48. Davis interview.

CHAPTER 19. A THOUSAND CALLEYS?

1. Ron Milam, *Not a Gentleman's War: An Inside View of Junior Officers in the Vietnam War* (Chapel Hill: University of North Carolina Press, 2009), 3.

2. This thesis is subject of some dispute. See for example Milam, *Not a Gentleman's War*, 27–29.

3. Milam, *Not a Gentleman's War*, 166.

4. Colonel Richard G. Hoffman, "Senior Officer Debriefing Report," January 5, 1972, NARA, 3.

5. Based on duty logs, Colonel Hoffman visited Pace only once during the twenty-seven-day siege.

6. For an excellent description of this issue, see Eric M. Bergerud, *Red Thunder Tropic Lightning* (Boulder, CO: Westview Press, 1993), 297, and "Carrot and Stick," *Newsweek*, May 25, 1970, 45.

7. John Saar, "You Just Can't Hand Out Orders," *Life*, October 23, 1970, 32.

8. Bergerud, *Red Thunder*, 307.

9. Interview with Jack Ryals, 1LT, FDO, B BTRY, P, July 22, 2010.

10. Headquarters, 2/35th Artillery, daily staff journal, January 12, 1971, (NARA), 5.

11. Interview with Robert Cronin, CPT, CO Bravo Co, 1/12th CAV, E, May 1, 2009.

12. Interview with Rich Coreno, 1LT, Plt Leader, B Co, E, November 9, 2009; interview with Nick Demas, SGT, Infantry, B Co, P, March 1, 2010; interview with Walt Wernli, SGT, Squad Leader, B CO, April 10, 2010.

13. Interview with Al Grana, SP4, Infantry, B Co, P, December 29, 2009.

14. Cronin maintains the order came from McCaffree, which is consistent with previous behavior. However, Cronin did not object as Adams had.

15. Interview with Paul Marling; SP4, MEdic, D Co, E, February 24, 2009.

16. Interview with Michael Stevens, SGT, Infantry, D Co, E, October 27, 2010.

17. Interview with Jack Adams, CPT, CO A Co, P, April 6, 2010.

18. Interview with Robert J. McCaffree, LTC, CO, 2/32 FA, P, December 15, 2008. Crater analysis was supposed to determine the type of projectile used and where it came from.

19. Written documentation of this incident is sparse, but it occurred at about the same time one of Charlie Battery's soldiers lost his legs to shrapnel wounds, which shows up in the battalion logs on October 5. Headquarters, 2/32d Artillery, *Consolidated Staff Journal*, October 5, 1971, NARA, 1.

20. This account is based primarily on the following: McCaffree interview; interview with Wayne Alberg, 1LT AXO, C BTRY, P, June 25, 2009; and interview with Michael Donze, SGT, Section Chief, C BTRY, P, April 20, 2010.

21. Ibid.

22. McCaffree interview.

23. This includes at least nine platoon leaders on the infantry side, and two fire direction officers and one assistant executive officer on the artillery side.

24. Interview with Ernest French, SP4, Infantry, B Co, P, April 8, 2010.

25. David Fulgham and Terrance Maitland, *The Vietnam Experience: South Vietnam on Trial, Mid 1970 to 1972* (Boston: Boston Publishing, 1984), 45; Ronald H. Spector, *After Tet* (New York: Vintage Books, 1994), 247–248.

26. Adams interview.

27. Department of the Army, Company B, 1/12th Cavalry, "Company Roster," September 1, 1971; courtesy of SP4 Bill Denton.

28. Grana interview.

29. Coreno interview.

30. Alberg interview; Donze interview.

31. Interview with Paul Cibolski, SSG, Section Chief, M and P, November 8, 2009.

32. Donze interview; Cibolski interview.

33. Operations Section, 23d Artillery Group, daily staff journal, October 10, 1971, NARA, 2.

34. Donze interview.

35. Adams interview; Alberg interview; Coreno interview; interview with Peter Hanson, CPT, BC, B BTRY, P, April 29, 2010.

36. William L. Hauser, *America's Army in Crisis: A Study in Civil-Military Relations* (Baltimore: Johns Hopkins University Press, 1973), 46.

CHAPTER 20. RICHARD BOYLE VS. THE POWERS THAT BE

1. See, for example, William M. Hammond, *Public Affairs: The Military and the Media, 1968–1973 (The U.S. Army in Vietnam)* (Washington, DC: Office of Military History, 1995), 617–627.

2. Charles C. Moskos Jr., *The American Enlisted Man* (New York: Russell Sage Foundation, 1970), 102–103.

3. Richard Boyle, *Flower of the Dragon: The Breakdown of the U.S. Army in Vietnam* (San Francisco: Ramparts Press, 1972).

4. Boyle, *Flower of the Dragon*, 217.

5. Ibid., 218.

6. Ibid.

7. Operation Sections 23rd Artillery Group, daily staff journal, October 5, 1971, NARA, 2.

8. Boyle, *Flower of the Dragon*, 218.

9. Uniform Code of Military Justice (UCMJ), Article 94, "Mutiny and Sedition," about.com, http://usmilitary.about.com/library/milinfo/ucmj/blart-94.htm (accessed May 22, 2010).

10. AP, "5 U.S. Troops Balk at Vietnam Patrol," *Washington Post*, October 12, 1971, A14.

11. Boyle, *Flower of the Dragon*, 264.

12. Ibid.

13. UPI, "Company Removed from Base after Soldiers Balk at Patrol," *Chicago Tribune*, October 12, 1971, 2.

14. Craig R. Whitney, "Army Says Some GI's Balked Briefly at Patrol," *New York Times*, October 12, 1971, 3.

15. David B. Guralink, ed., *Webster's New World Dictionary*, 2nd college ed. (New York: Simon & Schuster, 1980), 940.

16. Boyle, *Flower of the Dragon*, 217, 220, 231.

17. "Vietnam War," *CBS Evening News*, July 15, 1971 (VTNA #217981).

18. AP, "Foe Hits 11 Allied Bases along Cambodian Border," *New York Times*, September 27, 1971, 1.

19. AP, "U.S. Forces Support Saigon Border Drive," *Washington Post*, September 30, 1971, A1.

20. S&S Vietnam Bureau, "33 S. Viet Soldiers Hurt as Red Shelling Continues," *Pacific Stars and Stripes*, September 30, 1971, 6.

21. S&S Vietnam Bureau, "Reds Kill 18 ARVNs in Delta Base Attack," October 4, 1971, 6.

22. PFC Ken Schultze, "Mortars, B-52's Enliven Bunker Life," *Pacific Stars and Stripes*, October 9, 1971, 6.

23. Boyle, *Flower of the Dragon*, 231.

24. MG Adamson, "Mail Delivery Service," Message MAC 10570, November 6, 1971, Abrams Papers, MHI, Carlisle Barracks, PA, 1–2.

25. Boyle, *Flower of the Dragon*, 235.

26. Interview with Derek Paul, S4, Infantry, B Co, P, January 28, 2010; interview with Al Grana, SP4, Infantry, B Co, P, December 29, 2009; interview with Danny Farmer, SP4, Infantry, B Co, P, March 8, 2010.

27. Headquarters, 2/32d Artillery, daily staff journal, October 10, 1971, NARA, 1.

28. Ibid., October 11, 1971, 1.

29. Grana interview; interview with Mike McNamara, SP4, Infantry, B Co, E, November 14, 2009; interview with Reuben Topinka, SP4, Infantry, B Co, P, November 8, 2009; interview with Caesar Hastings, PVT, Infantry, B Co, P, March 30, 2009.

30. Grana interview.

CHAPTER 21. THE PRESS AND THE WHITE HOUSE

1. William M. Hammond, *Public Affairs: The Military and the Media, 1968–1973* (Washington, DC: CMH, 1995), 493–523.

2. Susan B. Carter et al., ed., *Historical Statistics of the United States* (New York: Cambridge University Press, 2006), 4:1056.

3. UPI, "Company Removed from Base after Soldiers Balk at Patrol," *Chicago Tribune*, October 12, 1971, 2.

4. David Halberstam, *The Powers That Be* (New York: Albert A. Knopf, 1979), 564–565.

5. Proquest Historical Newspapers, *New York Times*, September 27, 1971–October 4, 1971.

6. Ibid.

7. Ibid., *Chicago Tribune*, October 11, 1971–October 13, 1971.

8. Craig R. Whitney, "Army Says Some GI's Balked Briefly at Patrol," *New York Times*, October 12, 1971, 3.

9. Fox Butterworth, "U.S. Troops Leave Cambodian Border," *New York Times*, October 23, 1971, 2.

10. Proquest Historical Newspapers, *Washington Post*, October 2, 1971–October 25, 1971.

11. "Kennedy Asks Probe of GI Plea," *Washington Post*, October 16, 1971, A4.

12. UPI, "Second Refusal to Patrol at Firebase Revealed," *Washington Post*, October 22, 1971, A19.

13. Peter A. Jay, "U.S. Troops Removed from Vietnam Firebase," *Washington Post*, October 23, 1971, A1.

14. Peter A. Jay, "Combat Refusals Called Rare," *Washington Post*, October 25, 1971, A1.

15. Halberstam, *The Powers That Be*, 570.

16. Interview with Peter N. Jay, Saigon Bureau Chief, *Washington Post*, E, November 10, 2008.

17. Richard Boyle, *Flower of the Dragon: The Breakdown of the U.S. Army in Vietnam* (San Francisco: Ramparts Press, 1972), 273–274.

18. Proquest, Historical Newspapers, *Chicago Tribune*, October 11, 1971–October 23, 1971.

19. UPI, "Company Removed from Base after Soldiers Balked at Patrol," *Chicago Tribune*, October 12, 1971, 2.

20. Donald Kirk, "Find Viet Vets Feel Rejected, Deceived," *Chicago Tribune*, October 31, 1971, 1.

21. "About Stars and Stripes," *Stars and Stripes*, http://www.stripes.com/webpages.asp?id=97 (accessed April 22, 2010), 1, 2.

22. S&S Vietnam Bureau, "5 FB Pace GI's Balk at Night Patrol," *Pacific Stars and Stripes*, October 13, 1971, 6; UPI, "GI's Refuse to Go on Patrol in Second Incident at Pace," *Pacific Stars and Stripes*, October 23, 1971, 6.

23. PFC Ken Schultz, "Ambush Patrol 'Wasn't Our Job,' B Co. GI's Say," *Pacific Star and Stripes*, October 15, 1971, 6.

24. Interview with Michael Donze, SGT, Section Chief, P, April 20, 2010.

25. James Landers, *The Weekly War: News Magazines and Vietnam* (Columbia: University of Missouri Press, 2004), 4.

26. Ibid.

27. "A Question of Protection," *Time*, October 25, 1971, 38.

28. Dennis Mevèsi, "Nicholas Proffitt, 63, Novelist and War Correspondent, Is Dead," *New York Times*, November 17, 2006.

29. Nicholas Proffitt, "Soldiers Who Refuse to Die," *Newsweek*, October 25, 1971, 67.

30. Interview with Robert Cronin, CPT, CO Bravo Co, 1/12th CAV, E, May 1, 2009; interview with Rich Coreno, 1LT, Plt Leader, B Co, E, November 9, 2009. Unfortunately, First Lieutenant Shuler, the person most directly involved other than Cronin, passed away in 1998.

31. Ibid.

32. Wernli, Demas, and French all recall Cronin accompanying the patrol. Memories differ on whether or not Cronin talked about court-martialing anyone.

33. Proffitt, "Soldiers Who Refuse to Die," 68.

34. Ibid.

35. Keith W. Nolan, *Search and Destroy: The Story of an Armored Cavalry Squadron in Viet Nam* (Minneapolis: Zenith Press, 2010), 194, 346–347.

36. Ibid., 347.

37. Ibid., 348–353.

38. Interview with Richard Brummett, freelance photographer, P, September 13, 2010.

39. Ibid.

40. Hammond, *Public Affairs*, 106–107.

41. Ibid., 106.

42. "Vietnam / Patrol Refusal," ABC Evening News, October 11, 1971 (VTNA #12809) and "Vietnam/Troops," CBS Evening News, October 11, 1971 (VTNA #213222).

43. NBC Evening News, October 11, 12, 1971 (VTNA # 454183 and # 454205).

44. "Reluctant Company," ABC Evening News, October 13, 1971 (VTNA #12849).

45. "Journal (Vietnam Soldiers)," NBC Evening News, October 13, 1971 (VTNA #454241).

46. "Vietnam / Fire Base Pace," NBC Evening News, October 19, 1971 (VTNA #454324).

47. "Vietnam / Fire Base Pace," ABC Evening News, October 22, 1971 (VTNA #13014); "Vietnam / Fire Base Pace," CBS Evening News, October 22, 1971 (VTNA #213451); "Vietnam 1/2 CAV, Fire Base Pace," NBC Evening News, October 22, 1971 (VTNA #45416).

48. "Vietnam War," CBS Evening News, July 15, 1971 (VTNA #217981).

49. Interview with Stan W. Tyson, LTC CO, 1/12 CAV, E, March 6, 2009.

50. MG Wagstaff to GEN Abrams, "HOA 2217 Eyes Only," October 17, 1971, CMH, 2.

51. Hammond, *Public Affairs*, 159–165, 230; Halberstam, *The Powers That Be*, 593, 600.

52. "Vietnam," *News Summary*, October 12, 1971, NARA, Richard Nixon Presidential Library, 2.

53. Ibid., October 18, 20, 23, 1971. However, the White House Congressional Liaison Office did ask the Pentagon for a report on the incidents at Pace, apparently in response to Senator Kennedy's request. That report is included in Appendix D.

54. Hammond, *Public Affairs*, 380.

55. John L. Hess, "End of G.I. Combat Seen by Laird," New York Times, January 7, 1971, 1.

56. AP, "GI Combat Role in Viet Nearly Ended—Laird," Pacific Stars and Stripes, August 6, 1971, 5; UPI, "Laird: More Viet Cuts Due in Mid-November," Pacific Stars and Stripes, September 3, 1971, 24.

57. UPI, "Laird: Command Strategy Report Off Base, Labels It Speculation," Pacific Stars and Stripes, September 21, 1971, 6.

58. Ibid.

59. Ibid.

60. Graham A. Cosmas, MACV: The Joint Command in the Years of Withdrawal, 1968–1973 (Washington: CMH, 2007), 258–259.

61. Ibid.

62. Ibid.

CHAPTER 22. THE PRESS AND THE M-WORD

1. COL Robert D. Heinl Jr., "The Collapse of the Armed Forces," Armed Forces Journal, June 7, 1971 (TTVA #2131805053), 3.

2. William M. Hammond, Public Affairs: The Military and the Media, 1968–1973 (Washington, DC: CMH, 1995), 194.

3. Ibid., 194–198.

4. Horst Faas and Peter Arnett, "Told to Move Again on 6th Deadly Day, Company A Refuses," New York Times, August 26, 1969, 1.

5. AP, "Commander of Unit That Wouldn't Fight Relieved in Vietnam," New York Times, August 27, 1969, 1.

6. "Vietnam/Shurtz," ABC Evening News, August 27, 1969 (VTNA #6857); "Vietnam/ Shurtz," NBC Evening News, August 27, 1969 (VTNA #205237); "Vietnam / Brief Meeting," NBC Evening News, August 27, 1969 (VTNA #447116).

7. AP, "Officer Who Lost Command Visits Men of His Former Unit," New York Times, August 28, 1969, 2.

8. James P. Sterba, "G.I.'s in Battle Area Shrug Off the Story of Balky Company A," New York Times, August 29, 1969, 1.

9. AP, "Ex-C.O. of Company A Says Only 5 Defied Order," New York Times, August 30, 1969, 3.

10. "Vietnam / Fight / Mutiny Incident," CBS Evening News, August 28, 1969 (VTNA #205254).

11. "Vietnam / Temporary Mutiny," ABC Evening News, August 28, 1969 (VTNA #6874).

12. "Vietnam / Fight / Mutiny Incident," NBC Evening News, August 29, 1969 (VTNA #447154).

13. James Reston, "A Whiff of Mutiny in Vietnam," New York Times, August 27, 1969, 42.

14. James Sterba, "The 'Mutiny' and the Issue of Morale," New York Times, August 31, 1969, E-3.

15. "Incident in Song Chang Valley," Time, September 5, 1969, 22.

16. Hammond, Public Affairs, 203.

17. Ibid., 204.

18. Ibid., 205, 213–215.

19. John Laurence, The Cat from Hue (New York: Public Affairs, 2002), 634.

20. Ibid., 644–649; and Hammond, Public Affairs, 377–379.

21. Laurence, The Cat from Hue, 649–650.

22. Ibid., 670–673.

23. AP, "Troops Praised for Balking at CO's Order," Pacific Stars and Stripes, April 16, 1970, 6.

24. "Just Downright Refusal," Newsweek, April 20, 1970, 51.

25. Laurence, The Cat from Hue, 733–738.

26. Ibid., 773, 779.

27. John Laurence, "The Cat from Hue: A Vietnam War Story," Booknotes, http://www .booknotes.org/Program/?ProgramID-16595 (accessed January 1, 2006).

28. See, for example, J. D. Coleman, Incursion (New York: St Martin's Press, 1991), 246; William J. Shkurti, "A Minor Rebellion," Vietnam, June 2008, 50–55.

29. Hammond, Public Affairs, 379–380.

30. AP, "2 G.I. Platoons Near Laos Refuse Orders to Advance," New York Times, March 22, 1971, 1.

31. "South Vietnam / Orders Refused," CBS Evening News and ABC Evening News, March 22, 1971 (VTNA #14743, 21568).

32. AP, "53 GI's Balk at Order to Return to Viet Battle," Pacific Stars and Stripes, March 24, 1971, 6.

33. Heinl, "The Collapse of the Armed Forces," 3.

34. Ibid.

35. Ibid.

36. Iver Peterson, "Foe Kills 33 G.I.'s, Wounds 76 in Raid South of Danang," New York Times, March 29, 1971, 1; AP, "33 GI's Killed in Viet Raid," Washington Post, March 29, 1971, A1.

37. AP, "Reds Shell U.S. Base after Raid," *Chicago Tribune*, March 30, 1971, 6.

38. "South Vietnam / Enemy Attack," *ABC Evening News*, March 29, 1971 (VTNA #14844); *CBS Evening News*, March 29, 1971 (VTNA # 215791); *NBC Evening News*, March 29, 1971 (VTNA #456786).

39. "South Vietnam," *ABC Evening News*, March 30, 1971 (VTNA #14883); *CBS Evening News*, March 30, 1971 (VTNA #215834); *NBC Evening News*, March 30, 1971 (VTNA #456829).

40. SP5 Dan Evans, "Death and Destruction Crept in with the Fog," *Pacific Stars and Stripes*, April 1, 1971, 6.

41. Nicholas Proffitt, "The Hell at Mary Ann," *Newsweek*, April 12, 1971, 45.

42. Iver Peterson, "Pullout Is Not Seen as Threat to G.I.'s in Field," *New York Times*, June 1, 1971, 5.

43. Jeremy Kuzmarov, "The Myth of the Addicted Army" (Amherst: University of Massachusetts Press, 2009), 37–55, 209.

44. Hammond, *Public Affairs*, 215.

CHAPTER 23. SOUTH VIETNAMESE ALLIES

1. Jeffrey J. Clarke, *Advice and Support: The Final Years (The U.S. Army in Vietnam)* (Washington, DC: CMH, 1988), 408–409.

2. Ibid., 411.

3. President Nixon himself said, "at least six months and probably 8 months," at a May 8 press conference. "Transcript of President's News Conference on Foreign and Domestic Matters," *New York Times*, May 9, 1970, 8. See also Phillip B. Davidson, *Vietnam at War: The History, 1946–1975* (New York: Oxford University Press, 1991), 628; J. D. Coleman, *Incursion: From America's Choke Hold on the NVA Lifelines to the Sacking of the Cambodian Sanctuaries* (New York: St. Martin's Paperbacks, 1991), 271.

4. Ibid., 418–420, 423–425; Davidson, *Vietnam at War*, 629–631.

5. Shelby Stanton, *Vietnam Order of Battle* (Washington, DC: U.S. News Books, 1981), 334. See also tables 4.1 and 4.2

6. Clarke, *Advice and Support*, 408–417.

7. "Saigon's Forces Assume Primary Role at Borders," *New York Times*, August 12, 1970, 1.

8. Ha Mai Viet, *Steel and Blood: South Vietnamese Armor and the War for Southeast Asia* (Annapolis: Naval Institute Press, 2008), 58; AP, "South Vietnamese Attack in Cambodia Reported," *New York Times*, February 4, 1971, 1.

9. Viet, *Steel and Blood*, 59.

10. Craig R. Whitney, "Saigon's Cambodia Drive in Confusion after Death of Its Colorful Commander," *New York Times*, March 2, 1971, 3.

11. Clarke, *Advice and Support*, 478.

12. William M. Hammond, *Public Affairs: The Military and the Media, 1968–1973* (Washington, DC: CMH, 1995), 465.

13. Clarke, *Advice and Support*, 478.

14. Ibid.

15. Ibid.

16. Viet, *Steel and Blood*, 62.

17. Ibid., 63.

18. Jack J. Wagstaff, *Debriefing Report*, 27 May, 1971—15 December, 1971, CMH, 7.

19. Ibid., 8.

20. AP, "Enemy Reported to Capture Snoul," *New York Times*, June 1, 1971, 1.

21. Craig R. Whitney, "Much of Cambodia Still Held by Foe," *New York Times*, June 27, 1971, 1.

22. Wagstaff, *Debriefing Report*, 10.

23. Donn A. Starry, *Mounted Combat in Vietnam* (Washington, DC: Department of the Army, 1978), 177.

24. Peter Osnos, "Slugfest in Cambodia," *Washington Post*, March 2, 1971, A1.

25. Wagstaff, *Debriefing Report*, 11.

26. Clarke, *Advice and Support*, 102, 473.

27. Graham A. Cosmas, *MACV: The Joint Command in the Years of Withdrawal* (Washington, DC: CMH, 2007), 277; Davidson, *Vietnam at War*, 646.

28. Wagstaff, *Debriefing Report*, 11–12.

29. Ibid., 12.

30. Ibid., "HOA 2064," October 26, 1971, CMH, 3.

31. Ibid., "HOA 2108," November 1, 1971, CMH, 4.

32. Wagstaff, *Debriefing Report*, 7.

33. Ibid., 12.

34. Interview with Ray Rhodes, CPT, Adviser, 6th ARVN ABN, E, October 24, 2009.

35. AP, "U.S. Command Reveals 2nd Bombing Error," *Pacific Stars and Stripes*, October 23, 1971, 6.

36. Interview with Ray Rhodes, CPT, Advisor, 6th ARVN Airborne, E, October 24, 2009.

37. Richard Boyle, *Flower of the Dragon: The Breakdown of the U.S. Army in Vietnam* (San Francisco: Ramparts Press, 1972), 216.

38. Wagstaff, *Debriefing Report*, 10.

39. MG Wagstaff to GEN Abrams, "HOA 1993 Eyes Only," October 13, 1971, CMH, 2.

40. See, for example, Headquarters, 2/32d Artillery, daily staff journal, October 8, 1971, NARA, 1; October 13, 1971, 1; October 16, 1971, 1; October 20, 1971, 2.

41. MG Wagstaff to GEN Abrams, "HOA 1993 Eyes Only," October 13, 1971, CMH, 1.

42. C/2/32 to TOC (handwritten), "Casualties since 11 Oct," October 19, 1971, NARA, 1.

43. Clarke, *Advice and Support*, 466; Davidson, *Vietnam at War*, 630.

44. Clarke, *Advice and Support*, 411.

45. CO 2/32 to CO 23d Group, "Situation Report Update," October 4, 1971, NARA, 1.

46. MG Wagstaff to GEN Abrams, "HOA 1993 Eyes Only," CMH, 2.

47. Interview with Stan W. Tyson, LTC CO, 1/12 CAV, E, March 6, 2009; interview with Nick Demas, SGT, Infantry, B Co, P, March 2010; interview with Derek Paul, SP4, Infantry, B Co, P, January 28, 2010.

48. "A Question of Protection," *Time Magazine*, October 25, 1971, 38.

49. Clarke, *Advice and Support*, 390.

50. Interview with Jack Ryals, 1LT, FDO, B BTRY, 2/35 FA, P, July 22, 2009.

51. Interview with John LeVesque, CPT, B BTRY, 2/32 FA, P, March 26, 2009.

52. Headquarters, 2/35th Artillery, daily staff journal, January 22, 1971 (NARA), 3.

53. Clarke, *Advice and Support*, 479–480; Cosmas, *MACV*, 422; Davidson, *Vietnam at War*, 792.

54. Clarke, *Advice and Support*, 478.

55. Ibid.

56. Ibid.

57. AP, "A Saigon General Told a Lie to Boost His Troops' Morale," *New York Times*, October 7, 1971, 2.

58. AP, "S. Viets Claim 6-Month Hanoi Setback," *Washington Post*, October 24, 1971, 33.

59. MG Wagstaff to GEN Abrams, "HOA 2046," October 23, 1971, CMH, 1–2.

60. AP, "Saigon Ends Cambodia Drive," *New York Times*, December 31, 1971, 4.

61. Peter Osnos, "Saigon Relies Heavily on U.S. Air Support," *Washington Post*, October 10, 1971, 18.

62. Wagstaff, *Debriefing Report*, 12.

63. Ibid., 6.

64. AP, "Chup, in Cambodia, Seized Saigon Says," *New York Times*, December 15, 1971, 3.

65. Ibid.

66. AP, "Saigon Ends Cambodia Drive," 4.

67. Generals Tri and Wagstaff both supported an aggressive posture regarding NVA base areas in Cambodia, but General Minh did not. Lieutenant General Hollingsworth (Wagstaff's successor) supported Minh in pulling back, particularly from the Krek area, because of the number of troops required to keep the road open from Tay Ninh; however, this allowed the enemy build-up for the Easter Offensive to continue relatively unmolested. See Lewis Sorley, "COM US and Commandeers Update, December 28, 1971," *The Vietnam Chronicles* (Lubbock: Texas Tech University Press, 2004), 731.

68. Clarke, *Advice and Support*, 472–476; Davidson, *Vietnam at War*, 651–654.

69. Iver Peterson, "Resor in Vietnam, Expects Difficulties as Troops Pull Out," *New York Times*, May 4, 1971, 15.

70. MG Wagstaff to GEN Abrams, "HOA 838," September 17, 1971, CMH, 3.

CHAPTER 24. NORTH VIETNAMESE ENEMIES

1. Douglas Pike, *PAVN: People's Army of Vietnam* (Novato, CA: Presidio Press, 1986), 44.

2. Ibid., 47.

3. AP, "Red Offensive Crushed: Viet Gen.," *Pacific Stars and Stripes*, October 25, 1971, 6; MG Wagstaff to GEN Abrams, "HOA 2108," November 1, 1971, CMH, 1.

4. Headquarters, TRAC, daily staff journal, October 13, 1971, NARA, 13.

5. AP, "Fresh Enemy Unit in Border Clash," *New York Times*, October 9, 1971, 9.

6. Headquarters, 3/8th Infantry, "After Action Report, April 2, 1968," *Brave Americans*, http:www.braveamericans.org/History/ORLL/1_caar_2_April4th_inf.html (accessed April 8, 2008).

7. CO 2/32 to TOC, "Casualties since 11 Oct" (handwritten), October 19, 1971, NARA, 1.

8. "Strength, Equipment and Losses of 209th Regiment," October 19, 1971, TTVVA Item #2310912015.

9. Graham Cosmas, *MACV: The Joint Command in the Years of Withdrawal* (Washington, DC: CMH, 2007), 179–180.

10. Headquarters, 2/35th Artillery, ORLL, period ending April 30, 1971, NARA, 1.

11. 3d Brigade (Separate), 1st Air Cavalry Division, "Operation Katum, September 27–October 2 1971," *After Action Report*, October 7, 1971, author's collection, Annex B (Intelligence).

12. MG Wagstaff to GEN Abrams, October 12, 1971, "HOA 1986," CMH, 2.

13. AP, "U.S. Leaves Base Where GI's Balked," *Los Angeles Times*, October 23, 1971, 5.

14. Interview with Russell Davis, MAJ, XO/2/32, E, June 28, 2010; interview with Richard C. Ashley, CPT, BC, C BTRY, E, January 21, 2009; interview with Mark Diggs, 1LT, XO, C BTRY, E, February 5, 2009.

15. "Strength, Equipment and Losses of the 209th Regiment," 1.

16. Fire Support Element, 23d Artillery Group, daily staff journal, September 28, 1971–October 22, 1971, NARA. This document lists B-52 strikes by location. Only those within ten kilometers of Pace are counted.

17. Reuters, "Typhoon Limits Vietnam Action," *New York Times*, October 24, 1971, 9.

18. Paul Cibolski, "The Battle for Fire Support Base Pace," *Proud Americans*, http://proudamericans.homestead.com/stories.html (accessed August 1, 2009).

19. Interview with G. John LeVesque, CPT, S-3, 2/32 FA, P, March 26, 2009.

20. Headquarters, TRAC, October 2, 1971, 5; October 9, 1971, 1.

21. MG Jack Wagstaff, *Debriefing Report*, May 27, 1971–December 15, 1971, CMH, 12.

22. James H. Willbanks, *The Battle of An Loc* (Bloomington: Indiana University Press, 2005), 33.

23. See, for example, Ronald Spector, *After Tet* (New York: Vintage Books, 1993), 220–222; Phillip B. Davidson, *Vietnam at War: The History 1946–1975* (New York: Oxford University Press, 1991), 401–402; and Guenter Lewy, *America in Vietnam* (New York: Oxford University Press, 1978), 78–82.

24. Headquarters, U.S. Army Vietnam, "History of the 273 VC Regiment, July 1964–December 1969," September 5, 1970, TTVVA Item #2120217000, 4–6.

25. William LeGro, "The Big Red One," chap. 4, MS, TTVVA Item #13370164001, 2.

26. Donn A. Starry, *Mounted Combat in Vietnam* (Washington, DC: Department of the Army, 1978), 67.

27. Bernard W. Rogers, *Cedar Falls—Junction City: A Turning Point* (Washington, DC: Department of the Army, 1974), 147–148.

28. Tom Buckley, "196 Vietcong Killed in Ambush by GI's," *New York Times*, June 18, 1967, 1.

29. David Maraniss, *They Marched into Sunlight* (New York: Simon & Schuster, 2003), 346–347.

30. Headquarters, Pacific Air Force Command, "Ambush at XT 686576, 29 December 1967," *Project Contemporary Historical Evaluation of Combat Operations Report*, TTVVA Item #1683000125, 1.

31. David Ott, *Field Artillery, 1954–1973 (Vietnam Studies)* (Washington, DC: Department of the Army, 1975), 120–121.

32. Starry, *Mounted Combat in Vietnam*, 119–122.

33. "Viet Cong Order of Battle," Ron Leonard Collection, n.d., TTVVA Item #13680112004.

34. "History of 273 VC Regiment," 19.

35. Headquarters, 25th Division, "Combat After Action Report of the Battle of Tay Ninh, February 7, 1969," TTVVA Item #68300010347, 59–60.

36. R. Drummond Ayers Jr., "G.I. Unit Near Cambodia Repulses Foe, Killing 213," *New York Times*, April 27, 1969, 1.

37. J. D. Coleman, *Incursion: From America's Choke Hold on the NVA Lifelines to the Sacking of the Cambodian Sanctuaries* (New York: St. Martin's Paperbacks, 1991), 167–168.

38. Ibid., 207.

39. Headquarters, II Field Force Vietnam, ORLL, period of November 1, 1970–April 30, 1971, NARA, 16.

40. SP4 Frank Morris, "Enemy Wilts under Tank Pressure," *Tropic Lightning News*, August 24, 1970, http:www.25thida.org/TLN/+/D5-32.htm, accessed September 23, 2009.

41. Message from GEN Abrams, "MAC 10097," October 21, 1971, CMH, 2.

42. William Darryl Henderson, *Cohesion: The Human Element in Combat* (Washington, DC: National Defense University Press, 1985), 2.

43. Ibid., xvii.

CHAPTER 25. VIETNAMESE VERDUN

1. Graham A. Cosmas, *MACV: The Joint Command in the Years of Withdrawal, 1968–1973* (Washington, DC: CMH, 2007), 349.

2. Ibid., 356–358.

3. MACV, Intelligence and Security Division, DCSOPS, "Daily Intelligence Review," April 4, 1972, TTVNA #1070312014, 1. The M41 tanks were most likely captured from the South Vietnamese and may have been the ones spotted in the Chup Rubber Plantation in September.

4. Dale Andrade, *Trial by Fire: The 1972 Easter Offensive, America's Last Vietnam Battle* (New York: Hippocrene Books, 1995), 387–388.

5. Ibid., 495.

6. James H. Willbanks, *The Battle of An Loc* (Bloomington: University of Indiana Press, 2005), 120.

7. Ibid., 121–125.

8. Wallace S. Tyson, "Easter Offensive," *12th Cav*, http://12thcav.US/stories_112_ST _Easter_Offensive.htm (accessed February 7, 2010), 2.

9. Ibid.

10. Ibid., 3.

11. Willbanks, *The Battle of An Loc*, 147–149.

12. The number of French and Germans killed and missing in the Battle of Verdun has been of some dispute among historians. The best estimates seem to be about 82,000 Germans dead and missing (out of 700,000 engaged) and 182,000 Frenchmen dead (out of 1,200,000 engaged). This translates to about 12 percent for the Germans and 14 percent for the French. Roger Chickering and Stig Forster, *Great War, Total War: Combat and Mobilization on the Western Front, 1914–1918* (Cambridge, UK: Cambridge University Press, 2000), 114; "The Battle of Verdun and the Number of Casualties," *The Battle of Verdun 1916—The Greatest Battle Ever*, http://wereldoorlog 1418.nl/battleverdun/schactofferslhtm (accessed August 8, 2009), 1–3.

13. Willbanks, *The Battle of An Loc*, 144.

14. William M. Hammond, *Public Affairs: The Military and the Media, 1968–1973* (Washington, DC: CMH, 1995), 587.

15. Willbanks, *The Battle of An Loc*, 154–156.

16. Jeffrey J. Clarke, *Advice and Support: The Final Years* (Washington, DC: CMH, 1988), 485.

17. Willbanks, *The Battle of An Loc*, 163.

18. Ibid., 155.

19. Hammond, *Public Affairs*, 585–586.

20. Clarke, *Advice and Support*, 486.

21. Andrade, *Trial by Fire*, 377.

22. Ibid., 374, 377.

23. Clarke, *Advice and Support*, 486.

24. Ibid., 486.

25. Ibid., 416, 487.

26. Ibid., 483–489; Cosmas, *MACV*, 420; Andrade, *Trial by Fire*, 533.

27. Cosmas, *MACV*, 378–379; Andrade, *Trial by Fire*, 532–537; Clarke, *Advice and Support*, 488–489.

28. "Strength, Equipment and Losses of the 209th Regiment Cong Truong 7 Division," October 1971, TTVNA #231091215, 1.

29. Willbanks, *The Battle of An Loc*, 33.

30. Ibid., 132–134.

31. Ibid., 132.

32. Ibid., 139.

33. Ibid., 113, 120.

34. For a detailed critique of the North Vietnamese errors in judgment at An Loc, see Willbanks, *The Battle of An Loc*, 151–153; Andrade, *Trial by Fire*, 500; Phillip B. Davidson, *Vietnam at War: The History 1946–1975* (New York: Oxford University Press, 1991), 709–711.

35. Willbanks, *The Battle of An Loc*, 157–161.

36. Ibid., 161–164; Clarke, *Advice and Support*, 486.

37. Willbanks, *The Battle of An Loc*, 162.

38. Lewis Sorley, *A Better War* (New York: Harcourt, 1999), 217.

39. Ibid., 218.

40. See, for example, Andrade, *Trial by Fire*, 43; Clarke, *Advice and Support*, 471; Cosmas, *MACV*, 278.

41. MG Wagstaff to GEN Abrams, "HOA 838," September 17, 1971 (CMH), 3.

42. Donn A. Starry, *Mounted Combat in Vietnam* (Washington, DC: Department of the Army, 1978), 198.

43. Andrade, *Trial by Fire*, 500; Cosmas, *MACV*, 378.

44. Davidson, *Vietnam at War*, 731.

45. Sorley, *A Better War*, 218.

46. Drummond Ayres Jr., "Strain of the Vietnam War Weakens Army Elsewhere," *New York Times*, September 13, 1971, 1; Drew Middleton, "Drop in U.S. Capability Worries Military," *New York Times*, November 1, 1971, 3.

47. Stanley Karnow stated that Secretary Laird told him in an interview that he was "alarmed" by the Vietnam commitment's "debilitating effect on U.S. security obligations in Europe and elsewhere" (Stanly Karnow, *Vietnam: A History* [New York: Viking Press, 1983], 595). See also Dale Van Atta, *With Honor: Melvin Laird in War, Peace and Politics* (Madison: University of Wisconsin Press, 2008), 162, 366.

48. Stephen P. Randolph, *Powerful and Brutal Weapons: Nixon, Kissinger and the Easter Offensive* (Cambridge, MA: Harvard University Press, 2007), 114.

49. For a discussion of U.S. strategic policy goals in this period, see, for example, Robert Dallek, *Partners in Power: Nixon and Kissinger* (New York: Harper Collins, 2007), 617–619.

50. Randolph, *Powerful and Brutal Weapons*, 117–118.

51. Ibid., 118.

CHAPTER 26. PACE AS HISTORY

1. David Ott, *Field Artillery, 1954–1973 (Vietnam Studies)* (Washington, DC: Department of the Army, 1975), 221.

2. Dale Andrade, *Trial by Fire: The 1972 Easter Offensive, America's Last Vietnam Battle* (New York: Hippocrene Books, 1995), 387; James Willbanks, *The Battle of An Loc* (Bloomington: University of Indiana Press, 2005), 39–40.

3. Richard Boyle, *Flower of the Dragon: The Breakdown of the U.S. Army in Vietnam* (San Francisco: Ramparts Press, 1972), 216–268.

4. David Cortright, *Soldiers in Revolt: GI Resistance during the Vietnam War* (Chicago: Haymarket Books, 2005), 38.

5. Myra MacPherson, *Long Time Passing: Vietnam and the Haunted Generation* (Garden City, NY: Doubleday & Co., 1984), 343.

6. James Riordan, *Stone* (New York: Hyperion, 1995), 144.

7. Gerald Nicosia, *Home to War* (New York: Crown Publishers, 2001), 218.

8. William Hauser, *America's Army in Crisis: A Study in Civil-Military Relations* (Baltimore: Johns Hopkins University Press, 1973), 100–101.

9. Robert Jay Lifton, *Home from the War* (New York: Simon & Schuster, 1973), 332.

10. Richard R. Moser, *The New Winter Soldiers* (New Brunswick, NJ: Rutgers University Press, 1996), 46.

11. William M. Hammond, *Public Affairs: The Military and the Media, 1968–1973* (Washington, DC: CMH, 1995), 380.

12. "Fire Base Pace" Google search, November 5, 2008.

13. David Zeigler, director, *Sir! No Sir! The Suppressed Story of the GI Movement to End the War in Vietnam* (New York: Displaced Films, 2003).

14. Michael P. Kelly, *Where We Were in Vietnam: A Comprehensive Guide to the Firebases, Military Installations and Naval Vessels of the Vietnam War, 1945–1975* (Central Point, OR: Hellgate Press, 2002), 5–381.

15. Cortright, *Soldiers in Revolt*, 35–39.

16. Hauser, *America's Army in Crisis*, 101.

17. Keith W. Nolan, *Into Laos: The Story of Dewey Canyon II / Lam Son 719, Vietnam 1971* (Novato, CA: Presidio Press, 1986), 24.

18. Keith W. Nolan, *Sappers in the Wire: The Life and Death of Firebase Mary Ann* (College Station: Texas A&M University Press, 1995), xiii.

19. David Axe, "Was the 196th Light Infantry Brigade Really the Mutinous Outfit It Has Been Portrayed to Be?" *Vietnam*, October 2005, 16–17, 66.

20. William T. Allison, *Military Justice in Vietnam: The Rule of Law in an American War* (Lawrence: University of Kansas Press, 2007), 76.

21. J. D. Coleman, *Incursion: From America's Choke Hold on the NVA Lifelines to the Sacking of the Cambodian Sanctuaries* (New York: St. Martins Paperbacks, 1992), 209–211, 246; John Laurence, *The Cat from Hue: A Vietnam War Story* (New York: Public Affairs, 2002), 573–800.

22. Shelby L. Stanton, *The Rise and Fall of an American Army: U.S. Ground Forces in Vietnam, 1965–1973* (New York: Ballantine Books, 2003), 357.

23. Nolan, *Into Laos*, 24.

24. Geoffrey Perret, *A Country Made by War* (New York: Random House, 1989), 533.

25. Nolan, *Sappers in the Wire*, xii. 290–293.

26. Cortright, *Soldiers in Revolt*, 24–25.

27. Bruce P. Palmer Jr., *The 25-Year War: America's Military Role in Vietnam* (Lexington: University Press of Kentucky, 1984), 155.

CHAPTER 27. LESSONS LEARNED?

1. Melvin R. Laird, "Iraq: Learning the Lessons of Vietnam," *Foreign Affairs*, https://www.siaonet.org/olj/fa/fa_novdec05.d/html (accessed January 20, 2010), 1–10.

2. Dale Van Atta, *With Honor: Melvin Laird in Peace, War and Politics* (Madison: University of Wisconsin Press, 2008), 339.

3. Graham A. Cosmas, *MACV: The Joint Command in the Years of Withdrawal, 1968–1973* (Washington, DC: CMH, 2007), 141–145.

4. Laird, "Iraq," 4.

5. Jeffrey J. Clarke, *Advice and Support: The Final Years* (Washington, DC: CMH, 1987), 387–390.

6. Lewis Sorley, *A Better War* (New York: Harcourt, 1999), 70–72, 194–195, 221.

7. For a critique of SEER, see Clarke, *Advice and Support*, 387–390. For a critique of HES, see John Prados, *Vietnam* (Lawrence: University of Kansas Press, 2009), 323–326.

8. Secretary of Defense, "Vietnam War Deaths by Months," 1966–1971, *The American War Library*, http://members.aol.com./for country/kiamonth.htm (accessed January 13, 2004).

9. Laird, "Iraq," 3.

10. Ibid., 2.

11. Sorley, *A Better War*, 350–352.

12. James H. Willbanks, *Abandoning Vietnam* (Lawrence: University of Kansas Press, 2004), 277–278.

13. Cosmas, *MACV*, 178.

14. See for example the discussion of security breaches regarding B-52 strikes in William M. Hammond, *The Military and the Media, 1968–1973* (Washington, DC: CMH, 1995), 313. See also Larry Berman, *Perfect Spy: The Double Life of Pham Xuan An, Time Magazine Reporter and Communist Agent* (New York: Harper Collins, 2008) for more about the degree to which the North Vietnamese penetrated U.S. and South Vietnamese security.

15. Cosmas, *MACV*, 382.

16. Prados, *Vietnam*, 510.

17. Clarke, *Advice and Support*, 312–313. Minh was a nephew of Thieu's Prime Minister, Tran Van Huong.

18. Arnold R. Isaacs, *Without Honor: Defeat in Vietnam and Cambodia* (Baltimore: Johns Hopkins University Press, 1983), 121.

19. Laird, "Iraq," 6.

20. Van Atta, *With Honor*, 339.

21. Hammond, *The Military and the Media*, 518–521.

22. Fox Butterfield, "Reagan Meets Thieu in Saigon and Defends One-Man Race," *New York Times*, October 16, 1971, 5.

23. Laird, "Iraq," 4.

24. See for example, Defense Intelligence Agency, *Handbook of the Chinese Armed Forces*, 1976 (DD1-2680-32-76).

25. Headquarters, U.S. Army Vietnam, *History of the 273 VC Regiment*, September 5, 1970 (TTVA Item #2130317000), preface.

26. Sorley, *A Better War*, 329.

27. Isaacs, *Without Honor*, 491.

28. Cosmas, *MACV*, 289–292.

29. Ibid., 346–347.

30. Laird, "Iraq," 7.

31. Ibid., 8.

32. Hammond, *The Military and the Media*, 58–60, 73–75.

33. Ibid., 327–329.

34. Van Atta, *With Honor*, 339.

35. Cosmas, *MACV*, 258–259. See also additional discussion at the end of Chapter 21.

36. See Chapters 15 and 16.

37. Letter from Specialist Four Derek Paul, Infantryman, B Co, to his parents, October 14, 1971 (Courtesy of Derek Paul).

38. Laird, "Iraq," 9.

39. See, for example, Stephen P. Randolph, *Powerful and Brutal Weapons: Nixon, Kissinger and the Easter Offensive* (Cambridge, MA: Harvard University Press, 2007), 116–118.

40. Max Hastings, *The Korean War* (New York: Touchstone Books, 1988), 333–334. In fact, Hastings argues that the United States learned many of the wrong lessons from the experience in Korea.

41. Isaacs, *Without Honor*, 489.

42. Colin L. Powell, "U.S. Forces: Challenges Ahead," *Foreign Affairs* 71, no. 5 (Winter 1992): 32–45.

43. Ibid., 38.

Bibliography

This book is based on a number of sources. The baseline of dates, times, and places is taken from official documents, particularly the daily staff journals of the units involved and their higher headquarters. These journals also provide a rich source of detail on the day-to-day struggles of defending Fire Support Base Pace. Although these are official records, they are subject to human error and gaps in information. Most of them can be found in Record Group 472 at the National Archives II at College Park, Maryland. The messages from Lieutenant Colonel McCaffree to his superiors at 23d Artillery Group and from Major General Wagstaff to General Abrams at MACV are particularly revealing because they are much more candid than what may appear later in an official report. Colonel McCaffree's messages are included with the 2/32d Artillery's Daily Journals on file at the National Archives. General Wagstaff's messages are filed separately with General Abrams's papers at the Center for Military History.

Other than Richard Boyle's account, there are no books about Pace. However, numerous books provide important contextual information. Three volumes from the Army in Vietnam series have been particularly useful, including William M. Hammond's *Public Affairs: The Military and the Media, 1968–1973*, Graham Cosmas's *MACV: The Joint Command in the Years of Withdrawal, 1968–1973*, and Jeffrey J. Clarke's *Advice and Support: The Final Years*. General David Ott's *Field Artillery, 1954–1973* was also valuable in documenting the role of the field artillery in this period. Keith William Nolan's three volumes, *Ripcord*, *Into Laos*, and *Sappers in the Wire*, are the best descriptions of the war on the ground between the Cambodian Campaign and the Easter Offensive. John Shaw's *The Cambodian Campaign* provides a good overview of the events in the spring of 1970 that led to the border fighting in 1971. Dale Andrade's *Easter Offensive* and James Willbanks's *The Battle of An Loc* provide the best analysis of the 1972 campaigns in Military Region III. Shelby Stanton's *Vietnam Order of Battle* is an indispensable resource for tracking unit deployments.

Contemporary newspaper and magazine reports provide a great deal of information, particularly the *New York Times*, whose large staff allowed it to become the unofficial day-to-day record. These are available through Proquest, a digitized search service found in many large libraries, including the Ohio State University Thompson Library. The Pacific edition of *Stars and Stripes* also provided contemporary accounts of activities. These articles are available at the Stars and Stripes Web site in a digitized database as well. The Vanderbilt University Television News Archive in Nashville contains recordings of every NBC, CBS, and ABC Evening News broadcast from this period, as well as a searchable database.

Over the past ten years a number of Web sites have either expanded or appeared. Most helpful have been the *Proud Americans* site of the 2/32d Field Artillery, the site of the 12th Cavalry Regiment Association, the *Fly Army* site of the Vietnam Helicopter Pilots association, and Texas Tech University's *Vietnam Center and Archive* site. The Web site of the Vietnamese Veterans Memorial provides additional information on the soldiers who died in Vietnam, as well as personal remembrances of family and friends.

Dozens of Vietnam veterans involved in the defense of Fire Support Bases Pace and Lanyard gave their time to be interviewed by e-mail, letter, or telephone and provided a perspective and key details available nowhere else.

Sorting out events that happened almost forty years ago presented a number of challenges. Every effort has been made to reconcile key events from at least two independent sources. That has been possible in most cases, but not all. In those cases where sources conflict, it has been pointed out in the text or in an accompanying footnote. In other cases where there is no conflict, but also no corroboration, the author has had to apply his judgment as to the credibility of the source and the event. In all cases, sources are identified in the footnotes, and the reader is encouraged to refer to them as needed.

BOOKS

Allison, William Thomas. *Military Justice in Vietnam: The Rule of Law in an American War*. Lawrence: University Press of Kansas, 2006.

Andrade, Dale. *Trial by Fire: The 1972 Easter Offensive, America's Last Vietnam Battle*. New York: Hippocrene Books, 1995.

Appy, Christian G. *Working Class War: American Combat Soldiers and Vietnam*. Chapel Hill: University of North Carolina Press, 1993.

Bergerud, Eric. *Red Thunder Tropic Lightning: The World of a Combat Division in Vietnam*. Boulder, CO: Westview Press, 1993.

Boyle, Richard. *Flower of the Dragon: The Breakdown of the U.S. Army in Vietnam*. San Francisco: Ramparts Press, 1972.

Clarke, Jeffery J. *Advice and Support: The Final Years (The U.S. Army in Vietnam)*. Washington, DC: CMH, 1988.

Coleman, J. D. *Incursion: From America's Choke Hold on the NVA Lifelines to the Sacking of the Cambodian Sanctuaries*. New York: St. Martin's Paperbacks, 1992.

Cortright, David. *Soldiers in Revolt: GI Resistance during the Vietnam War*. Chicago: Haymarket Books, 2005.

Cosmas, Graham A. *MACV: The Joint Command in the Years of Withdrawal, 1968–1973 (The United States Army in Vietnam)*. Washington, DC: CMH, 2007.

Davidson, Phillip B. *Vietnam at War: The History 1946–1975*. New York: Oxford University Press, 1991.

Fulgham, David, and Terrence Maitland. *The Vietnam Experience: South Vietnam on Trial, Mid 1970 to 1972*. Boston: Boston Publishing, 1984.

Hammond, William M. *Public Affairs: The Military and the Media, 1968–1973 (The U.S. Army in Vietnam)*. Washington, DC: Center for Military History, U.S. Army, 1995.

Hauser, William L. *America's Army in Crisis: A Study in Civil-Military Relations*. Baltimore: Johns Hopkins University Press, 1973.

Henderson, William Darrell. *Cohesion: The Human Element in Combat*. Washington, DC: National Defense University Press, 1985.

Isaacs, Arnold R. *Without Honor: Defeat in Vietnam and Cambodia*. Baltimore: Johns Hopkins University Press, 1983.

Kelley, Michael P. *Where We Were in Vietnam: A Comprehensive Guide to the Firebases, Military Installations and Naval Vessels of the Vietnam War, 1945–1975*. Central Point, OR: Hellgate Press, 2002.

Kuzmarov, Jeremy. *The Myth of the Addicted Army*. Amherst: University of Massachusetts Press, 2009.

Landers, James. *The Weekly War: News Magazines and Vietnam*. Columbia: University of Missouri Press, 2004.

Laurence, John. *The Cat from Hue: A Vietnam War Story*. New York: Public Affairs, 2002.

Lavalle, A.J.C., ed. *Airpower and the 1972 Spring Invasion*. USAF Southeast Asia Monograph Series. Volume 2, monograph 3. Washington, DC: GPO, 1976.

Lewy, Guenter. *America in Vietnam*. New York: Oxford University Press, 1978.

Lipsman, Samuel, and Edward Doyle. *The Vietnam Experience: Fighting for Time, 1969–1970*. Boston: Boston Publishing, 1985.

Milam, Ron. *Not a Gentleman's War: An Inside View of Junior Officers in the Vietnam War*. Chapel Hill: University of North Carolina Press, 2009.

Nolan, Keith W. *Into Laos: The Story of Dewey Canyon II / Lam Son 719, Vietnam 1971*. Navato, CA: Presidio Press, 1986.

———. *Ripcord: Screaming Eagles under Siege, Vietnam, 1970*. Novato, CA: Presidio Press, 2000.

———. *Sappers in the Wire: The Life and Death of Firebase Mary Ann*. College Station: Texas A&M University Press, 1995.

Ott, David E. *Field Artillery, 1954–1973 (Vietnam Studies)*. Washington, DC: Department of the Army, 1975.

Prados, John. *Vietnam: The History of an Unwinnable War, 1945–1975*. Lawrence: University Press of Kansas, 2009.

Prugh, George S. *Law of War: Vietnam, 1964–1973*. Washington, DC: Department of the Army, 1975.

Randolph, Stephen P. *Powerful and Brutal Weapons: Nixon, Kissinger and the Easter Offensive*. Cambridge, MA: Harvard University Press, 2007.

Rogers, Bernard W. *Cedar Falls—Junction City: A Turning Point*. Washington, DC: Department of the Army, 1974.

Shaw, John M. *The Cambodian Campaign: The 1970 Offensive and America's Vietnam War*. Lawrence: University Press of Kansas, 2005.

Sorley, Lewis. *A Better War: The Unexamined Tragedy of America's Last Years in Vietnam*. New York: Houghton Mifflin Harcourt, 1999.

Stanton, Shelby L. *Anatomy of a Division: The 1st Cav in Vietnam*. New York: Warner Books, 1989.

———. *The Rise and Fall of an American Army: U.S. Ground Forces in Vietnam, 1965–1973*. New York: Ballantine Books, 2003.

———. *Vietnam Order of Battle*. Washington, DC: U.S. News Books, 1981.

Starry, Donn A. *Mounted Combat in Vietnam*. Washington, DC: Department of the Army, 1978.

Van Atta, Dale. *With Honor: Melvin Laird in War, Peace and Politics*. Madison: University of Wisconsin Press, 2008.

Viet, Ha Mai. *Steel and Blood: South Vietnamese Armor and the War for Southeast Asia*. Annapolis, MD: Naval Institute Press, 2008.

Willbanks, James H. *Abandoning Vietnam: How America Left and South Vietnam Lost Its War*. Lawrence: University Press of Kansas, 2004.

———. *The Battle of An Loc*. Bloomington: University of Indiana Press, 2005.

ARTICLES

AP. "Border Bases Hit; Troops that Balked Sent to New Base." *Washington Post*, October 13, 1971.

———. "Company Removed from Base after Soldiers Balk at Patrol." *Chicago Tribune*, October 12, 1971.

———. "Chup in Cambodia Seized, Saigon Says." *New York Times*, December 5, 1971.

———. "Enemy Commandos Kill 21 South Vietnamese." *New York Times*, September 21, 1971.

———. "Enemy Reported to Capture Snoul." *New York Times*, June 1, 1971.

———. "5 U.S. Troops Balk at Vietnam Patrol." *Washington Post*, October 12, 1971.

———. "Foe Hits 11 Allied Bases along Cambodian Border." *New York Times*, September 27, 1971.

———. "Fresh Enemy Unit in Border Clash." *New York Times*, October 9, 1971.

———. "GI Combat Role in Viet Nearly Ended." *Pacific Stars & Stripes*, August 6, 1971.

———. "Highway Is Objective." *New York Times*, September 30, 1971.

———. "Pentagon Reveals Rise in Fraggings." *New York Times*, April 29, 1971.

———. "S Viets Claim 6-Month Hanoi Setback." *Washington Post*, October 24, 1971.

———. "Saigon Ends Cambodia Drive." *New York Times*, December 31, 1971.

———. "A Saigon General Told a Lie to Boost His Troops' Morale." *New York Times*, October 7, 1971.

———. "Saigon Troops Lift Enemy Siege of Firebase along Border Area." *Washington Post*, October 2, 1971.

———. "Senate Study Finds Drug Abuse by G.I.'s a Rarity in Combat." *New York Times*, April 21, 1971.

———. "Typhoon Limits Vietnam Action." *New York Times*, October 24, 1971.

———. "2 GI's Left Behind at Isolated Base Consider It a Holiday." *Los Angeles Times*, October 24, 1971.

———. "U.S. Forces Support Saigon Border Drive." *Washington Post*, September 30, 1971.

———. "U.S. Leaves Base Where GI's Balked." *Los Angeles Times*, October 23, 1971.

Ayres, Drummond B. "Army Is Shaken by Crises in Morale and Discipline." *New York Times*, September 5, 1971.

Belair, Felix. "House Unit Cites Rise in GI Drug Use." *New York Times*, May 26, 1971.

Bond, Thomas C. "The Why of Fragging." *American Journal of Psychiatry* 133, no. 11 (November 1976): 1328–1330.

Bryant, Thomas G., Gerald B. Morse, Leslie M. Novak, John C. Henry. "Tactical Radar for Ground Surveillance." *Lincoln Laboratory Journal* 12, no. 2 (2000): 342–343.

Butterfield, Fox. "Reagan Meets Thieu in Saigon and Defends One-Man Race." *New York Times*, October 16, 1971, 5.

———. "U.S. Troops Leave Cambodian Border." *New York Times*, October 23, 1971.

Davis, Don. "GI's Refuse to Go Out on Patrol at Second Incident at Base." *Pacific Stars and Stripes*, October 23, 1971.

"Desertions among GI's Near Record High." *Washington Post*, August 11, 1971.

"Doubt on Vietnam Reported in Poll." *New York Times*, March 6, 1971.

Emerson, Gloria A. "G.I.'s Now Wear a Lot the Army Didn't Issue." *New York Times*, August 28, 1971.

———. "Grunts Wonder When Their Fighting Became 'Defensive.'" *New York Times*, January 22, 1972.

Evans, Rowland, and Robert Novak. "Last GI's in Bitter Mood." *Washington Post*, September 17, 1971.

"G.I. Use of Heroin Is Reported Cut." *New York Times*, July 27, 1971.

Glass, Andrew J. "Defense Report: Draftees Shoulder Burden of Fighting and Dying in Vietnam." *National Journal*, August 15, 1970, 1747–1755.

Gore, Albert. "Alert Engineers Repulse VC in Hand to Hand Fighting." *Pacific Stars and Stripes*, April 28, 1971, 23.

Graham, Fred P. "War Crimes Conviction Raises Series of Legal Conflicts for Foot Soldiers." *New York Times*, May 31, 1971.

Harris, Louis. "Drugs, Military." *Washington Post*, February 21, 1972.

Heinl, Robert Jr. "The Collapse of the Armed Forces." *Armed Forces Journal*, June 7, 1971 (TTVVA Item #2131805053).

Hess, John L. "End of G.I. Combat Foreseen by Laird." *New York Times*, January 1, 1971.

"Incident on Route 9." *Time*, April 5, 1971.

"Indochina: There's Still a War On." *Time*, January 24, 1972.

Jay, Peter A. "Combat Refusals Called Rare." *Washington Post*, October 25, 1971.

———. "U.S. Troops Removed from Vietnam Firebase." *Washington Post*, October 24, 1971.

"Kennedy Asks Probe of GI Plea." *Washington Post*, October 16, 1971.

Kirk, Donald. "Viet Vets Feel Rejected, Deceived." *Chicago Tribune*, October 31, 1971.

———. "Who Wants to Be the Last American Killed in Vietnam?" *New York Times Magazine*, September 19, 1971.

Laird, Melvin R. "Iraq: Learning the Lessons of Vietnam." *Foreign Affairs*, November/ December 2005, 22–23.

Montiel, Steve. "Troop Shift Surprised Reds." *Pacific Stars and Stripes*, October 7, 1971.

Naughton, James M. "President Gives 'Highest Priority' to Drug Problem." *New York Times*, June 2, 1971.

Osnos, Peter, and Peter Jay. "Slugfest in Cambodia." *Washington Post*, March 2, 1971.

———. "War Casualties: Leadership, Morale." *Washington Post*, September 15, 1971.

Peterson, Iver. "Enemy Saboteurs Invade U.S. Base and Blow Up Fuel." *New York Times*, May 25, 1971.

———. "Foe Kills 33 GI's, Wounds 76 in Raid South of Danang." *New York Times*, March 29, 1971.

———. "Pullout Is Not Seen as Threat to G.I.'s in Field." *New York Times*, June 1, 1971.

———. "Resor in Vietnam, Expects Difficulties as Troops Pull Out." *New York Times*, May 4, 1971.

———. "Saigon Denies Route by Enemy at Snoul." *New York Times*, June 2, 1971.

"Poll Finds Drugs No. 3 Issue in U.S." *New York Times*, July 27, 1971.

Proffitt, Nicholas. "The Hell at Mary Ann." *Newsweek*, April 12, 1971, 45.

———. "Soldiers Who Refuse to Die." *Newsweek*, October 25, 1971, 67–68.

"A Question of Protection." *Time*, October 25, 1971, 38.

Rich, Spencer. "Fear of Narcotics Wave among Vets Exaggerated." *Washington Post*, February 25, 1980.

Rueters. "Typhoon Limits Vietnam Action." *New York Times*, October 24, 1971.

Saar, John. "You Just Can't Hand Out Orders." *Life*, October 23 1970, 30–39.

"Saigon's Forces Assume Primary Role at Border." *New York Times*, August 12, 1970.

S&S Vietnam Bureau. "Ambush Patrol 'Wasn't Our Job' B Co. GI's Say." *Pacific Stars and Stripes*, October 15, 1971.

———. "Reds Kill 18 ARVNS in Delta Base Attack." *Pacific Stars and Stripes*, October 4, 1971.

———. "5 FB GI's Balk at Night Patrol." *Pacific Stars and Stripes*, October 13, 1971.

Schulti, Ken. "Mortars, B-52's Enliven Bunker Life." *Pacific Stars and Stripes*, October 9, 1971.

Shuster, Alvin M. "GI Heroin Addiction Epidemic in Vietnam." *New York Times*, May 16, 1971.

———. "Laird Expects Wider Pullout of Troops." *New York Times*, January 21, 1971.

Smith, Terrence. "Troop Withdrawals: Combat Role May End but Casualties Will Not." *New York Times*, January 10, 1971.

"The Troubled Army in Vietnam." *Newsweek*, January 11, 1971, 29–37.

UPI. "Blast Hurts 27 GI's during Vietnam Riot." *New York Times*, January 12, 1971.

———. "Company Removed from Base after Soldiers Balk at Patrol." *Chicago Tribune*, October 12, 1971.

———. "Laird: Command Strategy Report Off Base." *Pacific Stars & Stripes*, September 21, 1971.

———. "Laird: More Viet Cuts Due in Mid-November." *Pacific Stars and Stripes*, September 3, 1971.

———. "Second Refusal to Patrol at Firebase Revealed." *Washington Post*, October 22, 1971.

Whitney, Craig R. "Army Says Some GI's Balked Briefly at Patrol." *New York Times*, October 12, 1971.

———. "Saigon's Cambodia Drive in Confusion after Death of Its Colorful Commander." *New York Times*, March 2, 1971.

GOVERNMENT DOCUMENTS

Abrams, General Creighton W. Message MAC 100097, October 21, 1971. CMH.

CO 2/32 (LTC McCaffree) to CO 23d Group (COL Hoffman). "Situation Report Updated," October 1, 1971. NARA.

———. "Situation Update No. 2," October 4, 1971. NARA.

———. "Situation Update," October 6, 1971. NARA.

———. "Artillery Sitrep," October 6, 1971. NARA.

———. "Artillery Sitrep," October 9, 1971. NARA.

———. "Situation Update," October 9, 1971. NARA.

———. "Report on Pace," October 18, 1971. NARA.

C/2/32 to TOC (handwritten). "Casualties Since 11 October," October 19, 1971. NARA.

Department of the Army. *Field Artillery Cannon Gunnery (FM6-40)*. Washington, November 1969.

Department of the Army, Company B, 31st Engineer Battalion. "Aerial View of Fire Support Base Pace." July 19, 1971, CC 81146. NARA.

Headquarters, 2d Battalion, 32d Artillery. Daily staff journal, September 15, 1971–October 23, 1971. NARA.

Headquarters, 2d Battalion, 32d Artillery. ORLL, period ending April 30, 1971. NARA.

Headquarters, 2d Battalion, 32d Artillery. ORLL, period ending October 31, 1971. NARA.

Headquarters, Second Field Force Vietnam. ORLL, period of November 1, 1970–April 30, 1971. NARA.

Headquarters, 3d Brigade (Separate), 1st Cavalry Division (Airmobile), Operation Katum. *After Action Report*, October 7, 1971. Author's collection.

Headquarters, 3d Brigade (Separate), 1st Cavalry Division (Airmobile). ORLL, period ending October 31, 1971. NARA.

Headquarters, Third Regional Assistance Command. Daily staff journal, September 26, 1971–October 30, 1971. NARA.

Headquarters, 31st Engineer Battalion. ORLL, period ending October 31, 1971. NARA.

Headquarters, 23d Artillery Group. ORLL for period ending October 31, 1971. NARA.

Hoffman, Richard A. "Senior Officer Debriefing Report." January 5, 1972. NARA.

Kirwan, LTG Walter T., Jr. "White House Fact Sheet: Fire Support Base Pace Incidents." October 22, 1971. CMH.

Operations Group, 23d Artillery Group. Daily staff journal, September 15, 1971–October 31, 1971. NARA.

S2/S3 Sections 3d Brigade (Separate), 1st Cavalry Division (Airmobile). Daily staff journal, September 22, 1971–October 30, 1971. NARA.

Tozer, Major William S. "Report of Investigation Concerning Alleged Combat Refusal in B Company, 1st Bn, 12th Cavalry, October 12, 1971." NARA.

Wagstaff, Major General Jack J. *Debriefing Report*. Commanding General Third Regional Assistance Command, May 27, 1971–December 15, 1971. CMH.

Wagstaff, Major General Jack J. (CG TRAC) to General Creighton Abrams (COM US MACV). Message HOA 838, September 17, 1971. CMH.

———. Message HOA 1986, October 12, 1971. CMH.

———. Message HOA 1993, October 13, 1971. CMH.

———. Message HOA 2017, October 17, 1971. CMH.

———. Message HOA 2041, October 22, 1971. CMH.

———. Message HOA 2046, October 23, 1971. CMH.

———. Message HOA 2064, October 26, 1971. CMH.

———. Message HOA 2108, November 1, 1971. CMH.

WEB SITES

Biagini, Mark Fredrick. "The Vietnam Veterans Memorial." *The Wall*. http://thewall-usa.com/guest.asp?recid=3885 (accessed November 17, 2009).

Cibolski, Paul. "The Battle for Fire Support Base Pace." *Proud Americans*. http://www.proudamericans.homestead.com (accessed February 14, 2009).

Colaiezzi, Tom. "How FSB Pace Was Named." *Proud Americans*. http://proudamericans.homestead.com/stories.html (accessed February 8, 2009).

Comptroller, Secretary of Defense. "Vietnam War Deaths by Month, 1966–1971." *American War Library*. http://members.aol.com/forcountry/kiamonth.,htm (accessed January 13, 2004).

1st Cavalry Division Association. "Project Sky Trooper, 1st Battalion, 12th Cavalry—Vietnam." *Fallen Troopers, Vietnam Book of Honor*. http://lcda.org/boh_vn_1-12_Cav.htm (accessed July 5, 2008).

———. "Vietnam War." *Journals*. http://first-team.US/journals/12thregmt/1-8 (accessed July 22, 2008).

Gessell, Clifford. "Camp Thien Ngon." *The Red Dragon*. http://cliffordgessell.blogsdpot.com/2008/05/camp-thien-ngon.html (accessed July 24, 2008), 1–3.

Hahn, David Lee. "The Vietnam Veterans Memorial." *The Wall.* http://thewall-usa.com/info.asp? Recid=21179 (accessed January 3, 2010).

"Honor Roll for the 2/32 Field Artillery." *Proud Americans.* http://proudamericans.home stead.com/Honor_Roll~ie4.html (accessed July 5, 2008), 1–4.

"Jack J. Wagstaff." *Arlington Cemetery.* http://www.arlingtoncemetery.net/wagstaff.htm (accessed July 14, 2008).

"Lineage and Honors." *Proud Americans.* http://wwwproudamericans.homestead.com/files/History32.htm (accessed July 4, 2009).

Marling, Paul. "Personal Narrative—My Journey—Long." alt.war.vietnam. http://groups.google.com/group/alt.war.vietnam/msg/7a22016eacaaa53c?mode (accessed June 1, 2006).

Pace, Steve. "My Brother—My Hero." *The Wall.* http://www.the wall~usa.com/cgi-bin/search5.egi/ (accessed March 27, 2003).

12th Cavalry Regiment Association. "1st Battalion, 12th Cavalry Regiment Unit Decorations." *12th Cavalry Regiment.* http://www.12thcav.US/112_unit_decorations_list.htm (accessed July 4, 2009).

Tyson, Stanley W. "Easter Offensive." *12th Cavalry Regiment Association, Stories.* http://1/12thcav.us/stories_112_ST_Easter_Offensive.htm (accessed January 6, 2010).

"Vietnam 1963 to 1971." *Proud Americans.* http://proudamericans.homestead.com/history.html/ (accessed July 5, 2008).

Vietnam Helicopter Pilots Association. "Helicopter65-1c65-09548." *Fly Army.* http://flyarmy.org/incident/71093010.htm (accessed December 20, 2005), 1–2.

BROADCAST NEWS REPORTS

"Journal / Vietnam Soldiers." *NBC Evening News,* October 13, 1971, VTNA, 454241.

"Vietnam/Fighting." *CBS Evening News,* October 19, 1971, VTNA, 213369.

"Vietnam / Fire Base Pace." *ABC Evening News,* October 22, 1971, VTNA, 13014.

"Vietnam / Fire Base Pace." *CBS Evening News,* October 22, 1971, VTNA, 213451.

"Vietnam/Offensive." *CBS Evening News,* April 5, 1972, VTNA, 22805.

"Vietnam / Patrol Refusal." *ABC Evening News,* October 11, 1971, VTNA, 12809.

"Vietnam / Peace Talks / Firebase Pace." *NBC Evening News,* October 22, 1971, VTNA, 454416.

"Vietnam/Rebellion." *ABC Evening News,* October 12, 1971, VTNA, 12835.

"Vietnam / Reluctant Co." *CBS Evening News,* October 12, 1971, VTNA, 213253.

"Vietnam / Reluctant Co." *ABC Evening News,* October 13, 1971, VTNA, 12849.

"Vietnam / Thieu / Fire Base Pace." *NBC Evening News,* October 19, 1971, VTNA, 454342.

"Vietnam/Troops." *CBS Evening News,* October 11, 1971, VTNA, 213222.

"Vietnam War." *CBS Evening News,* July 15, 1971, VTNA, 217981.

INTERVIEWS

Interviews were conducted by e-mail (E), letter (L), or phone (P). Interviewees are listed with their 1971 rank and job description. Some interviews involved multiple dates because of dialogue back and forth in response to questions. Dates listed represents the major body of the interview.

2/32d Field Artillery

Atkin, Roger, SSG, Section Chief, E, March 22, 2010.

Alberg, Wayne, 2LT AXO, P, June 25, 2009.

Ashley, Richard C., CPT, BC, E, January 21, 2009.

Cibolski, Paul, SSG, Section Chief, M, 11/8/09, P, November 10, 2009.

Colaiezzi, Tom, 1LT FDO, E, May 9, 2009.

Crane, Mark, SP4, Commo Section, P, March 10, 2010.

Davis, Russell, MAJ, XO/2/32, E, June 28, 2010.

Diggs, Mark, 1LT, XO, E, February 5, 2009.

Donze, Michael, SGT, Section Chief, P, April 20, 2010.

Garner, Keith, MAJ, S-3, E, January 20, 2010.

Hinton, Lavell, PFC, FDC/2/32, P, June 23, 2010.

LeVesque, G. John, CPT, S-3, P, March 26, 2009.

Maxfield, Mark, SP4 Btry Recorder, E, January 8, 2009.

McCaffree, Robert J., LTC, CO, P, December 15, 2008.

McCormick, William, SP4, FDC, P, June 21, 2010.

Nagy, Ross, CPT, BC, E, January 16, 2010.

Oestrich, Bruce, SGT Commo Chief, P, November 18, 2008.

Timmons, Thomas H., CPT, BC, P, May 3, 2009.

1/12th Cavalry

Adams, Jack, CPT, CO A Co, P, April 6, 2010.

Bloomer, Morris, SGT, Infantry, B Co, L, April 8, 2009.

Coreno, Rich, 1LT, Plt Leader, B Co, E, November 9, 2009, and October 3, 2010.

Cowles, Greg, SP4, Medic, D Co, P, August 31, 2009.

Cronin, Robert, CPT, CO Bravo Co 1/12th CAV, E, May 1, 2009, and November 26, 2010.

Demas, Nick, SGT, Infantry, B Co, P, March 1, 2010, and July 8, 2010.

Denton, Bill, SP4, Infantry, E Co, L, January 13, 2010.

Dombrowsky, Thomas, CPT S-2, E, April 13, 2009.

Dye, Joseph E., MAJ S-3, L, January 13, 2009.

Farmer, Danny, SP4, Infantry, B Co, P, March 8, 2010.

French, Ernest, SP4, Infantry, B Co, P, April 8, 2010, and July 15, 2010.

Grana, Al, SP4, Infantry, B Co, P, December 29, 2009.

Hastings, Caesar, PVT, Infantry, B Co, P, March 30, 2009.

Lonchase, Steve, PFC, Mortars, E/1/12, P, July 6, 2010.

Marling, Paul, SP4, Medic, D Co, E, February 24, 2009.

McNamara, Mike, SP4, Infantry, B Co, E, November 14, 2009.

Paul, Derek, SP4, Infantry, B Co, P, January 28, 2010.

Reiger, Joe, SP4, RTO, B Co, E, March 16, 2010.

Stevens, Michael, SGT, D Co, E, October 27, 2010.

Topinka, Rueben, SP4, B Co, P, November 8, 2009.

Tyson, Stan W., LTC CO, E, March 6, 2009.

Wernli, Walter, SGT, B Co, P, April 10, 2010, and August 17, 2010.

White, Paul, SP4, RTO, D Co, E, November 21, 2009.

Other

Belt, Steve, SGT, Section Chief, D/71st ADA, E, July 28, 2009.

Boyle, Richard, Author, P, December 22, 2009.

Brummett, Richard, Photographer, P, September 13, 2010.

Colgan, Tim, SP4, Equipment Operator, 557 Engineers, P, January 11, 2010.

Crist, Mark, SP5, Crew Chief, 11 ACR, L, June 5, 2009.

Hanson, Peter, CPT, BC, B/2/35 FA, P, April 29, 2010.

Jay, Peter N., Saigon Bureau Chief, *Washington Post*, E, November 10, 2008.

Pace, Steven, Brother of Gary Pace, P, March 18, 2010.

Rhodes, Ray, CPT, Adviser, 6th ARVN ABN, E, October 24, 2009.

Ryals, Jack, 1LT, FDC, 2/35, P, July 22, 2010.

Tozer, William, MAJ, IG, 3d Bde, 1st CAV, E, October 5, 2009.

Index

1/1st Cavalry, U.S.
 Bravo Troop, 115–116, 189, 191
 combat refusal, 6, 116, 118, 148, 189, 191
1/12th Cavalry, U.S.
 An Loc siege and, 220
 arrival at Firebase Pace, 33, 34, 36, 89
 casualties, 89, 110–111, 136
 chain of command, 68
 combat performance, 94–96, 106–107
 commanders, 48, 95–96, 106, 138
 discipline issues, 103
 at Firebase Timbuktu, 34
 McCaffree's operational control, 53–54
 reconnaissance patrols, 36, 47–48, 49, 53–
  54, 63–64, 89
 relations with artillery units, 68, 69, 89
 return to United States, 82, 110
 Valorous Unit Award, 106, 270–271
 withdrawal from Pace, 73
 See also Bravo Company
1/26th Infantry Battalion, U.S., 213–214
1/27th Field Artillery, U.S., 17
1/46th Infantry, U.S., 121, 233–234
1/77th Cavalry, U.S., 116–117, 118, 137–138, 148
1/506th Infantry, 101st Airborne Division, U.S.,
  112–113
1st Brigade, 5th Mechanized Division, U.S., 114,
  115, 118, 119, 121
1st Cavalry Division, U.S.
 in Cambodian border area, 13–14, 215
 Cambodian invasion, 34
 combat performance, 109
 combat refusal incident (April 1970), 184,
  187–189, 190–191
 discipline problems, 109
 firebases, 109, 215
 fragging incidents, 103
 officers, 142
 units at Firebase Pace, 33, 34
 in Vietnam, 33–34
 withdrawal, 15, 108, 198
 See also 3d Brigade
1st Infantry Division, U.S., 10, 198, 213–214
2/7th Cavalry, U.S., combat refusal incident
  (April 1970), 93, 95, 187–189, 190–191, 232
2/8th Cavalry, U.S., 110, 220

2/12th Cavalry, 129
2/28th Infantry, 214
2/32 Field Artillery
 accomplishments, 232
 Battalion Headquarters, 69
 in Cambodia, 14
 casualties, 14, 81, 136
 combat performance, 106–107
 courts-martial, 98, 99(table)
 disciplinary actions, 100, 101(table)
 drug abuse, 100
 enemy attacks on (1970), 14
 headquarters, 11–12
 history of unit, 10
 leadership change, 65, 66–68, 102, 103, 135,
  144–145
 return to United States, 82, 211
 Tay Ninh West headquarters, 43, 78
 Valorous Unit Award, 106, 270–271
 veterans' Web site, 230
 weapons, 10–11
 See also Bravo Battery; Charlie Battery;
  McCaffree, Robert
2/35 Field Artillery, Bravo Battery, 18, 142–143,
  211
2/327th Infantry, 101st Airborne Division, 112
3/21st Infantry, U.S., 122, 232
3/31st Infantry, Americal Division, Alpha
 Company combat refusal, 184–187, 190
3d Armored Brigade, ARVN, 203
3d Brigade (Separate), 1st Cavalry Division, U.S.
 An Loc siege and, 220
 casualties, 109, 110
 commanding officers, 53, 68
 discipline problems, 87–88, 103
 firebases, 33, 34, 109
 inspector general, 69, 72, 90–91, 257–262
 mission, 108–109, 147–148
 operations, 109–110
 return to United States, 82, 110
3d Marine Amphibious Force, U.S., 111
III Corps, ARVN, 30, 197
5th Division, ARVN, 198, 219, 220, 221
5th Division, NVA, 35, 80, 200, 209, 219
5th Mechanized Division, U.S., 5, 111–112
6th Airborne Battalion, ARVN, 79, 104–105

7th Air Force, U.S., 39, 202
7th Division, NVA
  141st Regiment, 203–204, 209, 223
  165th Regiment, 209, 223
  209th Regiment, 50, 74, 80, 203–204, 209–213, 222–223
  An Loc siege, 219, 223
  attacks on ARVN, 199, 200, 202–204
  in Cambodian border area, 35, 209
  casualties, 206, 223
  retreat claimed by Minh, 80
9th Division, NVA
  271st Regiment, 213–216, 218, 219–220, 221, 223
  An Loc siege, 219–220
  attack on Firebase Illingsworth, 14, 215
  attacks on ARVN, 199
  in Cambodian border area, 35, 209
11th Armored Cavalry, U.S., 38, 40, 42, 93, 108, 110
12th Cavalry Regiment, U.S., 33–34. See also 1/12th Cavalry
18th Division, ARVN, 198
19th Maintenance Company, U.S., 104
21st Division, ARVN, 219, 221–222
22nd Division, ARVN, 111
23d (Americal) Division. See Americal Division
23d Artillery Group, U.S.
  casualties, 87
  combat refusal reported to, 56
  commanding officers, 43, 138–139
  courts-martial, 98
  drug abuse, 98, 99
  fragging incidents, 103
  intelligence reports, 35
  McCaffree and, 55, 74, 144
  redeployments, 141
24th Regiment, NVA, 218
25th Division, ARVN
  in Cambodian border area, 198, 207
  enemy attacks on, 218, 223
  at Firebase Pace, 32, 47, 204
  performance, 204
  reputation, 32, 204
25th Infantry Division, U.S.
  2d Brigade, 108
  battles, 214, 215
  firebases, 17, 18, 67, 215
  relations of officers and men, 142
  withdrawal, 17, 18, 108, 198
29th General Support Group, U.S., 104

31st Combat Engineers, U.S., 20–21, 27, 56, 100
33rd Regiment, NVA, 109
71st Artillery, U.S., 98, 104
79th Artillery, U.S., 70–71, 77–78
101st Airborne Division, U.S.
  accomplishments, 232
  Hamburger Hill assault, 61, 112, 130–131
  racial tensions, 118–119
  in Vietnam, 111, 112–113, 121
  in World War II, 85, 96
108th Artillery Group, U.S., 116–117
117th Assault Helicopter Company, U.S., 75–76
141st Regiment, 7th Division, NVA, 203–204, 209, 223
165th Regiment, 7th Division, NVA, 209, 223
173d Airborne Brigade, U.S., 111
185th Maintenance Battalion, U.S., 104
196th Light Infantry Brigade, U.S., 122
209th Regiment, 7th Division, NVA, 50, 74, 80, 203–204, 209–213, 222–223
271st Regiment, 9th Division, NVA, 213–216, 218, 219–220, 221, 223

ABC News
  combat refusal incidents reported, 185, 186, 187, 189
  coverage of Vietnam War, 180
  evening newscast, 163(photo)
  report on Firebase Pace evacuation, 80, 179, 180
  reports on combat refusal of October 9, 60, 61, 178–181
Abrams, Creighton
  combat operations, 131
  on combat refusal investigation, 72
  headquarters, 65
  investigation of Firebase Mary Ann defeat, 6, 120
  military strategies, 13, 182–183
  on North Vietnamese, 216, 242
  troop withdrawals, 238
  Wagstaff and, 25, 133
  Wagstaff's messages to, 78, 180, 202, 204–205, 206, 208, 211
AC-130 Spectre gunships, 40, 42, 50, 220
Adams, Jack, 34, 47–49, 143–144, 249
Afghanistan war, 96
African American soldiers
  assignments, 103–104
  racial tensions in Vietnam, 5, 103–104, 118, 119, 124, 127, 128

AFVN. *See* Armed Forces Radio and Television Networks

Agence France-Presse, 60, 92, 177

Airborne Division, ARVN
An Loc siege, 219, 220
artillery weapons, 68, 203
brigade near Pace, 47, 68
commanders, 222
counteroffensive in Tay Ninh, 38, 41, 42
at Firebase Pace, 104–105, 203
performance, 198, 202–203, 221
redeployment, 82, 207
as reserve, 201
task force at Krek, 202
training, 201
U.S. advisers, 79, 82, 104–105, 203

aircraft
AC-130 Spectre gunships, 40, 42, 50, 220
cargo, 40–41
See also helicopters

air support
of ARVN, 220
coordination by U.S. advisers, 226
importance, 223–224
at Katum, 40
in Military Region III, 224
at Pace, 40, 42, 50, 68, 133, 134
See also B-52 strikes

Alberg, Wayne, 24, 93, 144, 145, 249

Allen, Terry, Jr., 214

alliances, 239–241

Allison, William Thomas, 232

Alpha Battery, 2/32 Field Artillery, 42, 67

Alpha Company, 1/12th Cavalry
casualties, 89
commander, 143–144
departure from Pace, 49, 52
helicopter crew rescued, 144
Kit Carson scout, 35
at Pace, 34, 47–48, 89

Alpha Company, 3/31st Infantry, Americal Division, combat refusal, 184–187, 190

Ambrose, Stephen, 85, 96

Americal Division
1/46th Infantry, 121, 233–234
accomplishments, 118, 232
casualties, 122
combat refusal by 1/1st Armored Cavalry, 6, 116, 118, 148, 189, 191
combat refusal by 3/31st Infantry, 184–187, 190

departure from Vietnam, 122
Firebase Mary Ann defeat, 120, 121
My Lai massacre, 6, 130–132, 234
reputation, 234

Anderson, Mike, 79, 105

Andrade, Dale, 228

An Loc, siege of, 218–222, 223–224, 225

antiwar movement, 7, 230–231

AP. *See* Associated Press

Ap Bia Mountain, 130–131

Armed Forces Journal, 7–8

Armed Forces Radio and Television Networks (AFVN), 23, 57, 187

Army of the Republic of Vietnam (ARVN)
An Loc siege, 218–222, 223–224, 225
artillery units, 68, 203–204
battles (1971), 199–205, 210–211
in Cambodia, 15, 31, 197–199, 215–216
casualties, 204, 205(table)
collapse (1975), 224, 225, 236
combat operations, 111
counteroffensive in Tay Ninh, 38, 40, 42, 50, 80
defeats in Cambodia (1971), 199–201
at Firebase Lanyard, 17, 18
at Firebase Pace, 27, 28, 32, 47, 49, 57, 79, 105, 133, 204–205, 211, 239–240
friendly fire incidents, 74, 179, 203
growth, 3
infantry units protecting firebases, 17, 204–205
joint operations with U.S., 197
Kit Carson scouts, 35, 153(photo)
Lam Son 719, 5–6, 114–120
in Laos, 5–6, 114–115, 117, 199, 201, 226
leadership, 205–206
North Vietnamese agents, 239
paratroopers, 74, 79
performance, 17, 31, 198, 201, 202–203, 204–205, 221–222, 237
Rangers, 18, 205, 212, 219, 221
relations with U.S. troops, 105
retreat from Cambodia, 31
specialized units, 204
tanks, 203
Toan Thong (Total Victory) 1/71, 198–199
training, 198, 201
weaknesses, 198, 225–226, 238
weapons, 68, 198, 203
See also U.S. advisers; Vietnamization

Arnett, Peter, 185
Article 15 punishments, 100, 101(table), 123
artillery units
    combat performance, 100–102
    effects of troop withdrawals, 133
    equipment, 78–79
    exposure while loading and firing weapons, 44
    gun crews, 11, 100–102, 104
    importance in Vietnam, 10
    noncommissioned officers, 146
    at Pace, 98, 104
    redeployments, 30, 31(table)
    support of South Vietnamese, 15, 16(figure), 148, 199
    support troops, 11
    time-on-target exercises, 67
    training, 78, 101
artillery weapons
    of ARVN, 68, 203
    dangers, 100–101
    disabling to prevent capture, 35, 78
    Dusters, 16, 17, 159(photo)
    at Firebase Pace, 27–29, 43–44, 47, 53, 74–75, 101–102
    at firebases, 16, 17–18
    "Killer Senior," 67, 101
    laying guns, 46
    light, 11
    long-range, 10–11
    M107 175mm "Long Skinny" guns, 10–11, 43–44, 69, 72, 78, 104, 156(photo)
    maintenance, 104
    medium, 11, 17
    See also howitzers; Quad Fifties
ARVN. See Army of the Republic of Vietnam
Ashley, Richard, 66, 144–145, 249
Asner, Ed, 231
Associated Press (AP)
    combat refusal incidents reported, 116, 185, 186, 188
    Minh interview, 80
    photographers, 184–185
    report on Firebase Pace evacuation, 212
    reports from Vietnam, 200, 207
    reports on combat refusal of October 9, 60, 61, 169–170, 174, 175, 176, 179
    reports on siege of Pace, 170
    stories on Laird, 91–92
    story on Firebase Mary Ann, 191
    Vietnam bureau, 173

Atkin, Roger, 249
Axe, David, 232
Ayres, B. Drummond, 8

B-52 strikes
    NVA avoidance, 212
    in Pace area, 38–40, 42, 49, 50, 57, 68, 74, 133, 158(photo)
    support of ARVN, 199, 202, 219
Bacon, Robert, 184, 232
Baldwin, James C., 120
Bau Bang / Lai Khe, 213
Bazzi, Zack, 96
Behm, Chris, 41
Belt, Steven W., 79, 81, 249
Biagini, Mark F., 110–111
black soldiers. See African American soldiers
Bloomer, Morris, 249
Bolton, Donnelly, 92–93, 268–269
bombers. See B-52 strikes
Bond, Thomas C., 124
Border Rangers, 205
Boyle, Richard
    background and career, 58, 167, 177, 190, 249
    conspiracy allegations, 170–171, 172, 175
    criticism of ARVN, 203
    Firebase Pace visit, 58–60, 105, 170–172
    Flower of the Dragon, 91, 167–169, 228, 230
    inaccuracies, 172
    influence on press reports of combat refusal, 92, 170
    information on combat refusal, 59–60, 92
    interviews, 231
    lobbying of Congress, 80
    meeting with Kennedy aides, 61–62
    story on combat refusal, 60, 134, 135, 167–169, 171–172, 177, 189, 229
Bravo Battery, 2/32 Field Artillery
    evacuation of Katum, 42
    at Illingsworth, 14
    at Katum, 94
    redeployment, 211
    at Tay Ninh West, 65, 81
    time-on-target exercises, 67
Bravo Battery, 2/35 Field Artillery, 18, 142–143
Bravo Company, 1/12th Cavalry
    2d Platoon, 54, 57, 90, 171
    3d Platoon, 54, 55–56, 63–65, 91, 92
    arrival at Pace, 49, 52–53

Boyle's description, 171
casualties, 90
Cronin as commander, 54, 94, 95, 143, 167–168
daytime patrols, 63–64, 90, 91
at Firebase Timbuktu, 61, 134, 163(photo), 178, 179, 180
helicopter pilot rescued, 63, 95
press interviews, 61, 93, 134, 163(photo), 179, 180
soldiers scheduled for rotation home, 90–91
staff sergeants, 145–146
withdrawal from Pace, 61, 69, 91, 179
See also combat refusal, Bravo Company
Breeding, Gene L., 116
Brinkley, David, 179, 180
Brummett, Richard, 178, 249–250
Buchanan, Patrick, 180
Bunker, Ellsworth, 222
Burton, Jonathan R., 53, 65, 68, 69, 72, 137, 138
Butterworth, Fox, 174

Calley, William, 6, 132, 140
Cambodia
    ARVN offensive (November 1971), 206
    Chup Rubber Plantation, 15, 35, 81–82, 198–199, 200(figure), 207
    Lon Nol regime, 14
    mercenaries from, 205
    North Vietnamese Army in, 15, 197–198, 200, 206, 210, 215–216, 217, 224–225
    South Vietnamese army in, 15, 31, 197–199, 215–216
    Toan Thong (Total Victory) 1/71, 198–199
    U.S. airstrikes, 114
    U.S. invasion, 14–15, 31, 34, 215, 226
Cambodian border area
    artillery support of South Vietnamese in Cambodia, 15, 16(figure), 199
    bunker complexes, 18, 44, 216
    firebases, 14, 18, 209, 215
    fire support fans, 16(figure)
    Fishhook area, 13(figure), 129, 188
    forests, 12, 25
    Krek–War Zone C Battle, 38, 39(figure), 206–207, 209
    maps, 13(figure), 37(figure), 200(figure)
    North Vietnamese Army in, 12, 25–27, 32, 198, 207
    NVA attacks, 14, 215

Rock Island East, 129
    See also Tay Ninh Province
Campbell, Henry, 110
Campbell, James, 187
Camp Sentinel Radar (CSR III), 47, 71, 104
Capital Military District, 199
Carney, John J., 119
casualties
    North Vietnamese, 69, 202, 206, 212–213, 215, 223
    South Vietnamese, 49, 50, 55, 74, 153(photo), 204, 205(table)
casualties, American
    1/12th Cavalry, 89, 90, 110–111, 136
    2/32 Field Artillery, 14, 77, 81, 87, 103, 136
    3d Brigade, 1st Cavalry, 109, 110
    Americal Division, 122
    declining numbers, 4, 122
    in Dewey Canyon II, 119
    at Firebase Mary Ann, 120, 121
    at Firebase Pace, 34–35, 41, 49, 50–51, 72, 73, 77, 103, 104, 136
    at Hamburger Hill, 131
    infantry, 136
    in Junction City, 213
    at Khe Sanh, 119
    medical evacuations, 41, 50, 65, 71, 77, 104, 153(photo), 170
    in 1970, 4
    in Tay Ninh border area, 204, 205(table)
    in withdrawal period, 3, 24, 182, 237
CBS News
    combat refusal incidents reported, 185, 186, 187–189, 190, 232
    coverage of Vietnam War, 180
    reporters, 95
    report on Firebase Pace evacuation, 80, 179, 180
    reports on combat refusal of October 9, 60, 61, 170, 178–180
    team visit to FSB Pace, 23–24, 170
Center for Military History, U.S. Army, 230
Central Office for South Vietnam (COSVN), 12, 15, 188
Charlie Battery, 2/32 Field Artillery
    in Cambodia, 14
    casualties, 77, 87, 103
    commanders, 36–37, 43, 66, 144
    contingency plans for destroying weapons, 35
    defenses, 29

Charlie Battery, 2/32 Field Artillery, *continued*
   departure from Pace, 77–79, 211
   at Lanyard, 17, 100
   morale, 103
   noncommissioned officers, 146
   at Pace, 22, 42, 74, 98, 101
   relations with infantry, 136
   safety record, 101–102
   slow response times, 67, 102, 144
   time-on-target exercises, 67, 144
   weapons, 27
Charlie Company, 1/12th Cavalry, 33, 34, 89, 94
Charlie Company, 2/7th Cavalry, 93, 95, 187–
   189, 190–191, 232
Chicago Tribune, 60, 93, 174, 175, 176, 191, 230
Chup Rubber Plantation, 15, 35, 81–82, 198–
   199, 200(figure), 207
Cibolski, Paul, 90, 250
Claymore mines, 16, 56, 64, 89–90, 145
Clemson University, 20, 252
Colaiezzi, Tom, 230, 250
Coleman, J. D., 232
Colgan, Tim, 250
combat motivations, 95–96, 246–247
combat refusal, Bravo Company (October 9, 1971)
   Boyle's story on, 60, 134, 135, 167–169, 171–
     172, 177, 189, 229
   cancellation of order, 56, 60, 64–65, 90, 169,
     170
   Cronin's response, 63, 65, 90, 143
   described as mutiny, 60, 169, 172, 177, 189,
     229–230, 231
   discussions of night patrol, 53–54, 55–56,
     57, 143
   downplayed as just talk, 90, 92, 135
   effects on morale, 103, 107
   "Fact Sheet," 79–80, 263–266
   investigations, 69, 72, 90–91
   letter to Kennedy, 58–59, 60, 61–62, 79, 91,
     92, 94, 171
   not characterized as refusal, 60, 72, 80, 90,
     135, 169–170
   official statements, 60, 79–80, 135
   patrol on following day, 90, 92, 143, 145, 147
   press coverage, 60–61, 73, 92, 103, 107, 134,
     135, 169–170, 174–181, 189–191
   reasons, 56, 64, 89–91, 97, 136–137
   recorded statements, 59–60
   support of other troops, 57, 58–60, 73, 93, 94
   as temporary, 89–90, 96, 97, 137

combat refusal, Delta Company (October 13, 1971)
   described as mutiny, 231
   Dye's persuasion of men to go on patrol, 73,
     94, 137, 143
   "Fact Sheet," 79–80, 263–266
   not characterized as refusal, 80
   press coverage, 13, 80, 174–176, 190
   reasons, 73, 94
   support of other troops, 93
   temporary refusal, 73, 94, 96, 97, 137
combat refusals
   by 1/1st Armored Cavalry (March 1971), 6, 116,
     118, 148, 189, 191
   3/31st Infantry, Americal Division (1969),
     184–187, 190
   by Charlie Company, 2/7th Cavalry (1970), 93,
     95, 184, 187–189, 190–191, 232
   as exceptions, 97, 118
   interpretations, 228–231
   locations, 185(figure)
   military historians on, 85, 228–231
   military reactions, 232
   political context, 59
   press coverage, 184–191
   public perceptions, 85
   reasons, 90–91, 132, 142–143
   temporary, 97, 112–113
combat support troops
   appearances, 128–129
   discipline problems, 148
   fragging incidents, 124–125
   functions, 128
   at Pace, 98, 104
   performance, 119, 148
   proportion of troops in Vietnam, 294n1
   withdrawal, 108, 198
Comer, William C., 78–79
Congress
   Boyle's lobbying, 80
   hearings on military discipline in Vietnam, 86
   opponents of Vietnam War, 80
   Vietnam War funding limits, 114, 224, 237
   See also House of Representatives; Senate
Cook, Robert N., 120, 121
Cooper-Church Amendment, 114, 181
Coreno, Richard, 54, 90, 177, 250
Cortright, David, 86, 87, 88, 228–229, 231–232,
   234, 235
COSVN. *See* Central Office for South Vietnam
courts-martial, 6, 98, 99(table), 123, 132, 140

Cowles, Greg, 250
Crane, Marc, 250
crimes
    thefts by South Vietnamese troops, 105
    by U.S. soldiers, 87, 98
Crist, Mark, 250
Cronin, Robert
    Boyle and, 58
    Bravo Company command, 54, 94, 95, 143,
        167–168
    career, 54, 143, 250
    investigations of combat refusal, 69, 72
    patrol canceled, 56, 64–65, 90
    press and, 61, 176, 177
    reconnaissance patrols, 63, 64, 65, 136–137,
        145
    relations with troops, 143
Cronkite, Walter, 179
CSR III. See Camp Sentinel Radar
Cushing, Alanzo, 78

Dambe Valley, Cambodia, 199, 201, 208, 209, 247
Daugherty, Michael E., 118–119
Davidson, Michael S., 206, 224
Davidson, Phillip B., 105, 225–226, 228, 233
Davis, Russell, 66, 67–68, 74, 138, 139, 144–145,
    250
DeAngelis, Michael, 119
Defense Secretary. See Laird, Melvin R.
DeLeon, David, 104
Dellums, Ron, 80
Delta Company, 1/12th Cavalry
    arrival at Pace, 34, 48, 70–72, 92, 137
    departure from Pace, 78, 94
    helicopter crew rescued, 70–71, 73, 95, 145,
        155(photo)
    medic, 70, 71, 75–76
    platoon leaders, 145
    reconnaissance patrols, 73, 74, 75, 94
    remains of helicopter crew retrieved, 75–76,
        95, 147, 154(photo)
    See also combat refusal, Delta Company
Delta Company, 2/12th Cavalry, 129
Demas, Nick
    career, 250
    combat refusal, 56, 89–90, 137
    French and, 55–56
    leadership role, 146
    reconnaissance patrols, 63, 64, 92
Denton, Bill, 250

desertions, 86, 87, 123–124
Dewey Canyon II, Operation, 114–120
Diggs, Mark, 65–67, 68, 78, 138, 144–145,
    250–251
discipline of U.S. troops
    Article 15 punishments, 100, 101(table), 123
    in combat areas, 87, 99–100, 102, 103, 118–119
    combat performance and, 118–119
    courts-martial, 98, 99(table), 123
    crisis, 8
    desertions, 86, 87, 123–124
    differences between units, 87
    fragging incidents, 6–7, 103, 124–125, 128
    in Korean War, 123–124
    in last months of combat, 85–86, 96–97, 109,
        123–124
    press coverage, 124, 125–126, 173
    in rear areas, 88, 99, 118–119, 123, 124, 127–
        129, 148
    in withdrawal period, 235
    in World War II, 123–124
    See also combat refusals; drug abuse
Dodd, Thomas J., 125
dogs, tracker, 154(photo)
Dombrowsky, Tom, 251
Dong, Du Quoc, 222
Dong Ap Bia, 130–131
Donze, Michael, 77, 135, 146, 176, 251
Drudik, Robert, 188
drug abuse
    in combat areas, 98, 103, 118
    courts-martial, 98
    at Firebase Mary Ann, 6, 120, 121
    heroin, 99, 118, 125–126, 127
    incidence among U.S. troops in Vietnam, 7,
        86, 98–102, 103, 125–127, 235
    at Lanyard, 98
    marijuana use, 7, 72, 86, 99, 100, 125
    Nixon administration policies, 126, 127
    at Pace, 98
    press coverage, 125–126, 192
    public perceptions, 126–127, 192
    in rear areas, 103, 118, 121, 128
    Senate hearings, 125
    treatment and rehabilitation programs, 126
Drug Amnesty Program, 99
Dupree, Jim, 24
Dye, Joseph D.
    arrival at Pace, 68, 69, 137
    background and career, 68, 251

Dye, Joseph D, *continued*
  Delta Company and, 73, 74, 94, 95, 137, 143
  relations with McCaffree, 68

Easter Offensive (1972), 218–224, 219(figure),
  225, 227
Echo Company, 1/12/ Cavalry, 33, 34
Eckhardt, George S., 205
Edwards, Jessee, 81
Emerson, Gloria, 110
Evans, Rowland, 8
Ewell, Julian J., 197

Faas, Horst, 184–185
Farmer, Danny, 251
firebases
  in Cambodia, 14
  in Cambodian border area, 18, 209
  combat readiness, 120–121
  defenses, 16, 68
  enemy attacks on, 15–16
  evacuations, 42
  histories, 228
  infantry units, 16, 17, 33, 34
  living conditions, 23
  locations, 16
  opening, 109
  purpose, 15
  weapons, 16
Fire Support Base Alpha, 40, 202, 203, 209
Fire Support Base Bird, 68
Fire Support Base Burt, 214
Fire Support Base Elsenberg, 42
Fire Support Base Frontier City, 215
Fire Support Base Ike, 215
Fire Support Base Illingsworth, 14, 46, 215
Fire Support Base Katum
  air support, 40
  Border Rangers, 205
  defenses, 25
  evacuation, 32, 42, 65, 66, 81, 93, 134
  infantry units, 34
  location, 27
  VIP visits, 133
Fire Support Base Lanyard
  artillery units, 17, 142–143, 199, 211
  artillery weapons, 156(photo), 157(photo),
    160(photo)
  construction, 15

enemy attacks, 17, 18, 20, 21–22, 100, 121,
  146–147, 247
living conditions, 18–19
location, 15, 18
officers, 145
reconnaissance patrols, 142–143, 146, 205
significance, 246
site, 164(photo), 254
South Vietnamese troops, 18
Fire Support Base Lanyard II, 19, 20–21, 22. *See
  also* Fire Support Base Pace
Fire Support Base Mary Ann
  attack on, 6, 21, 120, 148, 191
  drug use, 6, 120, 121
  military historians on, 232, 233–234
  press coverage, 191
Fire Support Base Pace
  aerial views, 149(photo), 150(photo),
    151(photo)
  African American soldiers, 103–104
  artillery command change, 65, 66–68
  "black box," 40, 42
  cleared area surrounding, 27
  combat support troops, 98, 104
  commendation of soldiers, 106
  communications, 27
  construction, 22, 150(photo), 151(photo)
  defenses, 25, 29, 47, 48, 50, 68, 133, 141,
    167–168
  evacuation, 73, 77–79, 80, 81, 134, 139,
    174–175, 179, 211–212
  evacuation route blocked, 42
  Fire Direction Center, 27, 56–57, 102, 104
  ground surveillance radar, 27, 47, 56, 74, 104,
    136, 152(photo)
  infantry units, 33–34, 36, 69, 75, 88–89, 94,
    147
  isolation, 27
  lack of interest of military historians, 228
  layout, 27, 28(figure)
  living conditions, 22–24, 67–68, 74, 180
  location, 22, 27
  mail delivery, 171
  media visits, 23–24, 74–75, 160(photo),
    170–171, 179, 180
  medical evacuations, 34, 41, 47, 50, 170
  morale, 49, 59, 67, 68, 72, 74, 102–103, 107,
    180
  name, 22, 82

night patrols discussed, 47–48, 49, 53–54,
  55–56
officer performance, 133, 136–137, 138, 139,
  141, 143–145
RPG screen, 46, 144
significance, 32, 246
site, 164(photo), 254
slow response times, 44, 56–57, 66, 67, 102,
  138, 144
South Vietnamese troops, 27, 28, 32, 47, 49,
  57, 79, 105, 133, 204–205, 211, 239–240
supply helicopters, 22, 40–41, 75, 152(photo)
VIP visits, 24, 36, 69, 133, 138
withdrawal orders, 73
Fire Support Base Pace, siege of, 44–51, 52–55,
  201–205
  air support, 40, 42, 50, 68, 133, 134
  AK-47 fire, 63
  casualties, 34–35, 41, 49, 50–51, 72, 73, 77,
    103, 104, 136
  combat performance of U.S. troops, 105–107
  enemy accomplishments, 211 212
  enemy in forests surrounding, 40–41, 44,
    45(figure), 168–169
  enemy targets, 24
  helicopter crashes, 41, 63, 70–71, 72, 75–76,
    104, 154(photo), 155(photo)
  intelligence reports, 36–37, 49–50
  lulls, 171
  mortar launch sites, 44–46, 45(figure)
  mortar shelling, 34–35, 41, 44–47, 54–55, 73,
    74, 77, 210
  North Vietnamese goals, 203–204, 247
  RPGs and recoilless rifles, 46, 49, 68
  shelling damage to vehicles, 106
Fire Support Base Pace weapons
  artillery, 27–29, 43–44, 47, 53, 74–75, 101–
    102
  howitzers, 43–44, 46, 48, 65, 66–67, 69, 72,
    101, 158(photo)
  mortars, 161(photo)
  Quad Fifties, 27–29, 45, 63, 72
  safety record, 101–102
Fire Support Base Ripcord, 112–113, 148
Fire Support Base Rising Sun, 18
Fire Support Base Round Rock, 94
Fire Support Base Timbuktu, 34, 61, 134, 138,
  163(photo), 176, 178
Fire Support Base Tomahawk, 112, 148

Fort Sill, 67, 77–78
fragging incidents, 6–7, 103, 124–125, 128
France
  Agence France-Presse, 60, 92, 177
  battle of Verdun, 221, 307n12
  war with Viet Minh, 12, 210
French, Ernest
  background and career, 55, 251
  combat refusal, 56, 89–90, 92, 137
  Cronin on, 95
  Demas and, 55–56
  reconnaissance patrols, 63, 64, 92, 145
friendly fire incidents, 74, 179, 203

Garner, George, 81, 138, 251
Gettysburg, 78
Goldwater, Barry, 80
Grana, Al
  arrival at Pace, 52–53
  career, 251
  on Cronin, 54
  Cronin on, 95
  Kennedy's letter to, 79, 267
  letter to Kennedy, 58–59, 91, 92, 94
  press interviews, 61, 179
  support of combat refusal, 57
Gravel, Mike, 80
guns. See artillery weapons

Haig, Alexander, Jr., 214, 221
Halberstam, David, 175
Hamburger Hill assault, 61, 112, 130–131
Hamm, David L., 81
Hammond, William M., 124, 181, 187, 192–193,
  230, 233
Hanson, Peter, 251
Harris, Fred, 80
Harris, Louis, 127
Hastings, Caesar, 251
Hauser, William L., 148, 229, 231–232
Hebert, Fred, 41
Heckman, Wade, 104
Heinl, Robert, Jr., 7–8, 85, 86, 88, 128, 190–191,
  231, 235
helicopters
  anti-aircraft fire on, 41, 50, 65, 70, 72, 104
  command, 43
  crashes, 41, 63, 70–71, 72, 75–76, 104,
    154(photo), 155(photo)

helicopters, *continued*
  gunships, 41, 50, 63, 70, 72, 104, 199
  medical evacuations, 41, 50, 65, 71, 77, 104,
    153(photo), 170
  supply runs to Pace, 40–41, 75, 152(photo)
  support of South Vietnamese, 117–118
Henderson, Oren K., 6
Henderson, William Darryl, 216–217
heroin use, 99, 118, 125–126, 127. *See also* drug
  abuse
Highway 22. *See* Route 22
Hill, John D., 116, 189
Hinton, Levell, 103–104, 251
Ho Chi Minh, 241, 244
Ho Chi Minh Trail, 5–6
Hoffman, Richard, 43, 103, 138–139, 140–141,
  146, 297n5
Hollingsworth, James, 128–129, 221, 222,
  305n67
House of Representatives
  Appropriations Committee, 124
  studies of drug abuse in Vietnam, 126
  See also Congress
howitzers
  105mm, 11, 203
  155mm, 11, 17, 18
  of ARVN, 68, 203
  crews, 43–44, 66–67
  eight-inch, 10, 11, 48, 69, 72, 104, 144,
    157(photo)
  at firebases, 17, 18, 157(photo), 160(photo)
  loading and firing, 43–44
  M110, 10, 11, 104
  nicknames, 105
  at Pace, 43–44, 46, 48, 65, 66–67, 69, 72, 101
  XM546 beehive rounds, 68
Hughes, Harold E., 125
Hung Dao firebase, 201, 202, 209

infantry
  attitudes of soldiers, 95
  casualties, 136
  combat performance, 129
  effects of troop withdrawals, 133
  final patrols in Vietnam, 122
  at Firebase Pace, 33–34, 36, 69, 75, 88–89,
    94, 147
  firebases, 16, 17, 33, 34
  lieutenants, 145
  noncommissioned officers, 145–146

intelligence reports
  for Minh, 209
  for NVA, 239
  on NVA casualties, 215
  on NVA plans, 36–37, 49–50, 209
  on NVA positions, 24, 25–27, 35, 211
  on NVA units, 210, 213, 223
Iraq War, 96, 236
Isaacs, Arnold, 240, 242, 245

Jackson, Robert, 187–188
Jaffe, Jerome H., 127
Jay, Peter A., 86, 174–175, 192, 251
Jefferson Glen, Operation, 121
Johnson, Lyndon B., 7, 8, 182, 242, 243,
  244
Junction City, Operation, 12, 15, 213–214
Jury, Mark, 129

Karnow, Stanley, 228
Kelly, Michael P., 231
Kelly's Heroes, 85
Kennedy, Edward M., 80
  aides, 61–62
  criticism of U.S. military, 131
  letter to Grana, 79, 267
  request for Pentagon investigation, 174,
    180–181
  soldiers' letter to, 58–59, 60, 61–62, 91, 92,
    94, 171
Kenny, James, 118
Kerry, John, 7, 62
Kerwin, Walter T., Jr., 79–80
Khe Sanh, 29, 33, 102, 117, 119, 120–121
King, Martin Luther, Jr., 103
Kirk, Donald, 93, 127–128, 175
Kissinger, Henry, 182, 243
Kit Carson scouts, 35, 153(photo)
Korean War, 85–86, 123–124, 130, 239,
  244
Kratie, 199
Krek
  battles, 199, 201–202, 206–207, 208
  map, 200(figure)
  South Vietnamese troops, 27
  supply route to, 36, 37(figure)
Krek–War Zone C Battle (September 26–October
  22, 1971), 38, 39(figure), 206–207, 209. *See
  also* Fire Support Base Pace, siege of
Kuzmarov, Jeremy, 126, 129

Laird, Melvin R.
  candor, 243–244
  career, 243
  on lessons of Vietnam, 236–245
  on morale of U.S. troops, 5
  soldiers' letters to, 92–93
  statement that combat has ended, 59–60
  troop withdrawals, 4–5, 91–92, 93, 181–182,
    227, 238, 243
Lam Son 719, Operation, 5–6, 114–120, 173
Lanyard. See Fire Support Base Lanyard
Lao Bao, 117, 119, 120
Laos
  North Vietnamese Army in, 114–115
  South Vietnamese army in, 5–6, 114–115, 117,
    199, 201, 226
  U.S. airstrikes, 114
Laotian border area, 114, 130–131, 148. See also
  Lam Son 719
Laurence, John, 93, 95, 187–189, 190, 192, 232
LAWS. See Light Antitank Weapons Systems
Lee, Grady, 188
Lee, Richard, 70, 71, 145
LeVesque, G. John, 102, 212, 251
Lewy, Guenter, 124
lieutenants, 140–146
Life magazine, 142
Lifton, Robert Jay, 229
Light Antitank Weapons Systems (LAWS), 35
Loc Ninh, 218
Lonchase, Steve, 88, 251
Lon Nol, 14
Lord, Arthur, 74–75, 179, 180

M107 175mm "Long Skinny" guns, 10–11,
  43–44, 69, 72, 78, 104, 156(photo)
M110 Eight Inch howitzers ("Short Stubby"),
  10, 11, 104
MacFarlane, Jack, 111
machine guns. See Quad Fifties
MacPherson, Myra, 86, 87, 88, 100, 229, 231
MACV. See Military Assistance Command,
  Vietnam
Mansfield, Mike, 7
Maraniss, David, 214
marijuana use in Vietnam, 7, 72, 86, 99, 100,
  125. See also drug abuse
Marling, Paul, 70, 71, 75–76, 143, 230, 252
Martin, Ed, 61
Masters, 65, 66, 144–145, 146

Maxfield, Mark, 252
Maxwell, Michael, 187
McCaffree, Robert
  ARVN and, 204
  Boyle and, 58
  career, 43, 251
  combat refusals and, 56, 60, 65, 170
  command of artillery at Pace, 43, 46, 50, 51,
    65, 74, 81, 102–103, 106, 135, 138
  Diggs and, 66
  on drug abuse problem, 99
  infantry units and, 49, 52–54
  late reports of units, 55, 56–57, 102, 144
  patrol orders, 53–54
  relations with infantry, 68, 89, 136
  relations with press, 135–136
  reports about events at Pace, 47, 56, 60, 106, 135
  visits to Pace, 43, 47, 52–54, 58, 103, 144
  withdrawal from Pace, 73
McCaffrey, William J., 105, 128–129
McCloskey, Pete, 80
McCormick, William, 252
McCullum, Larry, 48, 64, 138
McGiffert, Donald, 224
McGuire Air Force Base, 93
McLaughlin, James, 71, 73
McNamara, Mike, 59, 252
McNamara, Robert, 241
media. See press coverage
medics. See Marling, Paul
Meyer, Richard M., 116–117, 118, 137–138, 148
Milam, Ron, 140
Military Assistance Command, Vietnam (MACV)
  An Loc siege and, 220
  attacks on NVA logistics, 113, 114–120
  Cambodian invasion and, 198
  Drug Amnesty Program, 99
  inspector general, 120
  Military History Division, 242
  press releases, 68
  strategy on Cambodian border, 15
  withdrawal timetable, 18, 82, 211, 239
Military Region I
  area, 26(figure), 111
  combat operations, 111–113, 148
  Dewey Canyon II, 114–120
  discipline problems, 127–128
  Hamburger Hill assault, 61, 112, 130–131
  morale, 128
  troop withdrawals, 121–122

Military Region II
  area, 26(figure), 111
  Vietnamization process, 111
Military Region III
  area, 26(figure), 111
  Easter Offensive (1972), 218–224, 219(figure)
  ground activity, 147–148
  Minh's command, 199
  order of battle, 255, 256
  redeployments, 29–30, 30(table), 31(table),
    108, 198, 207
  reserve troops, 34
  Vietnamization, 197
  See also Third Regional Assistance Command
    (TRAC)
Military Region IV
  area, 26(figure), 111
  U.S. ground troops withdrawn, 111
Military Review, 134
Miller, Ron, 61, 179, 180
mines, Claymore, 16, 56, 64, 89–90, 145
Minh, Nguyen Van
  career, 199
  command of Military Region III, 199, 205–
    206, 207, 239–240
  counteroffensive in Tay Ninh, 38, 50, 201–205
  intelligence for, 209
  offensive into Cambodia, 206
  performance, 205–206, 222
  relations with U.S., 211
  replacement, 222
  retreat from Cambodia, 31, 201, 222, 305n67
  as III Corps commander, 30, 201
  ties to Thieu, 240
  troops near Pace, 133
  victory claims, 80–81
Le Monde, 60, 167
morale of U.S. troops
  in combat areas, 128
  crisis, 8–9
  at Firebase Pace, 49, 59, 67, 68, 72, 74, 102–
    103, 107, 180
  Laird on, 5
  in withdrawal period, 8–9, 105, 118
Moser, Richard, 229–230, 231
Murphy, Morgan T., 126
mutinies
  Bravo Company combat refusal described as,
    60, 169, 172, 177, 189, 229–230

  definitions, 169, 170
  use of term, 186, 229
  See also combat refusals
My Lai massacre, 6, 130–132, 234

Nagy, Ross, 252
National Highway 22. See Route 22
nationalism, Vietnamese, 241–242
National Liberation Front (NLF), 209, 213
nation building, 241
NBC News
  combat refusal incidents reported, 178–180,
    185, 186, 187
  crew at Pace, 74–75, 160(photo)
  report on Firebase Pace evacuation, 80, 179,
    180
news magazines, 176–178. See also Newsweek;
  press coverage; Time
newspapers, 60, 173–176. See also press
  coverage; and individual newspapers
Newsweek
  combat refusal incidents reported, 188
  coverage of Vietnam War, 4, 176–178
  editorial opposition to Vietnam War, 178
  reports on combat refusal of October 9, 61,
    177, 181, 228–229
  Saigon bureau, 177
  story on Firebase Mary Ann, 121, 191
New York Times
  combat refusal incidents reported, 185, 186,
    187, 189, 190
  Pentagon Papers, 8, 175
  reports from Vietnam, 110, 111, 192, 200
  reports on combat refusal of October 9, 60,
    170, 174, 176
  reports on Pace, 170, 174
  Saigon bureau, 173–174
  stories on drug abuse in Vietnam, 125–126
  story on Firebase Mary Ann, 191
Nicosia, Gerald, 229, 231
Nixon, Richard M.
  on casualties in Vietnam, 24
  election (1968), 12
  press conferences, 24
  promise to end war, 12–13
  public opinion of, 6
  reelection campaign (1972), 80, 220, 237,
    239, 243
  on withdrawal plans, 181–182

Nixon administration
  Cambodian invasion, 14–15, 31, 34, 215, 226
  candor, 243–244
  combat refusal incidents and, 79–80
  goals in Vietnam, 236, 240
  military resources moved to Vietnam, 227
  Paris Peace Accords, 197, 207, 226, 236, 239
  peace negotiations, 242–243
  policy dilemmas in Vietnam, 240–241
  press coverage monitored, 180–181
  War on Drugs, 126
  See also Laird, Melvin R.; Vietnamization;
    Vietnam withdrawal
NLF. See National Liberation Front
Nolan, Keith William, 112–113, 118–119, 121,
    232, 233–234, 250
noncommissioned officers (NCOs)
  at Pace, 145–146
  roles, 145, 146
  training, 146
  See also fragging incidents
North Vietnam
  motivations, 241–243
  Paris Peace Accords, 197, 207, 226, 236, 239
  U.S. lack of understanding, 241–243
North Vietnamese Army (NVA)
  ambushes, 17, 18, 115, 117, 213–214
  anti-aircraft weapons, 40–41, 50, 65, 69, 78,
    104, 210
  attacks from Cambodia (1971), 199–205
  attacks on firebases, 15–16
  bunker complexes, 18, 44, 168–169, 216
  in Cambodia, 15, 197–198, 200, 206, 210,
    215–216, 217, 224–225
  in Cambodian border area, 12, 25–27, 32,
    198, 207
  casualties, 69, 202, 206, 212–213, 215, 223
  cover and concealment, 25, 109, 216
  draftees, 209, 215
  Easter Offensive (1972), 218–224, 225, 227
  errors, 223
  factors in success, 216–217
  infantry divisions, 35
  infiltration into South Vietnam, 209, 210, 216
  intelligence on ARVN, 239
  intelligence reports on, 35, 36–37, 49–50,
    209, 210, 211, 213, 215, 223
  lack of information on, 242
  in Laos, 114–115

  logistics, 5–6, 35–36, 112, 113, 114–120,
    197–198
  mortar launch sites, 44–46, 45(figure)
  offensive (Fall 1971), 209, 210–211
  organization, 216–217
  resiliency, 213–216, 222–223, 227
  tanks, 35
  Tet Offensive, 12, 29, 214–215
  unit cohesion, 216–217, 242
  weapons, 210
  See also Fire Support Base Pace, siege of
Novak, Robert, 8
NVA. See North Vietnamese Army

Oches, William, 188
Oestrich, Bruce, 252
officers
  fragging incidents, 6–7, 103, 124–125, 128
  leadership doctrine, 130
  lieutenants, 140–146
  majors, 48, 138
  moral authority, 147
  noncommissioned, 145–146
  performance at Firebase Pace, 133, 136–137,
    138, 139, 141, 143–145
  performance of junior, 140–141
  relations with men, 142–143
  relations with press, 135–136
  relations with troops, 141–142
  risks taken, 137
  roles in withdrawal from Vietnam, 130
  rotations, 132–133, 141
  training, 140
Ott, David, 228
Overseas Weekly, 167, 177

Pace. See Fire Support Base Pace
Pace, Gary Lynn, 162(photo)
  background, 20
  Clemson University honor, 252
  death, 21, 22, 147
  family, 22
  firebase named for, 22, 82
  heroism, 21, 100, 121, 145, 147
  at Lanyard, 20–21, 145
Pace, Steve, 22
Pacific Stars and Stripes. See Stars and Stripes, Pacific
    edition
Palmer, Bruce, 234–235

Paringaux, Roland, 60
Paris Peace Accords, 197, 207, 226, 236, 239
Paul, Derek, 243, 252
Pentagon Papers, 8, 173
Perret, Geoffrey, 232, 233, 234
Peters, William, 132
Peterson, Iver, 192
Pisor, Robert, 102
Pitt, Alfred B., 8
Pittman, Cecil, 161(photo)
Platoon, 214
Poveda, Carlos A., 115–116, 189
Powell, Colin, 245, 247
Powell Doctrine, 245
Prados, John, 105–106
press coverage
    of ARVN, 200
    bias in, 180, 191–192
    of Bravo Company combat refusal (October
        9, 1971), 60–61, 73, 92, 103, 107, 134, 135,
        169–170, 174–181, 189–191
    of combat refusal incidents, 184–191
    of Delta Company combat refusal (October
        13, 1971), 13, 80, 174–176, 190
    of discipline problems, 124, 125–126, 173
    of military drug abuse, 125–126, 192
    monitored by Nixon administration, 180–181
    of Vietnamization, 181–182, 192
    of Vietnam War, 173, 189, 191–193
    See also news magazines; newspapers;
        television network news; wire services
Proffitt, Nicholas C., 121, 177–178, 181, 191, 192,
    228–229, 252
Proud Americans. See 2/32 Field Artillery
public opinion, U.S.
    antiwar rallies, 7
    on drug abuse, 126–127
    influence of television news, 178
    of Nixon, 6
    of Vietnam War, 6

Quad Fifties (machine guns), 159(photo)
    crews, 98, 104
    at Firebase Lanyard, 17
    at Firebase Pace, 27–29, 35, 45, 63, 70, 72
    at firebases, 16

Rabel, Ed, 23–24
racial tensions, 5, 103–104, 118, 119, 124, 127,
    128

Ramparts Magazine, 167, 190
Randolph, Stephen P., 227
Rangers, ARVN, 18, 205, 212, 219, 221
Rauch, Rudolph, 109–110
Reagan, Ronald, 241
Reasoner, Harry, 163(photo), 179
Reiger, Joe, 61
Republic of Vietnam Armed Forces (RVNAF).
    See Army of the Republic of Vietnam;
    Vietnamese Air Force
Resor, Stanley R., 208
Reston, James "Scotty," 186–187
Reuters, 173
Reynolds, Lee, 142
Rhee, Syngman, 239
Rhodes, Ray, 82, 105, 203, 252–253
Rice, Al, 187–189
Rickenbacker, Eddie, Jr., 70–71, 73
Ricks, Ron, 41
Riordan, James, 229
rocket-propelled grenades (RPGs), 46, 49, 68
Rock Island East, 129
Route 9, 114, 115–117, 118, 148, 189
Route 22
    aerial view, 149(photo)
    ambushes on, 22, 35, 203–204, 209, 216
    bases protecting, 36
    blockage, 42, 65
    equipment evacuated from Pace, 81
    map, 37(figure)
    South Vietnamese clearing efforts, 50, 80
    as supply route, 27, 36, 38, 151(photo), 201
RPGs. See rocket-propelled grenades
Rumsfeld, Donald, 127, 236
RVNAF (Republic of Vietnam Armed Forces).
    See Army of the Republic of Vietnam;
    Vietnamese Air Force
Ryals, Jack, 164(photo), 253
Ryan, J. E., 55

Saar, John, 142
Santiago, Rafael, 146
Schultz, Ken, 176
Scott, David, 73
Scott, Hugh, 179
Senate
    Boyle's lobbying, 80
    Committee on Juvenile Delinquency, 125
    Cooper-Church Amendment, 114, 181
    Foreign Relations Committee, 7

Subcommittee on Alcoholism and Narcotics, 99–100
See also Congress; Kennedy, Edward M.
sergeants. See noncommissioned officers
Shuler, Ron, 163(photo)
    career, 253
    combat refusal incident, 55–56
    investigations of combat refusal, 69
    patrols led, 145
    as platoon leader, 54
    press interviews, 92, 176
    reconnaissance patrols, 63, 64
Shurtz, Eugene, 184, 185, 186
Shuster, Alvin M., 125–126
Sir! No Sir!, 230–231
Sky Troopers. See 1/12th Cavalry
Smith, Kenneth, 73, 143
Snoul, 200–201, 200(figure), 206, 208, 209
Sorley, Lewis, 224, 226, 237, 244
South Vietnam
    collapse of government, 237, 241, 245
    nation building, 241
    presidential election (October 1971), 41–42,
        173, 209, 241
    See also Thieu, Nguyen Van
South Vietnamese Army. See Army of the
    Republic of Vietnam
Special Forces Camps, 35–36, 215
Stansbury, Tom, 41, 104, 230
Stanton, Shelby, 109, 228, 233, 234
Starry, Donn A., 201, 225
Stars and Stripes, Pacific edition
    combat refusal incidents reported, 60, 80, 92,
        176, 187, 188, 189
    distribution in Vietnam, 175
    history, 175–176
    reports on siege of Pace, 170
    stories on Laird, 91, 181–182
    stories on withdrawal plans, 181–182
    story on Firebase Mary Ann, 191
Steele, Robert H., 126, 127
Sterba, James, 186, 192
Stevens, Michael, 72, 74, 138, 146, 253
Stone, Oliver, 214, 229, 249

Tao O Bridge, battle of, 223
Tay Ninh, Battle of (1968), 215
Tay Ninh City, 11–12
Tay Ninh Province
    ARVN counteroffensive, 38, 40, 42, 50, 80

Dog's Head area, 13(figure), 14, 15, 254
    enemy attacks in, 29
    forests, 12
    maps, 13(figure), 37(figure)
    NVA buildup, 211
Tay Ninh West
    2/32 Field Artillery headquarters, 43, 78
    camp, 65, 81
    casualties, 81
television network news
    bias in, 180
    combat refusal incidents reported, 185, 186,
        189
    coverage of events at Pace, 178–181
    impact on public perceptions of war, 178
    Nixon interview, 4
    reports from Vietnam, 191
    See also ABC News; CBS News; NBC News;
        press coverage
Tet Offensive, 12, 29, 214–215
Thien Ngon firebase
    airstrip, 65–66
    countermortar radar, 44
    enemy fire, 56
    NVA attacks, 36, 66, 72, 201
    South Vietnamese troops, 27, 35–36, 202
    as Special Forces Camp, 35–36, 215
    weapons, 36, 203
Thieu, Nguyen Van
    on Binh Long, 221
    government, 226
    military decisions, 115, 201
    military's connections to, 199, 205, 222, 240
    Minh and, 222
    presidential election (October 1971), 41–42,
        173, 209, 241
    promise to end war, 12–13
Third Regional Assistance Command (TRAC)
    commanders, 30, 206, 221, 222, 224
    firebase evacuation decisions, 42
    intelligence reports, 49–50, 209
    press releases, 61
    See also Military Region III; Wagstaff, Jack J.
Threlkeld, Richard, 186
Time magazine, 6, 109–110, 116, 176–177, 178,
    186–187
time-on-target (TOT) exercises, 67, 144
Timmons, Tom, 36–37, 49, 102, 144, 253
Toan Thong (Total Victory) 1/71, 198–199
Topinka, Reuben, 253

Tozer, William S., 69, 72, 90–91, 253
TRAC. See Third Regional Assistance Command
Tran Hung Dao, 40
Tri, Do Cao, 31, 197, 199, 205, 222, 305n67
Truman, Harry, 103
Tyson, Stan
  Adams and, 48, 49
  career, 253
  command of 1/12th Cavalry, 106, 220
  Cronin's reports to, 65
  Firebase Pace and, 138, 180
  Operation Thundering Hooves, 95–96
  orders to Alpha Company, 48

Uniform Code of Military Justice, 169
United Press International (UPI)
  reporters, 79
  reports on combat refusal of October 9, 60,
    170, 174, 175
  reports on combat refusal of October 13, 80,
    174, 176
  stories on withdrawal plans, 181–182
  Vietnam bureau, 173
U.S. advisers
  air support coordination, 226
  at An Loc, 221, 224
  at Firebase Pace, 79, 82, 104–105, 203
  functions, 224
  senior, 30
  training South Vietnamese, 3
U.S. Air Force, 39, 202, 227. See also air support
U.S. Army
  all-volunteer force, 247
  Center for Military History, 230
  challenges in withdrawal period, 3–9
  combat motivations, 246–247
  combat performance, 7–8, 105–106
  draftees, 142, 244
  effects of Vietnam War, 6, 227, 244
  mission in Vietnam (1971), 4–5, 181–183
  personnel policies, 132–133, 141
  public perceptions of GIs, 85
  relations with press, 192–193
  See also discipline of U.S. troops; Vietnam
    withdrawal
U.S. Command, 5, 40, 98, 211, 237, 242
U.S. Marines, 111, 122
U.S. Navy, 227
U.S. News and World Report, 176, 178
Utermahlen, Brian, 142

VA. See Veterans Administration
Van Atta, Dale, 241
VanOder, Dennis, 73
VC. See Vietcong
Verdun, battle of, 221, 307n12
veterans. See Vietnam veterans
Veterans Administration (VA), 126, 127
Vietcong (VC)
  attacks on firebases, 15–16
  in Cambodian border area, 12, 25–27, 209,
    213
  insurgency, 224
  survival skills, 216
Viet Minh, war with French, 12, 210
Vietnamese Air Force (VNAF), 202, 207
Vietnamese nationalism, 241–242
Vietnam Helicopter Pilots Association, 230
Vietnamization
  announcements, 91–92
  challenges, 207
  equipment, 30–31
  goals, 183
  increased responsibility of South Vietnamese
    military, 197, 204
  by military region, 111
  phases, 91, 182
  press coverage, 181–182, 192
  progress, 197–198, 206, 207–208, 225, 237
  success, 237, 238
Vietnam veterans
  antiwar, 7, 62
  lives after war, 247–248, 249–253
  perceptions of drug abuse, 126, 127, 192
  political views, 93
  recognition of, 246
  Web sites, 230
Vietnam Veterans Memorial, 76, 81
Vietnam War
  antiwar movement, 7, 230–231
  congressional funding limits, 114, 224, 237
  lessons of U.S. experience, 236–245
  Nixon administration goals, 236, 240
Vietnam withdrawal
  challenges, 3–9, 245
  combat operations, 75, 93, 109, 245
  cynicism of soldiers, 92–93
  effects on unit cohesion, 133
  impact on ground, 29–30
  Laird on plans, 4–5, 91–92, 93, 181–182, 227
  lessons of U.S. experience, 236–245

military historians on, 85, 233–235
morale of U.S. troops, 8–9, 105, 118
Nixon on, 24, 243
public relations, 91–93, 181–183
redeployments, 3, 29–30, 30(table), 31(table), 34, 108
state of U.S. troops, 85, 96
strategy, 4, 181–183
success, 238
timetable, 15, 17, 18, 82, 207, 208, 211, 238–239
U.S. casualties, 3, 24, 182, 237
U.S. objectives, 236, 240
See also Vietnamization
Virtual Wall Web site, 230
VNAF. See Vietnamese Air Force

Wagstaff, Jack J.
career, 133, 134, 253
casualty figures, 204, 212–213
combat operations, 133–135
Firebase Pace and, 25 27, 32, 51, 53, 61, 73, 78, 133–134, 135
Firebase Pace visits, 25–29, 135, 180
headquarters, 43
intelligence for, 209
on Krek-Pace campaign, 206–207
Minh and, 31, 205, 222, 239–240
relations with men, 135
relations with press, 134, 135, 175
on security situation, 208, 225
South Vietnamese army and, 201, 202–203, 204–206, 222
troop withdrawals and, 29–30, 133
War on Drugs, 126
wars
differences among, 244
last months of combat, 85–86
lessons from Vietnam, 236–245
War Zone C, 12, 13–14, 13(figure)
Washington, George, 241

Washington Post
combat refusal incidents reported, 60, 61, 80, 174–175, 176, 178, 190
reports on Army performance, 8
reports on desertions, 87
reports on Pace, 170, 174–175
rivalry with Times, 175
Saigon bureau, 173, 174–175, 176
stories on drug abuse in Vietnam, 127
story on Firebase Mary Ann, 191
weapons. See artillery weapons
Wernli, Walter (Tex)
background and career, 63–64, 253
combat refusal, 89–90, 136–137
leadership role, 146
press interviews, 61, 95
reconnaissance patrols, 63–65, 92
Westmoreland, William, 13, 29, 128, 132
Whitaker, M. R., 99
White, Paul, 92–93, 253, 268–269
Whitney, Craig R., 170, 174
Willbanks, James H., 221, 228, 238
Williams, Kenneth E., 21
Wilson, James, 93
wire services, 173. See also Associated Press; United Press International
World War I, battle of Verdun, 221, 307n12
World War II
combat motivations, 96
desertion rates, 87
discipline problems, 123–124
information on enemies, 241
patrols faked, 85

Xa Mat village, 15

Young, Harmon, 161(photo)

Zais, Melvin, 131
Zeigler, David, 230–231

CPSIA information can be obtained
at www.ICGtesting.com
Printed in the USA
BVHW010611170822
644757BV00022B/236